S0-BRE-187

ADA YARDENI • THE BOOK OF HEBREW SCRIPT

ADA YARDENI

THE BOOK OF HEBREW SCRIPT

HISTORY,
PALAEOGRAPHY, SCRIPT STYLES,
CALLIGRAPHY & DESIGN

Carta Jerusalem

THE BOOK OF HEBREW SCRIPT
Revised and expanded from the
original Hebrew edition
SEFER HAKTAV HA'IVRI © 1991

Translation, drawings and design by the author

ISBN 965-220-369-6

PRINTED IN ISRAEL

FOREWORD

While Arabic calligraphy is rightly famous for its exceptional beauty, and Latin calligraphy and letter design – for both artistic and practical purposes – have had a long and glorious history, Hebrew calligraphy has never gained similar attention. Professional scribes in Jewish communities have been trained since ancient times in the writing of the Sacred Scriptures and official documents, and instructions for the writing of Hebrew letters in Torah scrolls already appear in ancient literary sources, still Jewish society has usually paid more attention to content than to form.

When examining biblical manuscripts from different periods and localities, we may discover that, in spite of their varied appearance the letter-forms are constructed from similar basic components. With very little practice we are able to read Hebrew square script in ancient scrolls. However, together with the book-hand, many cursive and semi-cursive script-styles also evolved. Occasionally they differed so much from the dominant traditional square style that special training is needed to identify the individual letters.

Today's wealth of known inscriptions, documents and manuscripts in Hebrew script from different epochs and places can serve as inspiration and guidance for anyone interested in Hebrew lettering. This book presents a variety of Hebrew handwritings found in the epigraphical evidence from various periods and sites. Part 1 provides the historical background of Hebrew writing, from its beginnings until today. Part 2 deals with the graphic elements of the letters and the basic rules of Hebrew palaeography, including the various factors which influence the evolution of the letter-forms. Part 3 presents alphabetic tables of the most significant Hebrew script-styles, each accompanied by a detailed description of the main characteristics of the letter-forms. The last part of the book deals with modern Hebrew calligraphy, the design of Hebrew typefaces, and the factors which influence the harmony and balance of the script.

I wish to express my gratitude to teachers and colleagues connected with the writing of this book. Those who inspired me and shared their knowledge with me and those who gave me access to treasured inscriptions and manuscripts. In particular I wish to mention the late Yerahmiel Schechter, my teacher of calligraphy at the Bezalel school of art; Mr. Eliyahu Koren (Korngold) of the Koren publishing house, from whom I learned the design of Hebrew letters; Prof. Joseph Naveh, of the Hebrew University of Jerusalem, who introduced me to Semitic palaeography and epigraphy and encouraged me in my studies and work in that field; Prof. Bezalel Porten of the Hebrew University, with whom I have worked for many years in researching the Aramaic documents from ancient Egypt, and who invited me to examine and draw the original documents in museums and libraries throughout the world; to the late Prof. Shraga Abramson, and Prof. Malachi Beit-Arié, who engaged me in the Hebrew Palaeographical Project; to Prof. Colette Sirat of the Hebrew Palaeographical Project, for her constant encouragement and for arranging my first lectures in the field of palaeography; and to Magen Broshi, curator of the Shrine of the Book, who allowed me to examine the treasures of the Shrine and copy the documents in my drawings. I am deeply indebted to all of them.

Special thanks are due to the people involved with the publishing of this book: Baruch Sarel, chief editor of Carta, Jerusalem, for recommending the publication of the Hebrew edition of this book; to Dr. Mordechai Glatzer of the Hebrew Palaeographical Project, for reading and correcting the Hebrew version before it went to press; to Mr. David Maisel, for styling the English translation; to Barbara L. Ball for proof reading the book; and to Carta's publishers, Emanuel and Shay Hausman. I alone am responsible for errors. My apologies for any mistakes and my sincere thanks for bringing them to my attention.

Jerusalem, February 1997 — Ada Yardeni

TABLE OF CONTENTS

Part 1

HISTORICAL AND PALAEOGRAPHICAL BACKGROUND

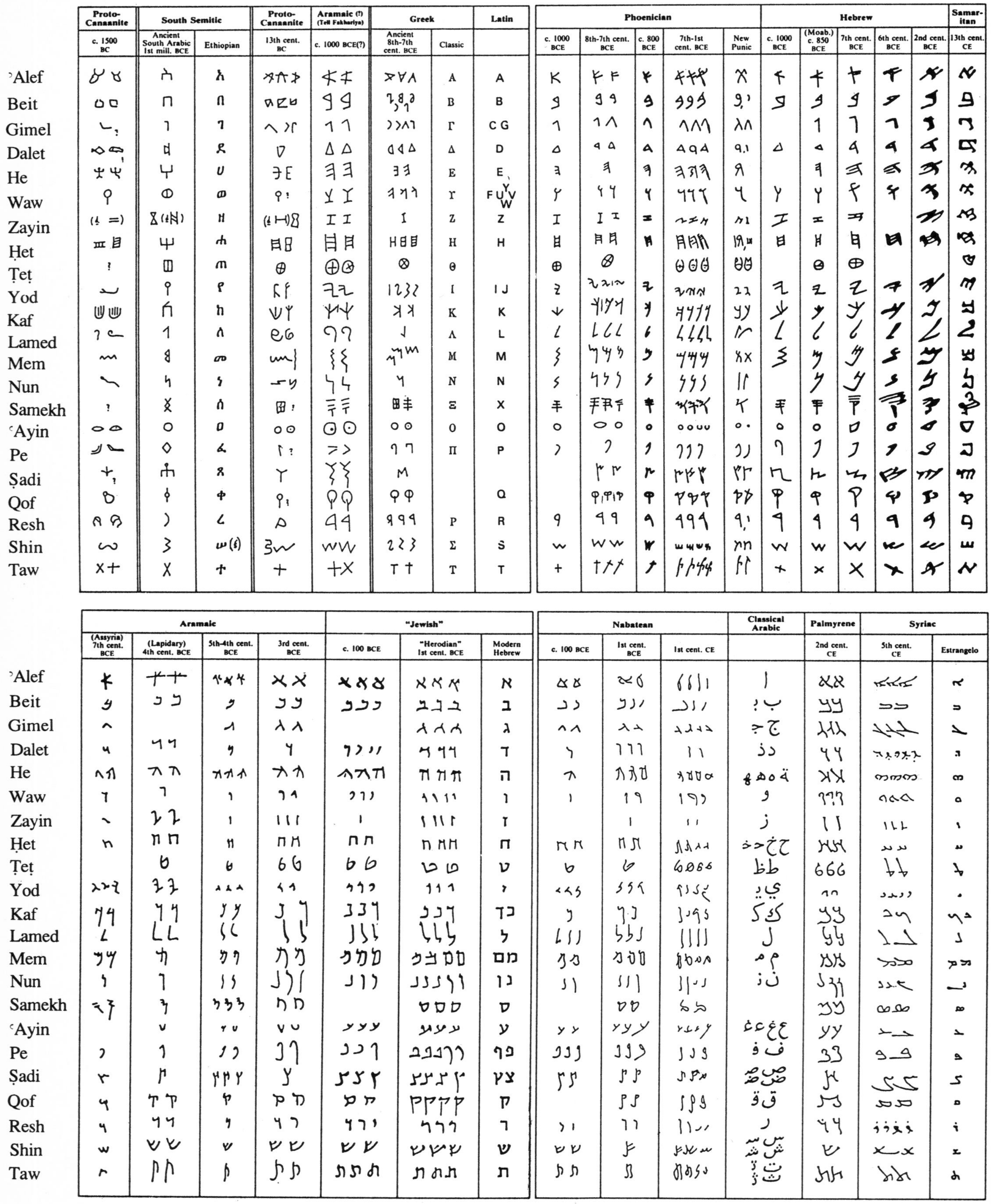

	Proto-Canaanite c. 1500 BC	South Semitic: Ancient South Arabic 1st mill. BCE	South Semitic: Ethiopian	Proto-Canaanite 13th cent. BC	Aramaic (?) (Tell Fakhariya) c. 1000 BCE(?)	Greek: Ancient 8th-7th cent. BCE	Greek: Classic	Latin	Phoenician: c. 1000 BCE	Phoenician: 8th-7th cent. BCE	Phoenician: c. 800 BCE	Phoenician: 7th-1st cent. BCE	Phoenician: New Punic	Hebrew: c. 1000 BCE	Hebrew: (Moab.) c. 850 BCE	Hebrew: 7th cent. BCE	Hebrew: 6th cent. BCE	Hebrew: 2nd cent. BCE	Samaritan 13th cent. CE
ʾAlef							A	A											
Beit							B	B											
Gimel							Γ	C G											
Dalet							Δ	D											
He							E	E											
Waw							Υ	F U Y V W											
Zayin							Z	Z											
Ḥet							H	H											
Ṭet							Θ												
Yod							I	I J											
Kaf							K	K											
Lamed							Λ	L											
Mem							M	M											
Nun							N	N											
Samekh							Ξ	X											
ʿAyin							O	O											
Pe							Π	P											
Ṣadi																			
Qof								Q											
Resh							P	R											
Shin							Σ	S											
Taw							T	T											

	Aramaic: (Assyria) 7th cent. BCE	Aramaic: (Lapidary) 4th cent. BCE	Aramaic: 5th-4th cent. BCE	Aramaic: 3rd cent. BCE	"Jewish": c. 100 BCE	"Jewish": "Herodian" 1st cent. BCE	"Jewish": Modern Hebrew	Nabatean: c. 100 BCE	Nabatean: 1st cent. BCE	Nabatean: 1st cent. CE	Classical Arabic	Palmyrene 2nd cent. CE	Syriac: 5th cent. CE	Syriac: Estrangelo
ʾAlef							א				ا			
Beit							ב				ب			
Gimel							ג				ج			
Dalet							ד				د ذ			
He							ה				ه			
Waw							ו				و			
Zayin							ז				ز			
Ḥet							ח				ح خ			
Ṭet							ט				ط ظ			
Yod							י				ي			
Kaf							כך				ك			
Lamed							ל				ل			
Mem							מם				م			
Nun							נן				ن			
Samekh							ס							
ʿAyin							ע				ع غ			
Pe							פף				ف			
Ṣadi							צץ				ص ض			
Qof							ק				ق			
Resh							ר				ر			
Shin							ש				س ش			
Taw							ת				ت ث			

Fig. 1. A comparative alphabetic chart

CHAPTER ONE:
A GENERAL SURVEY OF THE HISTORY OF THE ALPHABET TO THE BIRTH OF THE JEWISH SCRIPT

A. THE BEGINNING OF ALPHABETIC WRITING

Alphabetic writing began in the Near East during the first half of the second millennium BCE. At that time several writing systems were already used in the area and two of them had already been in existence for approximately 1500 years. In Babylon and Assyria the cuneiform script, which originated from Sumeric hieroglyphs, was used to indicate syllables, words and terms (ideographic writing), and in Egypt hieroglyphs were used to signify words, syllables and consonants. In the second millennium BCE, cuneiform and hieroglyphs were also used for alphabetic writing: that is, writing based on a limited number of signs, each indicating one consonant. Clay tablets discovered in Ugarit, dating from approximately the 14th and 13th centuries BCE, as well as single inscriptions discovered in the land of Israel, dating from the 13th or 12th century BCE, were written in the alphabetic cuneiform. Fragmentary inscriptions from the 17th-12th centuries BCE, in alphabetic hieroglyphs (acrophonic script: that is, a script in which each picture indicates the first consonant of the noun it describes), were also found in Israel. At that period, an Egyptian cultural influence was prevalent in the area. Longer inscriptions in alphabetic hieroglyphs were found in Sinai, in a place called Ṣerabiṭ el-Ḥadim (fig. 6). They date from the first half of the second millennium BCE. These inscriptions are also known as Proto-Sinaitic, or Proto-Canaanite. The beginnings of this script are unknown and there are several theories regarding its origin. The most widely accepted theory is that it was derived

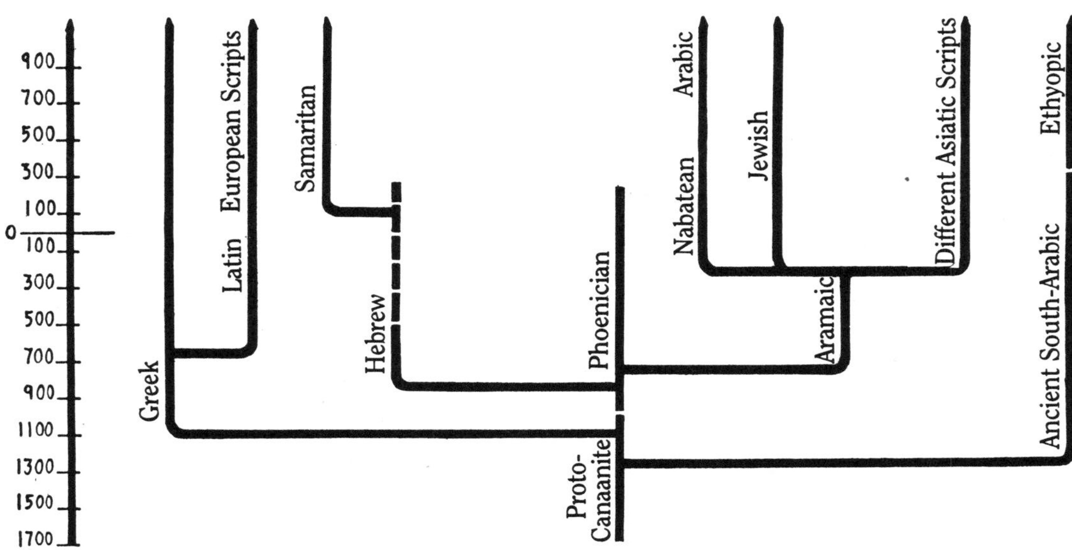

Fig. 2. The family tree of the Semitic linear scripts

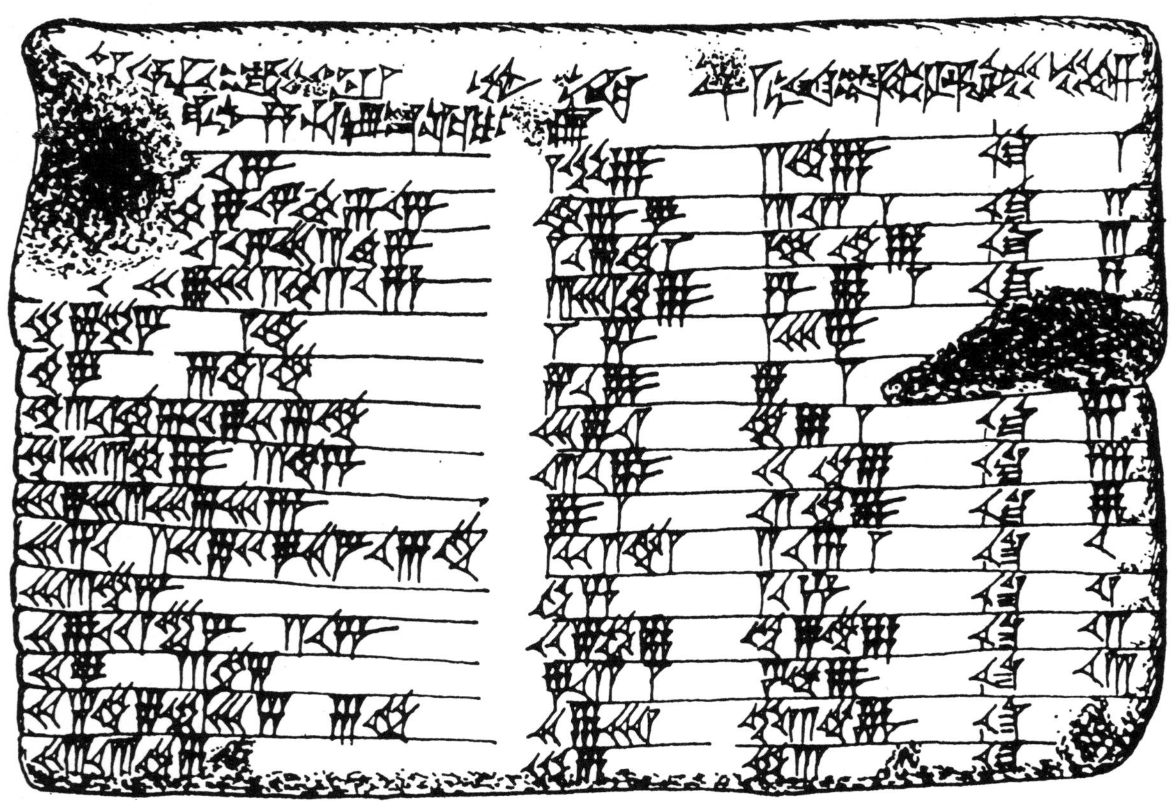

Fig. 3. A Babylonian mathematical clay tablet from the eighteenth century BCE (G. Ifrah, *From One to Zero* [Harrisonburg, Virginia 1985], 378)

Fig. 4. Assyrian and Aramaean scribes holding the stylus and the reed-pen on an Assyrian relief

Fig. 5. Egyptian scribes

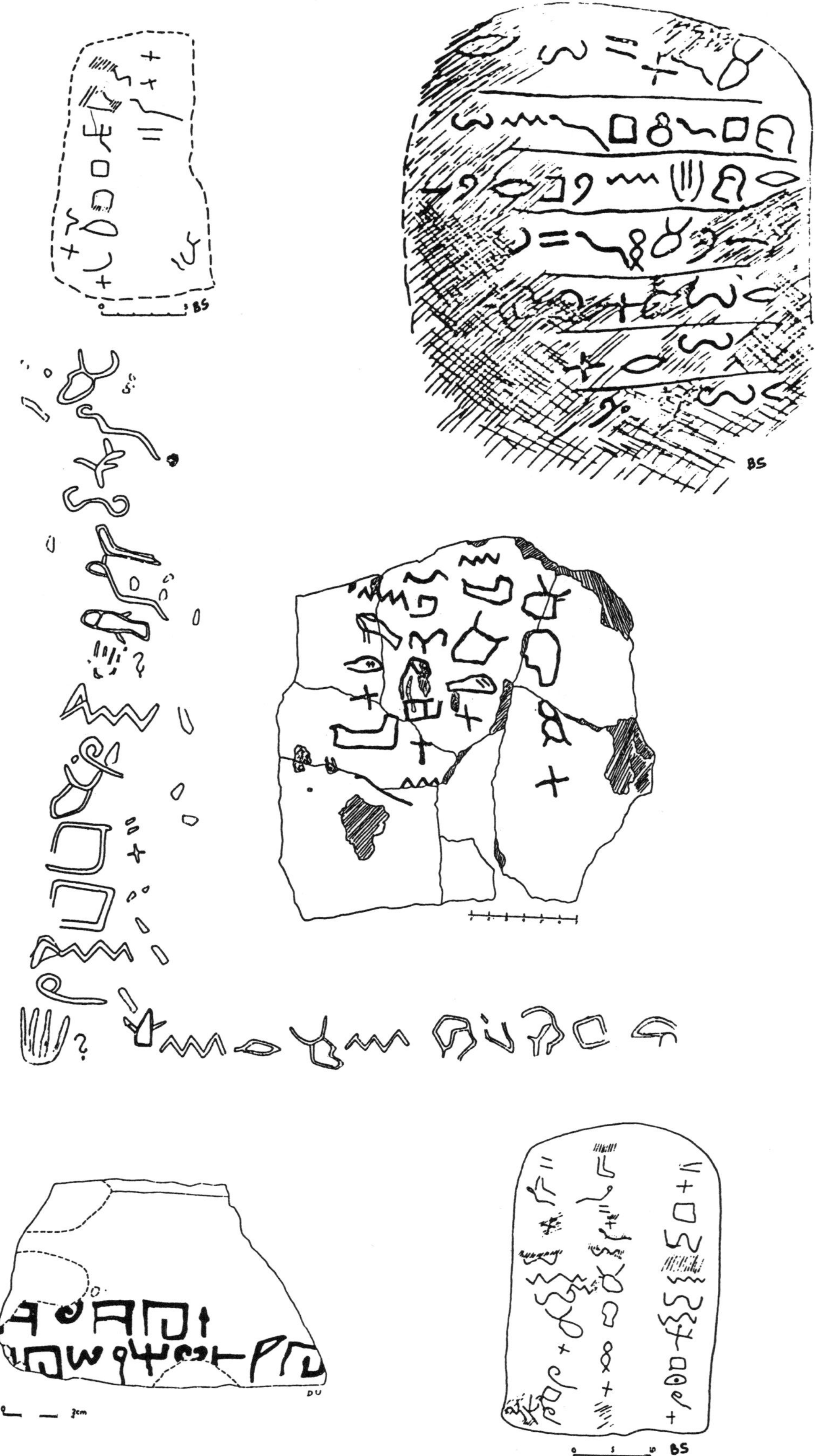

Fig. 6. Inscriptions in 'Proto-Canaanite' alphabetic signs (Cairo Egyptian Museum of Antiquities)

from the Egyptian hieroglyphs. The Ugaritic script had 30 signs and the Proto-Canaanite had approximately 28, which means that both these scripts had more than the 22 signs used in the Hebrew script today. In the Proto-Canaanite script, the lines were written in various directions – upwards, downwards, right and left, as well as backwards and forwards (a way of writing called *boustrophedon*, meaning 'ox turn' in Greek). The posture of the individual letter-signs was also irregular and they could face different directions.

Among the linear alphabetic scripts which derived from the Proto-Canaanite script were the Western Semitic scripts – the Phoenician script (fig. 7) and its descendants, the Aramaic script (fig. 8) and the ancient Hebrew script which Jewish literary sources term *Daʿatz* or *Raʿatz* (fig. 9); the Southern Semitic scripts – the ancient South Arabic script (fig. 10) and the Ethiopian script (fig. 11); and the ancient Greek script (fig. 12), from which all the European alphabetic scripts have derived. The Jewish script evolved from the Aramaic script in approximately the 3rd century BCE (see Chapter One, D-E), and this was the source of the Hebrew letters we use today.

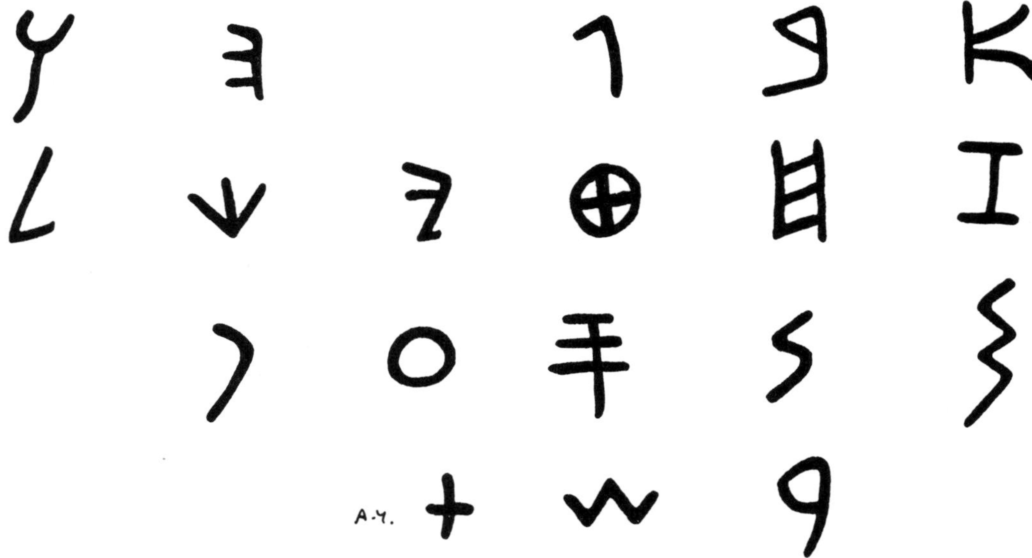

Fig. 7. Phoenician letters of the alphabet taken from the Aḥiram inscription (ca. 1000 BCE)

Fig. 8. Aramaic letters of the alphabet taken from a 5th century BCE papyrus deed from Elephantine (Cowley 20)

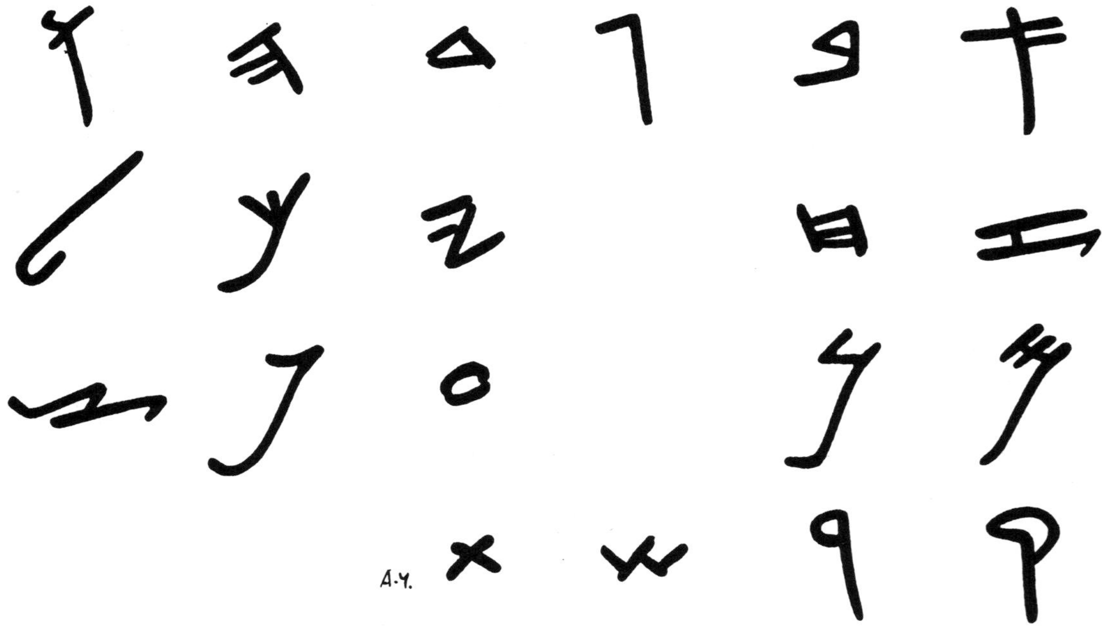

Fig. 9. The Ancient-Hebrew letters of the alphabet taken from the late 8th century BCE Siloam inscription

5. In Museo Massiliensi. CIH 492. Bustrophedon:

6. E Ġir'ān; nunc in Museo Britannico. CIH 286:

7. In al-Bayḍa. Hal. 282:.

8. In aggere Marib. Gl. 513, 514. Bustrophedon:

9. In Museo Luparensi. CIH 393:

10. In Constantinopoli. CIH 579:

Fig. 10. The South-Arabic script stylized for printing (from a book by K. Conti Rossini)

Alphabetic Chart

	The names of the letters	1° ă	2° u	3° i	4° a	5° e	6° ĕ	7° o	Transcription	
1	ሆይ ፡	ሀ	ሁ	ሂ	ሃ	ሄ	ህ	ሆ	h	ה
2	ላዊ ፡	ለ	ሉ	ሊ	ላ	ሌ	ል	ሎ	l	ל
3	ሐውት ፡	ሐ	ሑ	ሒ	ሓ	ሔ	ሕ	ሖ	ḥ	ח̇
4	ማይ ፡	መ	ሙ	ሚ	ማ	ሜ	ም	ሞ	m	מ
5	ሣውት ፡	ሠ	ሡ	ሢ	ሣ	ሤ	ሥ	ሦ	ś	שׂ
6	ርእስ ፡	ረ	ሩ	ሪ	ራ	ሬ	ር	ሮ	r	ר
7	ሳት ፡	ሰ	ሱ	ሲ	ሳ	ሴ	ስ	ሶ	s	שׁ
8	ቃፍ ፡	ቀ	ቁ	ቂ	ቃ	ቄ	ቅ	ቆ	q	ק
9	ቤት ፡	በ	ቡ	ቢ	ባ	ቤ	ብ	ቦ	b	ב
10	ታዊ ፡	ተ	ቱ	ቲ	ታ	ቴ	ት	ቶ	t	ת
11	ኀርም ፡	ኀ	ኁ	ኂ	ኃ	ኄ	ኅ	ኆ	ḫ	ח
12	ነሃስ ፡	ነ	ኑ	ኒ	ና	ኔ	ን	ኖ	n	נ
13	አልፍ ፡	አ	ኡ	ኢ	ኣ	ኤ	እ	ኦ	ʾ	א
14	ካፍ ፡	ከ	ኩ	ኪ	ካ	ኬ	ክ	ኮ	k	כ
15	ዋዊ ፡	ወ	ዉ	ዊ	ዋ	ዌ	ው	ዎ	w	ו
16	ዓይን ፡	ዐ	ዑ	ዒ	ዓ	ዔ	ዕ	ዖ	ʿ	ע
17	ዘይ ፡	ዘ	ዙ	ዚ	ዛ	ዜ	ዝ	ዞ	z	ז
18	የመን ፡	የ	ዩ	ዪ	ያ	ዬ	ይ	ዮ	j	י
19	ድንት ፡	ደ	ዱ	ዲ	ዳ	ዴ	ድ	ዶ	d	ד
20	ገምል ፡	ገ	ጉ	ጊ	ጋ	ጌ	ግ	ጎ	g	ג
21	ጣይት ፡	ጠ	ጡ	ጢ	ጣ	ጤ	ጥ	ጦ	ṭ	ט
22	ጰይት ፡	ጰ	ጱ	ጲ	ጳ	ጴ	ጵ	ጶ	p	פּ
23	ጸዳይ ፡	ጸ	ጹ	ጺ	ጻ	ጼ	ጽ	ጾ	ṣ	צ
24	ፀጰ ፡	ፀ	ፁ	ፂ	ፃ	ፄ	ፅ	ፆ	ḍ	צ̇
25	አፍ ፡	ፈ	ፉ	ፊ	ፋ	ፌ	ፍ	ፎ	f	פ̄
26	ፐ ፡	ፐ	ፑ	ፒ	ፓ	ፔ	ፕ	ፖ	p	(ס)פ

Fig. 11. The Early Ethiopian script stylized for printing

Fig. 12. An early Greek abecedary (ca. 7th century BCE)

B. THE PHOENICIAN SCRIPT – THE ANCESTOR OF THE ANCIENT HEBREW AND ARAMAIC SCRIPTS

Proto-Canaanite inscriptions from about the 13th century BCE had a smaller number of signs. By that time the number of consonants in the western Canaanite dialects had diminished. Towards the middle of the 11th century BCE the Canaanite hieroglyphs turned into linear letter-signs: that is, each letter was made up of a small number of lines, either straight or bent, and the pictures had become abstract forms. This script was used by the Canaanites who inhabited Phoenicia. Scholars name the Canaanite script of the mid 11th century BCE 'Phoenician script'. At that time the Phoenicians used 22 letter-signs of the Proto-Canaanite alphabet which designated only consonants; vowels were not indicated. Around that time the direction of writing from right to left and the position of the letters were also fixed.

The Phoenicians were a nation of traders and seafarers who left their mark throughout the Mediterranean, and Phoenician inscriptions have been found in numerous places in that area. The earliest Phoenician inscriptions are a fragmentary inscription from Nora, Sardinia, and one on a bowl from Crete. Their approximate date is the 11th century BCE. Other examples of Phoenician script are inscriptions from Gebal (Byblos), inscribed arrow heads from Lebanon and an inscription on a bowl from Crete of the first half of the 11th century BCE, and inscriptions from the beginning of the 10th century BCE, including writing on coffins from Gebal – e.g., the Aḥiram inscription of approximately 1000 BCE (fig. 13)

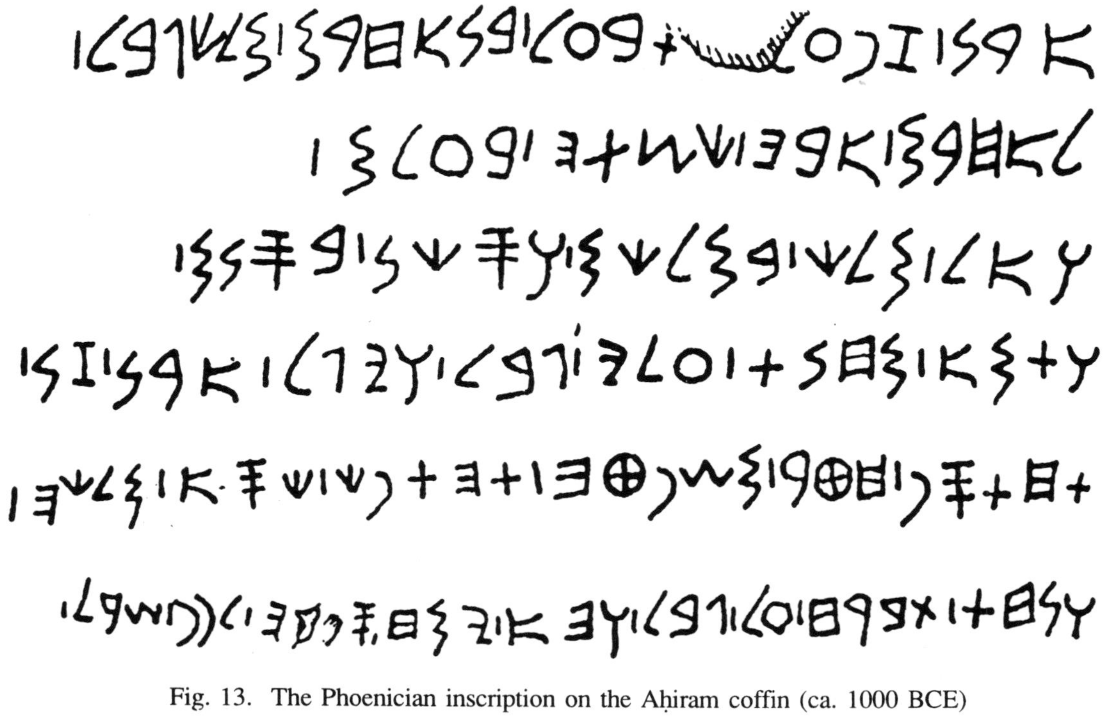

Fig. 13. The Phoenician inscription on the Aḥiram coffin (ca. 1000 BCE)

and the Yeḥimilk, Shifṭibaʿal, Abibaʿal and Elibaʿal inscriptions. Another inscription from Nora and one from Cyprus date from the 9th century, as does the inscription of Kilamuwa bar Ḥiyya from Zincirli (now in Berlin, fig. 14). The longest of the early Phoenician inscriptions known today is the Azitawadda inscription from the 8th century BCE, discovered in Karatepe in Cilicia.

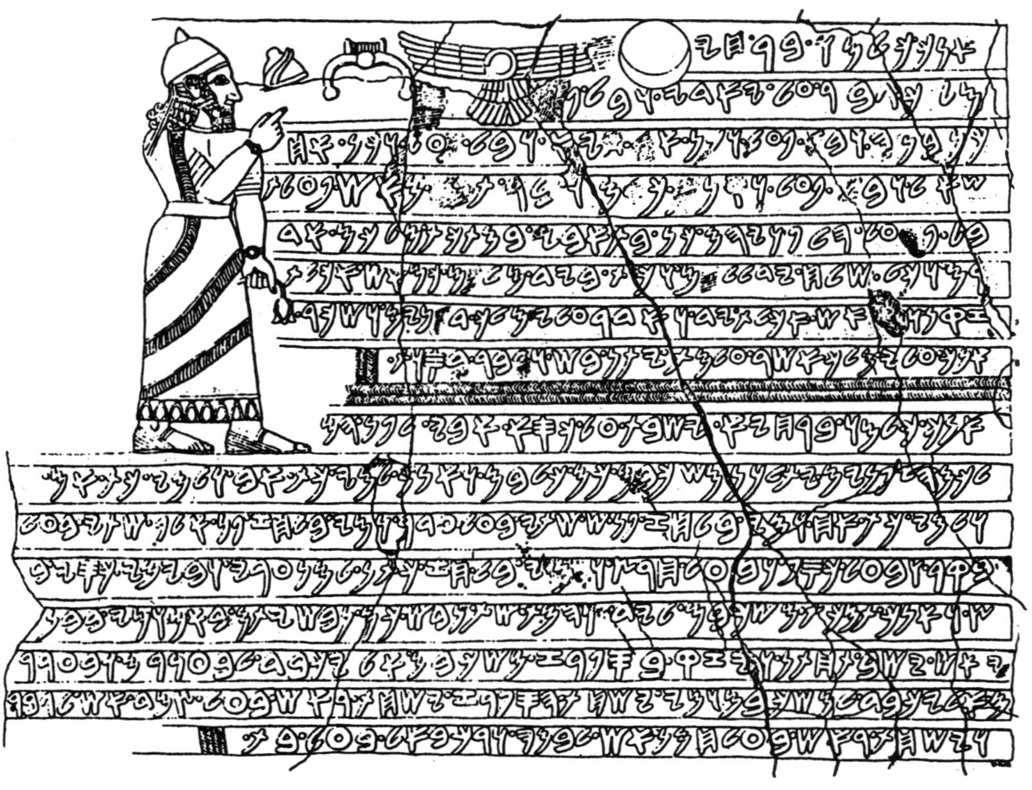

Fig. 14. The Inscription of Kilamuwa from Zincirli (9th century BCE; Berlin, Pergamon Museum)

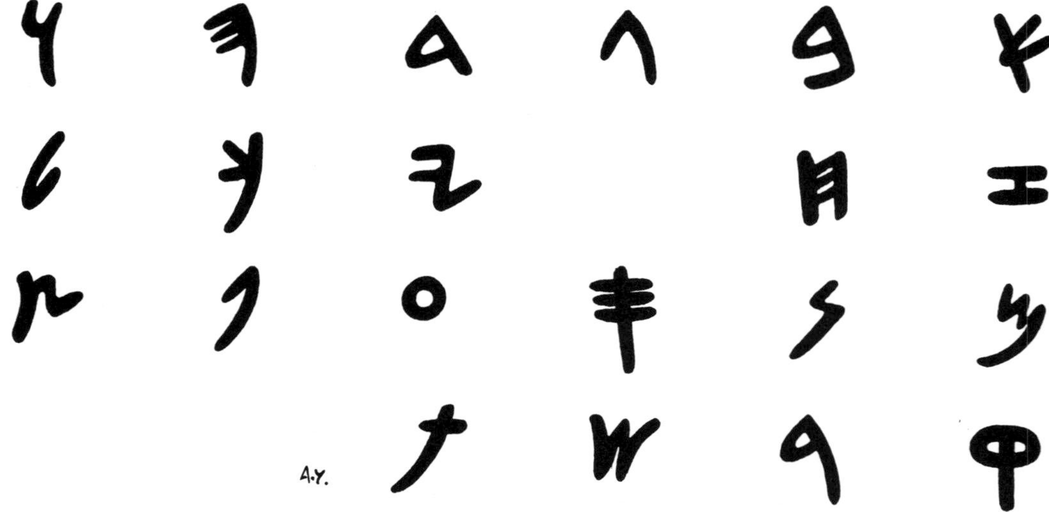

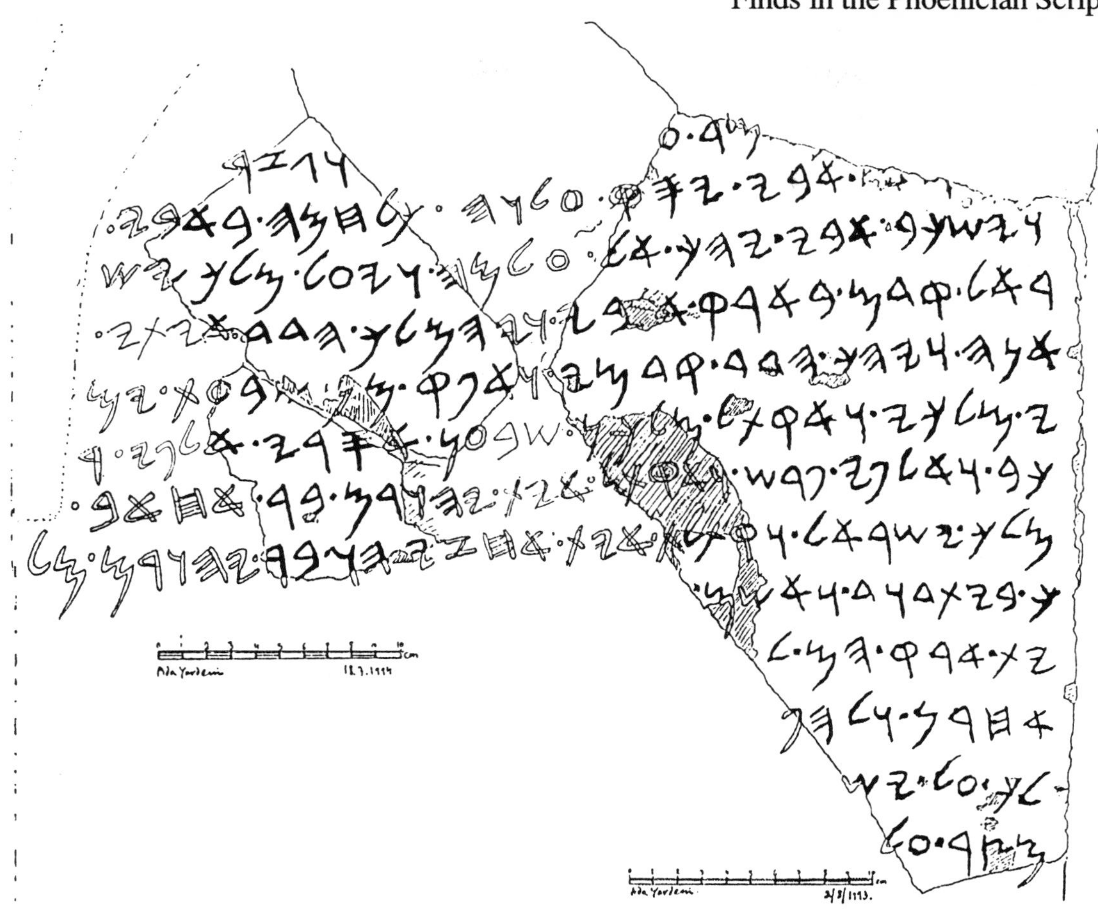

Fig. 15. A 9th century BCE Aramaic inscription from Tel Dan, mentioning the 'House of David'

The Phoenician script spread and was used for several dialects in regions near to Phoenicia. Thus, the Hadad and Panammuwa inscriptions found in Zincirli (today in Berlin) are written in a local dialect of Shamʾal (also called Yaʾudi) and in a Phoenician script of the 8th century BCE. Among the peoples who adopted the Phoenician script were the Hebrews and the Aramaeans. A bilingual inscription in Akkadian and Aramaic on a statue recently discovered in El-Faḫariyeh in Syria has ancient Phoenician letters. Scholars disagree about its date; some, judging from the script, say it is as early as the 11th century BCE, and some, guided by other criteria, put it as late as the 9th century BCE and explain the ancient forms of the script as an archaisation or a survival of ancient forms in peripheral areas. The ancient Aramaic inscriptions of the 9th and 8th centuries BCE are still written in Phoenician script. Among them is an inscription of the 9th century BCE on a piece of ivory from Arslan Tash, as well as three inscriptions on booty from the same period, all of which mention the name of King Ḥazaʾel; the Bar-Hadad inscription from Aleppo from approximately the middle of the 9th century BCE; the recently discovered Tel-Dan inscription mentioning the House of David and two kings who ruled in Israel and Judea in the middle of the 9th century BCE (fig. 15); the Zakkur inscription from the beginning of the 8th century; the Sfire (Sujin) inscription from approximately the middle of the 8th century BCE; and the Bar Rakkub inscriptions from the end of the 8th century BCE (now in Berlin and Paris).

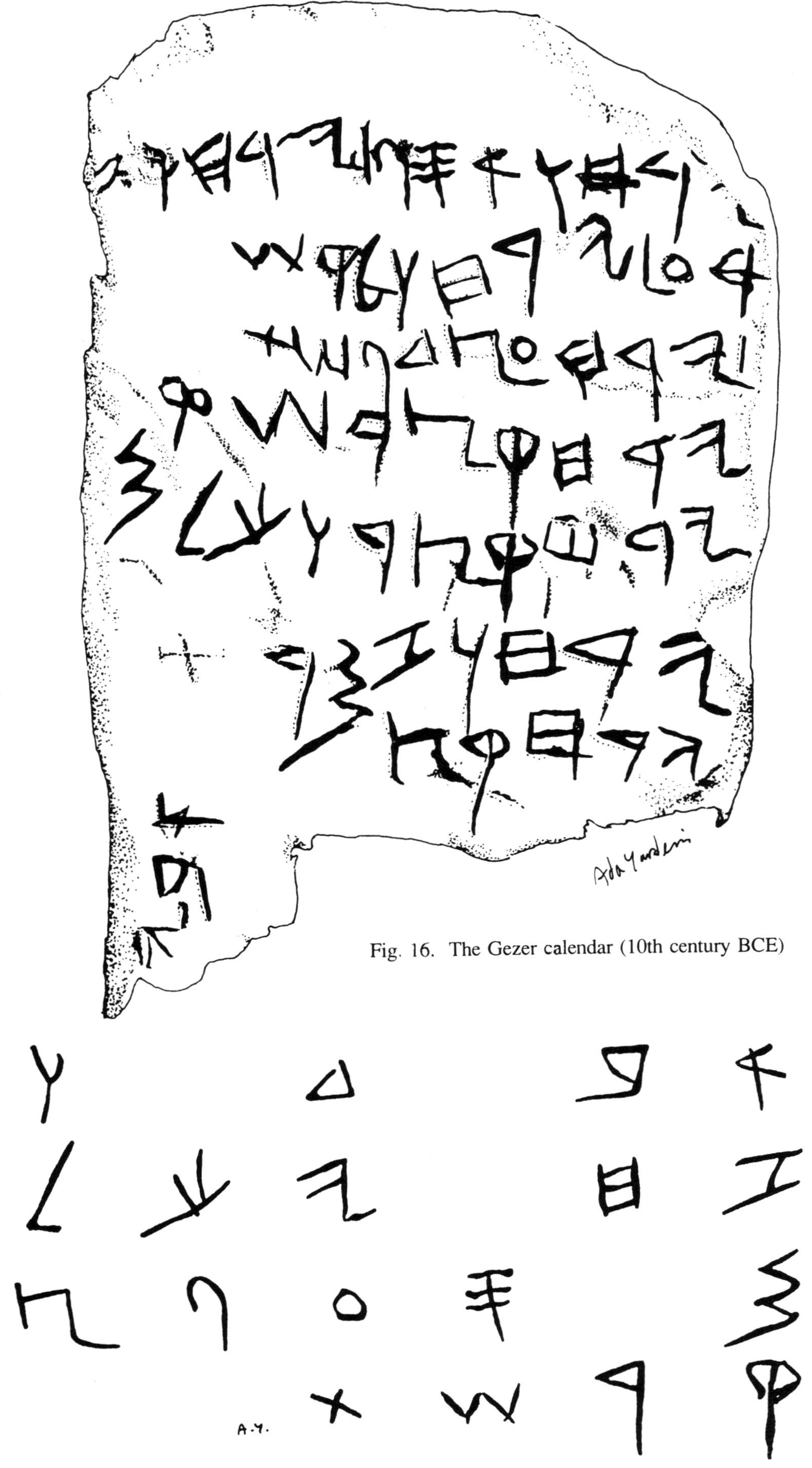

Fig. 16. The Gezer calendar (10th century BCE)

Several ancient Hebrew inscriptions in the Phoenician script have also been found, such as the Gezer calendar (which is written in Hebrew according to J. Naveh; fig. 16), and a few inscriptions from Ḥazor of the 9th century BCE. The Phoenician script served as an international script until approximately the 8th century BCE, and it then became a national script.

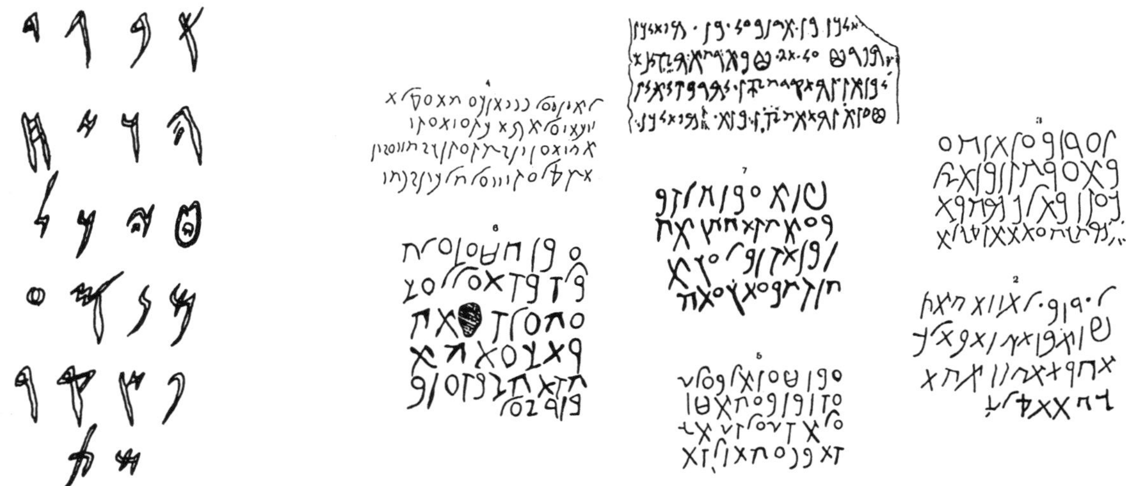

Fig. 17. The letters of the alphabet taken from inscriptions in Punic script

Fig. 18. Neo-Punic inscriptions

The Phoenicians, who ruled the sea, established colonies in the western Mediterranean. The most important was Carthage or Qarthadashat (meaning 'new city'), founded in 814 BCE (according to ancient tradition, although possibly a century later) on the northern coast of Africa (it is today a suburb of Tunis). In this way the Phoenician language developed several local dialects, and the Phoenician script evolved a number of different styles. In the Phoenician script three main stylistic groups may be discerned, which appeared in chronological order: the Phoenician script itself, the Punic script (fig. 17), used in the west Mediterranean colonies and particularly in Carthage, and the Neo-Punic script (fig. 18), which evolved in northern Africa after Carthage was destroyed in 146 BCE. The latest Neo-Punic inscriptions are from the 2nd century or the beginning of the 3rd century CE. After that the Phoenician script ceased to exist.

Fig. 19. Phoenician cursive script on an ostracon from Acre (M. Dotan, *EI* 20, 116-123)

Most of the Phoenician inscriptions which have been discovered, as well as thousands of Punic and Neo-Punic inscriptions, are carved or incised in stone in stonemasons' scripts while a few are written in ink or painted in cursive letters on papyri or ostraca (fig. 19). Inscriptions in cursive Phoenician letters date up to about 300 BCE. Coins with Phoenician script have been discovered in various places. The cursive Phoenician script influenced the lapidary script and the influence is reflected – in the Punic script, for example – in the thickening of the vertical strokes. Phoenician inscriptions have been found in a vast area extending from Mesopotamia to France and Spain, along the Mediterranean coast of Israel, near Eilat, and in Egypt as well (in Elephantine, for example).

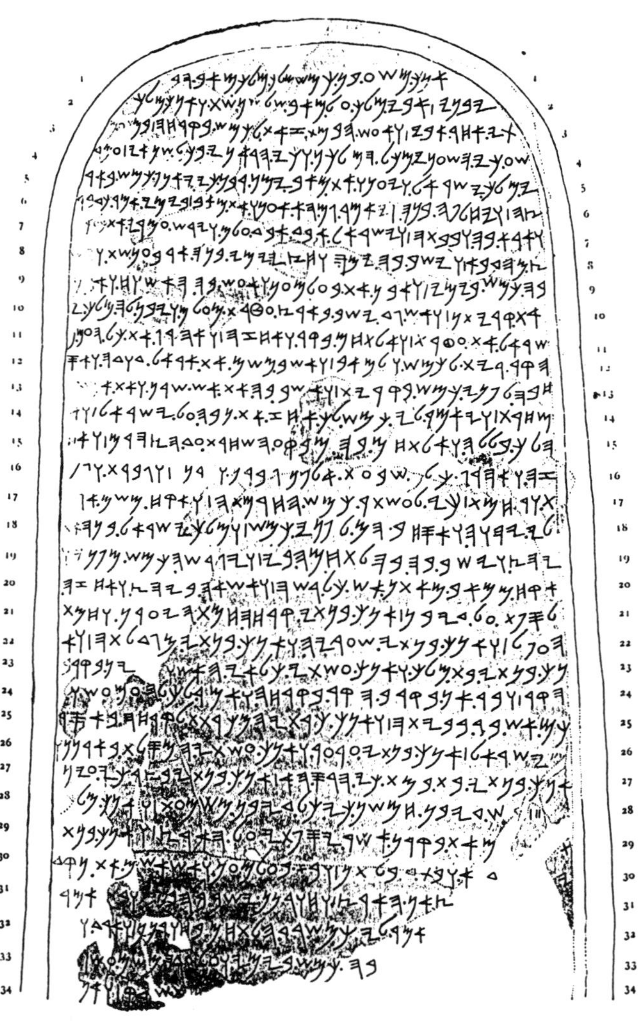

Fig. 20. The Moabite Meshaʿ stele (ca. mid-9th century BCE) representing an early phase of the Ancient-Hebrew script (Paris, Louvre)

C. THE MAIN FINDINGS IN THE ANCIENT HEBREW SCRIPT

The Israelite tribes who settled in the country were influenced by the Canaanite culture which prevailed in the area of Syria and the land of Israel, and adopted the Canaanite script around the 12th century BCE. The most ancient inscriptions with features differing from the Phoenician script, which are attested in Hebrew inscriptions from then on, are Moabite inscriptions from approximately the middle of the 9th century BCE. The most famous inscription is to be found on a black granite stele erected by Meshaᶜ King of Moab, in which ᶜOmri King of Israel is mentioned (it is now in the Louvre in Paris; fig. 20). The fragment of an inscription mentioning Meshaᶜ's father, Kemoshyat King of Moab, has also been found, as well as another fragment of an inscription in ancient Hebrew letters from approximately the same period. So far no earlier inscriptions in Hebrew script have been found.

In its early stages, the Hebrew script differed from the Phoenician script mainly in a certain cursive tendency, reflected in the curving to the left of the downstrokes in the 'long-legged' letter-signs, as well as in the consistent use of a Waw with a concave top and of the x-shaped Taw.

Hebrew Inscriptions dating from the end of the 9th century were discovered in Quntilet ᶜAjrud, a cultic site near the Sinai border, and other inscriptions of approximately the same time were found in Ḥazor and in ᶜArad. A Hebrew ostracon bearing the first five letters of the alphabet was found in Lachish and apparently belongs to the same period.

The ancient Hebrew script (fig. 9) is not the ancestor of the modern Hebrew script. The latter evolved from another branch of the Phoenician script – the Aramaic script (see below). Despite the fact that in the Hebrew language, and in Aramaic as well, the number of consonants was larger than in Phoenician, the 22 letter-signs of the Phoenician alphabet served to indicate all the consonants in the Hebrew and in the Aramaic languages, and no other signs were added. Thus, certain signs were used to indicate more than one consonant (e.g., one sign was used for both Shin and Sin).

The number of findings in the ancient Hebrew script increases from the 8th century BCE onwards. Several findings from Samaria belong to that period, including the fragment of a stele inscription, the famous Samaria ostraca which bear short inscriptions, most of them written in ink (fig. 21), and an inscription in Hebrew letters on a bowl. Fragments of an ivory inscription, sent from Samaria, were found in Nimrud (Calaḥ).

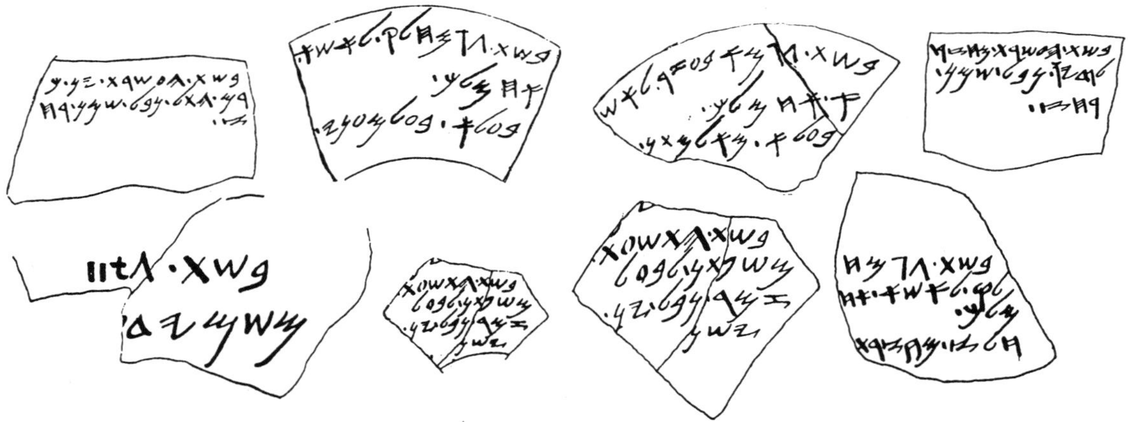

Fig. 21. The Ancient-Hebrew script on ostraca from Samaria (ca. 8th century BCE)

Fragments of two ostraca inscribed in the ancient Hebrew script were found in Tell Qassileh and may also be dated to the 8th century BCE. A fragmentary Hebrew ostracon from Tel-Dan and fragmentary jar inscriptions from Ḥazor are also from that period.

A few years ago, a minute ivory pomegranate dating from the 8th century BCE was bought in Jerusalem (it is now in the Israel Museum in Jerusalem). It bears a Hebrew inscription which mentions priests and the House of the [Lor]d. This may have been a cultic object from the First Temple in Jerusalem. The 'Jar of the Gate' inscription from Tel Kinrot is of approximately the same period.

Some inscriptions of the late 8th century BCE were discovered in the region of Judea, among them the famous Siloam inscription (fig. 22) dating from the end of the century (it is now in Istanbul), the Royal Steward inscription (now in the British Museum in London), burial inscriptions from Jerusalem of the same period, burial inscriptions from El-Kom in the Judean hills, a rock inscription in ink from a site near En-Gedi, and some of the earliest ʿArad ostraca. A fragment of a Hebrew ostracon from Gezer and an ostracon from Tel ʿIra are also from that period.

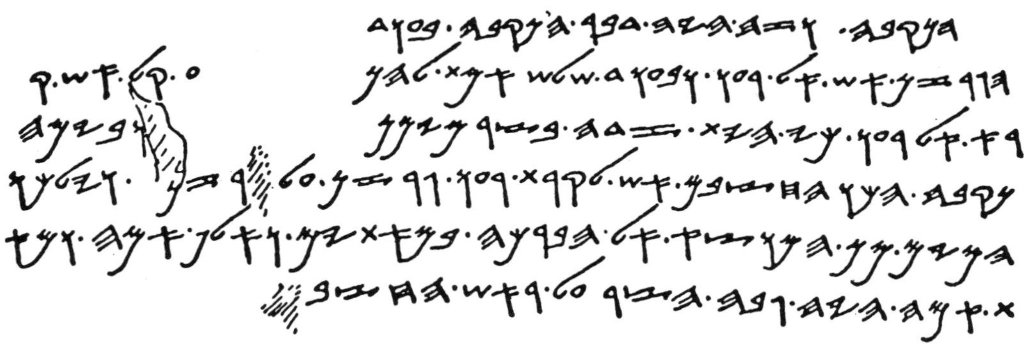

Fig. 22. The Siloam inscription (now in Istanbul)

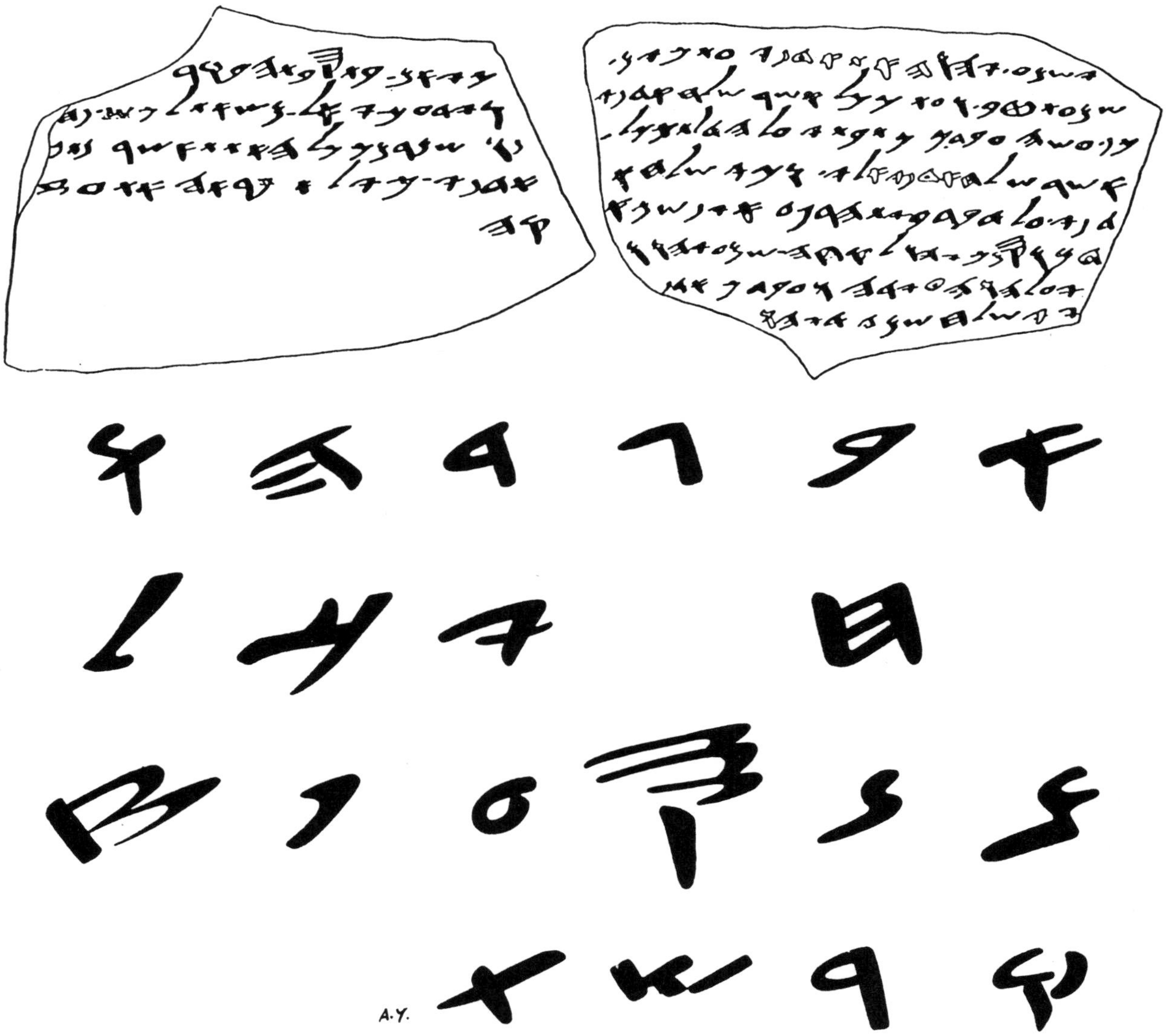

Fig. 23. A 6th century BCE ostracon from Lachish and the Ancient-Hebrew letters of the alphabet taken from an early 6th century BCE ostracon from Arad

Many seals of the 8th-6th centuries, carved in semi-precious stones, have been found in excavations throughout the land of Israel. Hundreds of jar handles dating to the 8th-7th centuries BCE, with seal-impressions inscribed

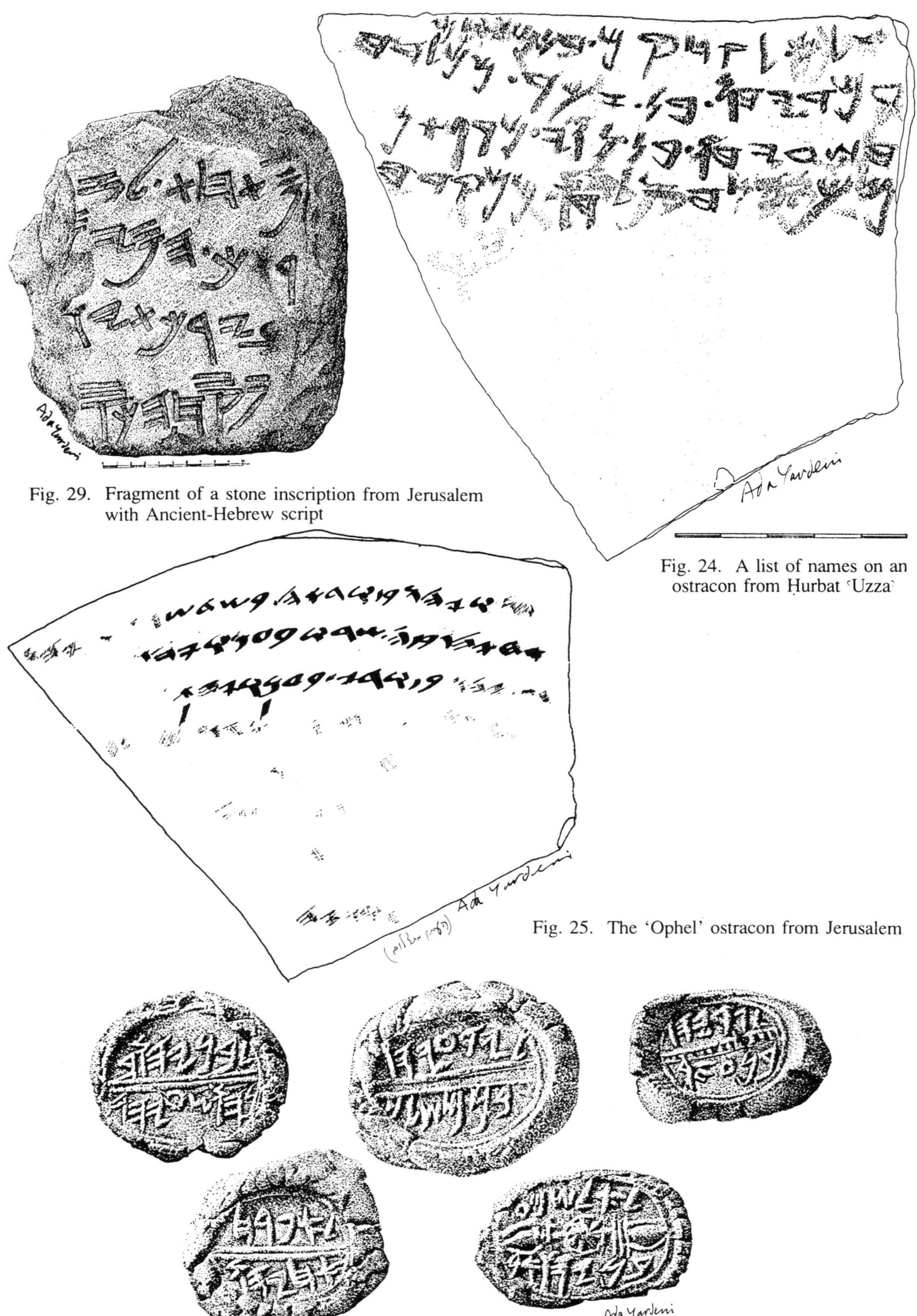

Fig. 29. Fragment of a stone inscription from Jerusalem with Ancient-Hebrew script

Fig. 24. A list of names on an ostracon from Ḥurbat ʿUzza

Fig. 25. The 'Ophel' ostracon from Jerusalem

Fig. 26. Bullae with Ancient-Hebrew script from the City of David (enlarged)

'La-Melekh' ('belonging to the king') were found in Judea, as well as many jar inscriptions, usually noting the name of the owner or the quantity, and seal impressions from the same period bearing the names of officials. Early Hebrew letters also appear on stone weights from the 7th-6th centuries BCE, unearthed in various sites in the country. Fragments of two alabaster vessels with early Hebrew lettering found in Susa are also from that period. A large group of Hebrew ostraca dating from the 7th and early 6th centuries BCE was discovered in ʿArad. Among them are several letters. Another group of letters was discovered in Lachish (see the script in fig. 23), dating to the early 6th century BCE, shortly before the city was conquered by the Babylonians. Recently, about 30 Hebrew ostraca dating from the late 7th century BCE were found in Ḥurbat ʿUzza (fig. 24). Another small group of ostraca and jar inscriptions with ancient Hebrew letters was discovered recently in Ḥirbet al-Muqannaʿ (ancient ʿEkron). Single Hebrew ostraca from the late First Temple period were discovered

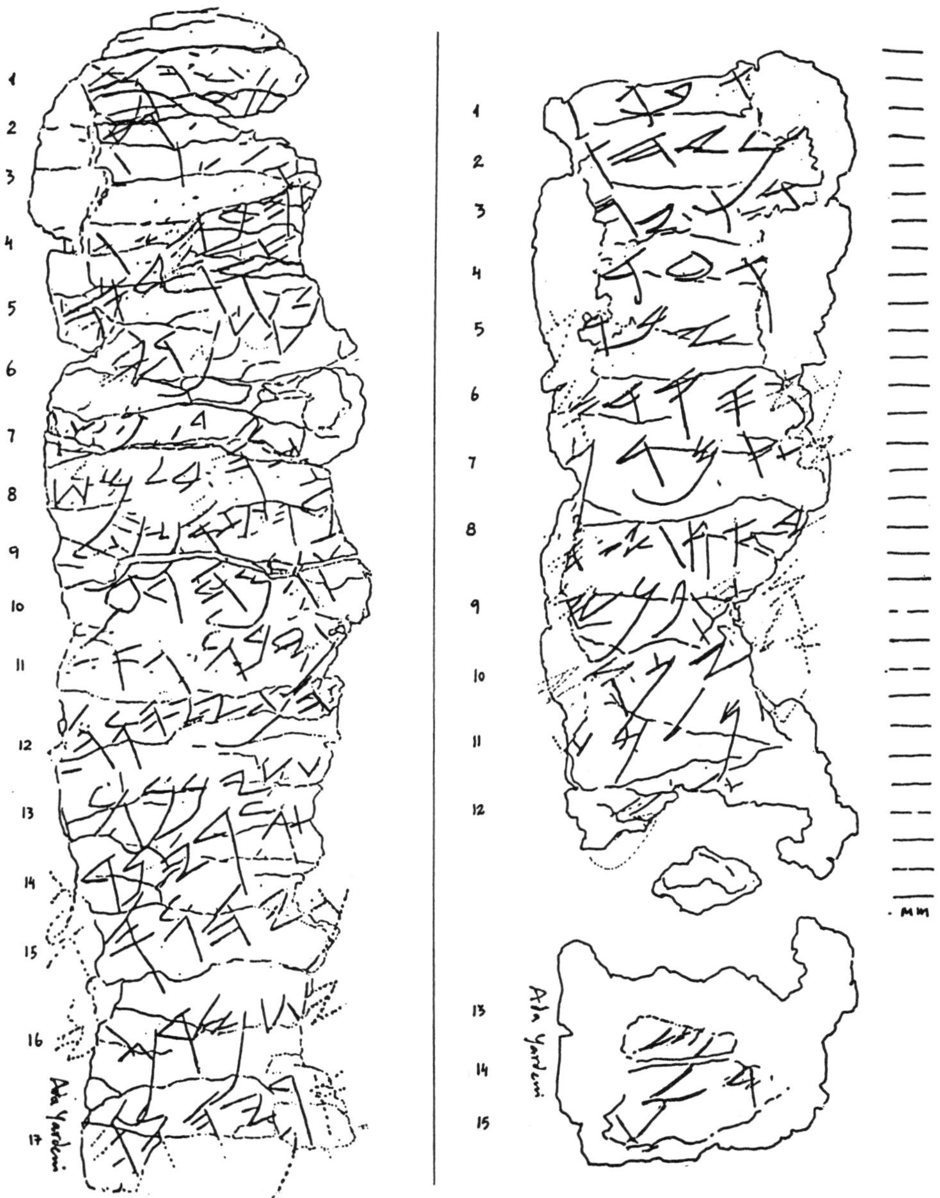

Fig. 27. The 'Priestly Blessing' amulets from Ketef Hinnom in Jerusalem (early 6th century BCE; enlarged)

in various places throughout the country, among them the 'Meṣad Ḥashaviahu' ostracon (on display in the Israel Museum in Jerusalem), the 'ʿOphel' ostracon from Jerusalem (fig. 25), and others. Ostraca from that period are still occasionally discovered in excavations in various sites in Israel.

Most of the ostraca were written on with ink and a few had letters incised in them. In addition to the findings mentioned above, many clay vessels with short inscriptions and large groups of bullae (seal impressions on silt used for sealing papyrus and leather documents) were discovered in Jerusalem and its vicinity (fig. 26), as well as in Lachish. Some inscriptions on jar-handles from Gibeʿon and perhaps the cave inscriptions from Ḥirbet Beit Leyyi also form part of the epigraphical material from that period. Two amulets with the priestly blessing from approximately the same period were discovered in Ketef Hinnom in Jerusalem (they are now in the Israel Museum in Jerusalem; fig. 27). Only one document on papyrus, from the 7th century BCE, has survived from the First Temple

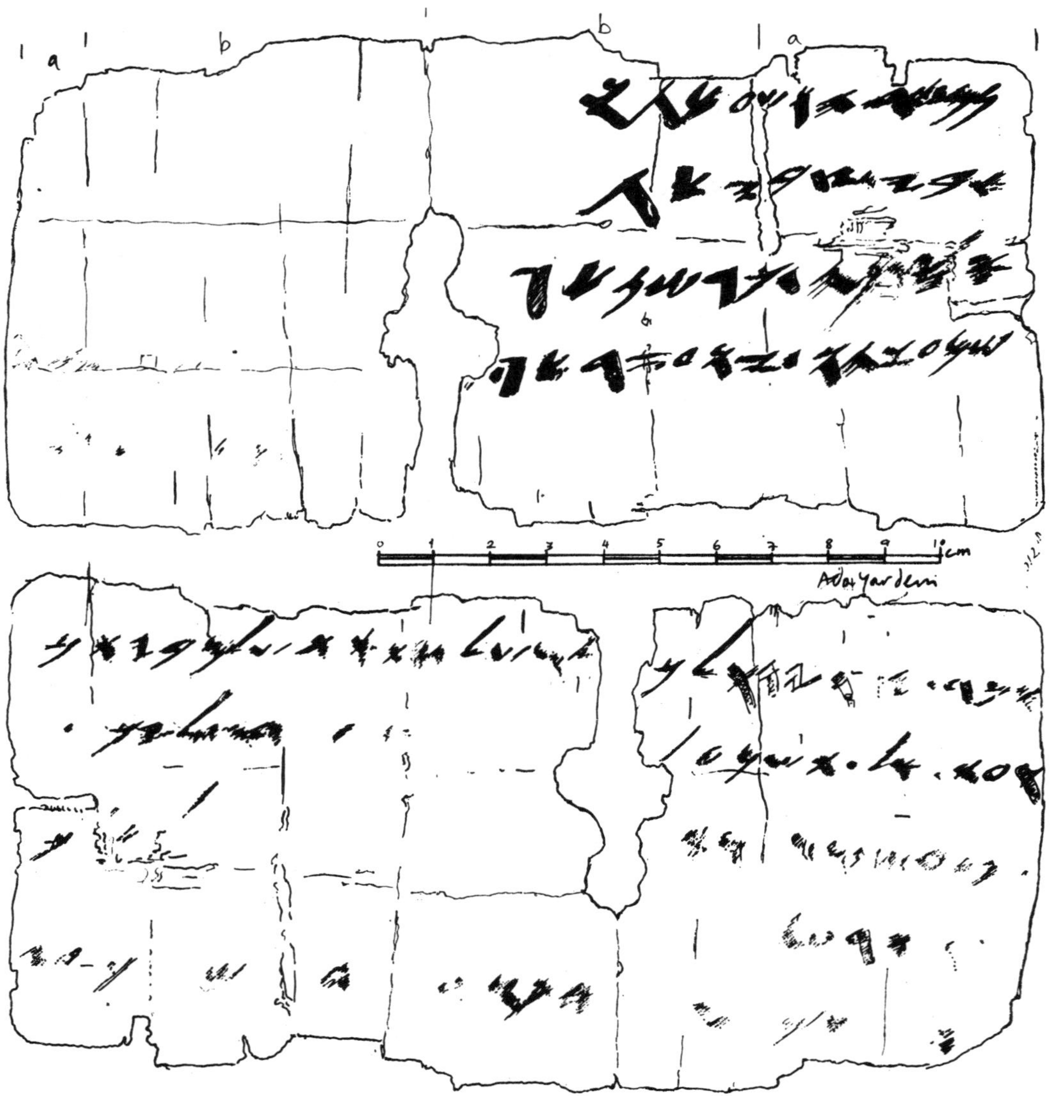

Fig. 28. The Ancient-Hebrew script on a papyrus fragment from Wadi Murabbaʿat (7th century BCE; Jerusalem, The Israel Museum; reduced)

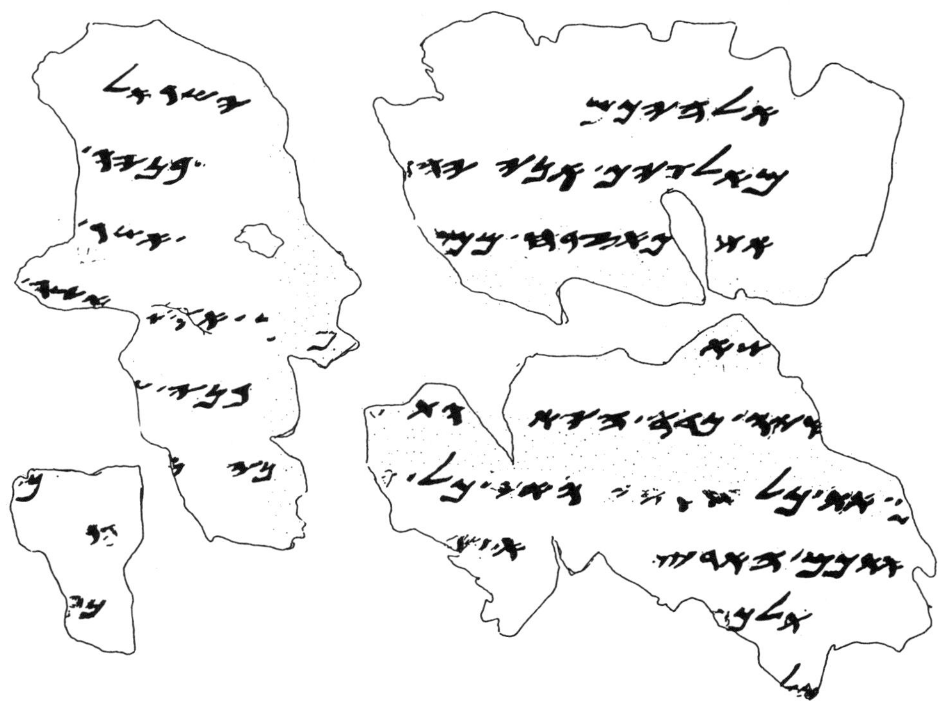

Fig. 30. Fragments of a Leviticus scroll from Qumran in Ancient-Hebrew script (ca. 3rd century BCE; The Rockefeller Museum of Antiquities, Jerusalem)

period (fig. 28). It was found in a cave in Wadi Murabbaʿat in the Judean desert and is today on display in the Israel Museum in Jerusalem. The impressions of papyrus fibers, which survived on the back of many bullae of that period, testify to the common use of papyrus for writing in that region.

The ancient Hebrew script was used continuously for Hebrew writing until the end of the First Temple period, i.e., the early 6th century BCE. At that time, the use of the Aramaic script began to prevail throughout the region and by the beginning of the Second Temple period it was already the official script of the Persian empire. The Jews in the Babylonian exile, as well as those who remained in the land of Israel, adopted the Aramaic script and both the official and everyday use of the ancient Hebrew script was gradually neglected. The epigraphical material in that script from the Second Temple period is relatively poor. The main finds were coins, seal impressions and impressions on jar handles bearing the names of Judea or Jerusalem. A fragment of an inscription on marble, and a fragment of a limestone tablet inscribed with elaborated letters in the ancient Hebrew script (fig. 29) were also found in Jerusalem.

Fragments of the Pentateuch written in the ancient Hebrew script dating from the 3rd or 2nd century BCE survived in caves in the Judean desert (fig. 30). The tetragrammaton and the word 'ʾEl' in ancient Hebrew letters occasionally appear in several scrolls otherwise written in the Jewish script (see below). Hasmonaean coins and coins from the Bar Kokhba revolt (132-135 CE), as well as a few ostraca found in Masada, predating the fall of the fortress in 74 CE, bear ancient Hebrew letters.

As epigraphical material is unearthed from time to time in archaeological excavations which are constantly taking place in Israel, findings are made which have not been published so far.

The ancient Hebrew script was a quite conservative one and its formal evolution was slow. Already at an early period a certain semi-cursive style evolved, apparently through writing with brush and ink, and it remained almost unchanged for centuries. Unlike the royal and dedication inscriptions found in neighbouring countries, only single fragments of Hebrew monumental inscriptions have been discovered so far. Some of them show the influence of letter-forms written in ink – an influence mainly reflected in the differences between bold and thin strokes running in different directions. Despite the use of brush and ink, the ancient Hebrew script did not develop an extreme cursive style (a style in which the letter-signs become similar in their forms or are joined to each other with ligatures).

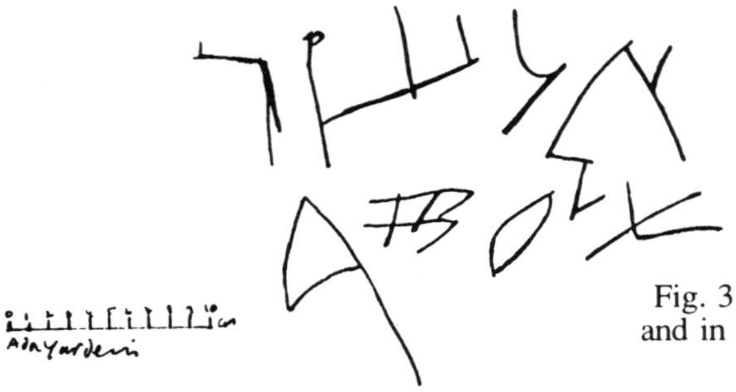

Fig. 31. The name ʾElʿazar in the Ancient-Hebrew script and in the Jewish script incised on a coffin from Jerusalem (the Herodian period)

The most cursive forms of ancient Hebrew letters appear in the name Elʿazar inscribed on an ossuary from Jerusalem (fig. 31). Most of the inscriptions and documents in the ancient Hebrew script are now kept in various museums and institutes in Israel, while a few important inscriptions are in other countries, especially England, France and Turkey. It seems that after the failure of the Bar Kokhba revolt the ancient Hebrew script was completely abandoned by the Jews. The heirs of that script were the Samaritans. Two seal impressions with ancient Hebrew letters were found in Wadi ed-Daliyeh near Jericho, together with Aramaic documents written in Samaria and dated to the 4th century BCE. Several stone inscriptions in ancient Hebrew letters were recently discovered on Mount Gerizim. These testify to the continuous use of the script in that region. The Samaritans continued to use the ancient Hebrew script and it became their national script. It was used by them for writing in Hebrew as well as in the Samaritan Aramaic dialect. In the course of its long history the Samaritan script developed several styles (e.g. fig. 32), and it is still in use.

Fig. 32. The letters of the alphabet in the Samaritan script

Epigraphical material from ancient Moabite, Ammonite, Edomite and Philistine sites shows that these peoples used the Hebrew script when under Israelite cultural and political influence. (A stone inscription in ancient Hebrew letters from the 7th century BCE, mentioning the name of the Philistine site ʿEkron, was recently discovered in Ḥirbet al-Muqannaʿ – ancient ʿEkron). Later the Moabite and Edomite scripts were exposed to the influence of the early Aramaic script, while the Philistine script shows the influence of the Phoenician script. Ammonite inscriptions show a strong similarity to the early Aramaic letter-forms, and scholars are uncertain whether it is an independent script or a local variant of the Aramaic script.

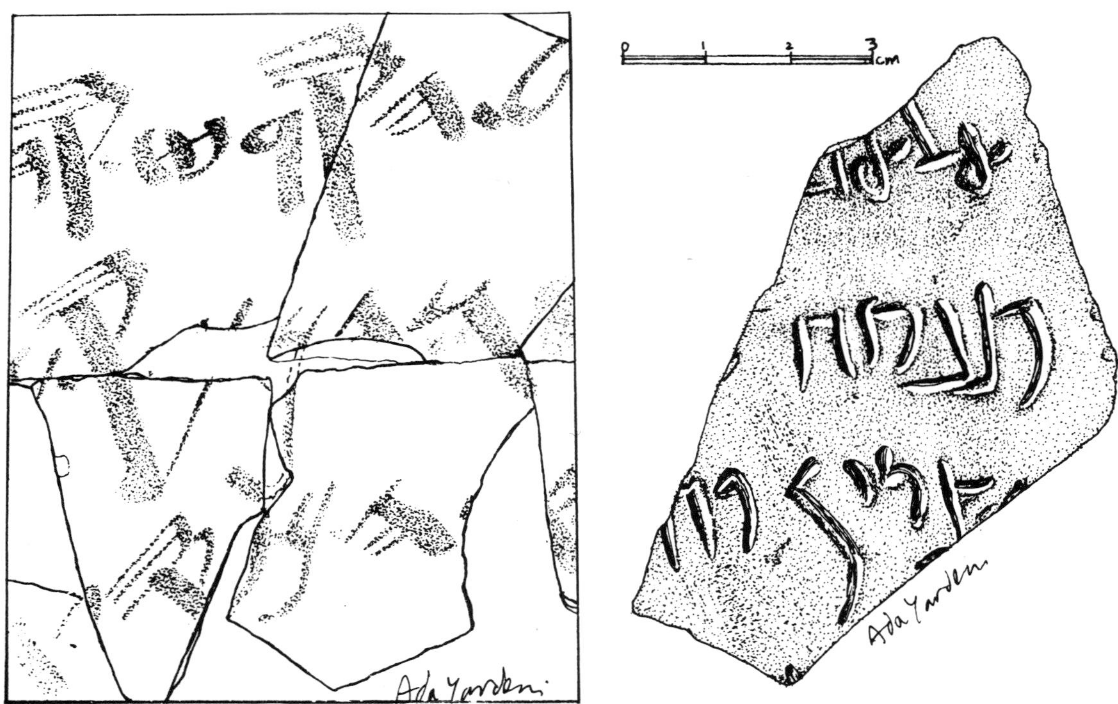

Fig. 33. Two ostraca from the City of David, Jerusalem:
one written in ink in the Ancient-Hebrew script and the other incised (before burning) in a late Aramaic script of the 3rd or 2nd century BCE

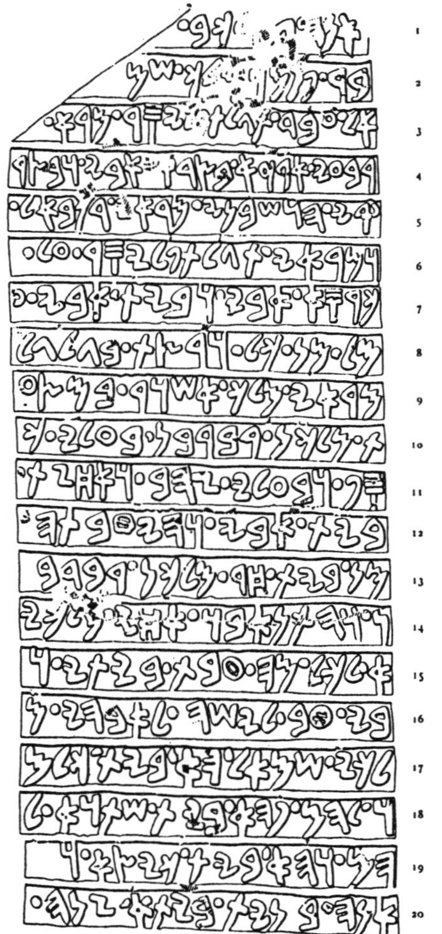

Fig. 34. Early Aramaic script engraved on the Bar Rakkub stele (8th century BCE)

D. THE MAIN FINDINGS IN THE ARAMAIC SCRIPT

The Aramaeans were Semitic tribes mentioned in various sources from the 2nd half of the 2nd millennium BCE. Around the beginning of the 1st millennium BCE they settled permanently in the area of Syria and Mesopotamia. Like the Hebrews, the Aramaeans adopted the Phoenician script. Inscriptions in Aramaic from the 9th century BCE were still written in the Phoenician script (see e.g. fig. 15). Around the mid 8th century, the Aramaic script began to exhibit characteristics which distinguished it from the Phoenician script, in particular an opening at the tops of the letters. Already in the 7th century BCE, the Aramaic script, which was easy to write and contained a small number of signs, began to replace the complex cuneiform script with its hundreds of signs in the Neo-Assyrian empire. The Aramaic language became the lingua franca and the Aramaic alphabet began to be used for the official correspondence between the nations of the Neo-Assyrian, and later the Babylonian empires. They consequently became the language and script of the clerks and scribes. When the Persians conquered Babylon in 539 BCE, they gave the Aramaic language and script an official status throughout their enormous empire which stretched from Asia Minor, Egypt and North Arabia in the west, to Afghanistan and India in the east. Though the Aramaic script served for the writing of official documents and letters at that period, it was rarely used for stone-carved royal inscriptions, which were usually written in the traditional language and script of the respective nations in the empire.

Among the earliest inscriptions in the Aramaic script are bricks from Ḥammat from the mid 8th century, the Bar Rakkub stone inscriptions (fig. 34), ivory inscriptions from Nimrud (Calaḥ), several seals, dated inscriptions on bronze weights from Nineveh, and an ostracon from Nimrud from the end of the 8th century. Scholars differ on the dating of a plaster inscription from Deir-ʿAlla, in which Bilʿam son of Beʿor is mentioned. Some place it around the mid 8th century BCE, others at the end of that century, classifying it with Ammonite inscriptions. A Phoenician inscription in Aramaic script dating from approximately the beginning of the 7th century BCE was discovered in Arslan Tash in northern Syria. A long letter in ink on an ostracon, 'the Assur Ostracon' (now in Berlin; fig. 35), dates from approximately the 2nd half of the 7th century. Another letter, on papyrus, from the early 6th century, named the 'Adon letter', was found in Saqqara and was probably written in ʿEkron (it is now in Cairo; fig. 36). Two burial inscriptions from Nerab and an inscription from Gözne in Asia Minor date from the 7th century BCE. The 'blsrʾṣr' inscription and the 'psmšk' ostracon apparently date from the same period. A group of dated clay tablets from Nineveh and Aramaic dockets from Assur and Tell Ḥallaf also belong to the 7th century BCE. An Aramaic contract on a clay tablet of unknown provenance is dated to the 34th year of Nebuchadnezzar 571/70 BCE (it is now in the Louvre). Dated Aramaic clay tablets from Nerab and from Babylon are from the 6th century BCE. A dated lease document from 515 BCE was found in Egypt (the 'Bauer-Meissner Papyrus'; now in Munich); A group of eight private letters from the late 6th or early 5th century BCE which did not reach its

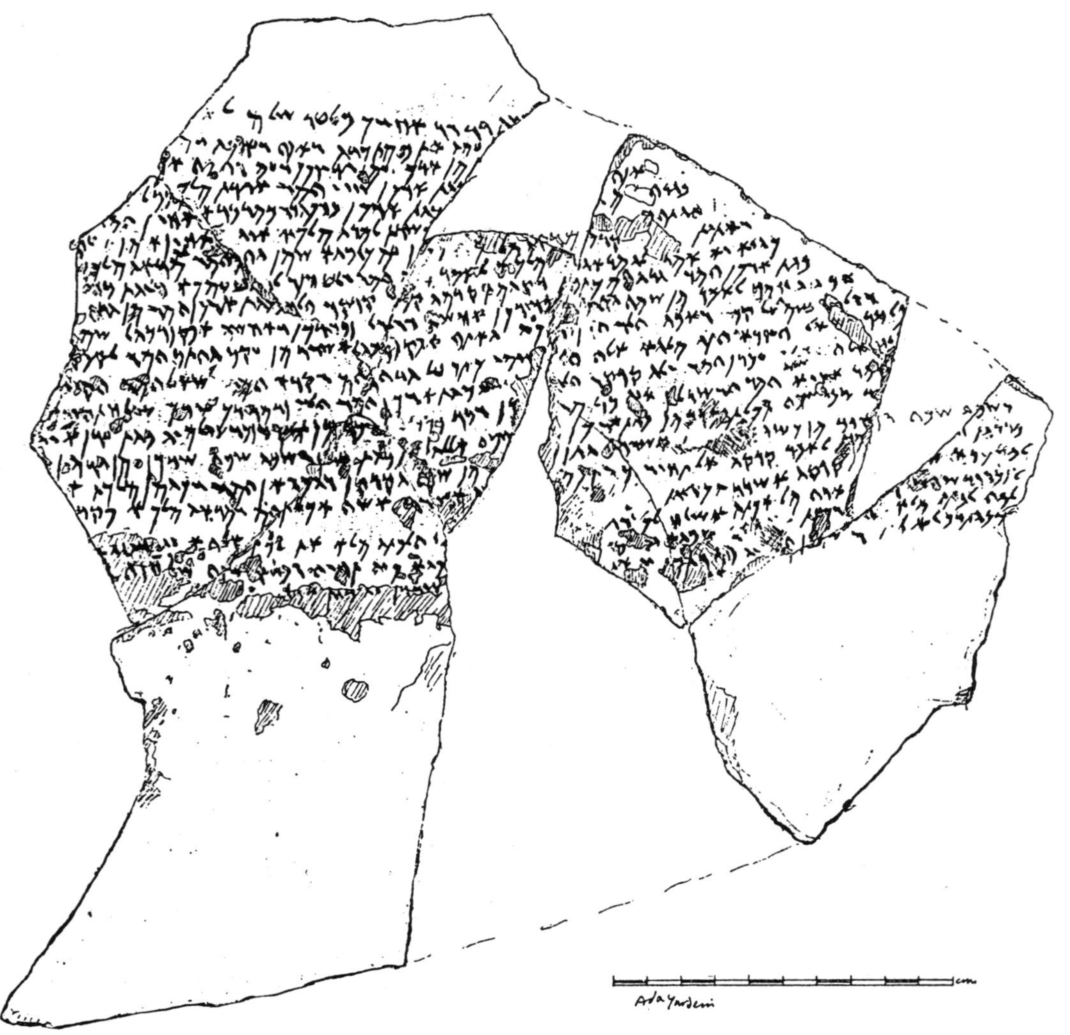

Fig. 35. 7th century BCE Aramaic script written in ink on the 'Assur ostracon' (now in Berlin; reduced)

destination was discovered in Hermopolis (it is now in the University of Cairo). Another three fragments of documents on papyrus discovered in Egypt belong to the same period (two are now in Cairo [Cowley 52 and Richie 15] and one is in Göttingen).

The Aramaic formal script is attested in inscriptions and documents from a period of over 400 years – from the 7th to the 3rd centuries BCE. The formal Aramaic script of the Persian period, which flourished in the 5th century BCE, is fairly uniform in style. A vast number of Aramaic documents of the Persian period has been discovered in the countries which belonged to the Persian empire, particularly Egypt, Israel, Jordan, Asia Minor, Tema (North Arabia), Syria, Iran, Iraq, India and Afghanistan. Most of the material is now to be found in museums and libraries around the world, and the chief collections are in Cairo, Berlin, Oxford, London, and New York. The largest and most important group of Aramaic documents of the Persian period was discovered in Egypt – mainly on the island of Elephantine on the Nile and in Saqqara. The island's Jewish inhabitants were part of the Persian garrison which included Aramaeans and people of other nationalities as well. The findings

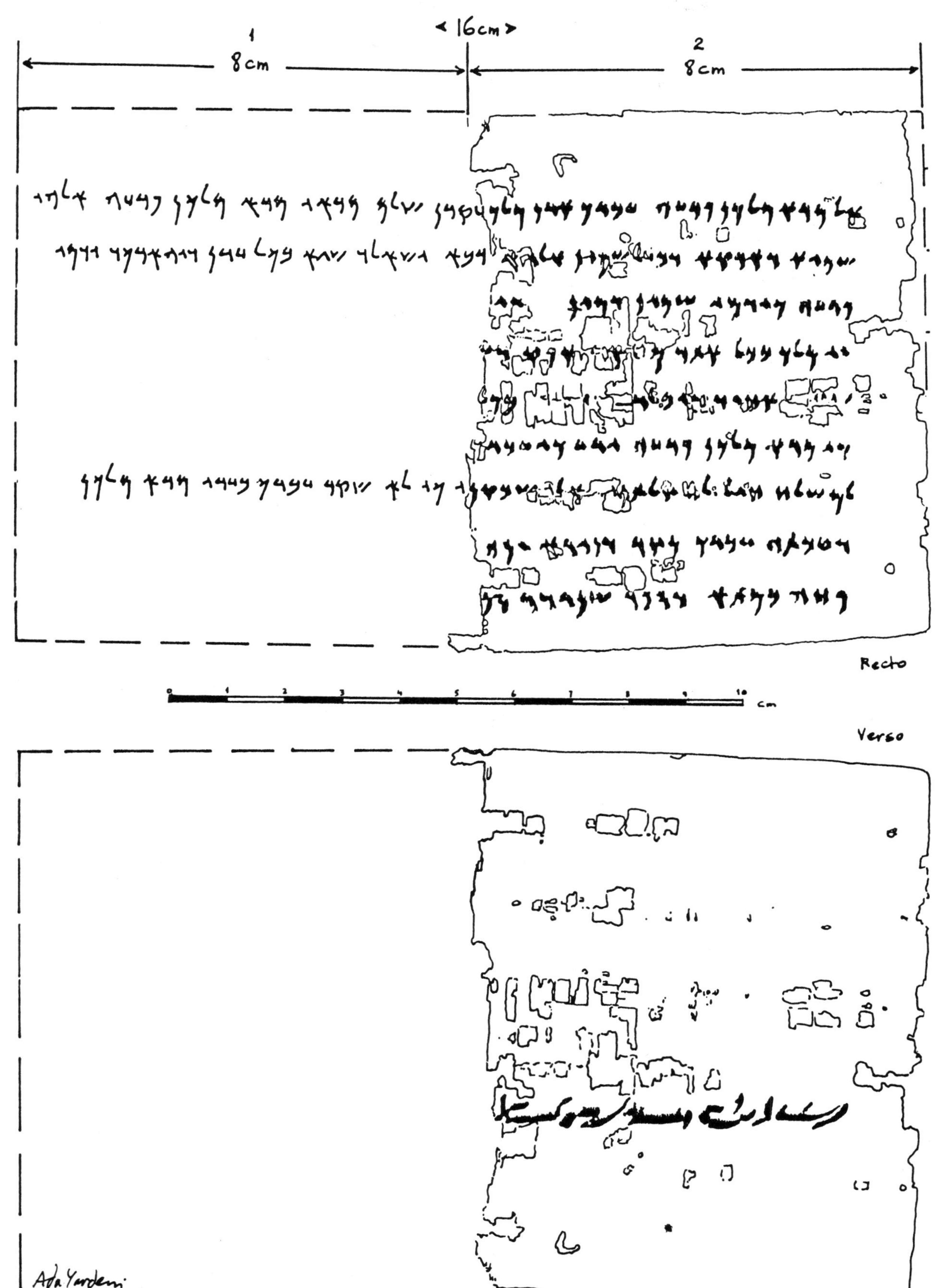

Fig. 36. The late 7th century BCE Aramaic script written in ink on papyrus in the 'Adon letter' from Saqqara (real size)

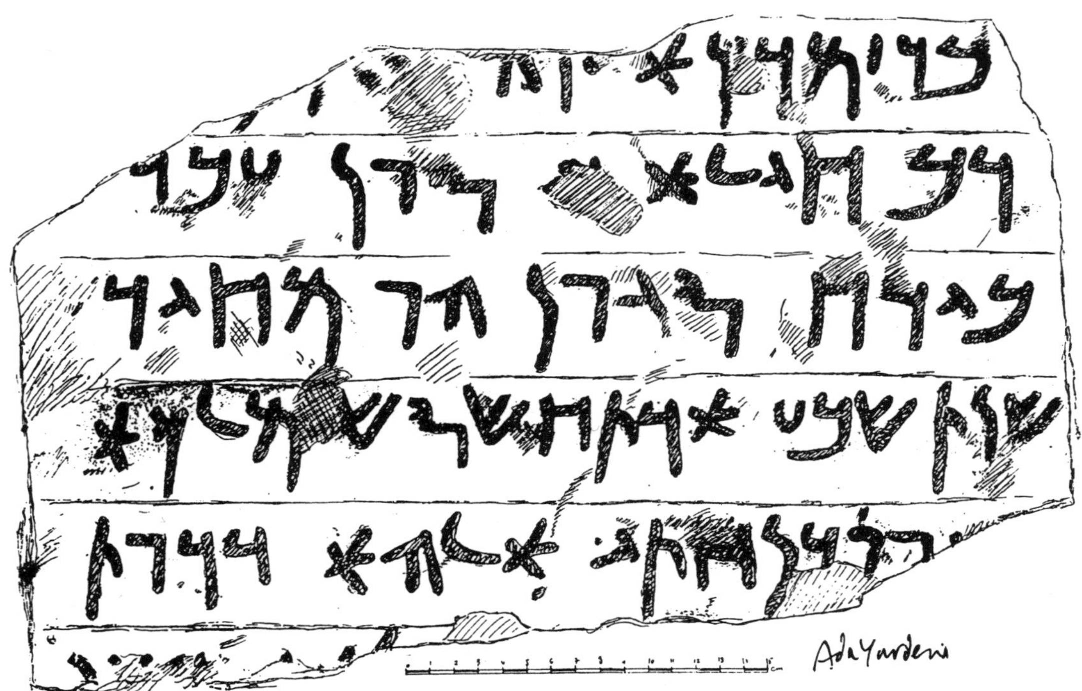

Fig. 37. An Aramaic inscription dating from the seventh year of Artaxerxes I (458 BCE)

include hundreds of documents written on various materials, such as papyrus, clay, stone, wood and metal. Together with the large number of dated contracts and lists, there are a few dated inscriptions, such as a funerary inscription (lost in World War II) of the year 482 BCE and a small stele of year seven of the reign of Artaxerxes (458 BCE; it is now in Cairo; fig. 37).

The excavations on the island, which started at the end of the 19th century and still continue, unearthed hundreds of documents on papyrus, some intact and most of them fragmented. Among them are more than fifty

Fig. 38. The formal Aramaic script in a detail of a papyrus deed, dating from the year 495 BCE (Cowley 1; real size)

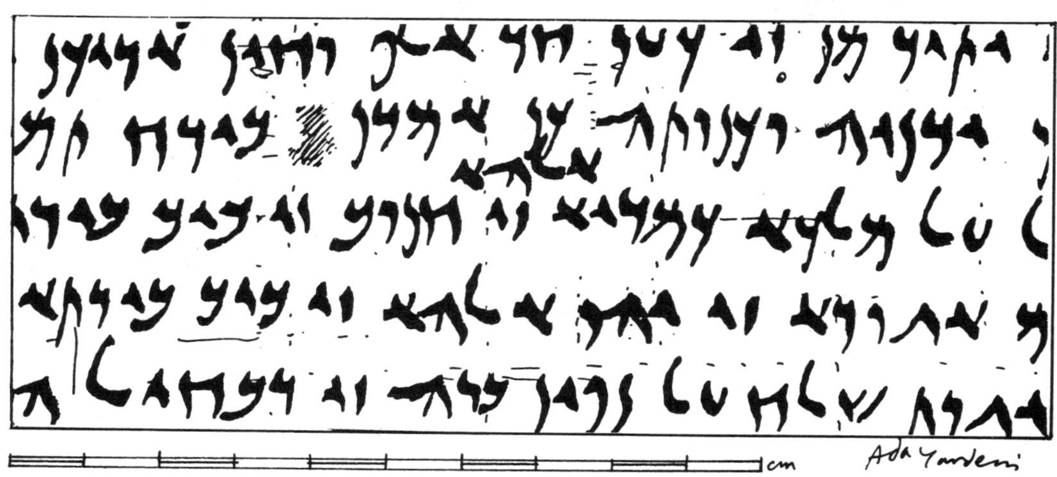

Fig. 39. Detail of an Aramaic letter on papyrus sent by Jews from Egypt to priests in Jerusalem at the end of the 5th century BCE (Cowley 30; real size)

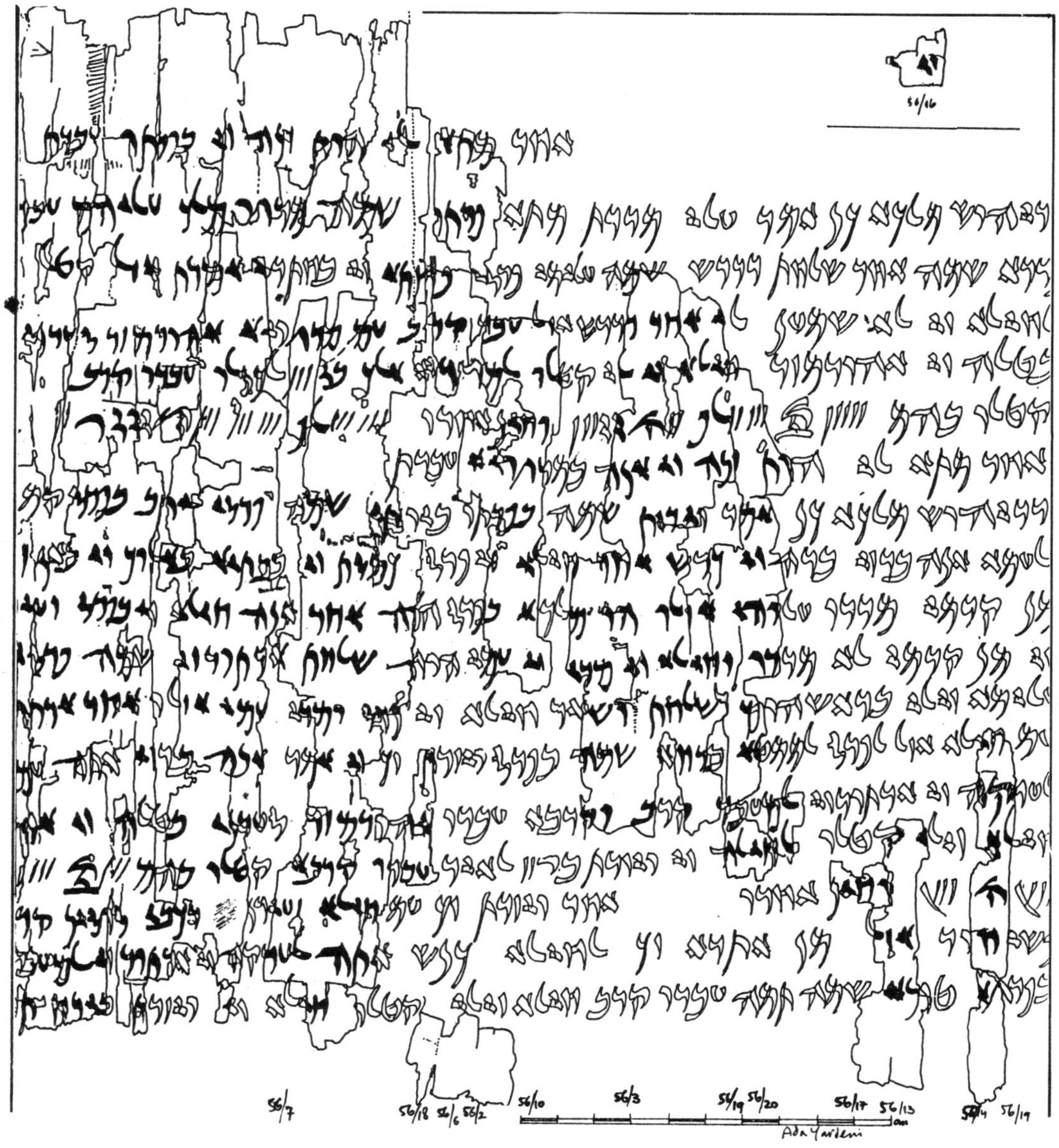

Fig. 40. Detail of the 5th century Aramaic copy of the 'Behistun inscription' of Darius I on a papyrus scroll from Elephantine (with part of the text restored; reduced)

contracts, many of which bear dates from the beginning to the end of the 5th century BCE (fig. 38); formal and private letters, among which are two copies of a letter sent by Elephantine Jews to Jerusalem (fig. 39); a copy of the Behistun inscription of Darius I (fig. 40); fragments from a scroll of Aḥiqar's fables (fig. 41); fragments of a literary text; and lists and accounts. The longest non-literary text is an erased customs account over which Aḥiqar's text was written. It contained some 60 columns (40 of which have partly survived) listing taxes collected from Ionian and Phoenician ships for the king's house in the year 475 BCE. Also excavated were hundreds of ostraca (some of which are as yet unpublished), mostly letters and some lists of names. Among sixteen Aramaic letters written on hide, which were sent by Persian officials to Egypt, are two dated letters

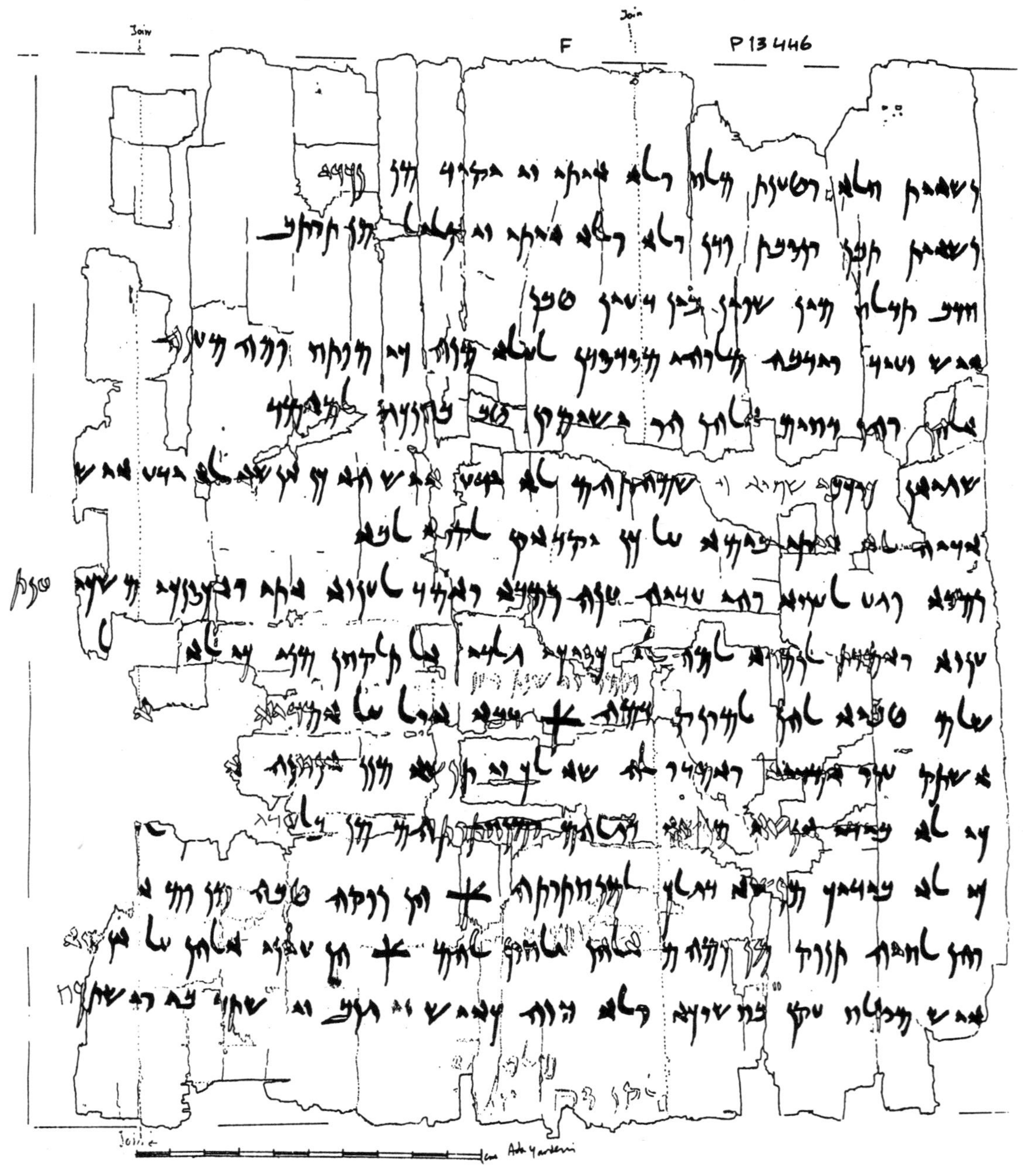

Fig. 41. Detail of the 5th century Aramaic version of the Fables of Aḥiqar on a papyrus scroll from Elephantine (reduced)

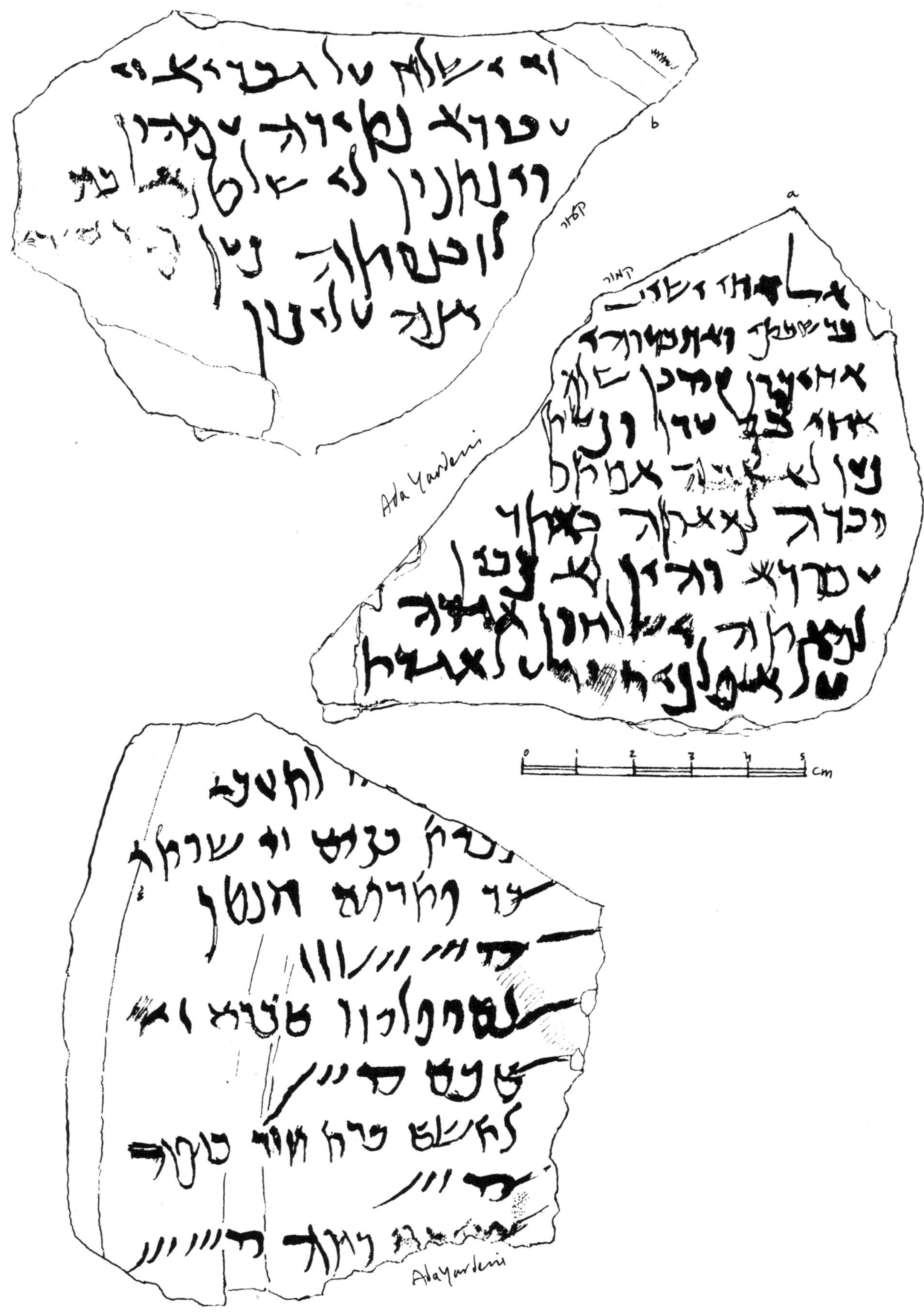

Fig. 42. Two Aramaic ostraca from Edfu, Egypt, from the 4th and 3rd centuries BCE (real size)

of 427 and 411 BCE. Some 200 Aramaic papyrus fragments and a few ostraca were discovered in Saqqara in the nineteen-sixties. The Aramaic epigraphical material from Egypt also includes inscriptions on various objects such as jars, statuettes, funerary stelae, tombstones, coffins, labels of mummies, scribal palettes, silver bowls, seals and bullae. Remnants of a long Aramaic literary text of about the early 5th century BCE survived on the walls of a cave in Sheikh Faḍil. Aramaic graffiti appear among Phoenician and Greek graffiti on the walls and pillars of the the temple of Osiris in Abydos. Aramaic documents of the Hellenistic period were found in Edfu, including documents on papyrus and ostraca (fig. 42) as well as tomb inscriptions. An ostracon found in Zawiyet el-Maytin (Kom el-ʾAḥmar; fig. 43) is also from that period.

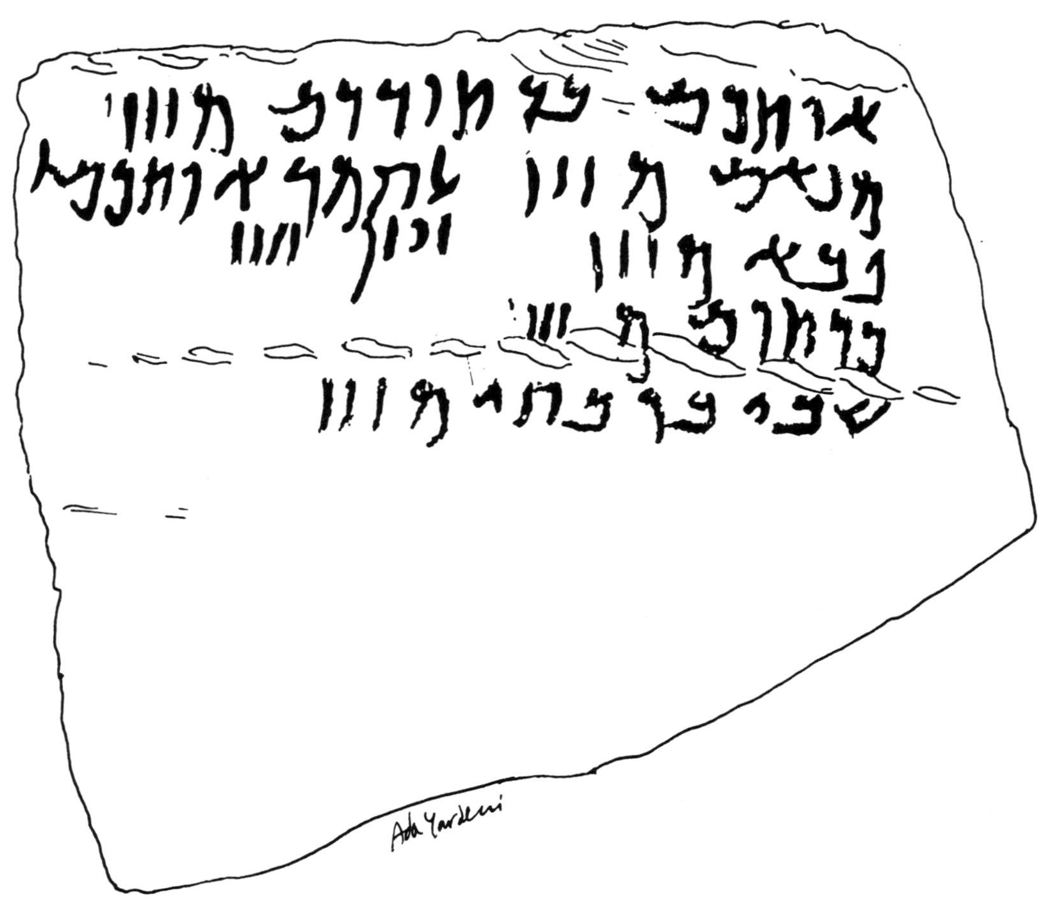

Fig. 43. The late Aramaic script on an ostracon from Kom al-ʾAḥmar (ca. 3rd century BCE; Louvre E. 23566; reduced)

The number of Aramaic epigraphical findings from the Persian period outside Egypt is much smaller. Aramaic inscriptions and ostraca as well as clay tablets, seals and coins from that period have been discovered throughout the area of the Persian empire. A considerable number of finds were made in Israel. Because of their direct connection with the Jewish script, I will now list the most important findings. Most of the Israeli material in Aramaic script is on ostraca, generally written in ink, and in a few cases incised, before or after the clay was burnt. A small group of ostraca and jar inscriptions from the 5th century BCE were found in Tell

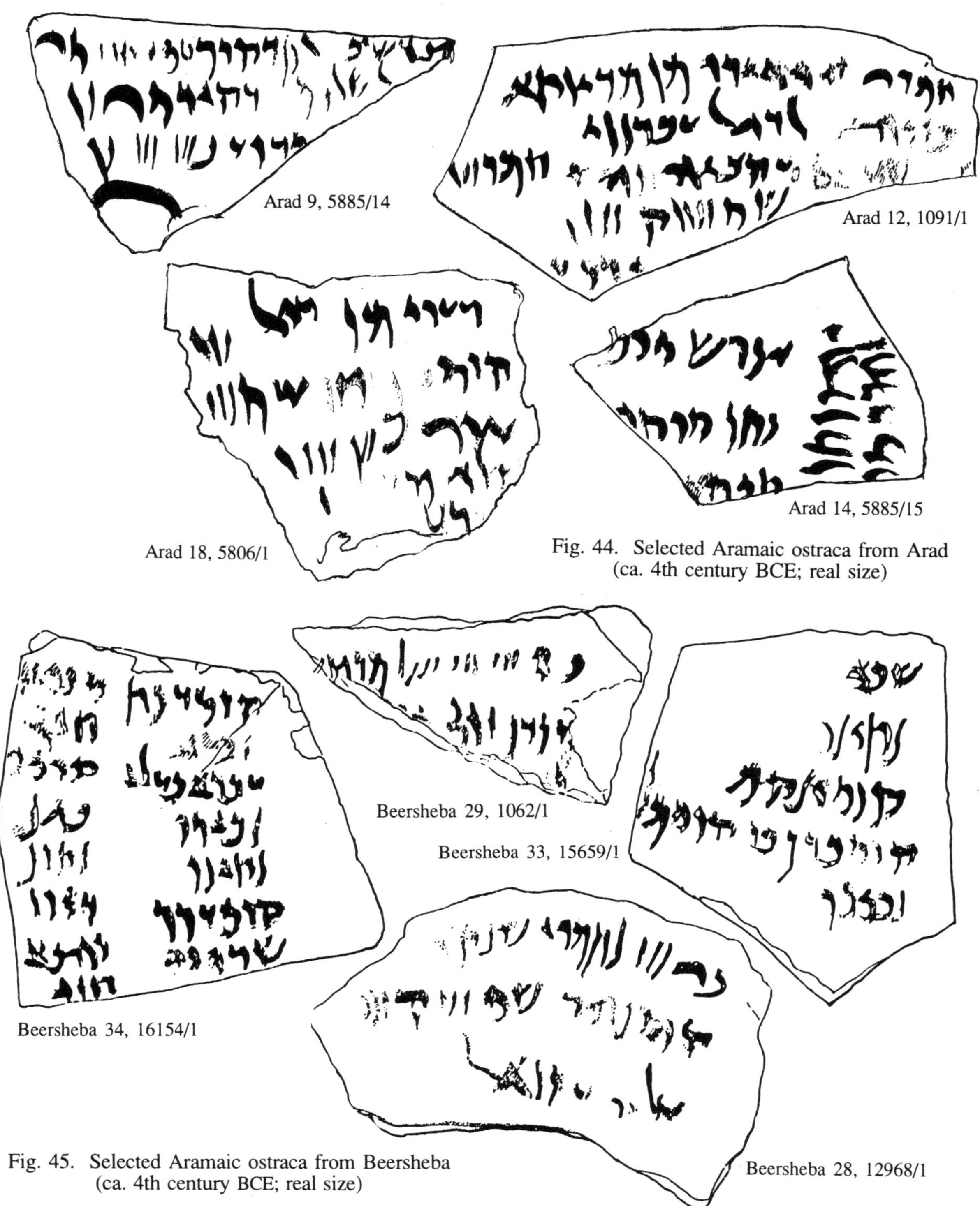

Fig. 44. Selected Aramaic ostraca from Arad (ca. 4th century BCE; real size)

Fig. 45. Selected Aramaic ostraca from Beersheba (ca. 4th century BCE; real size)

Jemmeh and single ostraca from the 5th and 4th centuries were found in various sites throughout the country, such as Tell el Farʿah, Yaṭṭa, Raphiaḥ, Tel ʿIra, Tel Yokneʿam, Gibeʿon, Ashdod, Eilat, ʿEn Gedi and elsewhere. An incense altar of the Persian period bearing Aramaic letters was found in Lachish. A large group of Aramaic ostraca, mostly from about the late 5th to the early 4th centuries BCE, was found in ʿArad (fig. 44), and another large group from the same period was found in Beersheba (fig. 45). A large group of papyri in Aramaic script written in Samaria and dated to the 4th century BCE was discovered in Wadi ed-Daliyeh near

Fig. 46. Detail of an Aramaic deed on papyrus from Wadi ed-Daliyeh near Jericho (SP 1) dating from the year 335 BCE (Jerusalem, The Israel Museum; real size)

Jericho (fig. 46), and another papyrus with a list of names from roughly the same period was recently discovered in a cave near Jericho (named the 'Abiʾur cave' after a person mentioned in the document). Some 800 ostraca bearing short texts in Aramaic script, many of them dated to the middle of the 4th century BCE, have become known recently and about half of them have already been published (about 200 of these ostraca are in the Israel Museum and another group is in the Bible Lands Museum in Jerusalem; about 50 are in the Jewish Theological Seminary in New York; the others are still in private collections). A group of ostraca (still unpublished) from the same period was recently discovered in Mareshah. A few 3rd century BCE ostraca, one of them dated, were found in el-Kom (fig. 47). Short Aramaic inscriptions on stone from around the 3rd century BCE were discovered recently on Mt. Gerizim. A most important discovery was recently made of a dated Idumean marriage contract on an ostracon found in Mareshah. The ostracon (fig. 48), written in a semi-formal Aramaic script, is dated to the year 136 of the Seleucid era: i.e., 176 BCE. It provides the missing link between the late Aramaic script and the Jewish Hasmonean semi-formal script.

Fig. 47. Aramaic ostraca from El-Kom (mid-3rd century BCE)

The formal evolution of the letter-signs in the ink-written Aramaic clerical script was faster than in the case of the lapidary script. Carving or incising letter-signs in stone or other hard materials takes much longer than writing with brush and ink or paint. Aramaic inscriptions in the lapidary script from the 4th century BCE include, for instance, a tri-lingual inscription from Xanthos dating from year 2 of Artaxerxes III (358 BCE) and a bi-lingual inscription from Sardis dating from year 10 of this king (350 BCE). The forms of the lapidary letter-signs were generally precise and conservative. Writing in ink naturally tends to change and evolve faster than writing on a hard material. It creates rounder and more cursive shapes. The scribe avoids lifting his hand from the writing surface in order to increase the speed of writing, and in this way ligatures or semi-ligatures are sometimes created between consecutive strokes. Interrelationships develop between the lapidary and the cursive scripts, and they influence each other. In this way intermediate shapes are created: cursive forms are introduced into the lapidary script and vice versa. Few ink inscriptions use

Fig. 48. The late Aramaic script in an Idumean marriage contract on an ostracon dating from 176 BCE

the letter shapes of the Aramaic lapidary script and the letters Yod and Zayin are remarkable in preserving their archaic forms longer than the other letters. The clerical script required clear and legible forms as it was used in official documents. It was therefore generally carefully written by professional scribes and, although cursive in character, the Aramaic official script was calligraphic and highly legible. In most of the documents the letter-signs are relatively large and not connected by ligatures. The letters differ from each other in shape and size to such an extent that they can sometimes be identified even when only small parts of them survive. The Aramaic clerical script which appears in hundreds of documents discovered throughout the Persian empire 'from India to Kush' reveals only minor local differences in the execution of the basic forms.

Gradually, the cursive tendency created a difference between the medial and final forms of certain letters: i.e., the forms of the letters when appearing in the middle of the word or at its end. This tendency already began in the 5th century BCE but did not become a fixed pattern in the Aramaic script. The Aramaic writing tradition began to weaken when Alexander the Great conquered Persia in 323 BCE. A process began, which gave rise to a multitude of variations of shape and different types of letters in different parts of the empire. Greek replaced Aramaic as the administrative language and the Greek script replaced the Aramaic script in official documents. As a unifying element no longer existed, the Aramaic script developed local forms around the end of the 3rd century BCE which eventually evolved into independent scripts used for different languages. Some of these scripts continued to evolve and are still in use. There is a distinction between the eastern and western branches of the forms of writing which grew out of the Aramaic script. The eastern branch comprises the Syriac scripts, the Manadic script, the Palmyrene script, the script of Ḥatra, the script of Nissa (Turkmenistan), the script of Armazi (Georgia), the ᶜElamean script and others. The western branch comprises the Nabatean and the Jewish scripts.

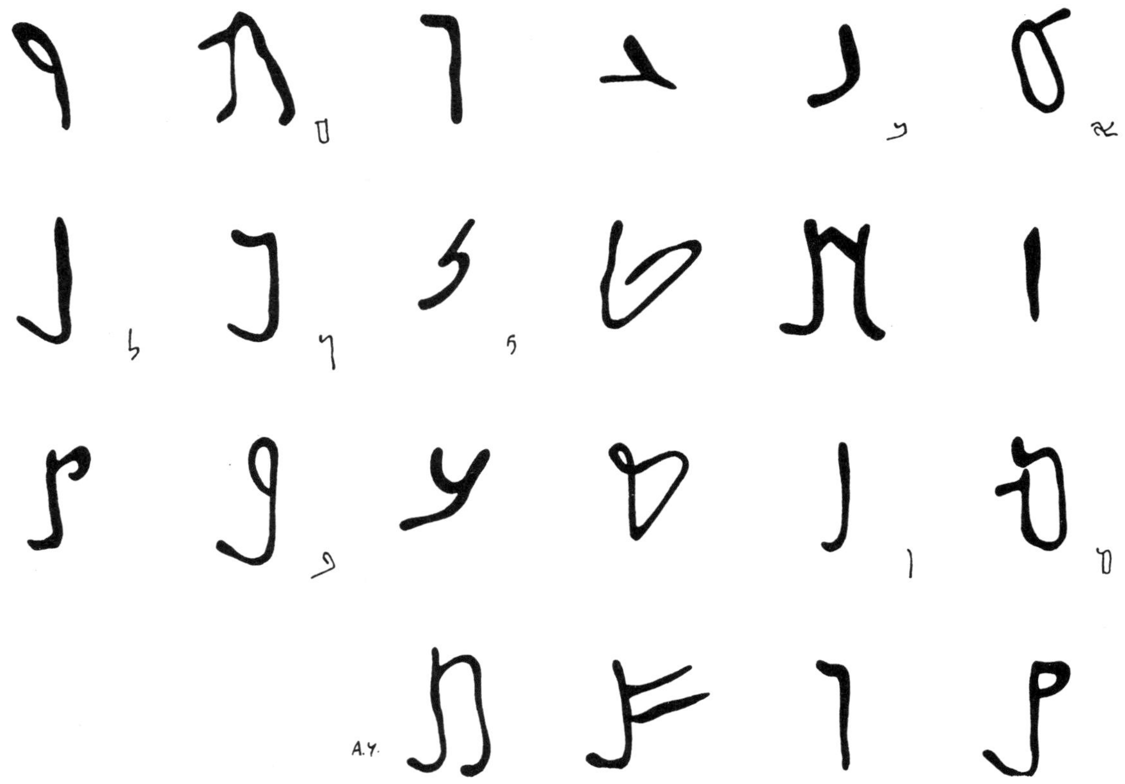

Fig. 49. Nabatean alphabet taken from a papyrus deed from the late 1st century BCE

The Nabatean script was used throughout the Nabatean kingdom, and is the ancestor of the Arabic script. After the Roman conquest of Nabatea in 106 it continued to exist in the Roman province of Arabia, which included the Nabatean region. The Nabatean script (figs. 49, 50) rapidly developed an extreme cursive quality expressed in ligatures and in the formal similarity of several letter-signs. This cursive script evolved into the classical Arabic script. The earliest known Arabic inscriptions date from the 5th century CE.

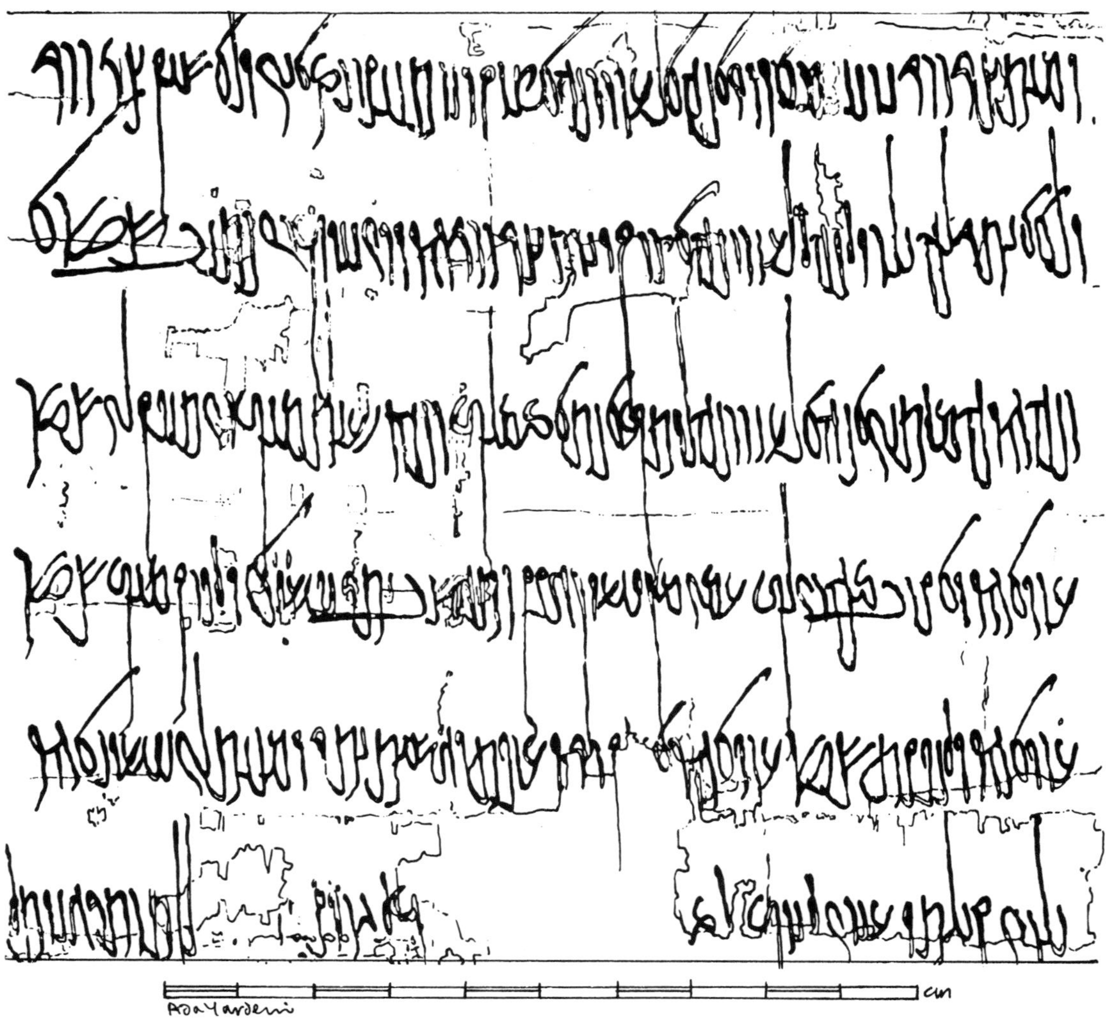

Fig. 50. Detail of a papyrus deed from Naḥal Ḥever (pap. Starckey) written in an elegant cursive Nabatean hand (real size)

The Jewish script, which the sources call 'Assyrian' or 'Square', adopted various forms and styles in the lands of the Jewish Diaspora, but the basic structure of the letter-signs inherited from the Aramaic script can still be recognised today in the modern Hebrew script.

E. THE ABANDONMENT OF THE ANCIENT HEBREW SCRIPT IN FAVOUR OF THE ARAMAIC SCRIPT, AND THE BIRTH OF THE JEWISH SCRIPT

At the beginning of the 6th century BCE, Judea was situated between the two dominant superpowers of that period – Babylon in the east and Egypt in the south-west. Egypt's attempts to take over Mesopotamia by an alliance with Assyria at the end of the 7th century BCE compelled the rulers of Babylon to conduct a series of campaigns against Egypt. This confrontation caused a political crisis in Judea, which had become a thoroughfare for the Babylonian army. It resulted in the destruction of the First Temple by Nebuchadnezzar's army in 586 BCE, and the exile to Babylon of a major part of the urban population, the upper classes, the priesthood, and Judea's ruling families. The urban lower classes and the rural population remained in the country.

The language spoken in the land of Israel before the exile to Babylon was Hebrew, and the ruling and upper classes understood Aramaic as well. The Jews who were exiled to Babylon were influenced by their environment, and so began speaking and writing Aramaic in order to communicate with their neighbours and for the writing of official documents. When the Temple was destroyed, the Jews lost their main place of worship, and the sacrifices and services in the Temple were replaced by the study of the Torah and prayers in the synagogue. The use of Hebrew and the ancient Hebrew script apparently served as a unifying factor in the Jews' attempt to maintain their native Hebrew heritage and in preserving the hope of salvation and return to their land. It is therefore difficult to understand why scrolls of the Bible were written in Aramaic script rather than the ancient Hebrew script, when the sanctity of the Torah was so important to the Jews! That, perhaps, is what prompted certain Jewish sages to claim that Ezra the scribe received the Torah in the Aramaic language.

Scholars are divided as to whether or not a written canon of the Pentateuch existed before the Babylonian exile. The book of the Torah found by King Josiah in the Temple was probably the Book of Deuteronomy. It is possible, however, that the Jews of the Diaspora already possessed at least part of the Torah in writing or that they began to collate the written Torah in their desire to maintain the national heritage. We may assume that sacred books and literary works in the Israel of the pre-exilic period were written on papyrus. In Babylon they may have used hide, as papyrus does not grow there. Those scrolls were sewn together similarly to the papyrus scrolls in which a number of sheets are attached to each other.

Some of the Jewish exiles began to return to Israel shortly after Babylon was conquered by the Persians in 539 BCE. The first group returned with Sheshbazzar. Another group came with Zerubbabel during the reign of Darius I. A large wave of immigrants came with Ezra the scribe in 458 BCE (some scholars believe Ezra returned at the beginning of the 4th century BCE, later than Nehemiah).

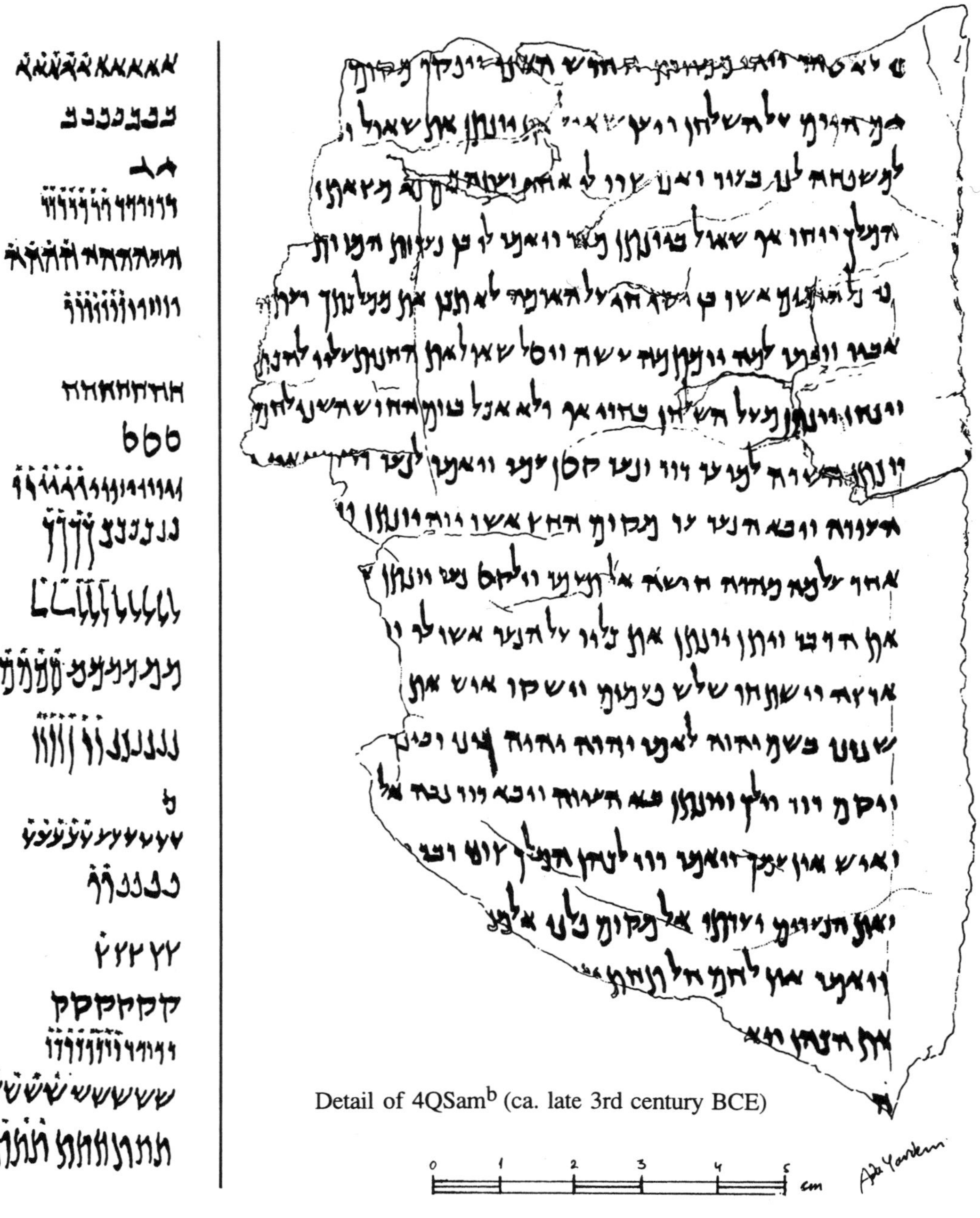

Detail of 4QSam[b] (ca. late 3rd century BCE)

Fig. 51. Details of early Qumran biblical scrolls from the late 3rd and early 2nd centuries BCE (4QEx[f], 4QSam[b], 4QJer[a]; The Rockefeller Museum of Antiquities, Jerusalem)

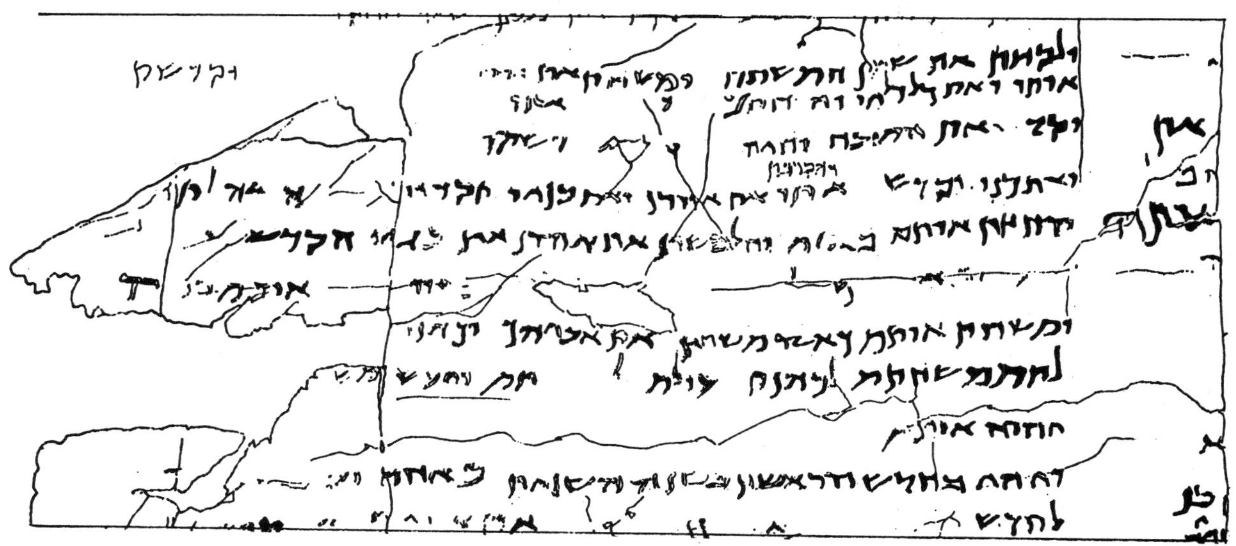

Detail of 4QEx[f] (ca. early 2nd century BCE)

Detail of 4QJer[a] (ca. late 3rd century BCE)

The Jews who remained in Judea had not been immune to the influence of their conquerors and neighbours. The vulgar Hebrew which they spoke assimilated foreign elements which changed the grammar and vocabulary. The writing of Hebrew seems to have survived only among a small group of scribes, perhaps belonging to the Sadducean priesthood. When the Babylonian exiles returned they found a mixed language spoken in Judea. Nehemiah (13:24) relates: “And their children spake half in the speech of Ashdod, and could not speak in the Jews’ language, but according to the language of each people.” Those coming back from Babylon seem to have wanted the Jewish people to return to its national origins, and Ezra gathered the people in the Temple for the reading of the Torah (445 BCE). In order to make sure that they understood it, the Torah was read in Hebrew and translated into Aramaic. Tradition connects Ezra the scribe with the use of Aramaic script for the writing of the Torah. Some scholars claim that in Babylon Ezra assembled those parts of the Torah which are said to have a priestly origin (P) and read this new Torah to the people. As there is no definite evidence, the historical picture remains unclear. However, all the Hebrew inscriptions predating the beginning of the Second Temple period are in the ancient Hebrew script, and no biblical texts predating the end of the 3rd century BCE or thereabouts have been found. The material from Qumran contains fragments of Exodus and Leviticus, for instance, in the ancient Hebrew script together with fragments from an Exodus scroll in the pre-Jewish cursive script. Some scholars believe that not all the people participated in the change-over from the ancient Hebrew to the Aramaic script, and that in the Second Temple period the Sadducean sect continued to preserve the ancient Hebrew scribal tradition. The Hebrew script of this period is also called ‘the Paleo-Hebrew’ script. It seems that the final rejection of the ancient Hebrew script by the Jews occurred because it came to be identified with the Samaritans.

The early biblical scroll fragments from Qumran in pre-Jewish script (from the books of Samuel, Jeremiah and Exodus; fig. 51) testify to the continuous evolution of a Judean variant of the Aramaic script of the 4th and 3rd centuries BCE. Similar types of letter-signs appear in late Aramaic documents from the land of Israel and Egypt and in these early scroll fragments from Qumran. The 1QIsa^{a} scroll from the late 2nd or early 1st century BCE already reveals a developed scribal tradition of the Jewish script (fig. 53). The renewal of the national life in Judea in the Second Temple period led to a flourishing of the spoken Hebrew vernacular, while classical Hebrew with a certain Aramaic influence remained the literary sacred language. The local Judean script in most of the biblical scrolls from Qumran, as well as in extra-biblical apocryphal scrolls, is called 'Jewish script' by modern scholars. In some of the scrolls the tetragrammaton and occasionally the word 'ʾEl' appear in the ancient Hebrew letters. In others, from a somewhat later period, the tetragrammaton appears as four short downstrokes (these first became three and then two Yods in manuscripts from the Middle Ages).

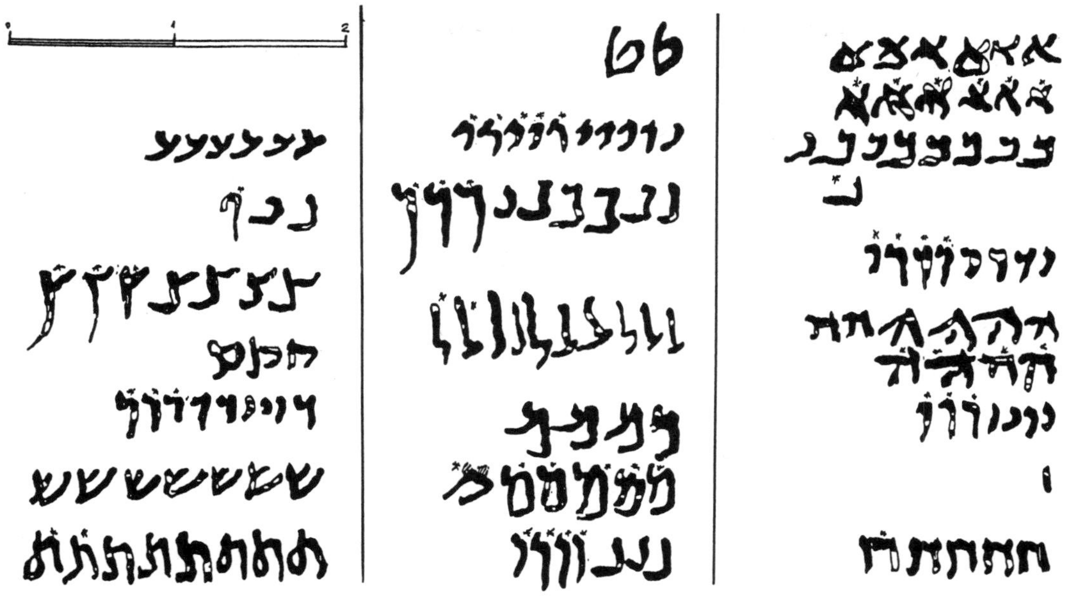

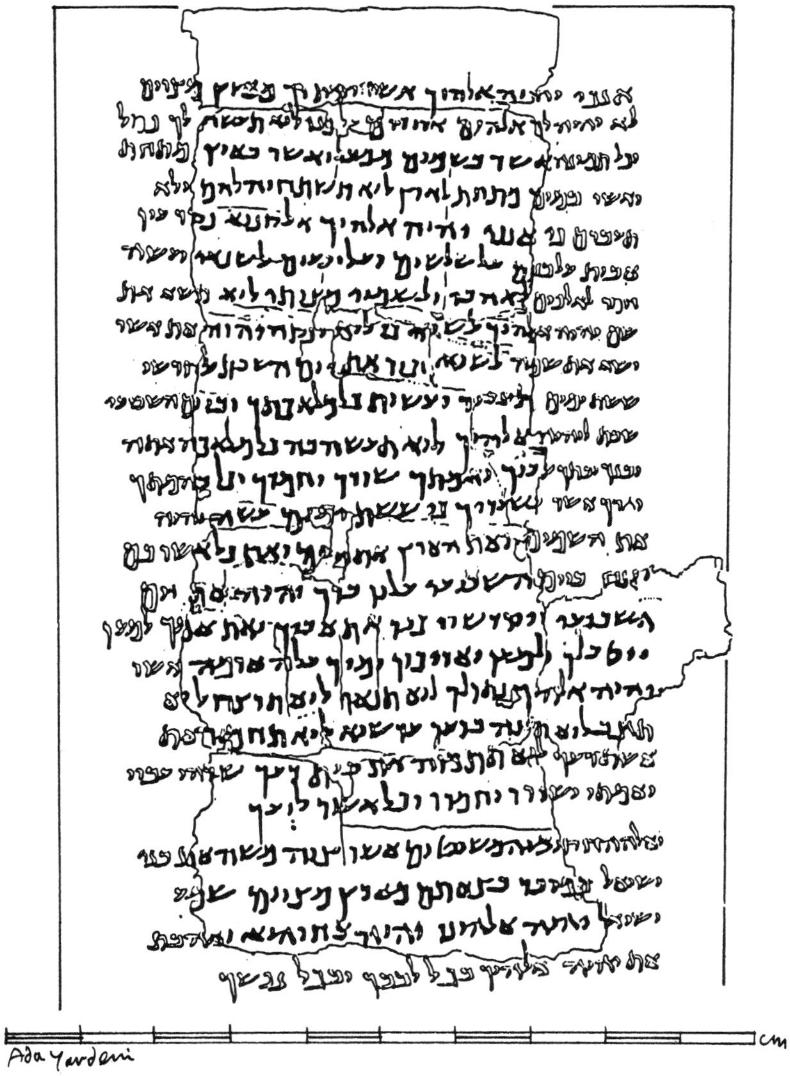

Fig. 52. The Ten Commandments and part of *Shema' Yisra'el* in a papyrus fragment from Egypt (the Nash papyrus) from about the middle of the 2nd century BCE (Cambridge University Library Or. 233; real size)

Fig. 53. Detail of the 1QIsa[a] scroll (late 2nd or early 1st century BCE; Jerusalem, Shrine of the Book; real size)

CHAPTER TWO: A GENERAL SURVEY OF THE FINDS IN THE JEWISH SCRIPT AND THE 'SQUARE' HEBREW SCRIPT

A. THE SECOND TEMPLE PERIOD TO THE END OF THE BAR KOKHBA REVOLT (FROM THE 3RD CENTURY BCE TO 135 CE)

The earliest documents in the local Judean script discovered so far are fragments of biblical scrolls of Exodus, Samuel and Jeremiah, found in Qumran cave 4 (fig. 51). Until the discovery of the documents from the Judean Desert, the Nash papyrus (fig. 52) was the earliest known document in the Jewish script. This is a papyrus fragment from the Hasmonean period of the Ten Commandments and part of *Shemaʿ Yisraʾel* written in a semi-cursive script.

In 1947, ancient scrolls in Hebrew letters were found by Bedouin in a cave in the Judean Desert. Three of them were purchased by Professor E.L. Sukenik of the Hebrew University of Jerusalem, who realized their great antiquity and called them 'Megillot Gnuzot' ('Hidden Scrolls'). Another four scrolls were purchased by a Syriac bishop. They were taken to the United States where they were later purchased by a Jewish philanthropist. Today the scrolls are kept in the Shrine of the Book in Jerusalem.

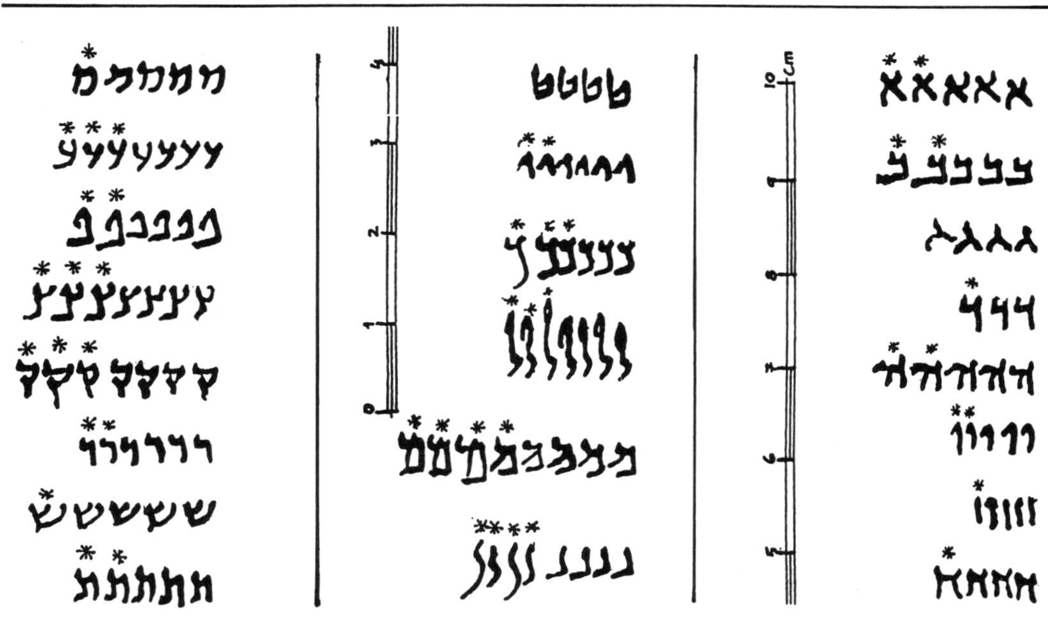

←

Palaeographic Comparative Chart of 4Q448

Lower columns | Upper column

cursive | semi-cursive | book-hand | cursive | semi-cursive | book-hand

(!)

(?)

(?)

(?)

0 1 2 3 4 5 cm

Ada Yardeni

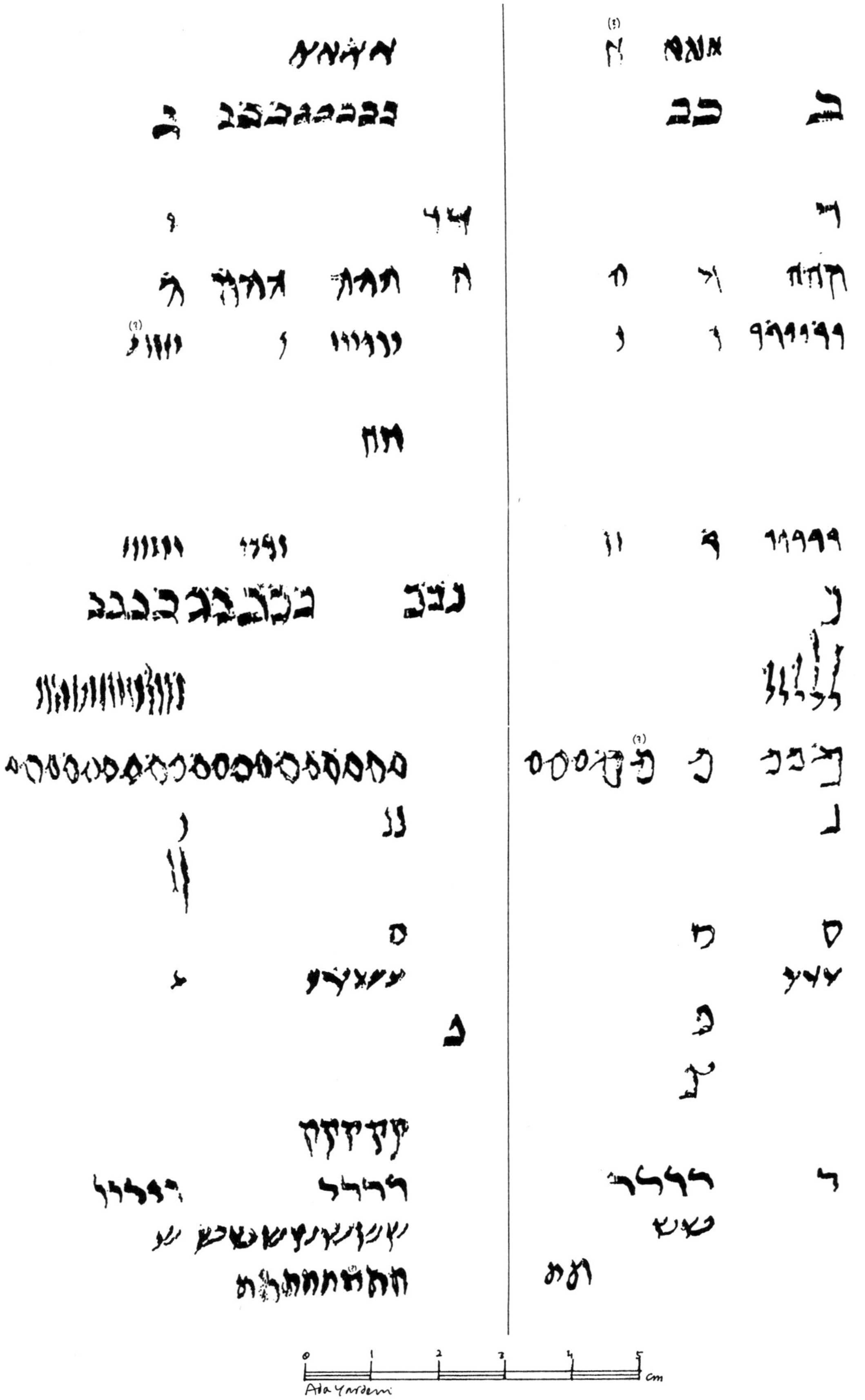

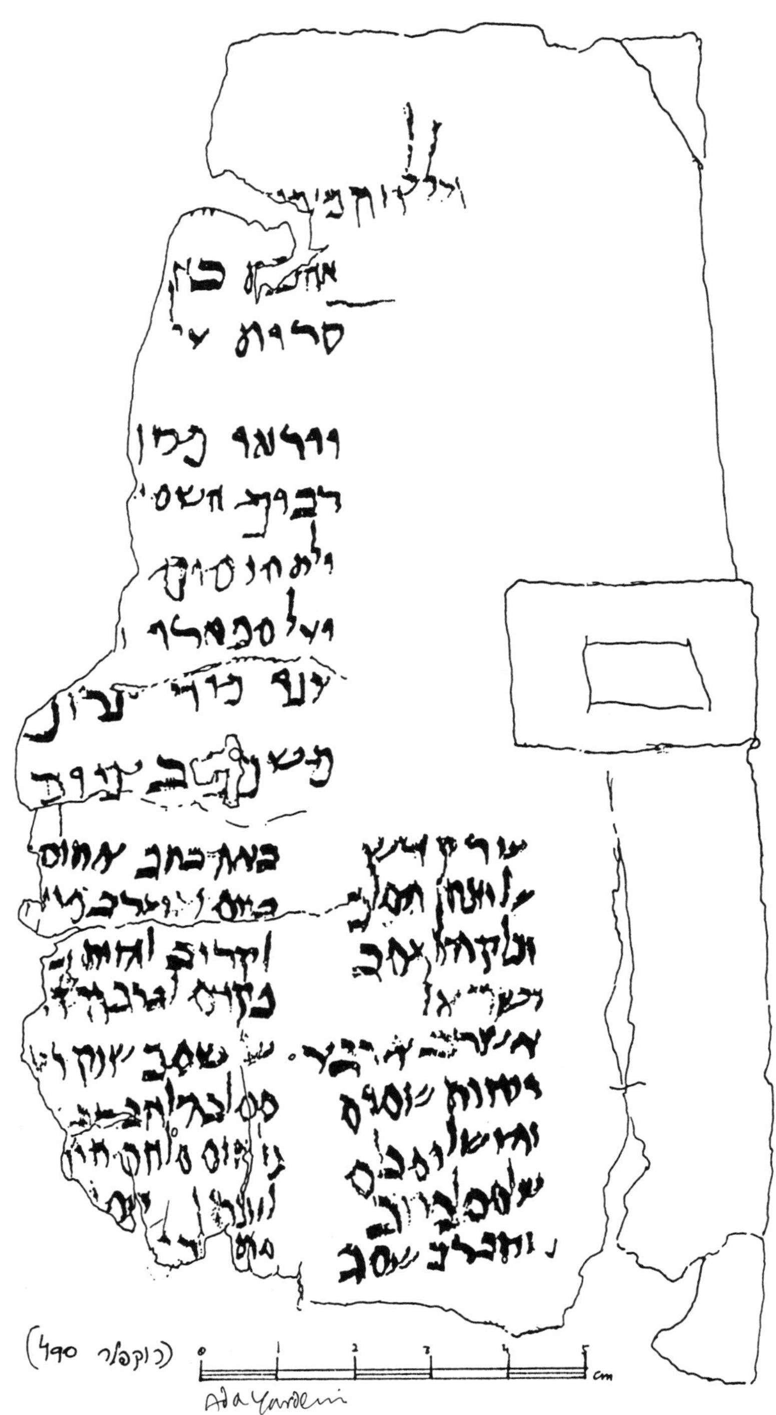

Fig. 54. A semi-cursive Hasmonean script in a liturgical poem from Qumran (4Q448) mentioning Jonathan the King (Alexander Jannaeus)

Following the discovery, the caves were investigated by archaeological expeditions from Jordan, as well as by the Ecole Biblique et Archéologique in Jerusalem. In the years 1956-1957 written documents were found in ten more caves in the Judean Desert. Amongst the finds were some almost intact hide scrolls as well as fragments of a copper scroll. In Qumran hundreds of fragments were found, mostly written on hide, from the late 3rd century BCE to ca. 68 CE. Most of the material was brought to the Rockefeller Museum in Jerusalem which came under Israeli control in 1967, after the Six-Day War. Other caves in the Judean Desert were also searched, by Bedouin as well as by the expeditions mentioned above and by Israeli archaeological expeditions. Material found or purchased by the Israelis is now located in the Shrine of the Book in Jerusalem as well as in the Rockefeller Museum; this includes finds from Naḥal Ḥever and Masada. Some other finds, including the copper scroll, are now in the Archaeological Museum in Amman, Jordan, and a few plates are in Paris. The majority of the Qumran finds are of a literary nature. The material includes fragments of scrolls of all the books of the Bible except for Esther, some in more than one copy. Two scrolls of Isaiah were found, one almost intact (fig. 53), from the late 2nd or early 1st century BCE. Together with the biblical scrolls, fragments of many works of sectarian character and apocryphal scrolls were discovered, among them works that were previously unknown. Most of the scrolls are in Hebrew and a few are in Aramaic. Part of the material is still unpublished.

No document among the finds from Qumran is explicitly dated, but there are scrolls and documents that may be dated by events or names which are mentioned in them, such as the fragment of a scroll in a semi-cursive script bearing the name of King Jonathan (Alexander Jannaeus) which may be dated to the early 1st century BCE (fig. 54).

Most of the finds are written in a Jewish book-hand with a thin calamus (reed-pen), in carbon-ink, and some are written in iron-ink (fig. 183). The finds from Masada, which belong to the period before 74 CE, include some fragments of biblical and non-biblical scrolls (now in the Rockefeller Museum of Antiquities in Jerusalem) and hundreds of ostraca with short inscriptions (now in the Institute of Archaeology on Mount Scopus). Large groups of documents, dating from the period from the middle of the 1st century CE to the end of the Bar Kokhba revolt in 135, were found in the Caves of Wadi Murabbaʿat and Naḥal Ḥever. Among them were fragments of biblical scrolls, phylacteries, deeds in Greek, Aramaic (fig. 59), Nabatean and Hebrew (fig. 60), as well as letters to and from Bar Kokhba (fig. 61), most of them in Hebrew and some in Aramaic and in Greek. Most of the deeds and letters are written on papyrus. One letter is on wood and one deed on hide. The material from Naḥal Ḥever includes the archives of a woman named Babatha, which reveal certain events in her life. Part of the documents from these groups are located in the Rockefeller Museum and another part in the Shrine of the Book, where some of them are on display.

Many of the deeds are dated. The literary material, however, is undated but may be arranged in a rough chronological order, based chiefly on palaeographical grounds.

Scholars distinguish four main periods in the evolution of the Jewish script (from the palaeographic point of view, this is an arbitrary classification, as the evolution of the script was a continuous process):

Fig. 55. Detail of the Ḥabakkuk Commentary from Qumran
(the Herodian period; The Rockefeller Museum of Antiquities, Jerusalem)

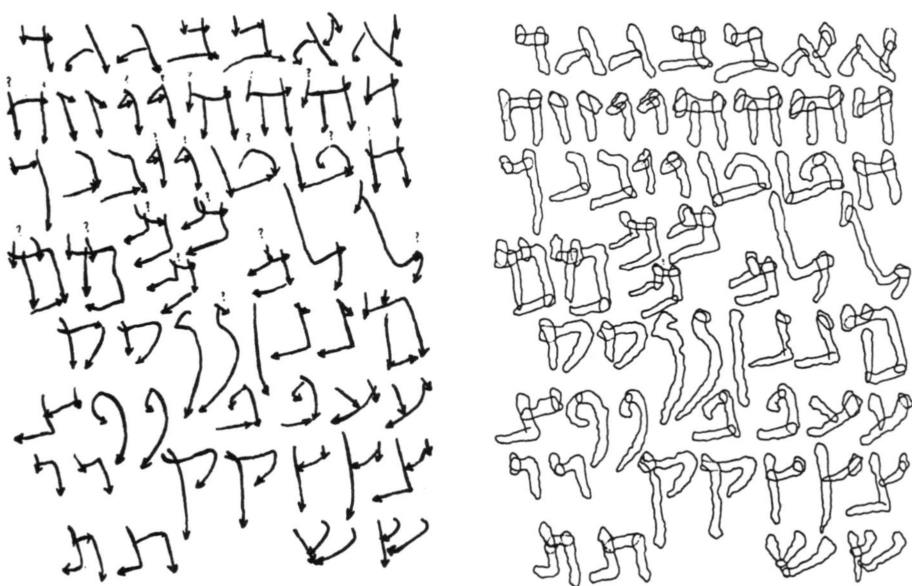

1. The proto-Jewish script (ca. 250 - ca. 150 BCE);
2. The Hasmonean script (ca. 150 - ca. 30 BCE);
3. The Herodian script (ca. 30 BCE - ca. 70 CE);
4. The post-Herodian script (ca. 70 - 135 CE).

Fig. 56. Detail of the 'Temple Scroll' from the Judean desert, showing stitches at the join of two hide sheets

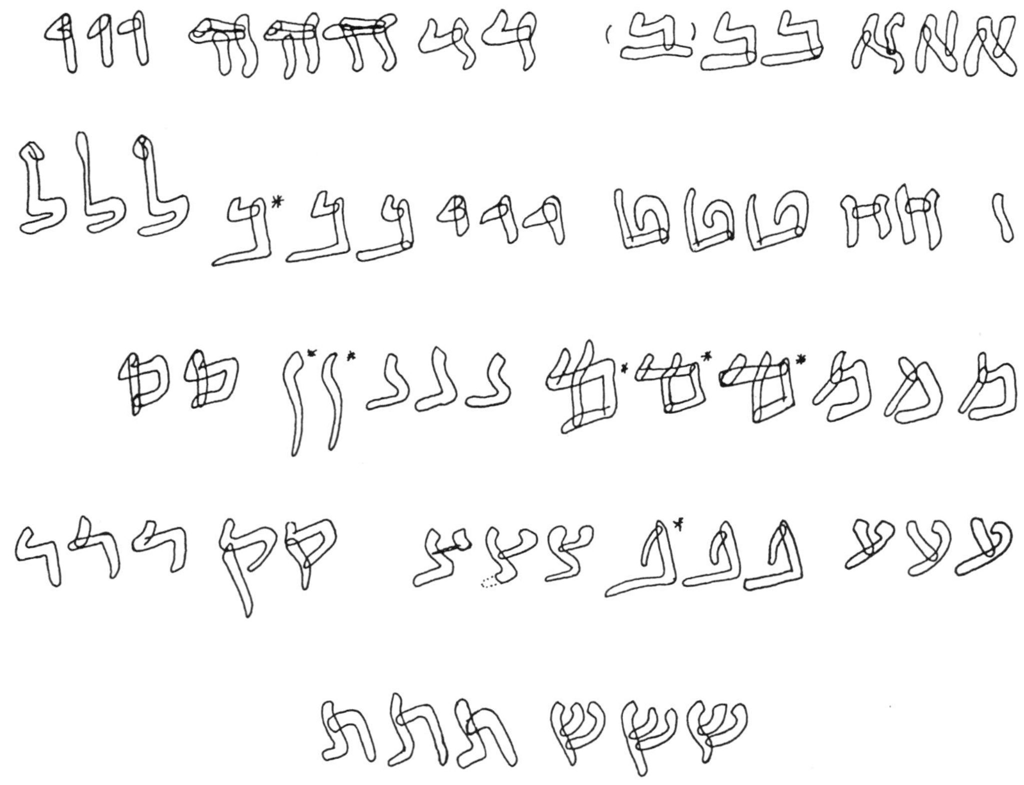

Fig. 57. Early Herodian letters of the alphabet in the Jewish book-hand taken from the MMT scroll from Qumran (4Q397; The Rockefeller Museum of Antiquities, Jerusalem; enlarged)

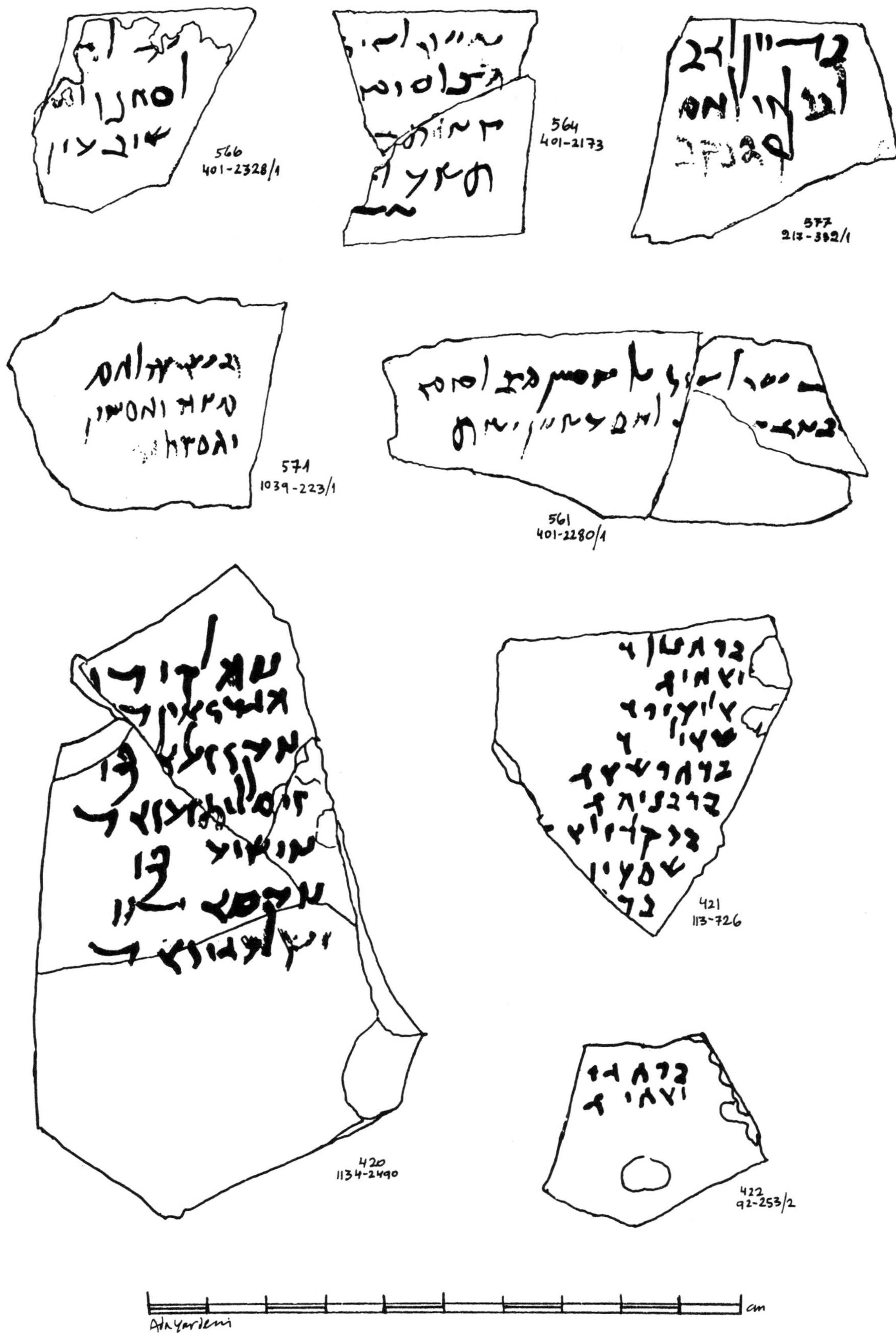

Fig. 58. Selected ostraca from Masada written in a Jewish cursive script (ca. mid-1st century CE; real size)

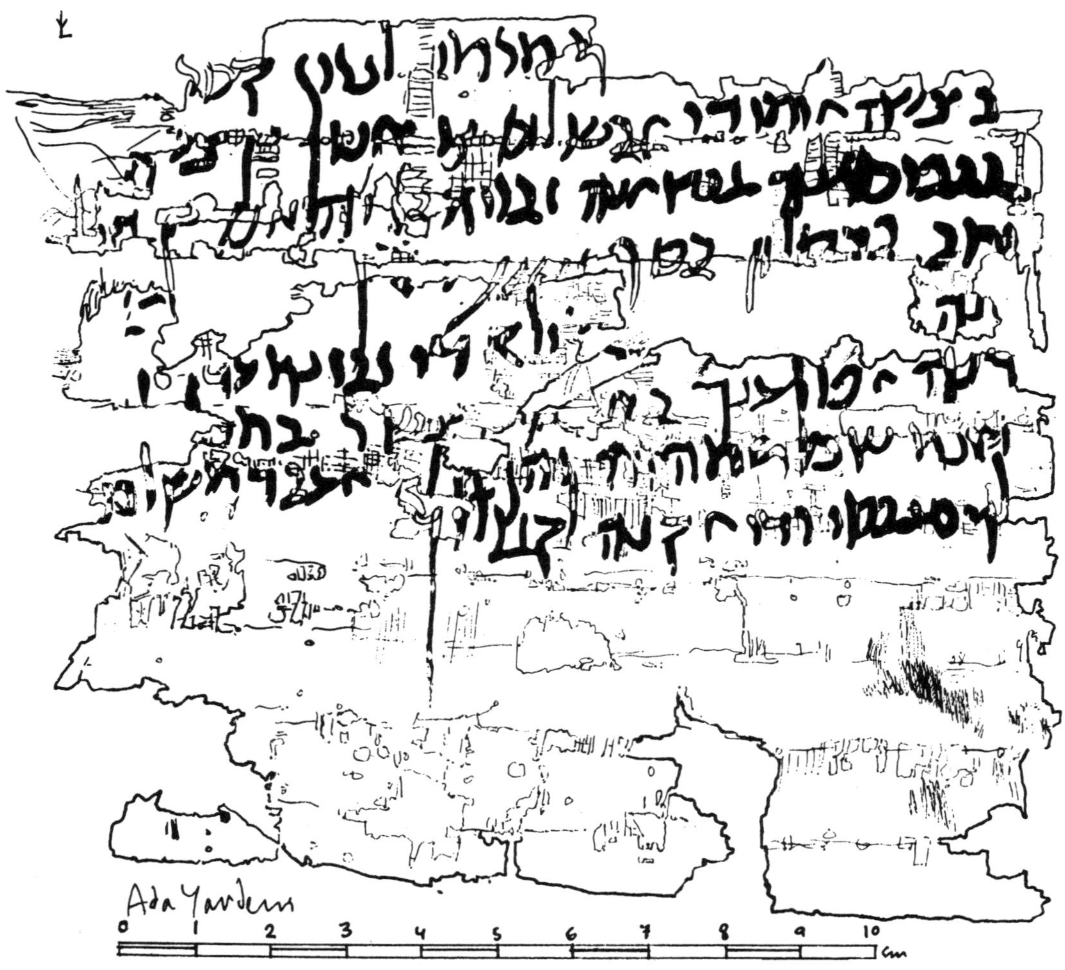

Fig. 59. An Aramaic papyrus deed from Wadi Murabba'at (Mur. 18) in cursive Jewish script dating from the second year of Neron (55 CE; The Rockefeller Museum of Antiquities, Jerusalem; real size)

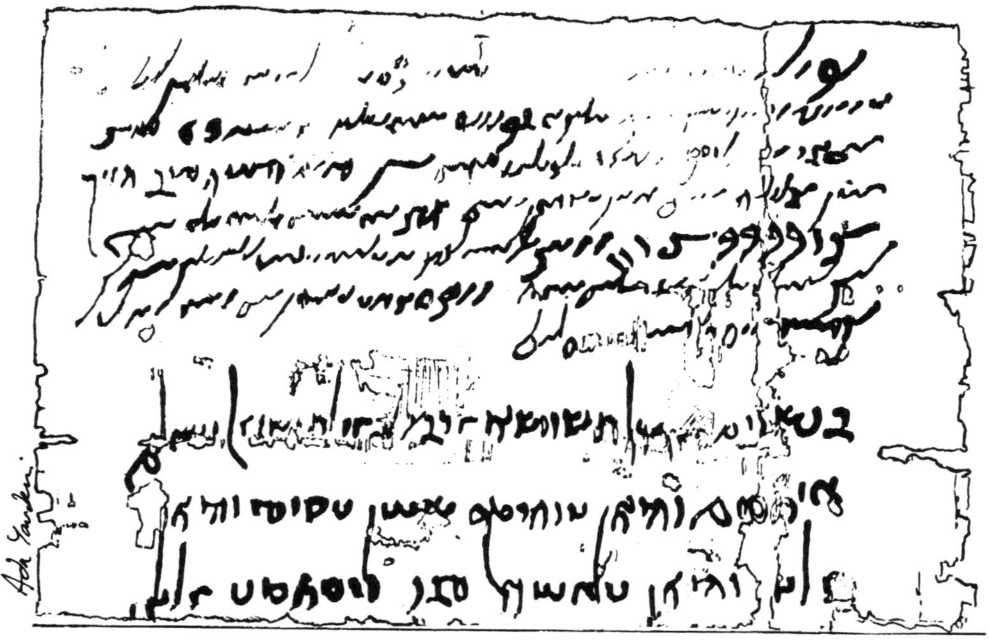

Fig. 60. Detail of a Hebrew papyrus deed from Wadi Murabba'at (Mur. 30) in an extreme cursive script (134 CE; The Rockefeller Museum of Antiquities, Jerusalem; real size)

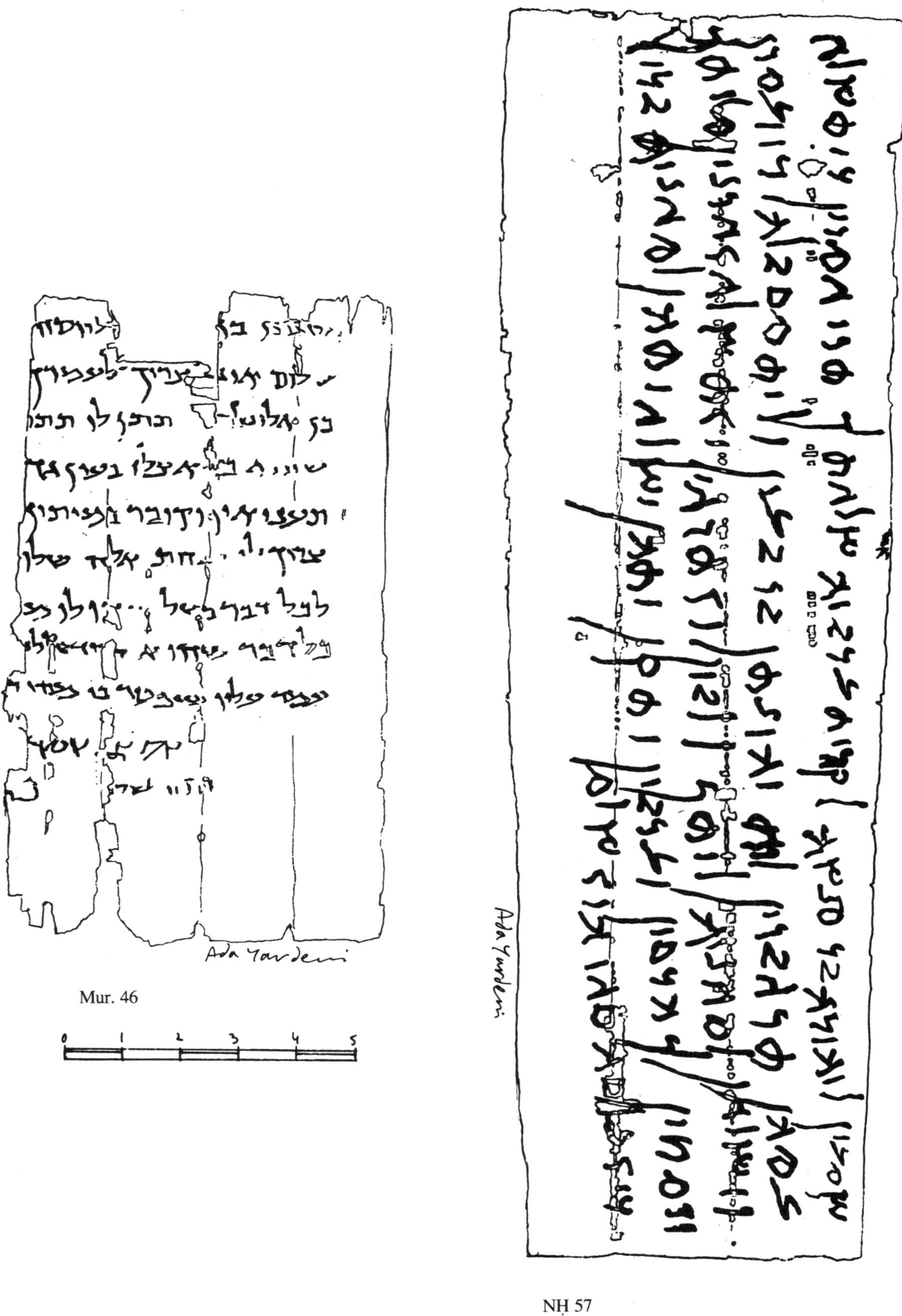

Mur. 46

NḤ 57

Fig. 61. Two letters of Shimʿon son of Kosiba (Bar Kokhba) from the time of the revolt (NḤ 57; Mur. 46; 132-135 CE; Jerusalem, Shrine of the Book; real size)

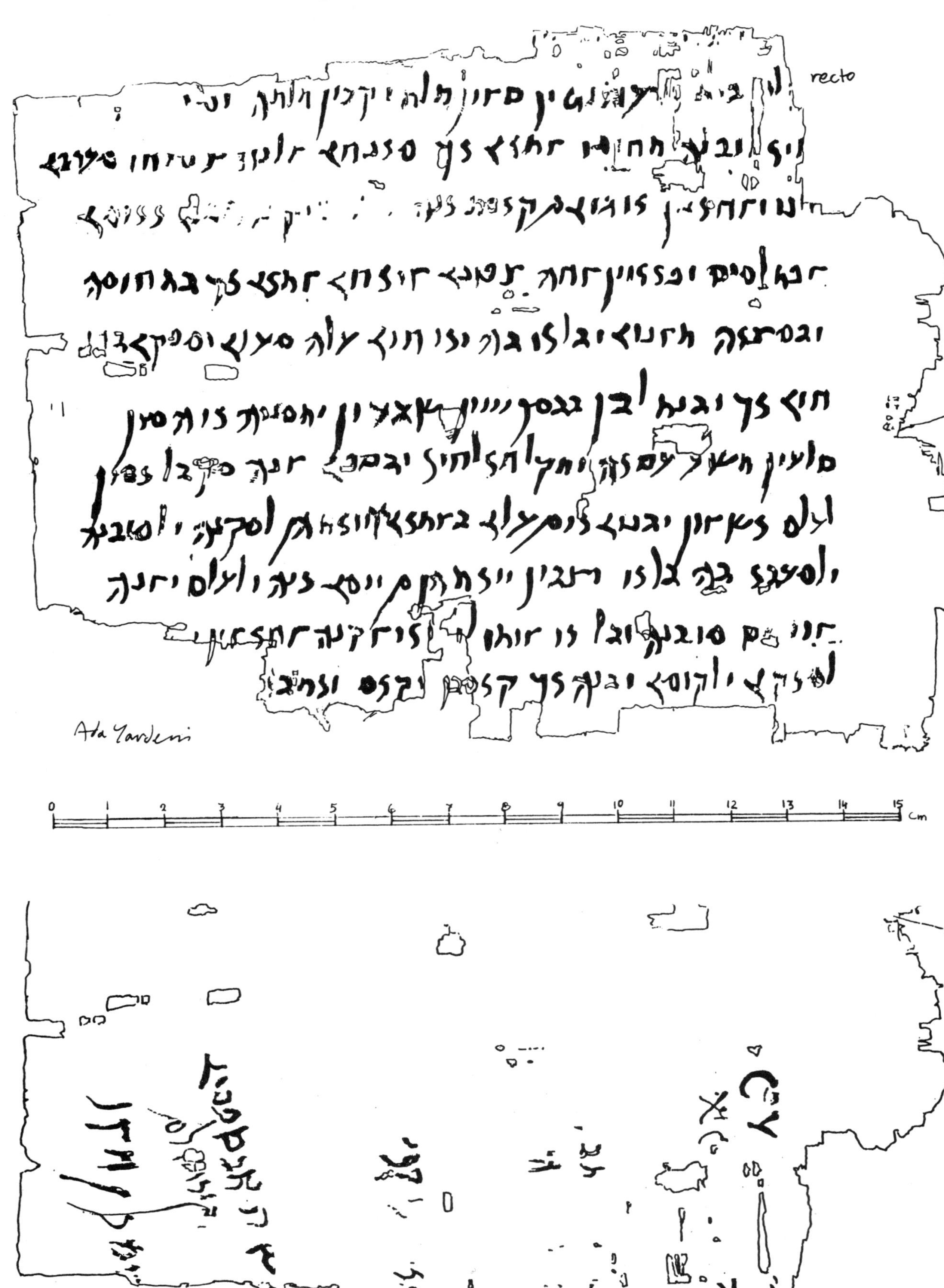

Fig. 62. Part of a papyrus deed in the Jewish cursive script from Wadi Murabba'at (XḤev/Se 50; Institut Catholique de Paris, BTS 7163; real size)

Fig. 63. The Jewish Herodian book-hand in the Psalms scroll from Qumran (11QPs; The Rockefeller Museum of Antiquities, Jerusalem)

In addition to the chronological classification, three main categories of writing may be discerned:

1) A calligraphic book-hand, which is an elaborated version of the script that evolved from the Aramaic official script. Several formal variations of it exist as well as examples of earlier and later phases of its evolution.

2) A cursive script which partly reflects certain types of cursive letter-signs in the Aramaic script and partly reflects cursive forms which evolved independently from the Jewish book-hand. To this category belong several cursive hands, including an extreme cursive writing.

3) Together with these two main styles, several intermediate scripts of various degrees of fluency and in various phases of evolution exist in the documents.

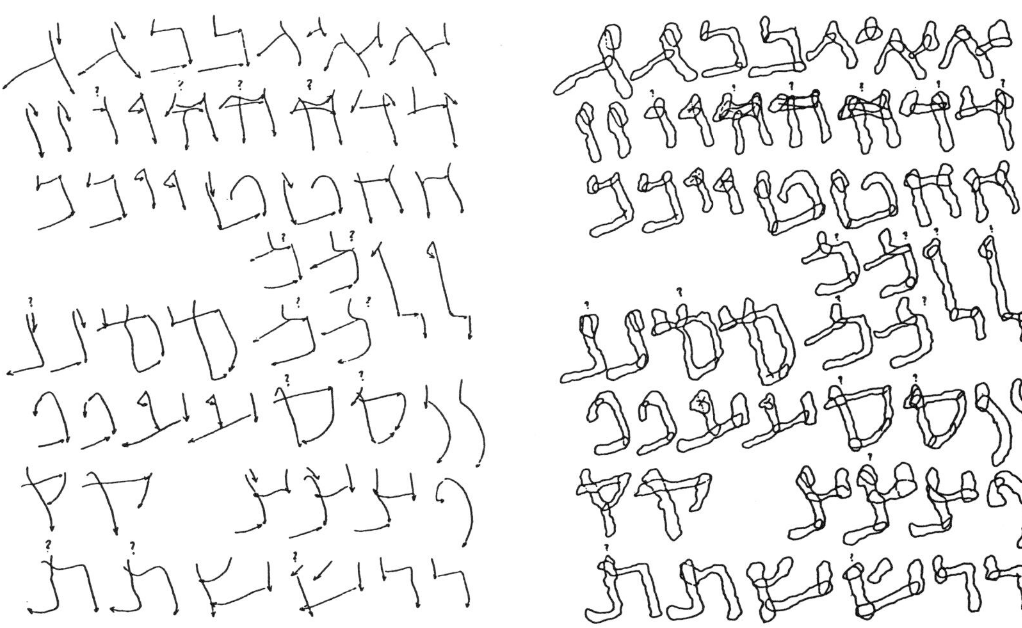

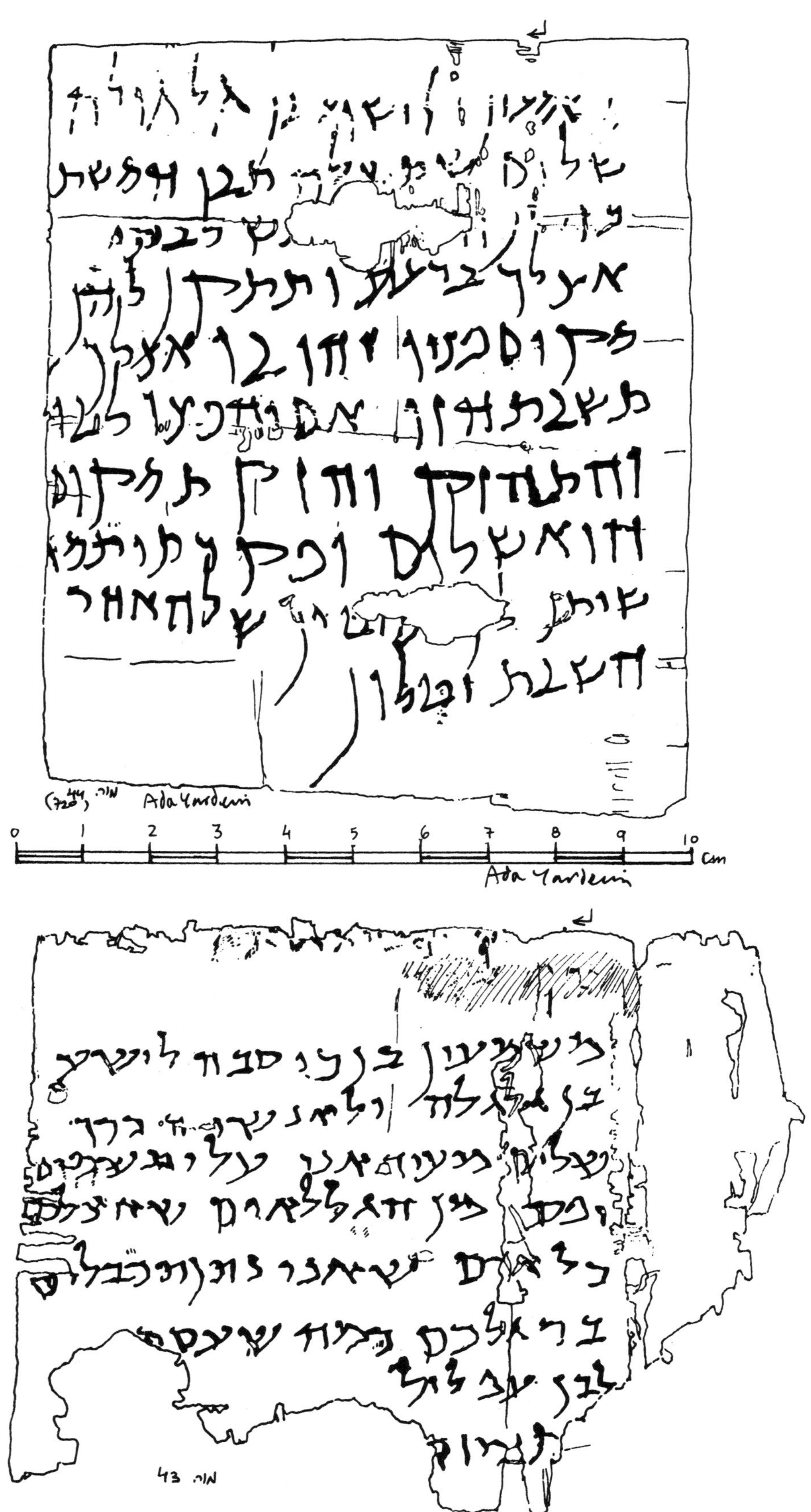

Fig. 64. Non-calligraphic Jewish script in two letters of Shimʿon son of Kosiba (Bar Kokhba) from the time of the revolt (Mur. 43; Mur. 44; 132-135 CE; The Rockefeller Museum of Antiquities, Jerusalem; real size)

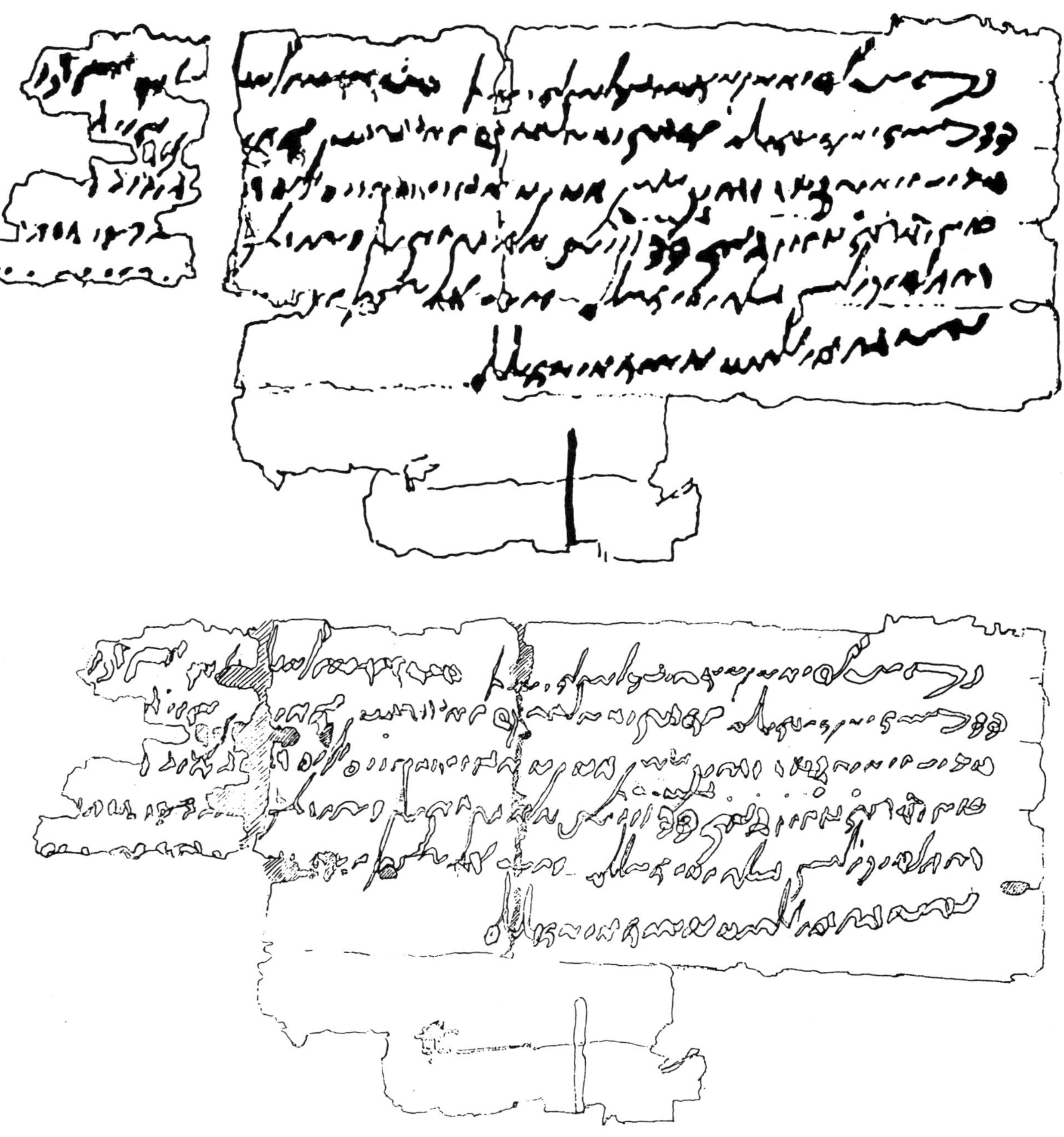

Fig. 65. An extreme cursive script in a fragment of a Hebrew 'double' deed from Wadi Murabbaʿat (Mur. 22; 135 CE; The Rockefeller Museum of Antiquities, Jerusalem; enlarged)

The classification into these categories assists in dating the manuscripts and in arranging them into chronological groups.

In addition to the manuscripts from the Judean Desert there are other epigraphic finds from the late Second Temple period. These include burial inscriptions, such as the Benei Ḥezir inscription from the 1st century BCE

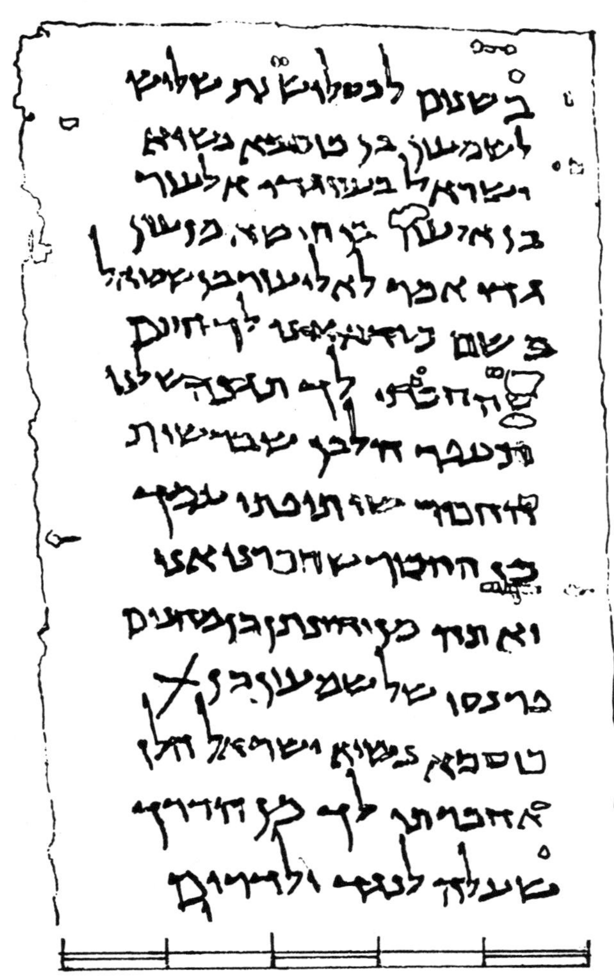

Fig. 66. A detail of a Hebrew deed in an elegant book-hand (NḤ 45; 134 CE; Jerusalem, the Shrine of the Book; real size and enlarged)

and the ʿUzziah epitaph (fig. 67), as well as Queen Helena's inscriptions and hundreds of ossuary inscriptions in square and cursive scripts from the Herodian period (fig. 68), many of them from Jerusalem and Jericho; a few monumental inscriptions, such as the 'House of Trumpeting' fragmentary inscription (fig. 69), and various other inscriptions such as those on border stones in Gezer ascribed to the 1st century BCE; seals; weighing stones, such as the 'Bar Qathros' weight found in the Burnt House in Jerusalem (fig. 70); Herodian inscriptions, recently discovered together with earlier Aramaic inscriptions on Mount Gerizim; and a weight with the inscription 'Shimʿon son of Kosiba (Bar Kokhba), Prince of Israel' which was recently discovered (fig. 72), and is the third of its kind found so far. Another discovery recently made and still unpublished is an ostracon from Qumran with a Hebrew inscription.

Fig. 67. The ʿUzziah epitaph engraved with Jewish letters from the Herodian period (Jerusalem, The Israel Museum)

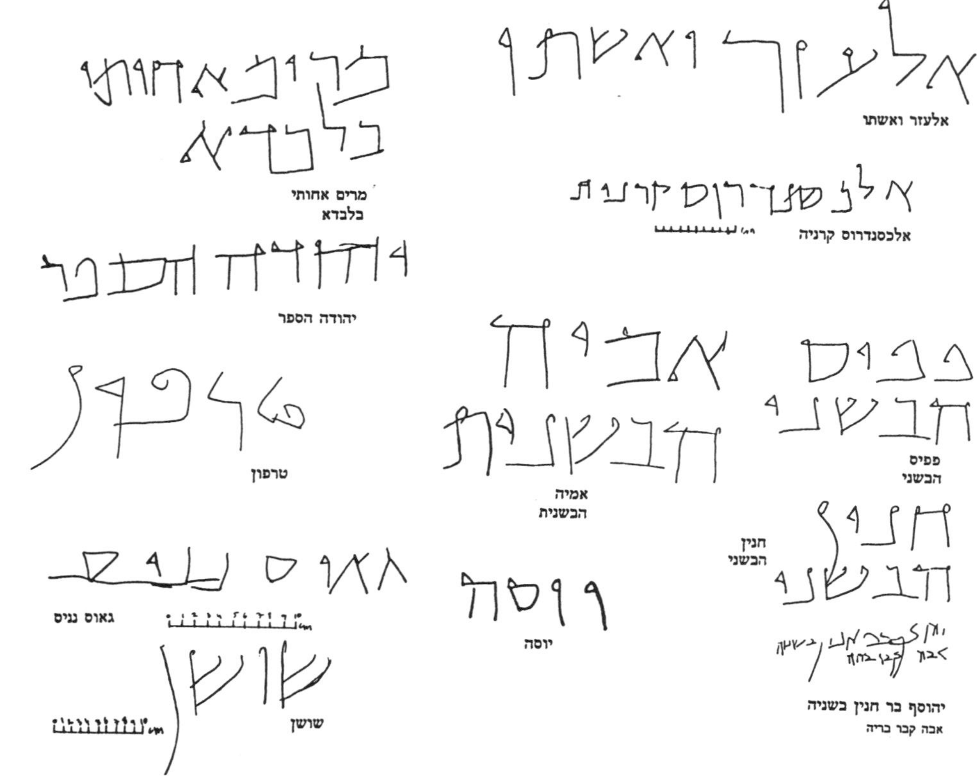

Fig. 68. Selected ossuary inscriptions from the Herodian period

Fig. 69. A fragment of a monumental stone inscription from Jerusalem saying: 'To the House of Trumpeting, ...["

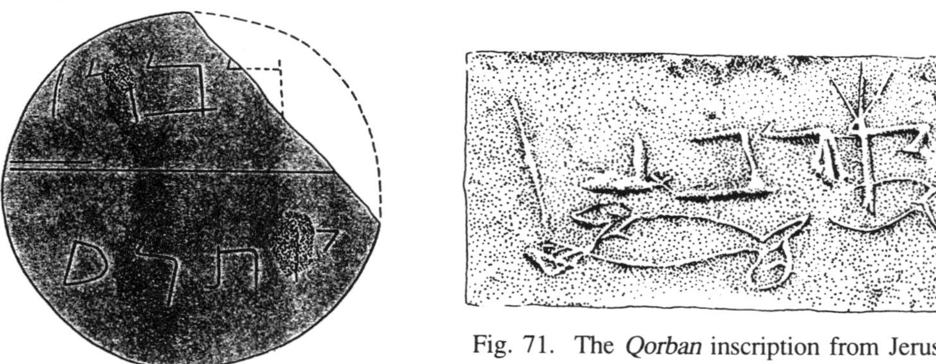

Fig. 71. The *Qorban* inscription from Jerusalem

Fig. 70. The *Bar Qathros* weight from the Herodian period (Jerusalem, the 'Burnt House')

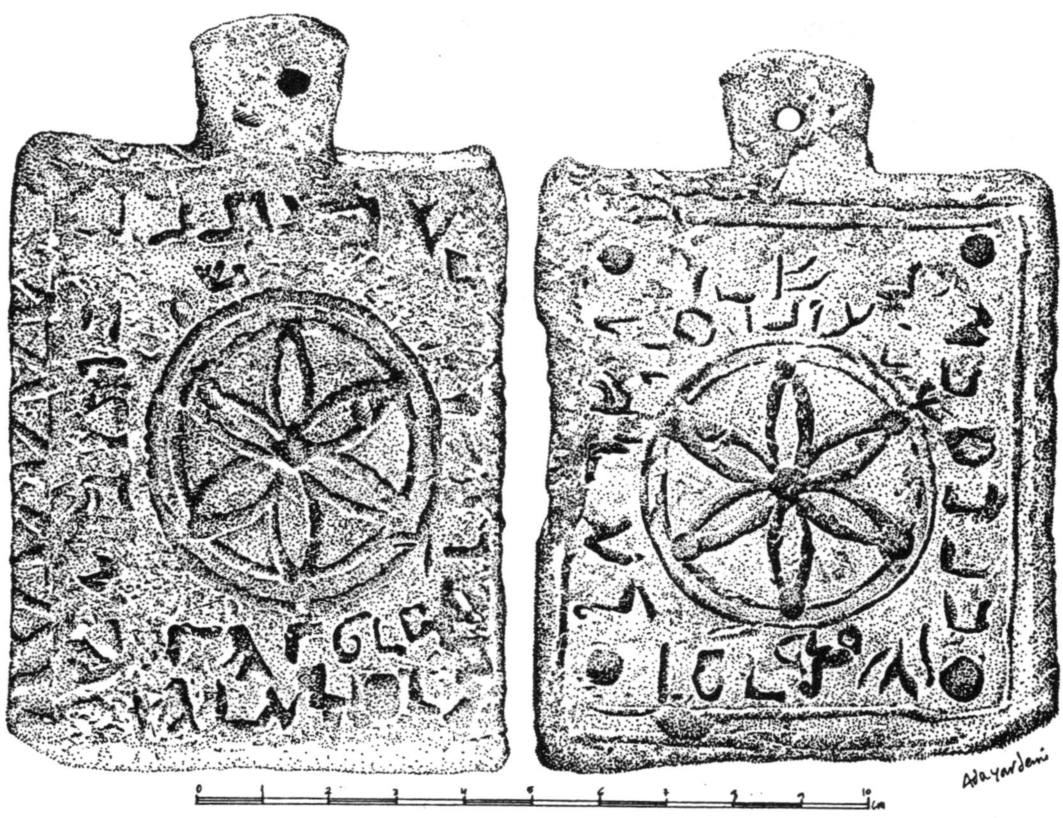

Fig. 72. A weight bearing the name of Shimʿon son of Kosiba (Bar Kokhba; 132-135 CE)

In some of the monumental inscriptions engraved in stone the letter-signs show the influence of cursive forms written with ink, reflected mainly in the formation of the extreme ends of the strokes. Only single inscriptions show the influence of the contemporary Greek and Latin stone and marble inscriptions that were engraved in elegant scripts. This style of engraving (fig. 73) is later found a great deal in stone inscriptions of the Byzantine period.

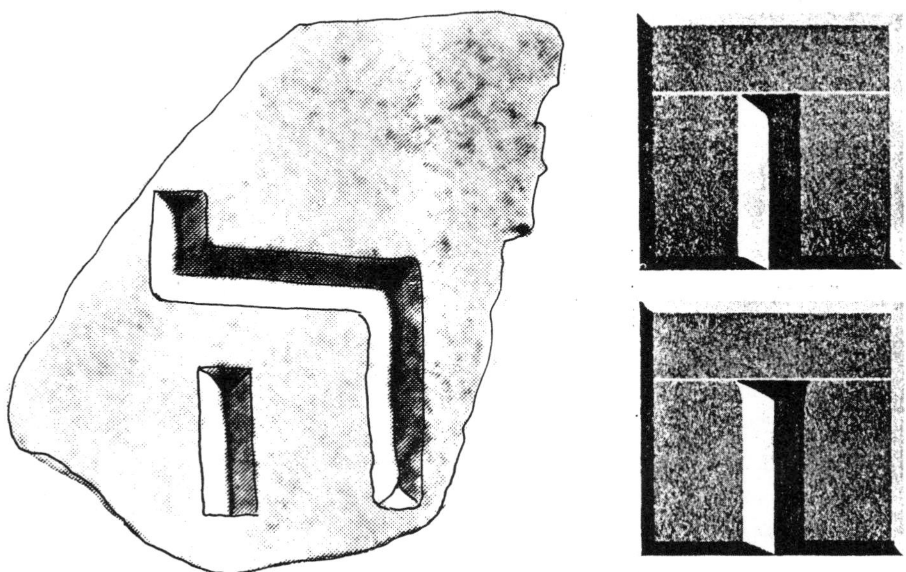

Fig. 73. Hebrew letters in Byzantine stone inscriptions sometimes reflect the influence of the Roman technique of letter engraving

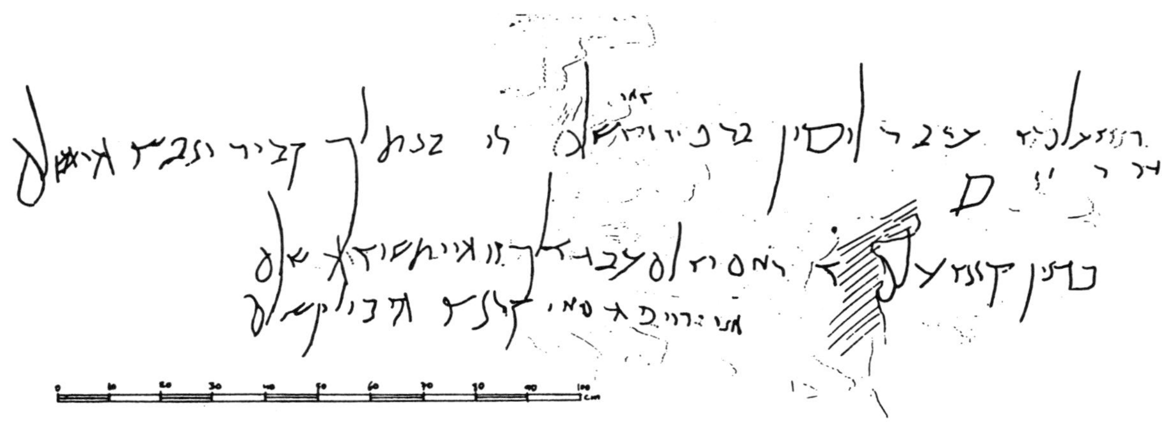

Fig. 74. Jason's tomb inscription, in cursive Jewish script (Jerusalem, Alfasi Street)

A non-calligraphic cursive script appears in the Jason burial inscription from Jerusalem (fig. 74). Cursive script appears in a large number of ossuary inscriptions (fig. 75) as well as on a sarcophagus lid from Bethphage (fig. 76).

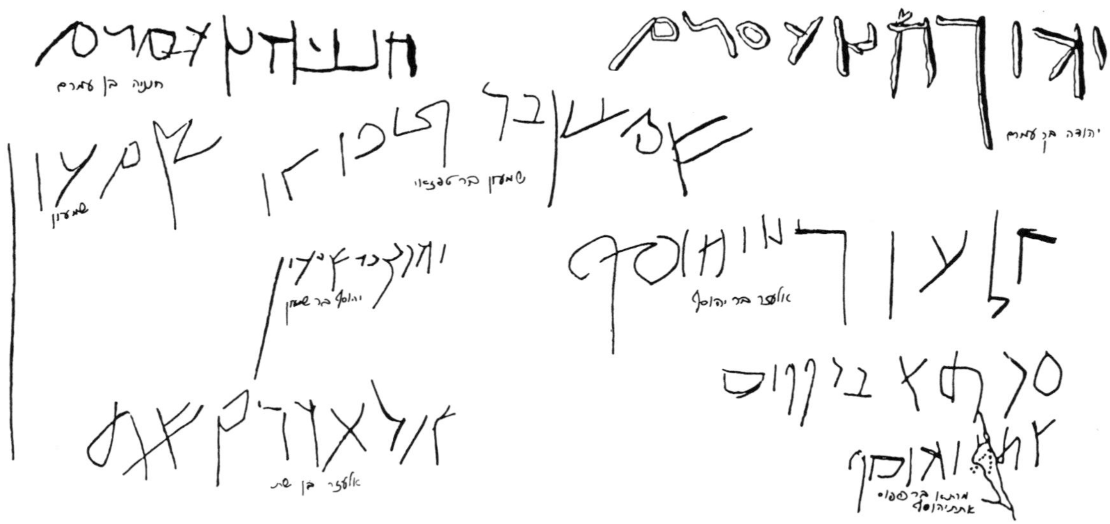

Fig. 75. The cursive Jewish script on ossuary inscriptions from the Herodian period

A few abecedaries were also found, written on different materials. Among them was a complete abecedarium on an ostracon of the 1st century BCE from Qumran and another one in Herodian letter-forms found in a burial cave in Ḥirbet ʿAiṭun. A Herodian abecedarium appears on an ostracon from Herodium. An almost complete abecedarium of the Second Temple period appears on the wall of a cistern in Naḥal Mikhmas and another abecedarium of that period, together with a list of names in alphabetical order extending to the letter ʿAyin, appears on an ostracon purchased in 1967 from a dealer in Jerusalem.

Most of the epigraphical material dating from the period from the time of the Second Temple to the end of the Bar Kokhba revolt is today located in museums and institutions in Israel, especially the Israel Museum, the Rockefeller Museum, the Bible Lands Museum, the Institute of Archaeology at the Hebrew University on Mount Scopus and the Hebrew Union College, all of them in Jerusalem. Smaller collections are located in the Museum of Tiberias, the Hecht Museum in Haifa University and in various archaeological sites all over the country.

In the late Second Temple period spoken Hebrew was the language used in schools, and after the destruction of the Temple the Mishnah was written in that language. The scribal tradition of writing the Torah was then gradually crystallized and the scribal rules for the form of the letter-signs were fixed.

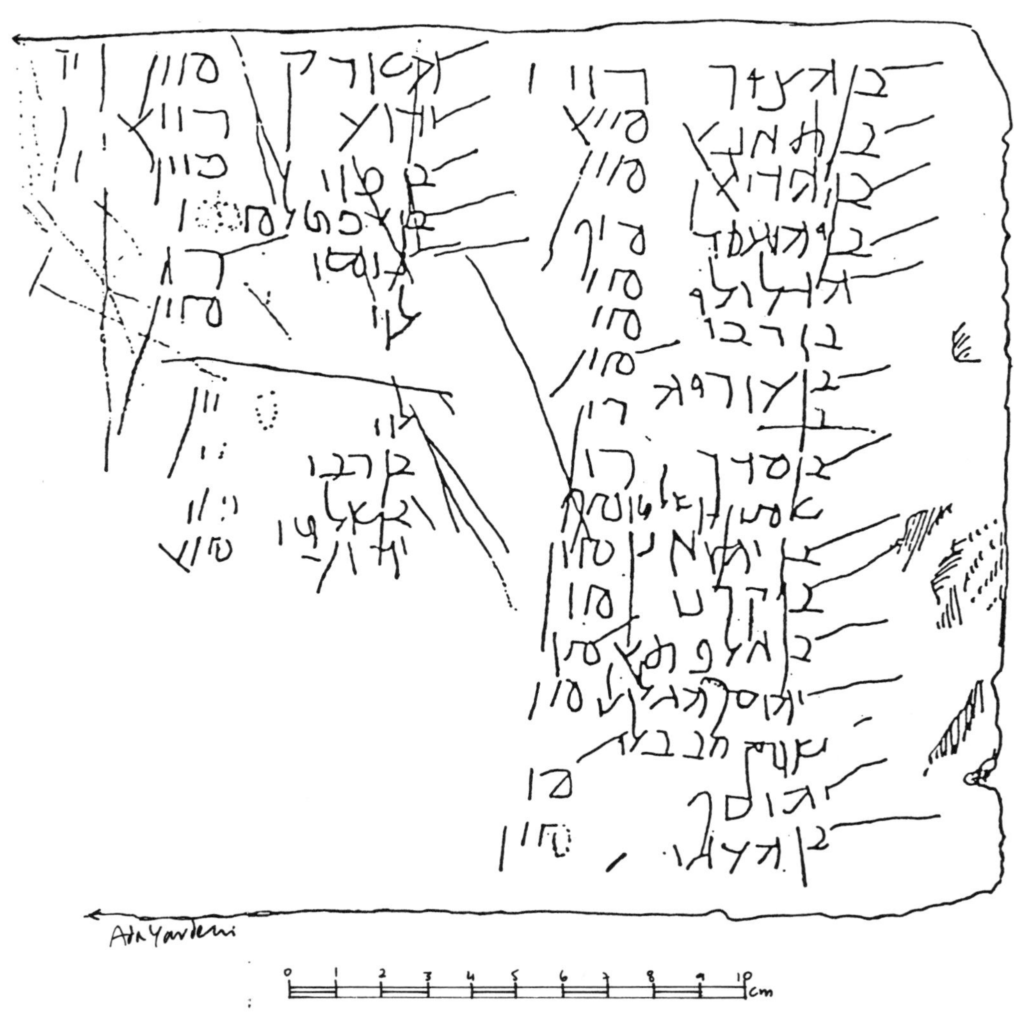

Fig. 76. List of names in the Jewish cursive script on an ossuary lid from Bethphage (Paris, Louvre AO 7487; reduced)

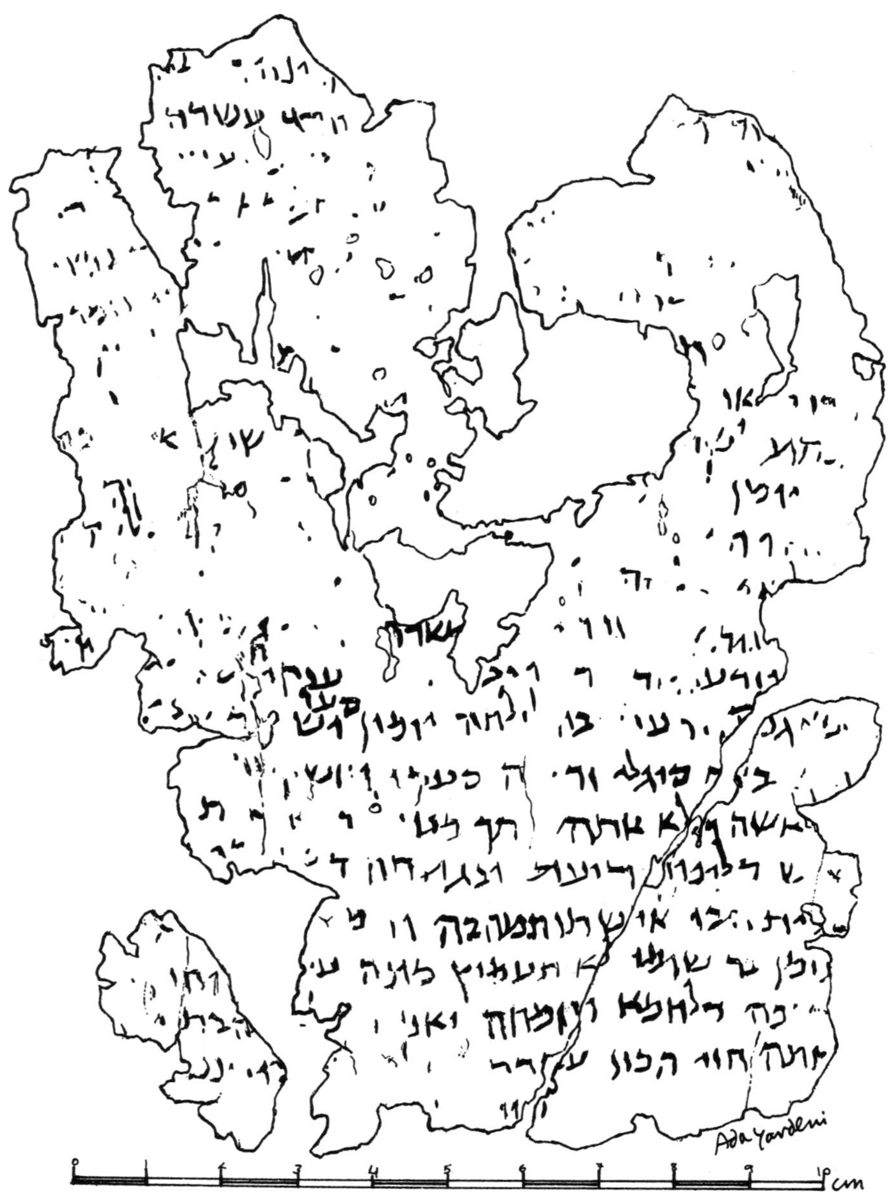

Fig. 77. A fragment of a hide document from Dura-Europos written in a semi-cursive script (late 2nd or early 3rd century CE; Paris, Bibliothèque nationale, suppl. GR 1354; real size)

Frey 821

Frey 822

Fig. 78. Inscriptions on the doorposts of a house in Palmyra from the 3rd century CE

B. FROM THE END OF THE BAR KOKHBA REVOLT TO THE CAIRO GENIZAH (135 CE TO THE 9TH CENTURY)

Most of the epigraphic material in the Hebrew script from the end of the Bar Kokhba revolt to the end of the Byzantine period was discovered in the land of Israel. The majority of the finds are undated, but a relative chronology may be conjectured according to the archaeological context.

Fig. 79. Hebrew inscriptions on coffins and marble plates in Beit She'arim and Jaffa (3rd and 4th centuries CE)

Despite the fact that Jewish communities outside the land of Israel existed from an early period, no examples of Hebrew script have been found outside Israel predating the late 2nd century CE. The early finds include an inscription bearing the name *Ywdn*, as well as a few papyrus fragments from Egypt (see below). The inscriptions from the Dura-Europos synagogue, which was destroyed in the year 256, also form part of these early finds. These include fresco inscriptions and graffiti as well as two fragments on hide (one is located in the Bibliothèque Nationale in Paris [fig. 77] and the other in the Art Gallery in New Haven, Conn. in the U.S.A.). One inscription bears the date 245. In Palmyra, Hebrew inscriptions were found on the doorposts ('Mezuzah') of a house, among them the text of *Shemaʿ Yisraʾel* (fig. 78). These inscriptions predate the destruction of Palmyra in 273 CE.

About 30 Hebrew inscriptions on coffins and marble plates were found in the necropolis of Beit Sheʿarim in Israel (fig. 79). They date from the period from the early 3rd to the middle of the 4th century (the cemetery was destroyed in the revolt against Gallus in 351). An inscription recently found in the synagogue of Meroth in the Golan is possibly also from the 4th century (fig. 80). About six funerary inscriptions from about the 4th century were found in Jaffa and Jerusalem, and other burial inscriptions of that period were found in Zippori (one of them is perhaps earlier in date). Another group of inscriptions dating from the 3rd to the 5th centuries was found in the Golan Heights.

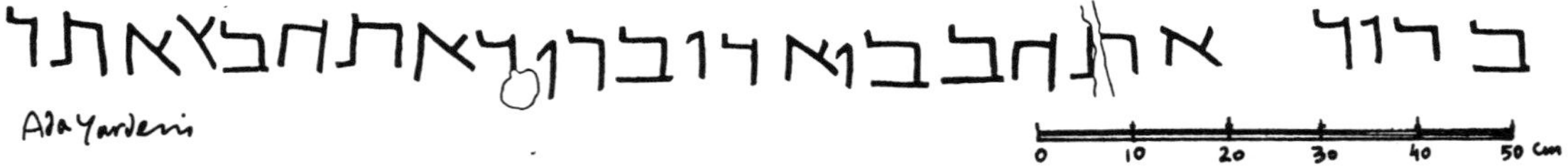

Fig. 80. A Hebrew synagogue inscription from Ḥurbat Meroth (ca. 4th century CE?; Jerusalem, The Israel Museum)

A few burial inscriptions with Hebrew script from the Byzantine period were found outside Israel, mainly in France, Spain and Italy, including a 5th century tri-lingual tombstone from Tortosa, Spain. A burial inscription from the Byzantine period with Hebrew script was discovered recently in the Crimea (fig. 81).

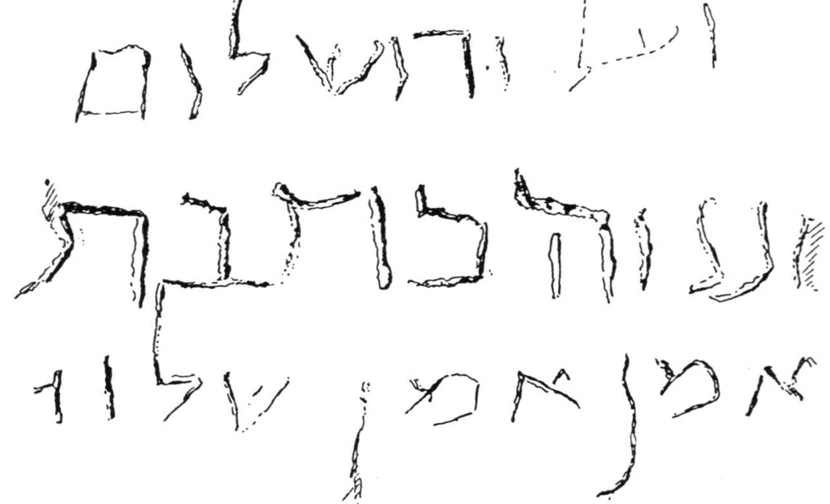

Fig. 81. A Hebrew burial inscription from the Crimea (the Byzantine period)

Fig. 82. An epitaph from Zoʿar dated to Ṭebet, year 386 of the destruction of the (Second) Temple (457 CE)

Fig. 83. Fragments of synagogue inscriptions from Tiberias (the Byzantine period)

A find of great importance is about 15 dated epitaphs from Zoʿar, south of the Dead Sea. The earliest of these appears to be from the 4th century (the date is difficult to decipher), and the others date from the 5th century (fig. 82). Scores of Aramaic and Hebrew synagogue inscriptions of the Byzantine period have been discovered all over Israel, and a few have been found outside the country. Some of them are engraved in stone (fig. 83) and others formed in mosaic (figs. 84, 85). They date from the 4th-7th centuries.

Fig. 84. A mosaic inscription from the Ḥammat Gader synagogue (the Byzantine period)

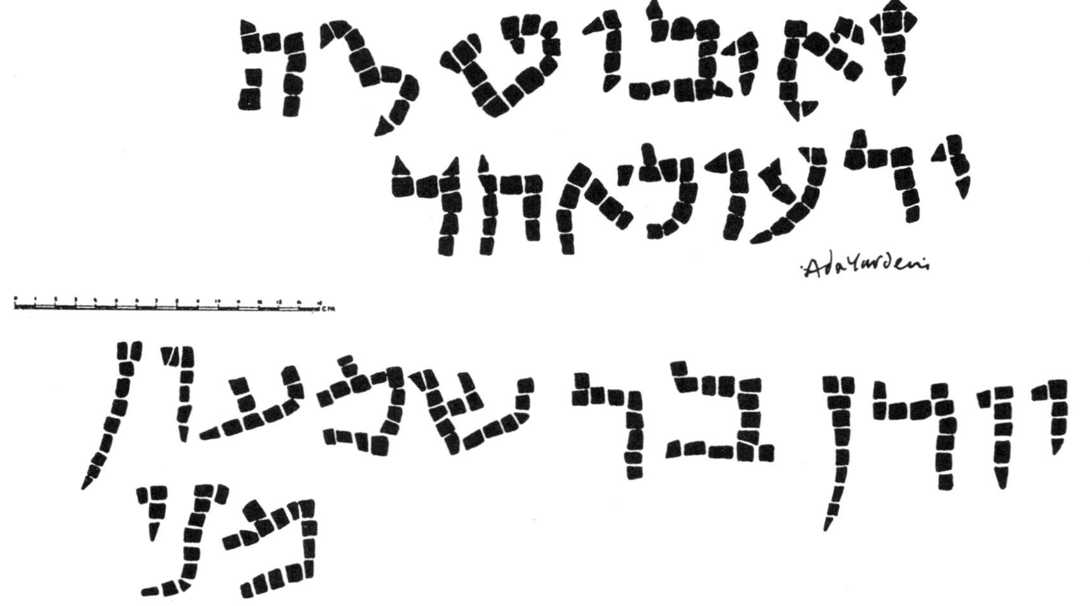

Fig. 85. Mosaic inscriptions from the synagogue of Meroth
(the Byzantine period; Jerusalem, The Israel Museum)

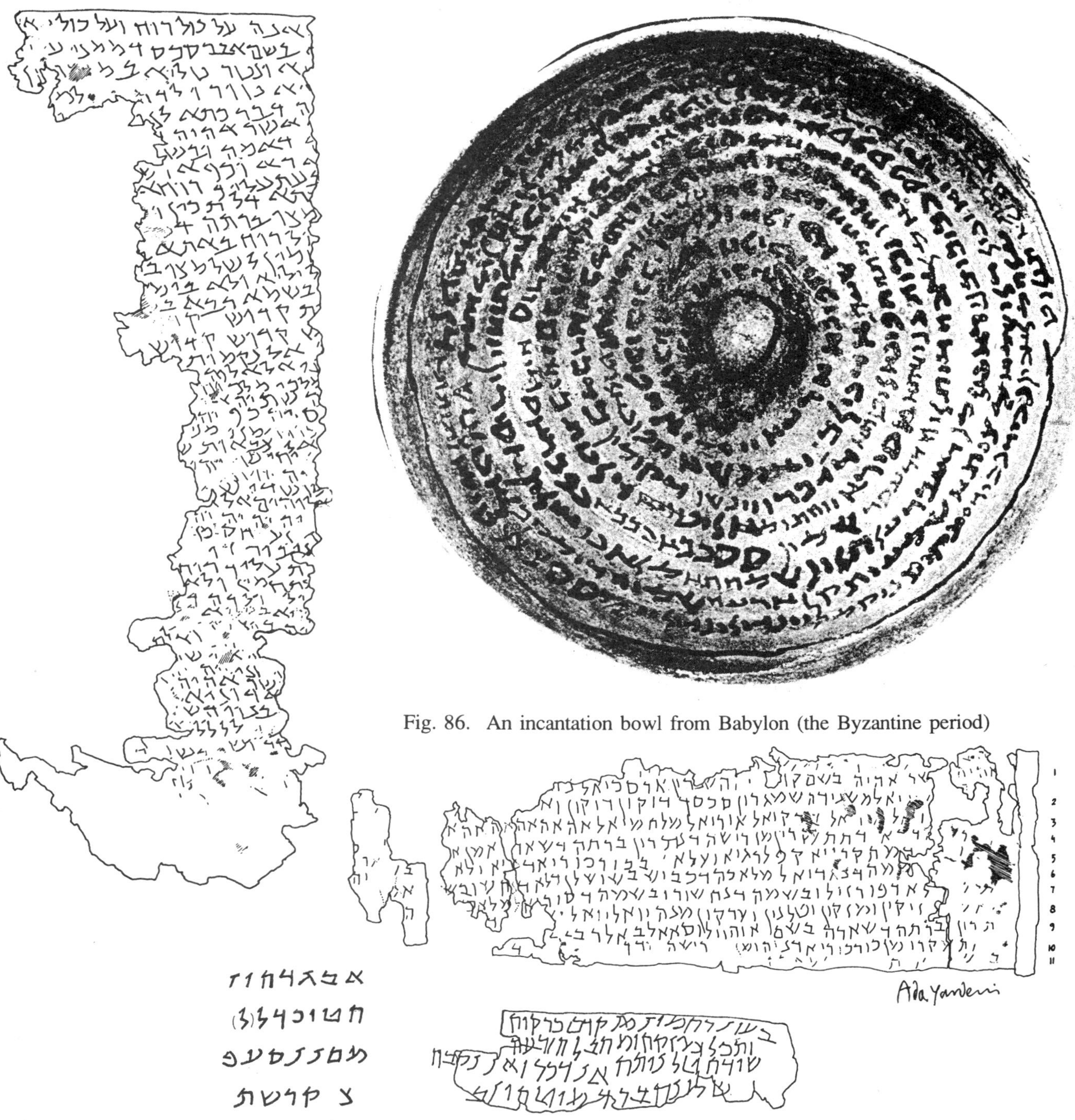

Fig. 86. An incantation bowl from Babylon (the Byzantine period)

Fig. 87. Selected amulets from the Byzantine period

Hundreds of clay incantation bowls, most of them found in Iraq (fig. 86), and about fifty undated amulets incised on metal – copper, silver or gold – (fig. 87), belong to approximately the same period.

A large group of Hebrew epitaphs dating from the 9th century was found in southern Italy, about twenty of them in Venossa (fig. 88), and a few other epitaphs were found in France and Spain. One epitaph from Narbonne bears the date 688. An epitaph from Baʿalbek in Lebanon bears the date 837/8 (fig. 89).

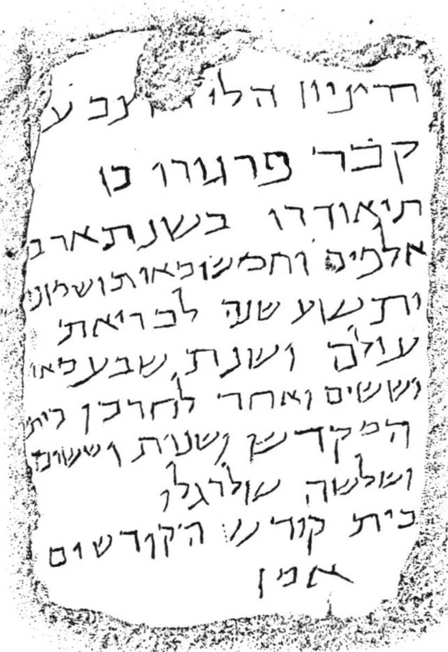

Fig. 88. Jewish epitaphs in Hebrew script from Venossa, Italy (9th century CE)

Fig. 89. Hebrew script incised in a stone epitaph from Ba'albek, Lebanon, dating from the year 837/8

About 150 papyrus fragments bearing inscriptions in Hebrew letters, in the Hebrew, Aramaic or Arabic languages, were found mainly in Egypt, and are now located in various places throughout the world. They span a period of about 500 years (from the 3rd to the 8th centuries), and include, inter alia, a small biblical fragment (fig. 90), liturgical poems (fig. 91), and deeds and letters (fig. 92). Only one of them is dated – a marriage contract written in Antinoupolis in Egypt in the year 417 (fig. 93). It is now located in Cologne. Two letters, one in Aramaic and one in Hebrew, were purchased in Cairo in 1899. Their provenance is unknown (fig. 94).

Fig. 90. A fragment of an Exodus papyrus scroll (2nd or 3rd century CE; Oxford, Bodleian Library, Ms. Heb. d.89(p); real size)

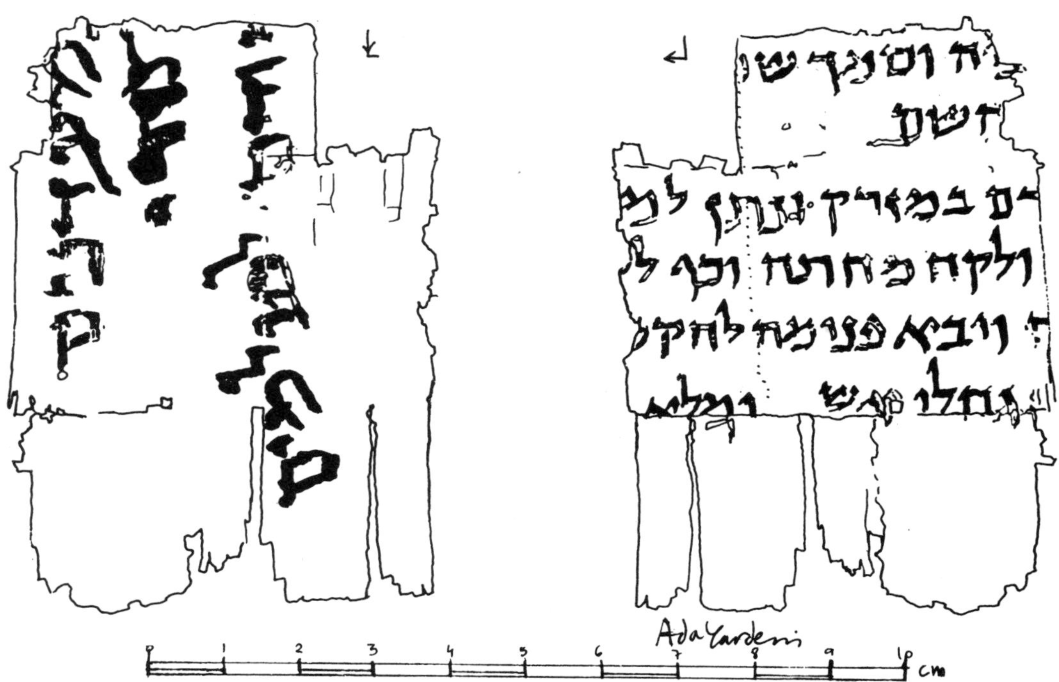

Fig. 91. A papyrus fragment with liturgical poems in Hebrew script (the Byzantine period; Moscow, Pushkin Museum, I 1.b 1028; real size)

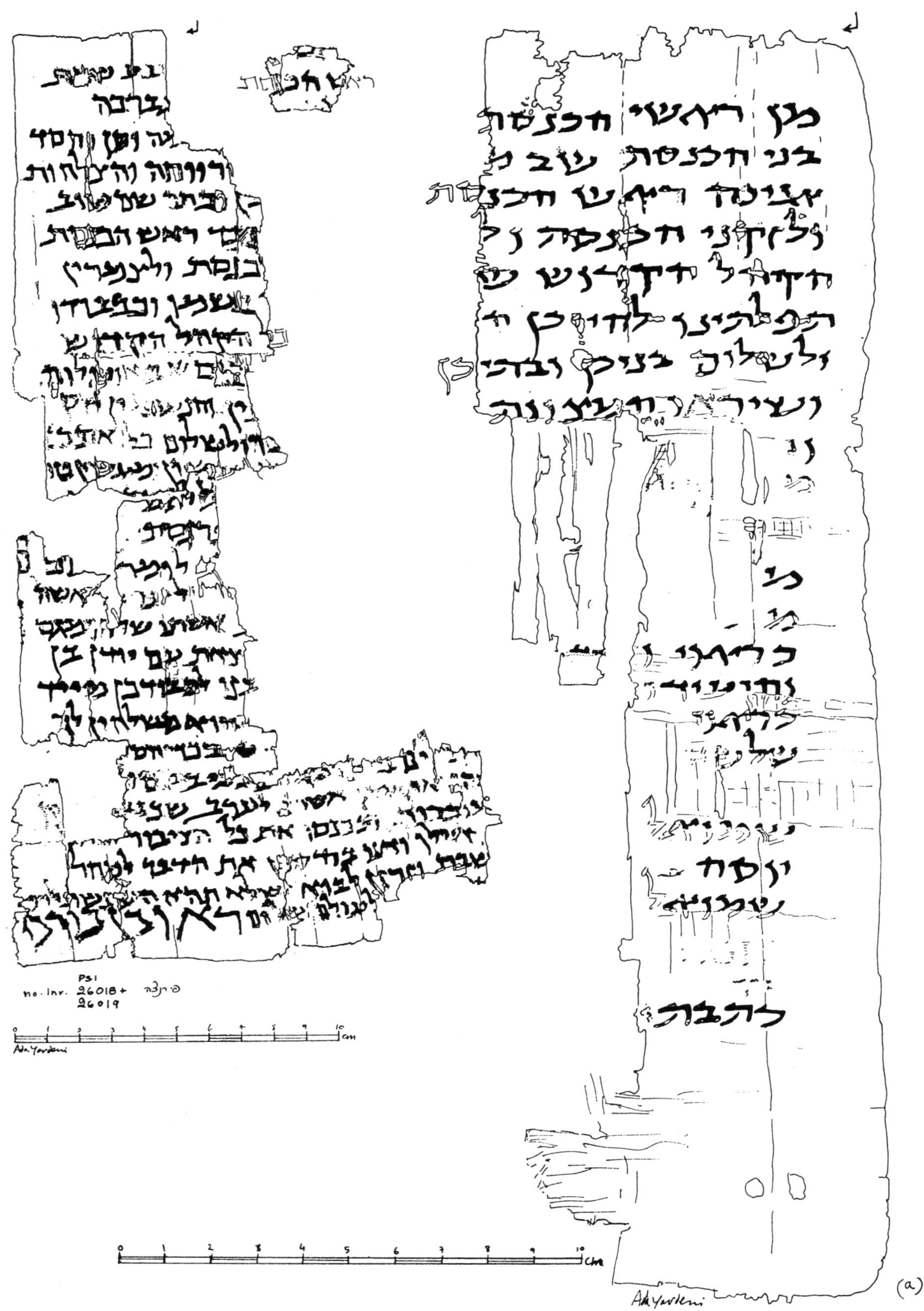

Fig. 92. Papyrus letters in Hebrew script (the Byzantine period; Oxford, Bodleian Library, Ms. Heb. C57(P); Florence, Biblioteca Medicea Laurenziana, Inv. 26018, 26019; reduced)

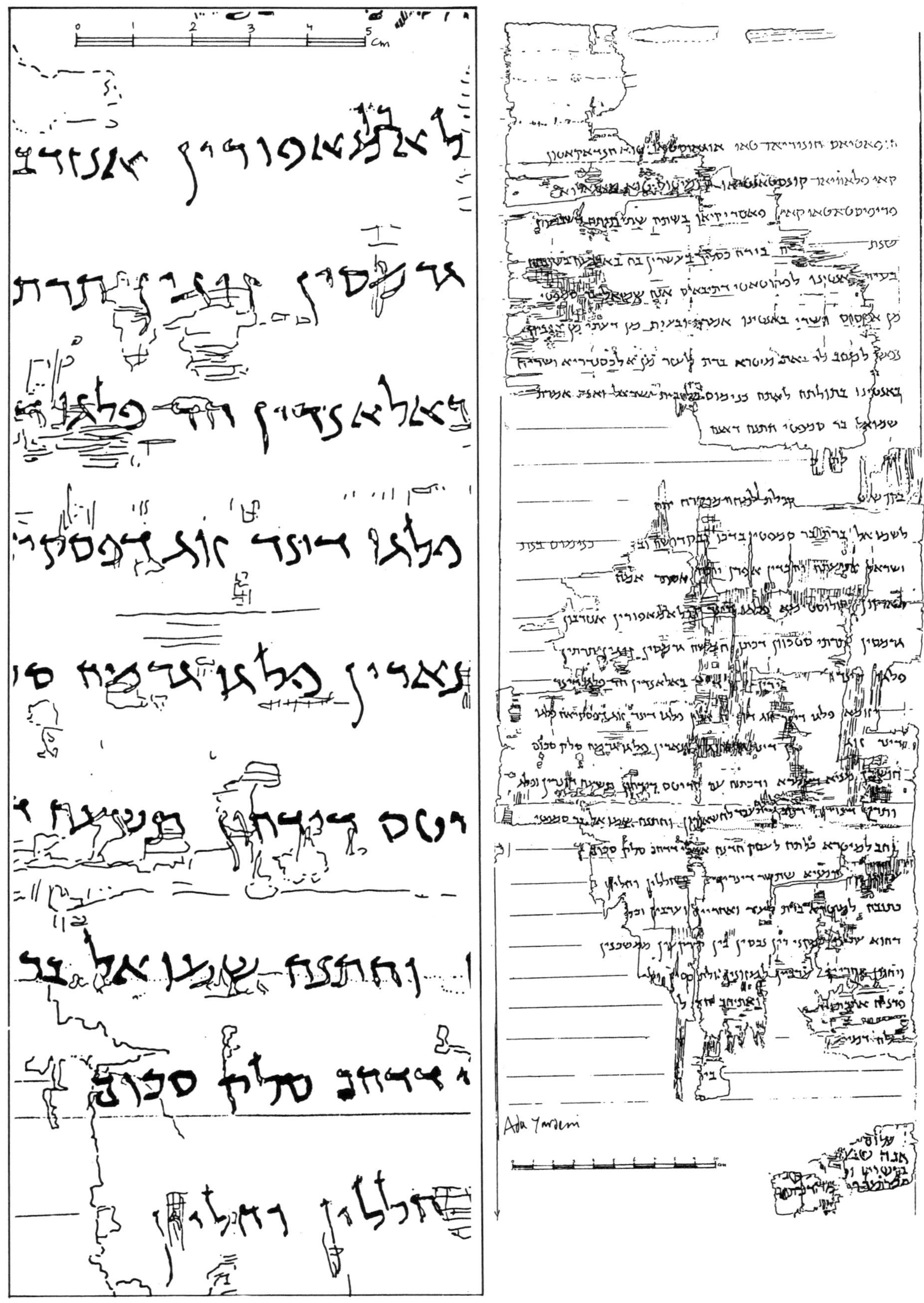

Fig. 93. A Jewish *Ketubbah* on papyrus, written in Antinoupolis in 417 CE (Cologne, Institut für Altertumskunde der Universität zu Köln, Papyrussammlung, Inv. no 5853; reduced, and detail in real size)

A number of papyrus fragments with Hebrew script, which were found together with Greek documents in Oxyrhynchus, are now located in the Bodleian Library in Oxford. Another four, found in Antinoupolis, are now in the Ashmolean Museum in Oxford and there is yet another fragment in Berlin. The small fragment of Exodus, which may be from the 3rd century, as well as the two letters mentioned above and another, earlier letter in Aramaic, are now in the Bodleian Library in Oxford.

The main collections of these papyrus fragments are in the Bodleian Library and Ashmolean Museum in Oxford, the Erzherzog Rainer Papyrussammlung in Vienna, the British Library in London, and the Papyrussammlung of the Staatliche Museen zu Berlin. There are single papyrus fragments in the Louvre in Paris, the Universities of Heidelberg and Cologne, the Macquarie University Library in Australia, the Ann Arbor Library, Michigan, in the U.S.A., San Cugat del Valles in Spain, the John Rylands Library in Manchester, the Bibliotheca Medicea Laurenziana in Florence, the Pushkin Museum in Moscow, and the University Library in Cambridge.

Fig. 94. A papyrus letter with an elegant Hebrew script (the Byzantine period; Oxford, Bodleian Library, Ms. Heb. f.114 [P]; real size)

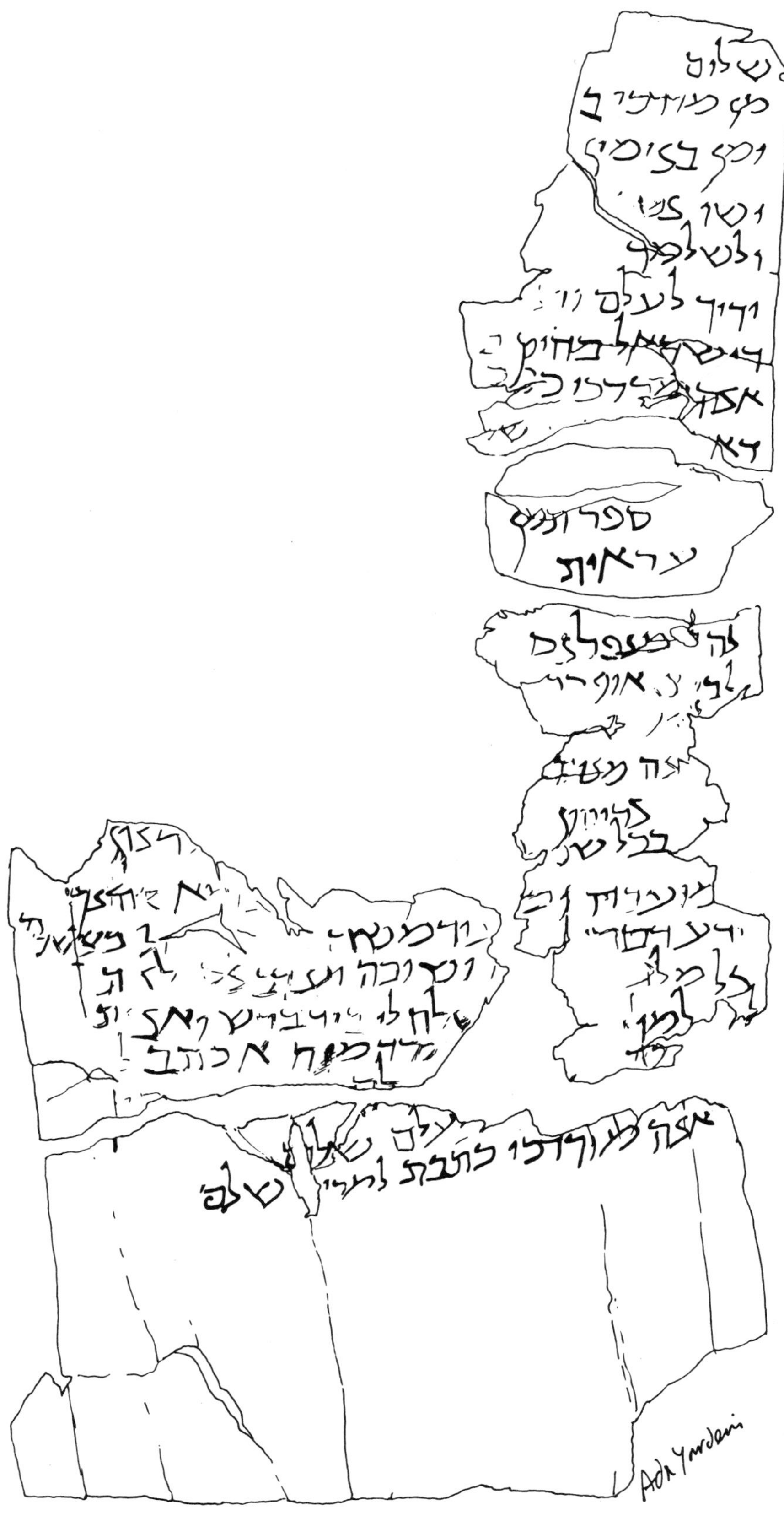

Fig. 95. A fragment of a letter from Oxyrhynchus (5th or 6th century CE; Oxford, Bodleian Library, Ms. Heb. C58 [P]; real size)

Fig. 96. Hebrew script on chinese paper from about the early 9th century, with Babylonian vowelization

In addition to the papyri, there are documents written on hide, the most important of which are a letter from Oxyrhynchus now located in Cologne (fig. 95), small fragments with palimpsests, the erased texts of which are in Hebrew letters and the superimposed text in Latin, from the 8th century (now in the National Bavarian Library in Munich), and a liturgical text (or an amulet?) of the early 8th century (now in the British Library in London). A Jewish letter in Persian from Turkestan (also in the British Library) perhaps belongs to the second half of the 8th century, and a liturgical text on chinese paper (now in the Bibliothèque Nationale in Paris) perhaps dates from the early 9th century (fig. 96).

A few manuscripts from the Cairo Genizah (see below) probably predate the 9th century; among them palimpsests of the Mishnah, Talmud and Midrash as well as *piyyutim* (liturgical poems) of Yannai. Two fragments of a Genesis scroll, in a calligraphic book-hand, probably written in the 8th century, are now in the University Library in Cambridge (fig. 97).

The majority of the material from the Byzantine and Arab periods is in a non-calligraphic or loose style of writing, mostly executed by unskilled writers. Only a few papyri and hide fragments and synagogue inscriptions testify to a tradition of elegant calligraphy preserving the basic forms of the ancient Jewish letter-signs together with their ornamental additions. In fact, these ornamental additions occasionally also appear in various forms in non-calligraphic writing and the tracing of their evolution assists in determining their relative chronology (see below in part 2).

As well as the almost complete absence of finds in a calligraphic book-hand, there is no evidence of the development of a cursive script-style during this period. The cursive Jewish script that reached its peak at the time of the Bar Kokhba revolt is not found afterwards and the cursive scripts that appear in the manuscripts of the Cairo Genizah are unrelated to it. In the Arab period – i.e. from the 7th century onwards – a certain influence of the cursive Arabic script may be recognized in the Hebrew script (figs. 100, 101), anticipating the later Eastern cursive script that appears in Genizah manuscripts (see below) from about the 11th century onwards.

Fig. 97. Detail of a fragmentary Genesis scroll from Egypt (ca. 8th century CE; Cambridge, University Library T-S NS 3.21; real size [with part of the text restored])

C. THE CAIRO GENIZAH

Thousands of manuscripts in Hebrew letters have survived from the period from the early Middle Ages to the 15th century, when print gradually superseded the handwritten book. The largest store of manuscripts of that period was discovered in the Ben Ezra synagogue in Fuṣṭāṭ (old Cairo), where a Jewish community existed for several centuries which had close connections with other Jewish communities, such as those in Babylonia, Palestine, North Africa and Spain, which were under Islamic authority.

The synagogue of Fuṣṭāṭ was founded in the 9th century. During the time of its existence thousands of manuscripts of various kinds were placed in an upper storeroom (in Hebrew called 'Genizah'). The sole entrance to the storeroom was a hole high in the wall of the women's gallery, which could be reached only by a ladder. The existence of the Genizah had been known to scholars for a long time, but rumours of the misfortunes that might befall those who removed material from it prevented people from trying to investigate the place. It was not until the 19th century that scholars and dealers succeeded in persuading the synagogue officials to permit the removal of material from the Genizah. Fragments of Genizah manuscripts began to appear in various places. The Imperial Library of St. Petersburg in Russia purchased a collection of manuscripts from the Russian Karaite Abraham Firkowitch and another collection was acquired by the Russian Archimandrite Anthonius in Jerusalem. Some fragments were brought to London by Elkan Adler, and others were brought to Philadelphia by Dr. Cyrus Adler. Towards the end of the 19th century, the Bodleian Library in Oxford began to purchase fragments from the Genizah. However, the actual source of all this material had not yet been located. In 1896, the twin sisters Agnes Lewis and Margaret Gibson showed a fragment they had purchased in Egypt to the Jewish scholar Solomon Schechter for identification. Schechter identified the fragments as belonging to the Hebrew book of Ben Sira (Ecclesiasticus) and realized that all the material came from a common source. With a letter of recommendation from Cambridge University to the heads of the Jewish community in Cairo and a large amount of money provided by Charles Taylor, he set off for Cairo to try and discover the source of the manuscripts and obtain permission to ship the manuscripts to England. In the Ben Ezra synagogue he discovered a hoard of manuscripts, including a 10th century copy of an ancient text, which he named 'Zadokite Document A' (fig. 99; the early version of this document was later discovered among the Dead Sea Scrolls and is now known as the 'Damascus Document' [fig. 98]). According to unofficial sources, some manuscripts had earlier been removed from the synagogue by members of the Jewish community and buried in the Basatin cemetery in Cairo. In June 1898 Schechter and Taylor delivered a collection of about 100,000 manuscripts to the senate of the university of Cambridge. Additional Genizah material was later donated to the Cambridge University Library by other people and it is now the largest existing collection of Genizah material. Other large collections are in Oxford and in the British Museum in London, in St. Petersburg in Russia, in the

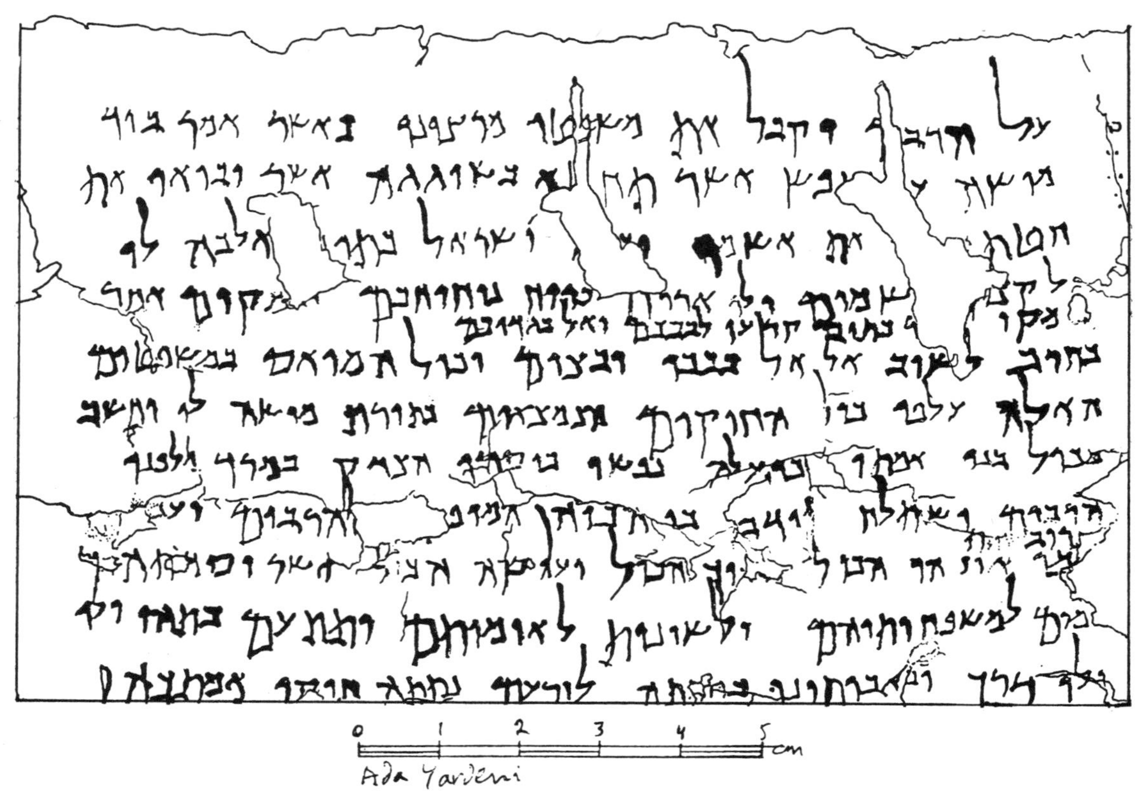

Fig. 98. Detail of the Damascus Document Ms. A (4Q266)

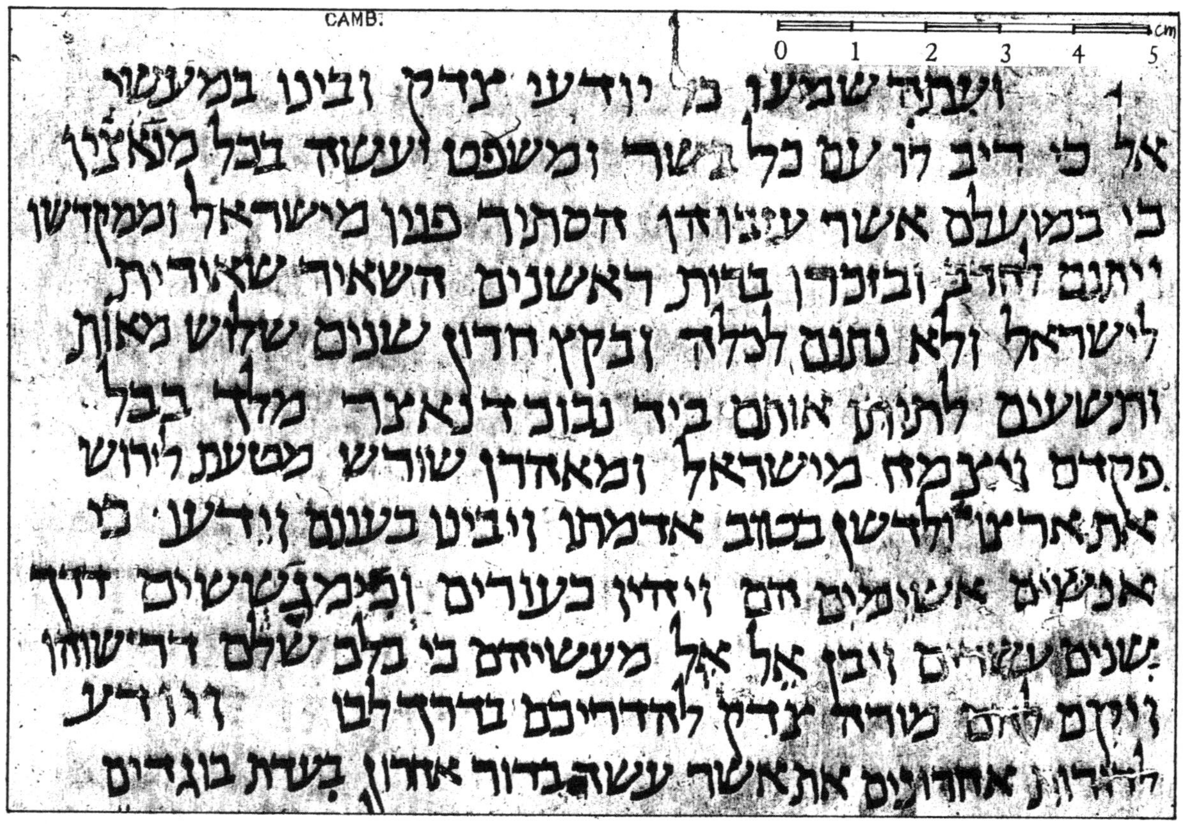

ועתה שמעו כל יודעי צדק ובינו במעשי
אל כי ריב לו עם כל בשר ומשפט יעשה בכל מנאציו
כי במועלם אשר עזבוהו הסתיר פניו מישראל וממקדשו
ויתנם לחרב ובזכרו ברית ראשנים השאיר שאירית
לישראל ולא נתנם לכלה ובקץ חרון שנים שלוש מאות
ותשעים לתיתו אותם ביד נבוכדנאצר מלך בבל
פקדם ויצמח מישראל ומאהרן שורש מטעת לירוש
את ארצו ולדשן בטוב אדמתו ויבינו בעונם וידעו כי
אנשים אשימים הם ויהיו כעורים וכימגששים דרך
שנים עשרים ויבן אל אל מעשיהם כי בלב שלם דרשוהו
ויקם להם מורה צדק להדריכם בדרך לבו ויודע
לדורות אחרונים את אשר עשה בדור אחרון בעדת בוגדים

Fig. 99. Detail of a page of the Zadokite Document A (Cambridge University Library, T-S. 10 K 6)

Jewish Theological Seminary in New York and in Dropsie College in Philadelphia. All in all, about 200,000 Genizah fragments exist in various collections throughout the world, dating from about the 9th to the 19th centuries. They include literary and non-literary texts of all kinds in Hebrew, Aramaic, and Judeo-Arabic written with Hebrew letters, as well as palimpsests with Greek and Syriac texts.

Ever since its discovery, the Genizah material has been investigated and studied by numerous scholars. However, part of the material still awaits publication. The Genizah manuscripts vary not only in their subject-matter but also in their styles of writing. They contain an abundance of Hebrew script-styles which permit the tracing of the formal evolution of the Hebrew letter-signs over a period of a thousand years.

Microfilms of the Genizah manuscripts are to be found at the Institute of Microfilms of Hebrew Manuscripts in the building of the Jewish National and University Library in Givat Ram, Jerusalem, and there is a collection of photographs at the Hebrew Palaeography Project in the same building.

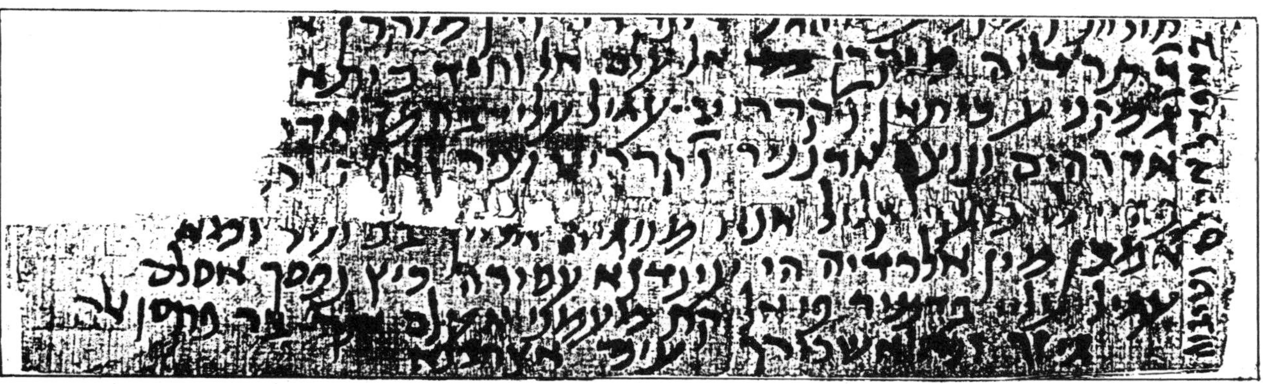

Fig. 100. Detail of a papyrus document in Hebrew script reflecting the influence of the Arabic script (Vienna, Österreichische Nationalbibliothek, Papyrussammlung, Papyrus Erzherzog Rainer, H 33)

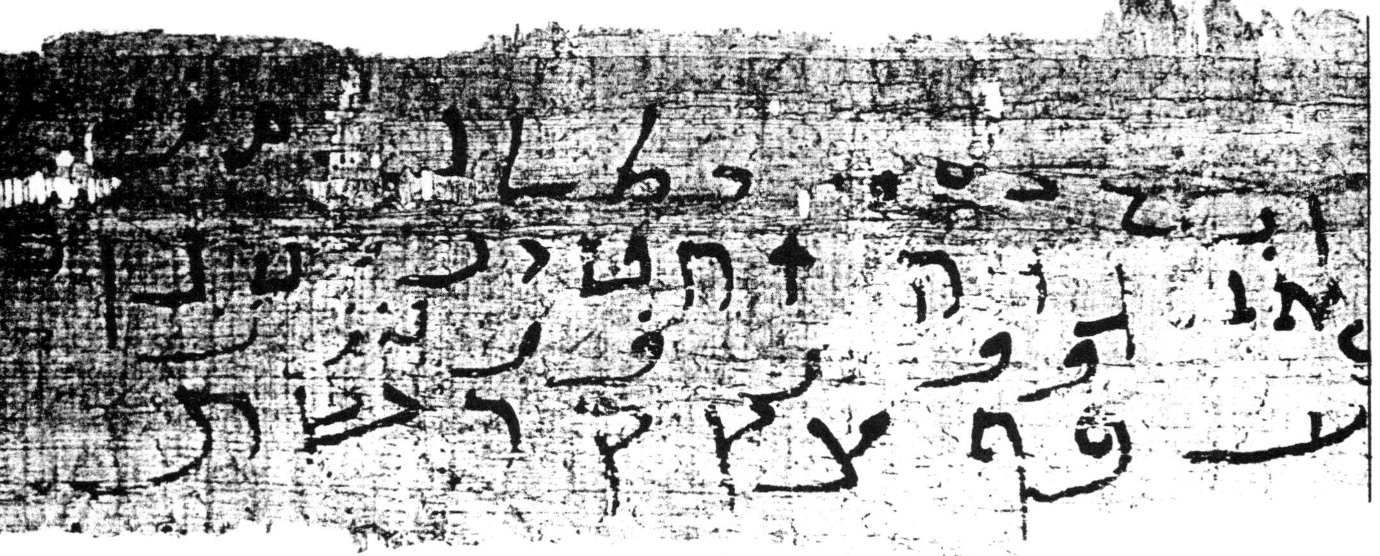

Fig. 101. Arabic and Hebrew abecedaries on papyrus (Vienna, Österreichische Nationalbibliothek, Papyrussammlung, Papyrus Erzherzog Rainer, AP 1256)

D. THE SPREAD OF THE HEBREW SCRIPTS FROM THE EARLY MIDDLE AGES TO THE MIDDLE OF THE 15TH CENTURY

The script in some of the early manuscripts from the Cairo Genizah testifies to the continuity of a scribal tradition that preserved the letter-signs of an elegant book-hand. Its beginnings are already to be found in documents from the Judean Desert (fig. 102) and its later stages of evolution may be seen in some papyrus fragments of the Byzantine period (fig. 94) and in biblical fragments predating the 9th century (figs. 97, 103). The outstanding features of this elegant calligraphic book-hand are

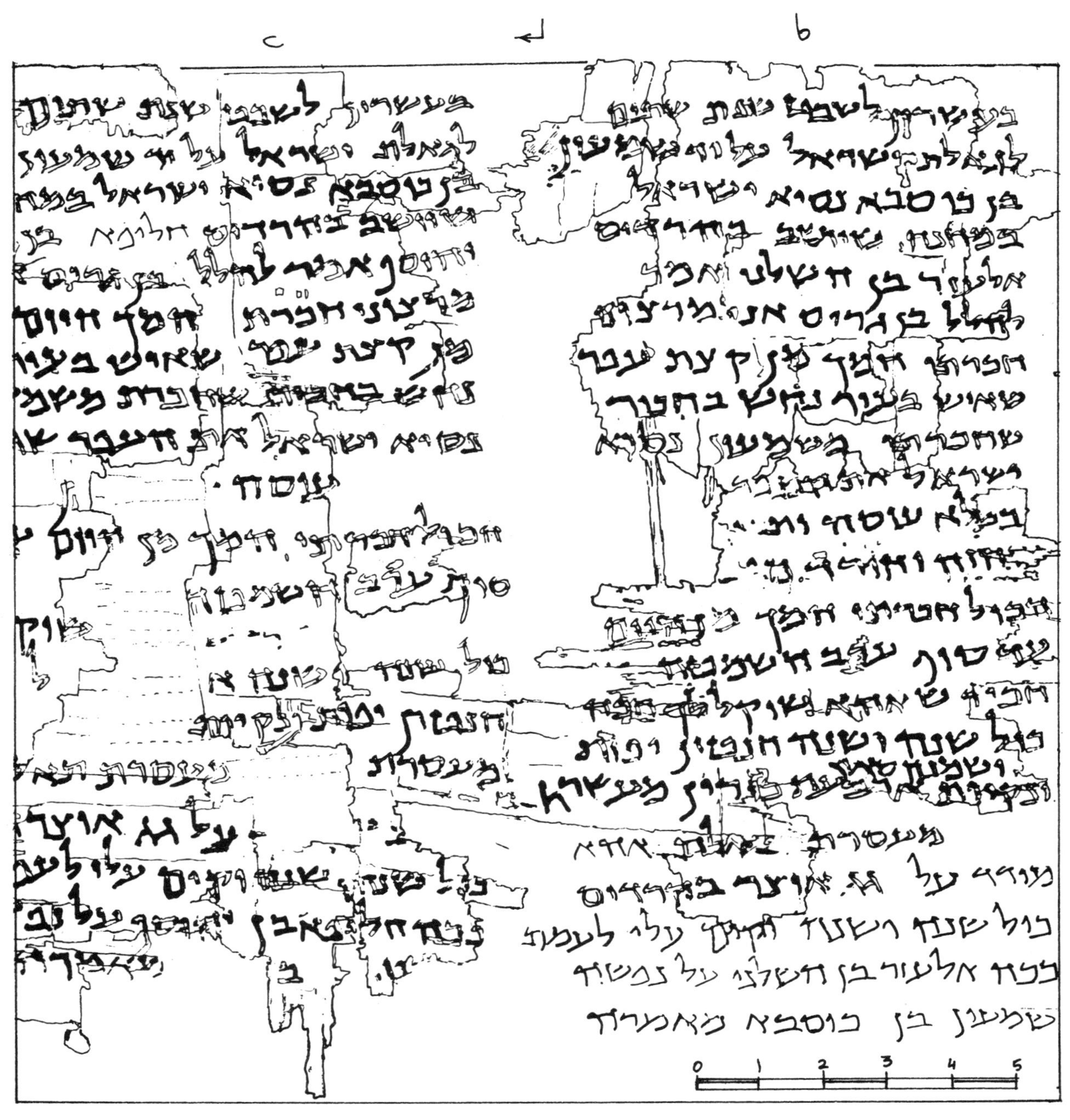

Fig. 102. Detail of a papyrus deed in an elegant Jewish book-hand from 133 CE (Mur. 24; The Rockefeller Museum of Antiquities, Jerusalem, Inv. no. 828; real size)

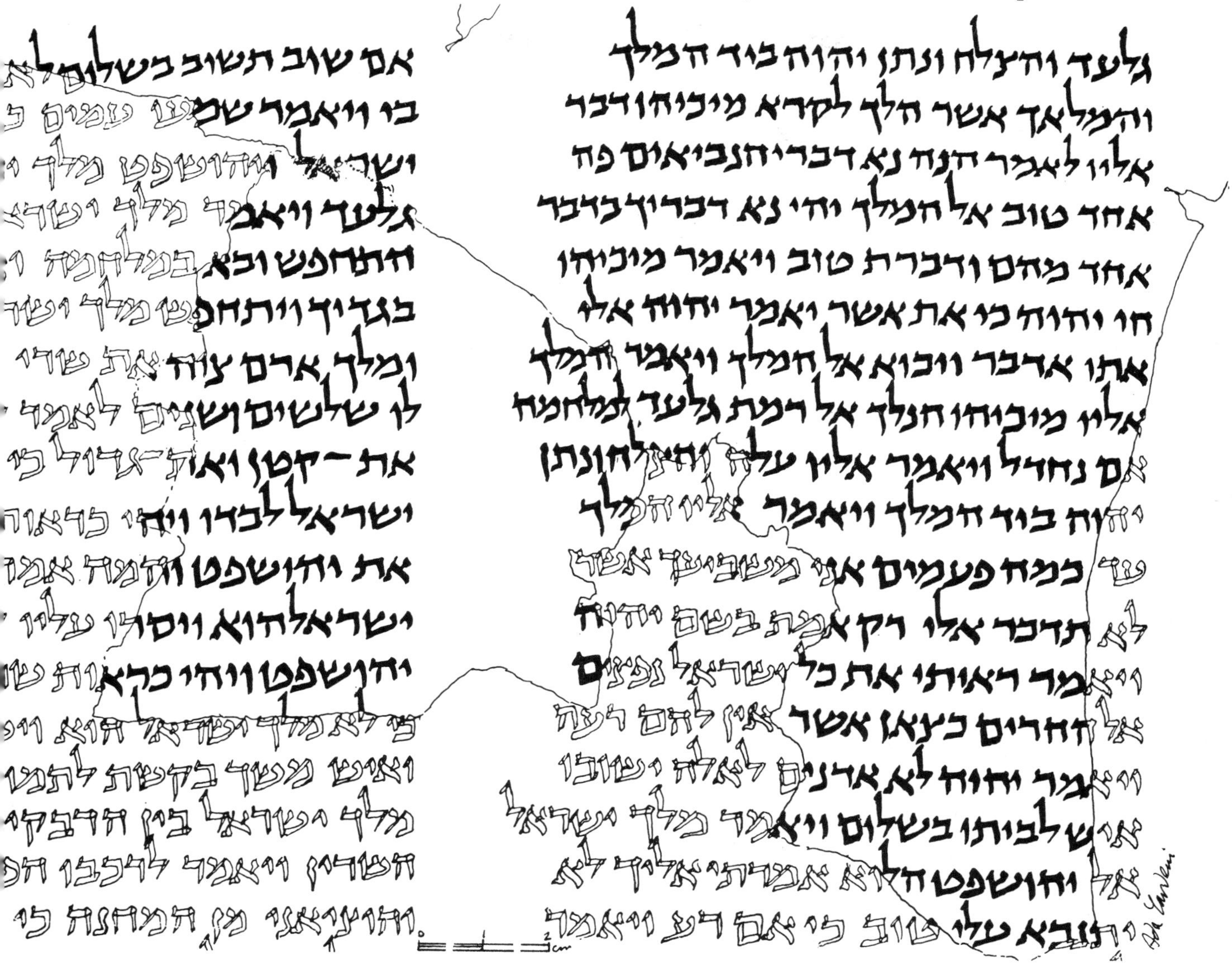

Fig. 103. A fragment of a biblical scroll (I Kings, 22), written in Antinoupolis in ca. the 8th century CE (Oxford, Ashmolean Museum, Antinoupolis papyri no 47)

the regularity of the letter-signs (one form for each letter in the alphabet as against the variant forms in most of the non-calligraphic scripts) and of the traditional ornamental additions that appear in various forms in accordance with the different styles of script. In the non-calligraphic and cursive scripts the number of strokes of the individual letter-signs was occasionally reduced as a result of fluent writing and the ornamental additions were often simplified or omitted altogether.

The elegant Hebrew calligraphic book-hand reached its peak in the late 9th to the 11th centuries (fig. 104). The Hebrew biblical manuscripts surviving from that time are the most beautiful of their kind. That script, referred to as the 'Eastern' Hebrew script, was dominant at that period in the whole of the Middle East, from Babylonia to Palestine, Egypt, Syria and Lebanon, and started to spread into North Africa and Spain on one hand, and Italy and Central and Western Europe on the other. From this 'Eastern' script, several major and secondary script-styles evolved. The Sephardi and Ashkenazi book-hands, which were later adapted to printing

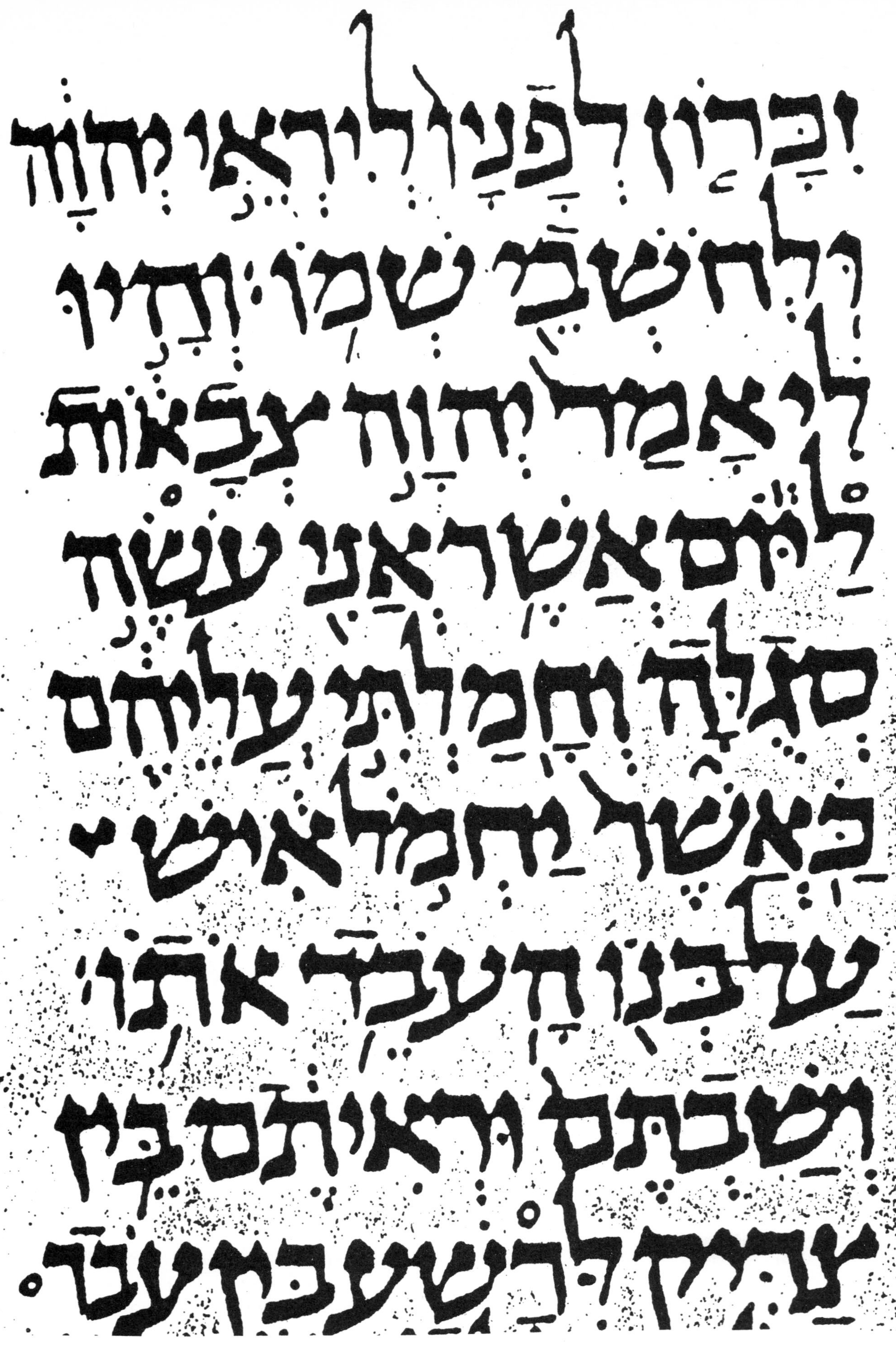
זכרון לפניו ליראי יהוה
ולחשבי שמו: והיו
לי אמר יהוה צבאות
ליום אשר אני עשה
סגלה וחמלתי עליהם
כאשר יחמל איש
על בנו העבד אתו:
ושבתם וראיתם בין
צדיק לרשע בין עבד

Fig. 104. An elegant Hebrew book-hand in a detail of a biblical manuscript from the 10th century CE, ascribed to Moshe Ben Asher. (The date in the colophon, corresponding to the year 895, is uncertain) techniques, were the direct descendants of the 'Eastern' book-hand, which is therefore of major importance for the evolution of the modern Hebrew script (see below, Part 3, dealing with the styles of script). The elegant calligraphic book-hand appears mainly in Torah manuscripts and occasionally in other literary manuscripts and official documents. It was elaborated through the extensive Masoretic activity in the 8th and 9th centuries; however, its roots lay in the early centuries CE with the sanctification of the Hebrew letter-signs and the fixing of rules for preserving the Torah scribal tradition.

עצים אל משה ואל אהרן
ואל כל העדה:
ויניחו אתו במשמר כי לא
פרש מה יעשה לו:
ויאמר יהוה אל משה מות
יומת האיש רגום אתו
באבנים כל העדה מחוץ
למחנה:

Fig. 105. An elaborate 'Eastern' script and a cursive 'Eastern' script in a page of a Karaite manuscript written in Jerusalem in 1373 (Paris, Bibliothèque nationale, héb. 283)

The copying of the sacred Scriptures was done exclusively by professional scribes, who were specially trained for that work. It needed profound knowledge of the relevant Halachot (legal prescriptions), and any minor deviation from the rules made the manuscript unfit for ceremonial use.

Despite the strict tradition, the letter-signs underwent stylistic changes due to a natural process of evolution, and a variety of script-styles evolved in different Jewish communities. Unlike the practice in the Christian world, where books were copied mainly in monasteries and later in universities by professional scribes, book-copying was widespread in Jewish society not only in scribal schools but also among private people, and for private use. From about the 11th century, centres of learning in various Jewish communities in Europe were engaged in the writing and copying of books. The widespread existence of writing activity among non-professional writers caused a rapid evolution of the letter-forms and deviations from the standard traditional writing.

Together with the elegant calligraphic script, more or less cursive non-calligraphic scripts evolved, which were used for private and occasionally official purposes. There is no evidence of real cursive writing until the late 11th or 12th century. The extreme cursive Jewish script that was used up to the end of the Bar Kokhba revolt disappeared without leaving a trace. A semi-cursive script appears on a fragment from Dura-Europos (fig. 77) from the late 2nd or early 3rd century. From the 7th century onwards, with the influence of the cursive Arabic script, the beginnings of a cursive Hebrew script-style appear next to the 'Eastern' book-hand. Documents in an extreme cursive hand from the early 12th century (fig. 106) bear witness to a long history of that style, which perhaps began in the early Islamic period.

In the Genizah documents from the early 12th century onwards, three main 'levels' of writing may be discerned: 1) The calligraphic book-hand used for sacred, ritual and official documents, executed by professional scribes; 2) an extreme cursive hand; and 3) a semi-cursive hand in a variety of forms and of types of writing, some of which later evolved into semi-cursive script-styles. The 'Eastern' Hebrew script spread westwards in two main directions – via Byzantium and Italy into Central and Western Europe (in 980 Jews moved into Central Europe from northern Italy), and via North Africa into Spain. In the course of time differences developed in the letter-forms due to the use of different writing implements (the reed pen versus the quill pen), as well as the influence of non-Hebrew scripts – particularly Arabic and Latin – used by Jews dwelling in the different areas. Writing in the foreign scripts naturally also influenced their way of holding the writing implement for drawing the different strokes.

The differences in the writing were part of the general differences in the techniques of book-making. From about the 4th century the codex gradually superseded the scroll, particularly in the Christian world. The Jews, however, continued to use a scroll for writing the Torah, as they still do. Papyrus was in common use in the Middle East until about the 8th

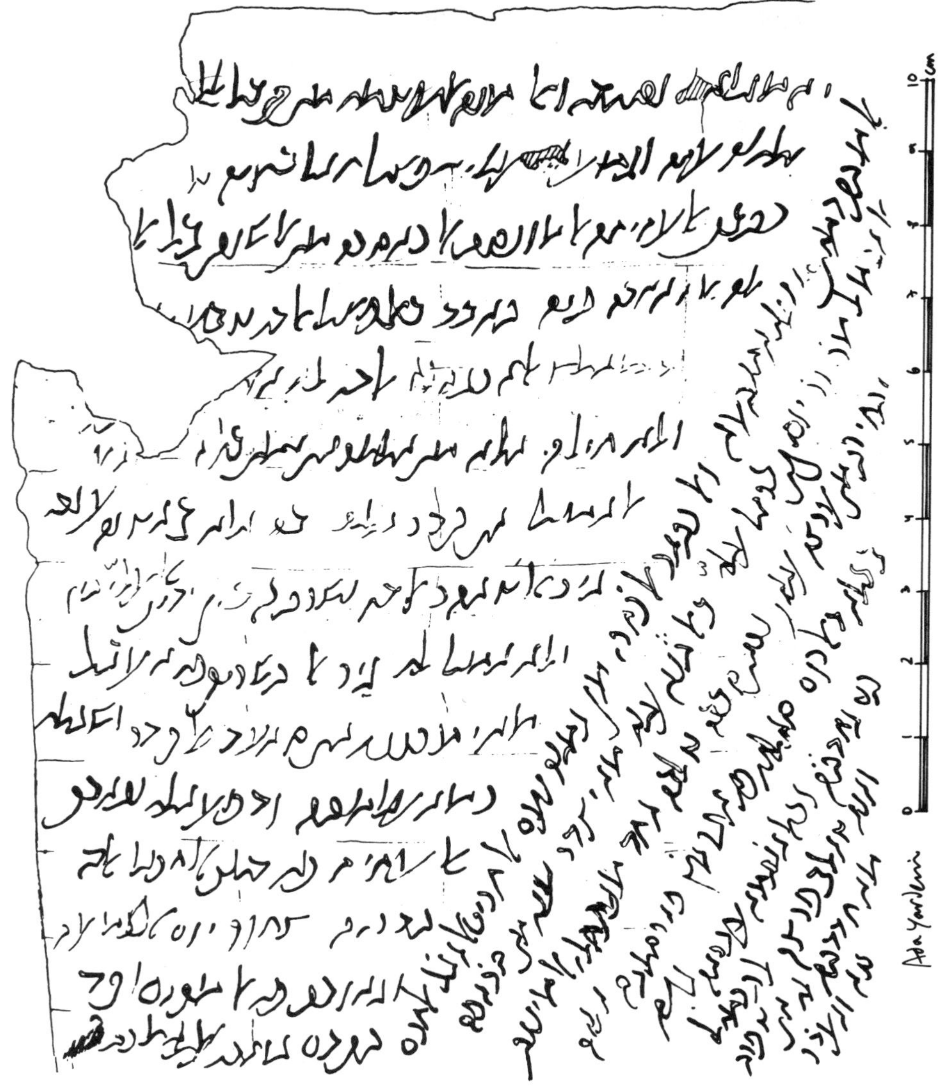

Fig. 106. A letter by Yehudah ha-Levi in the Arabic language and in an extreme cursive 'Sephardi' script (before 1140; New York, JTS, ENA, NS I.4.5; real size)

א	י	ק
ב	כ	ר
ג	ל	ש
ד	מ	ת
ה	נ	ך
ו	ס	ם
ז	ע	ן
ח	פ	ף
ט	צ	ץ

century. After the 11th century it was replaced by vellum or parchment. (The last known dated papyrus is a bull of Pope Victor the Second from the year 1057.)

In the different countries, various techniques of book-making developed with regard to size, the number of pages in the folded sheets which made up the book, the pagination, the format and design of the writing surface, the drawing of the lines and margins, the filling-out of the spaces at the end of lines, the ornamentation and the illustrations. All these technical details help in dating undated manuscripts and identifying their provenance. However, in the case of the Jews, because of their many migrations in the course of their history, these factors alone are not sufficient to enable us to determine the date and provenance of a manuscript.

Two prominent cultures influenced Hebrew book-making and the Hebrew script in the Middle Ages – the Islamic culture with its Arabic script and the Christian culture with its Latin script. In the early Middle Ages, the reed-pen was still the usual writing implement in the Islamic countries while the quill-pen was the main writing implement in Christian Europe. The quill-pen is more flexible than the calamus, or reed-pen, but on the other hand less adjustable to rapid writing, and as such is hardly suited to an extreme flowing script.

The 'Islamic' branch of Hebrew script included that of the Jewish communities in the Middle East, Central Asia, North Africa, Spain and southern France. In the 'Islamic' branch, two main families may be discerned – an 'Eastern' family and a 'Western' one. The 'Eastern' family of Hebrew script-styles may be found in manuscripts from Egypt, Palestine, Syria, Iran, Persia, Asia Minor and Yemen (although, from about the 13th century, the Yemenite Hebrew script shows independent features). The earliest dated manuscripts in the 'Eastern' script are from the late 9th century. The 'Western' family of the 'Islamic' branch – the 'Sephardi' script-style – may be found in manuscripts from North Africa, Spain (including Catalonia), Portugal and southern France. The earliest known dated Hebrew manuscript from Spain was written in Gerona in the year 1184. The earliest known dated codex in Hebrew letters from Southern France – which has characteristics similar to those of the manuscripts from Spain – is from the year 1282. Eleventh-century manuscripts in cursive script from Catalonia (under Christian rule from 801) represent a type of script that was used in Christian Europe. The *Reconquista* (Christian reconquest) in Spain, however, did not obliterate the Sephardi script-style, which spread northwards and also became dominant in Catalonia and Provence.

The 'Christian' branch of the Hebrew script included that of the Jewish communities in Italy, Central and Western Europe and later in Eastern Europe as well. In the 'Christian' branch there were also two main types of Hebrew script. One emerged in the late 12th century under the influence of the Gothic style in central and northern France, Germany and possibly

England (before the expulsion of the Jews in 1290), and at a later period also in Eastern Europe (no Hebrew manuscripts from Eastern Europe have so far been found dating from before the 11th century). The other type is found mainly in manuscripts from Italy (the earliest dated manuscript is from 1072/3). From about the late 13th century onwards, the 'Ashkenazi' script-style became dominant in northern Italy, while mediaeval manuscripts from southern Italy reveal the influence of the Sephardi style. Manuscripts in the Hebrew cursive script from western Turkey, Greece, the Balkans and Crete, which belonged to the Byzantine empire, show independent features from about the 11th century onwards.

The 'Eastern' Hebrew book-hand continued to exist in Babylonia and Persia until the late Middle Ages, when it absorbed the characteristics of the Sephardi Hebrew script-style. With the Karaite sect the 'Eastern' Hebrew script-style survived for a longer period, and an elegant Hebrew 'Eastern' book-hand as well as an 'Eastern' cursive hand still appear in Karaite manuscripts of the 15th century (fig. 105).

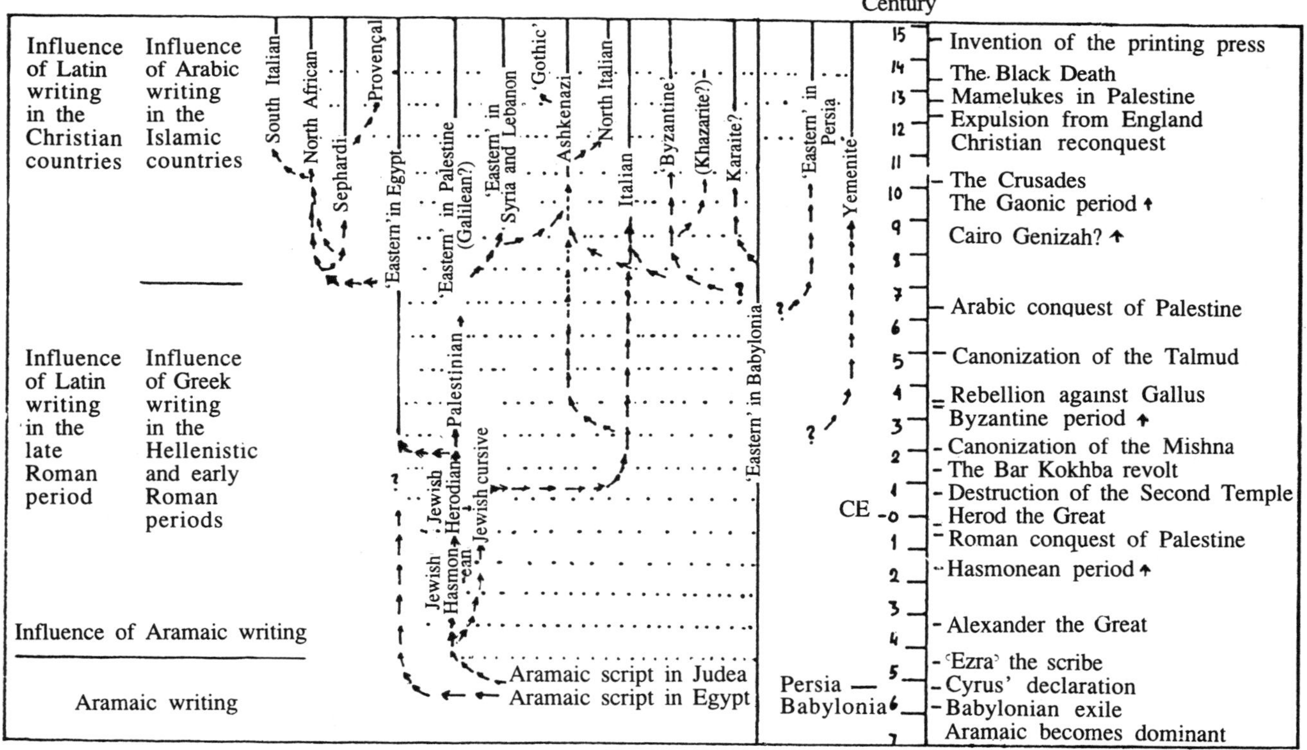

Fig. 107. A schematic description of the dissemination of the Hebrew scripts

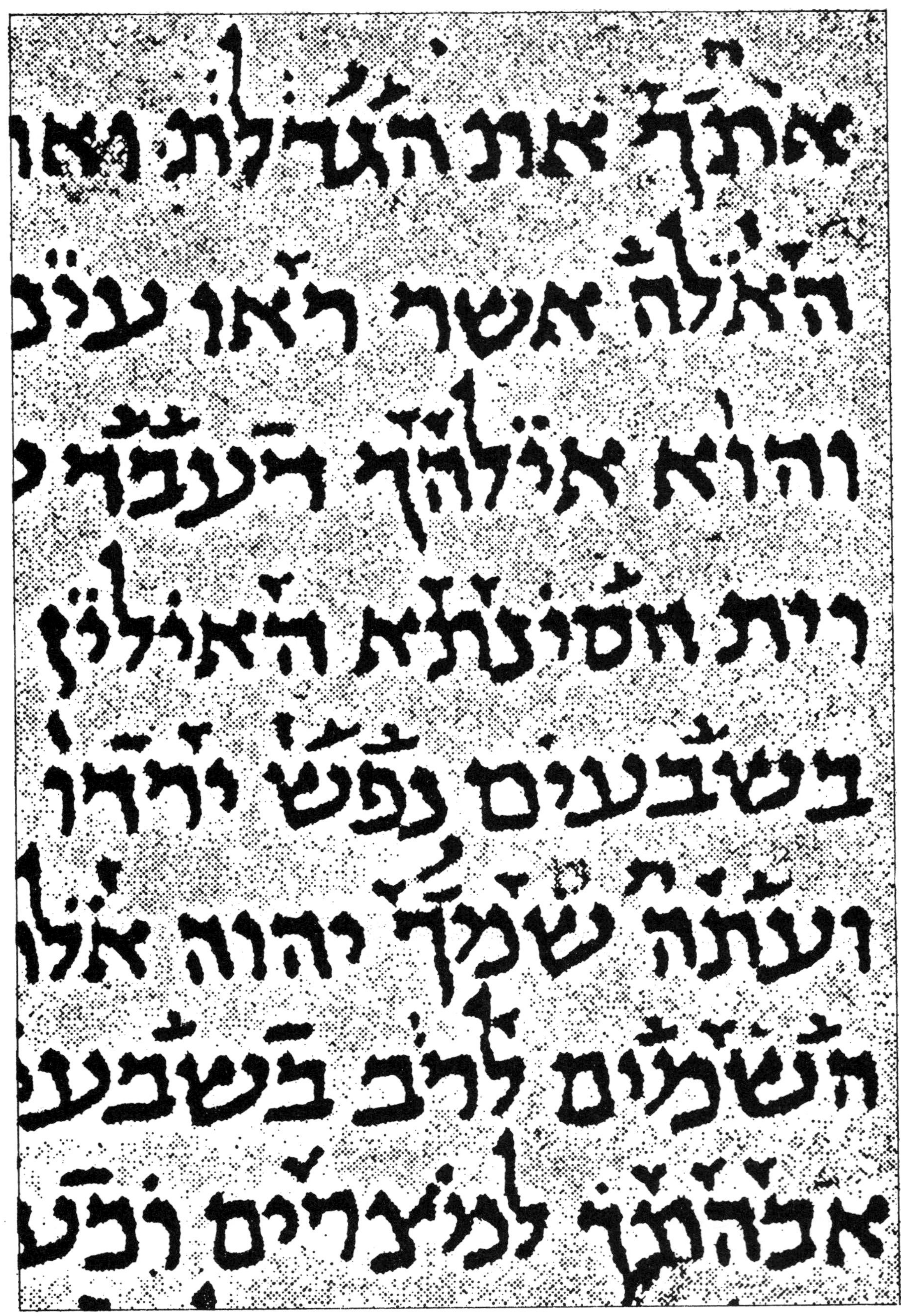
אתך את הגדלת
האלה אשר ראו
והוא אלהך דעבד
וית חסינתא האילין
בשבעים נפש ירדו
ועתה שמך יהוה
השמים לרב בשבע
אבהתך למצרים

Fig. 108. Detail from a Deuteronomy manuscript with early Babylonian vowelization (ca. 9th century; Oxford, Bodleian Library, Ms. Heb. d.26; enlarged)

E. EARLY BIBLICAL MANUSCRIPTS IN THE 'EASTERN' BOOK-HAND

The elegant square book-hand preserved the ancient scribal traditions of Torah copying. Those traditions were elaborated by skilled professional scribes and followed strict scribal rules.

Among the early manuscripts from the Cairo Genizah are fragments of biblical scrolls, one of the earliest of which is a Genesis scroll (fig. 97) which perhaps dates from the late 7th or early 8th century. These fragments include examples from Ezekiel and Daniel with vowelization and accentuation marks. Fragments of six biblical scrolls, the text of which was erased and overwritten with 13th century Greek medical texts, were recently published. Their script resembles that of the 10th century manuscripts. These fragments are located in the Biblioteca Medicea Laurenziana in Florence. Fragments of early biblical codices were also found, including a codex of Exodus from the 9th or 10th century. There are also biblical fragments from before the 10th century with Palestinian or mixed Tiberian and Palestinian vowelization marks, as well as Babylonian or Babylonian and Tiberian vowelization marks. None of the manuscripts are dated, and the dating is based on palaeographical, codicological and linguistic criteria. Scholars distinguish a number of stages in the evolution of the Hebrew vowelization systems which permits a relative chronology of the manuscripts to be determined. From about the 10th century the Tiberian vowelization system gradually superseded the other systems.

Examples of early biblical manuscripts with Babylonian vowelization are texts of Deuteronomy (today in the Bodleian Library in Oxford [Ms. Heb. d 26; fig. 108]) and Samuel ([Ms. Heb. 2, 49]), a manuscript of Isaiah (in the Jewish Theological Seminary [Ms JTS 505.9]); a manuscript of Joshua (in the National Library in Jerusalem [Heb. 4^{0} 577.4]); a large manuscript of Chronicles (in Berlin [Or.Qu. 680] and New York [Ms JTS 510]); manuscripts in the Cambridge University Library – Isaiah (MS T-S A38.6), I Chronicles (MS T-S A39.15), Job (MS T-S A39.20) and Joshua (MS T-S A39.4); and a manuscript of Job (Firk. II 1546, 1547) and of I Chronicles in St. Petersburg (Anthonin Collection 366.1).

An early manuscript of Deuteronomy with Palestinian vowelization is today in the Cambridge University Library (MS T-S NS 249.15). The Leningrad (St. Petersburg) manuscript of the latter prophets written in 916 (Heb. B.3; fig. 109) is one of the early dated biblical manuscripts with mixed Babylonian and Tiberian vowelization. An early biblical manuscript with Tiberian vowelization is a text of the prophets with a colophon stating that it was written in 895. The manuscript is ascribed to Moshe ben Asher but scholars claim that it was written somewhat later. The Aram-Zobah Bible (fig. 110) was written by Shelomo ben Boyaʿaʾ and vowelized by Aharon ben Asher in the first half of the 10th century. The Sassoon Ms. No. 507 of the Torah and a manuscript now located in the British

אליו לאמר בן אדם שים
פניך על הר שעיר והנבא
עליו ואמרת לו כה אמר
אדני יהוה הנני אליך
הר שעיר ונטיתי ידי
עליך ונתתיך שממה
ומשמה עריך חרבה
אשים ואתה שממה
תהיה וידעת כי אני יהוה
יען היות לך איבת עולם

Fig. 109. Detail of a biblical manuscript in an elaborate 'Eastern' calligraphic hand (916 CE; St. Petersburg, Heb.B.3.; enlarged)

Museum (Or. 4445) belong to the same period. Several early manuscripts predating the 10th century, as well as one dated 1009, are in St. Petersburg. A dated manuscript from 1106 is located in Jerusalem (Heb. 8.2238). The Reuchlin manuscript from Karlsruhe, dated 1105/6, and the Vatican manuscript Urb.2 which, according to its colophon, was written in 979 (although the date is uncertain), are examples of manuscripts with Ben Naphtali's expanded Tiberian vowelization. The Erfurt 3 manuscript from Berlin (Or. Fol. 1213) dates from the 11th century. Many biblical manuscripts of the 12th century have survived.

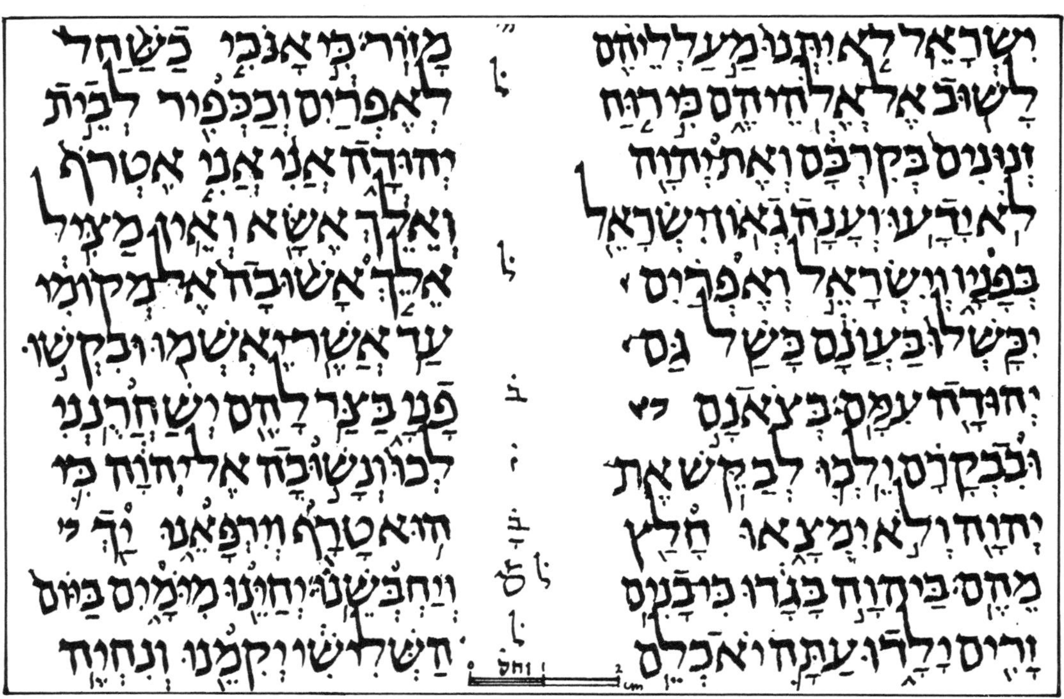

Fig. 110. Detail of the Aram-Zobah manuscript of the Bible (first half of the 10th century; Jerusalem, The Israel Museum)

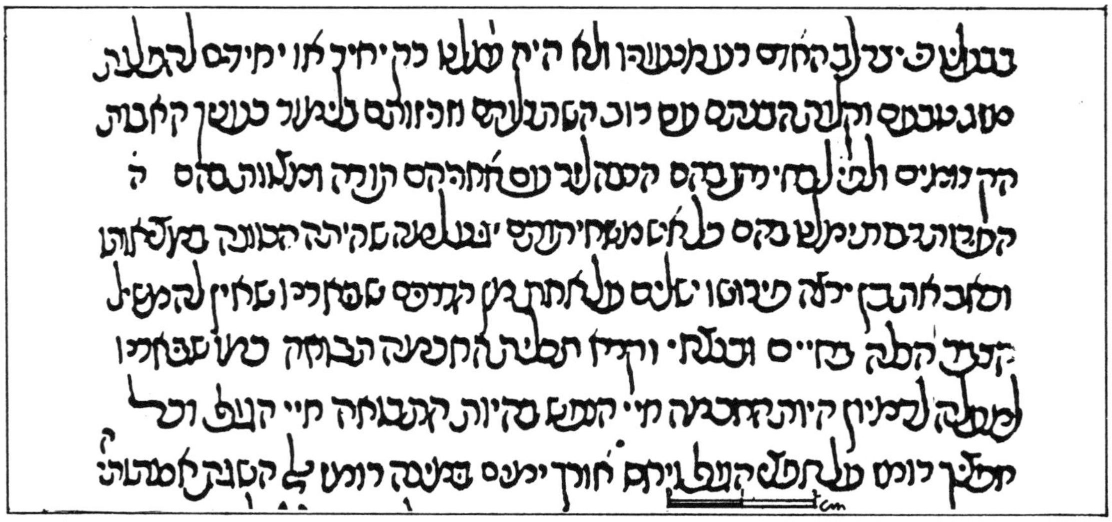

Fig. 111. A semi-cursive ‘Sephardi’ script in a manuscript from Toledo (1477; Frankfurt, Universitätsbibliothek, Ms. Hebr. 8056)

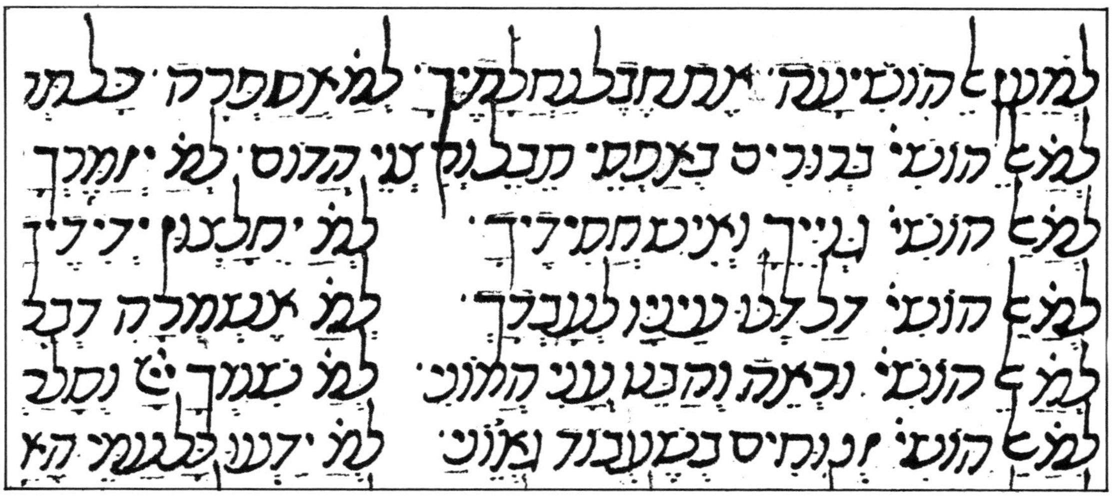

Fig. 112. A variant of Hebrew ‘Sephardi’ semi-cursive script in a manuscript from Fez (1332; Oxford, Bodleian Library, Or. 611 [1164])

Fig. 113. An extreme cursive Hebrew ‘Sephardi’ script in a mathematics book in the Arabic language from Qalaʿat Aiyub, Spain (1475; Paris, Bibliothèque nationale, H. 1125)

F. THE DISSEMINATION OF THE SEMI-CURSIVE AND CURSIVE SCRIPTS

The elegant square book-hand was used a great deal for sacred and ritual texts as well as official documents. Together with that book-hand, various cursive and semi-cursive hands were used which served for private as well as official and literary writings. Some of these semi-cursive hands, called 'half-a-calamus' or *Meshiṭa*ʾ in contemporary literary sources, developed into stylized calligraphic scripts. Among them was the semi-cursive Sephardi script-style (fig. 111), which emerged toward the 13th century and was later used for printing (the first dated Hebrew printed book – Rashi's commentary to the Torah – employed that script, which was consequently named 'Rashi script'). This script-style is still used by some Yemenite Jews, and a modern version of it is occasionally used by Jews from North Africa. A second semi-cursive hand that appears in manuscripts from Spain and North Africa (fig. 112) reached its culmination in the 14th century. An extreme cursive Sephardi hand (fig. 113), which evolved as a result of the influence of the cursive Arabic script, is found in documents of the early 12th century; a semi-cursive Ashkenazi hand (fig. 114) emerged in the 13th century under the influence of the Gothic Latin forms; a cursive Ashkenazi hand (fig. 115), from which the modern cursive Hebrew script developed, is to be found in documents of about the same period (already in documents of the 15th century, some of the letter-signs show a striking resemblance to the modern forms); a semi-cursive Italian hand (fig. 116) reached its culmination in the 15th century, while a cursive version of it appears in documents from the 16th century onwards. An elaborated 'Eastern' semi-cursive is found in documents from about the 12th century onwards (fig. 117). In Yemen a unique semi-cursive script appears in the 13th century (fig. 118), together with the 'Eastern' cursive script (which was later replaced by the Sephardi cursive).

The cursive and semi-cursive hands in other regions did not become stylized into calligraphic scripts. However, some scripts developed local characteristics, such as the semi-cursive 'Persian' hand (fig. 119) or the cursive 'Byzantine' hand (fig. 120). The influence of the Sephardi semi-cursive and book-hand styles penetrated eastwards at a relatively early period and produced a mixture of forms that did not evolve into an independent script-style. Some of the semi-cursive and cursive hands continued to develop and others gradually disappeared with the invention of the printing press which caused a revolution in book-making in the middle of the 15th century.

> The Ashkenazi cursive script evolved into the modern official Hebrew cursive script used in Israel. The Jews in the Arab countries followed the Sephardi writing-tradition, including the Sephardi semi-cursive script, and many of them still use it today.

Fig. 114. A semi-cursive Hebrew 'Ashkenazi' script in the Gothic style in a manuscript from Besançon, France (1397; Cambridge, University Library, Add. 490.1)

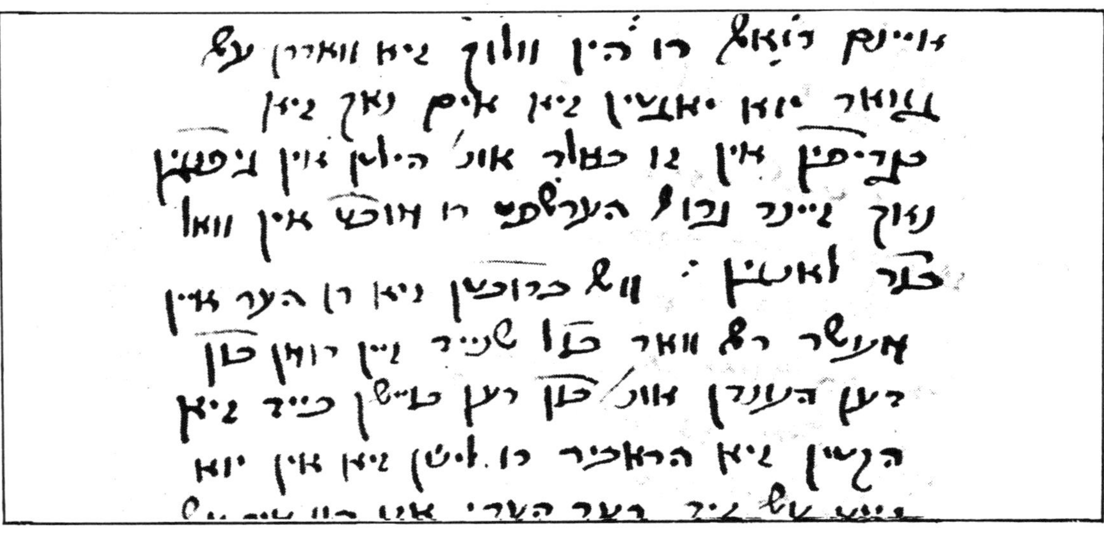

Fig. 115. A cursive Hebrew 'Ashkenazi' script in a manuscript from Italy (1510/11; Parma 2513, Cod. Pol. 1.)

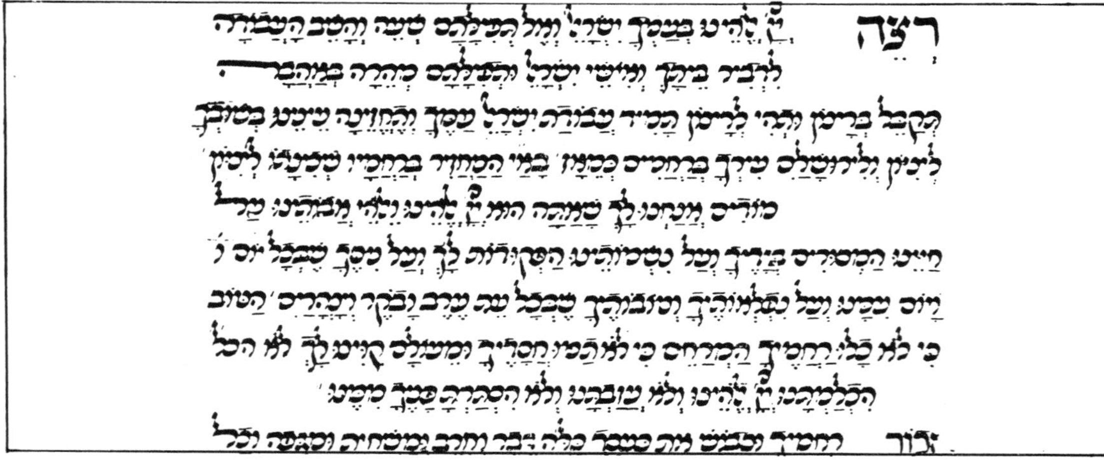

Fig. 116. A semi-cursive script of Italian style written by the scribe Abraham Fariṣol (1488; New York, JTS, ENA 1230)

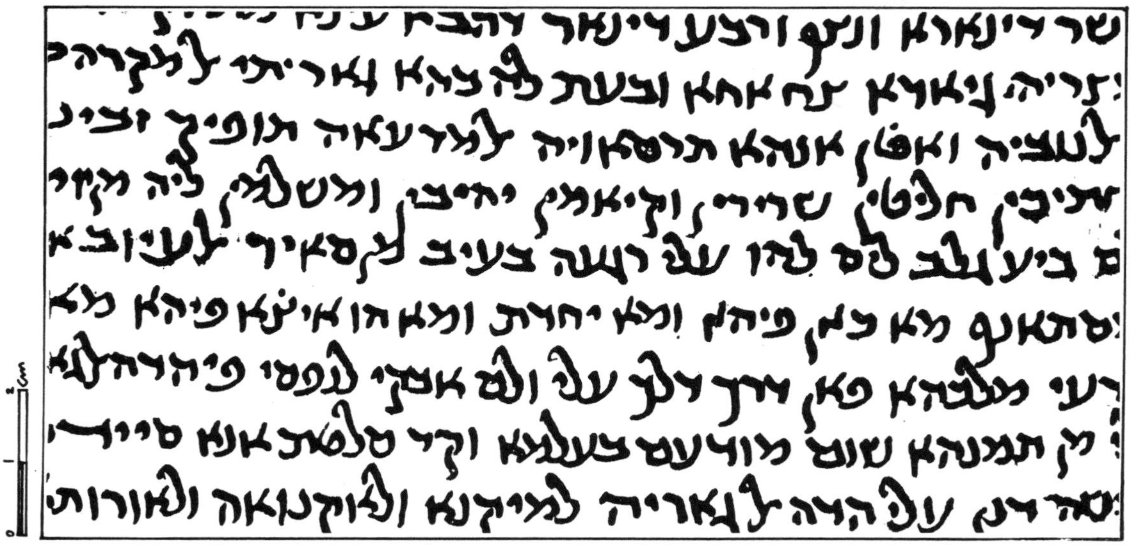

Fig. 117. A semi-cursive 'Eastern' script in a manuscript from Fusṭāṭ (old Cairo; 1100; Oxford, Bodleian Library, Ms. Heb. 12)

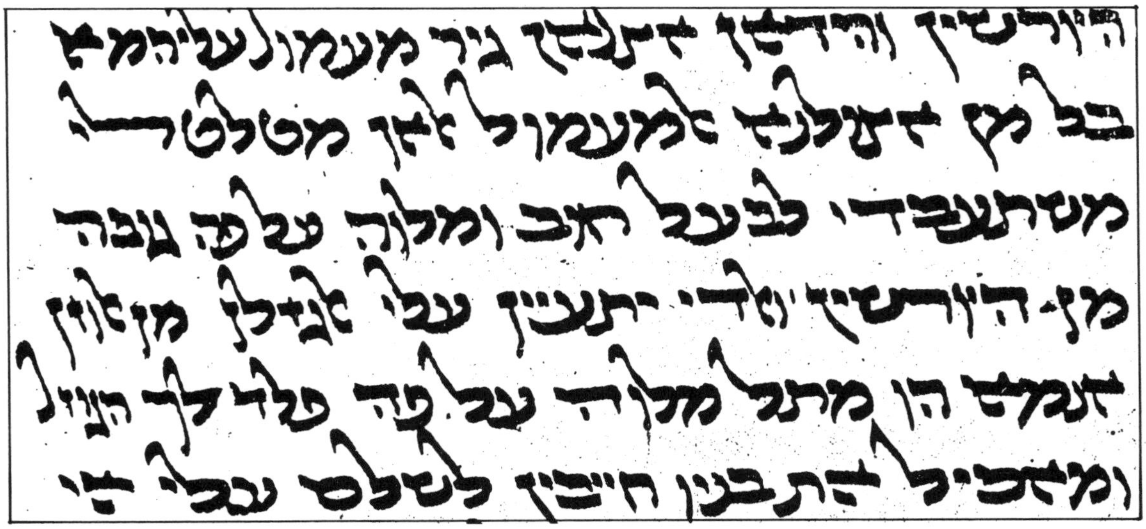

Fig. 118. A semi-cursive Yemenite script in a manuscript written in ʿAden by the scribe Saʿadiah son of Yaḥiah son of Khalphon el-ʿAdani (1222; Berlin, Nationalbibliothek, Qu. 568 Or. Ms.)

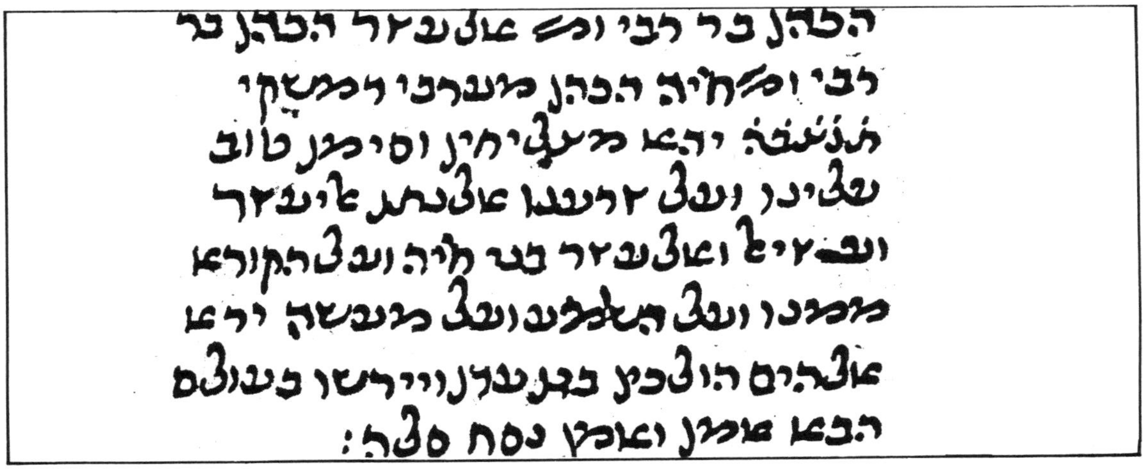

Fig. 119. An 'Eastern' semi-cursive script of Persian style in a manuscript from Bukhara (1497; Moussaieff collection, Ms. Heb. 130)

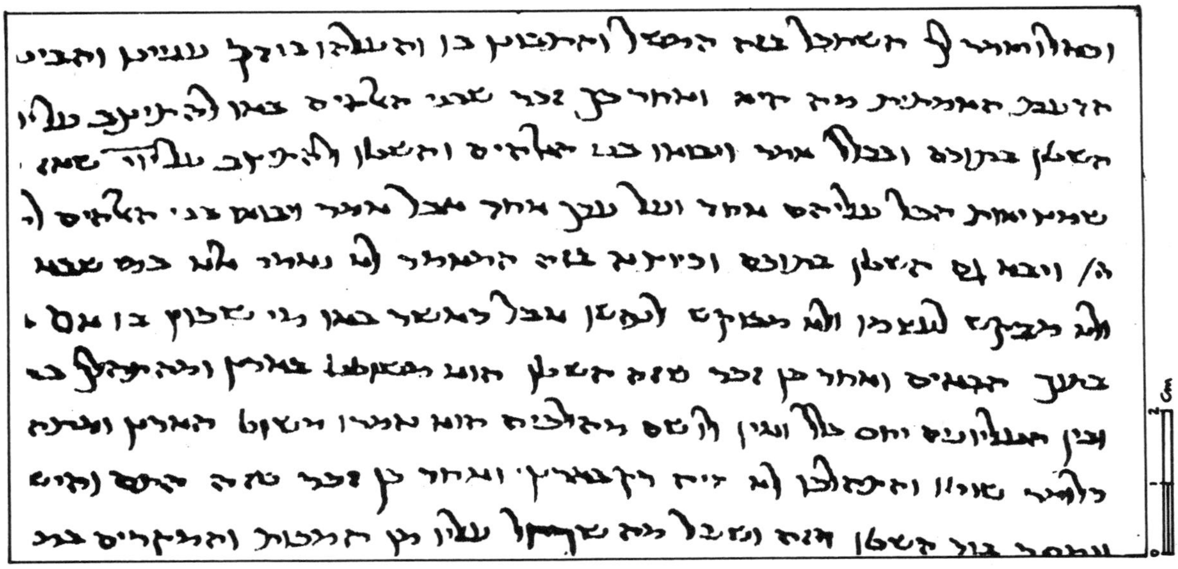

Fig. 120. A semi-cursive script of Byzantine style in a manuscript from Salonica (1329; Leipzig, Karl-Marx-Universitätsbibliothek B.H.13)

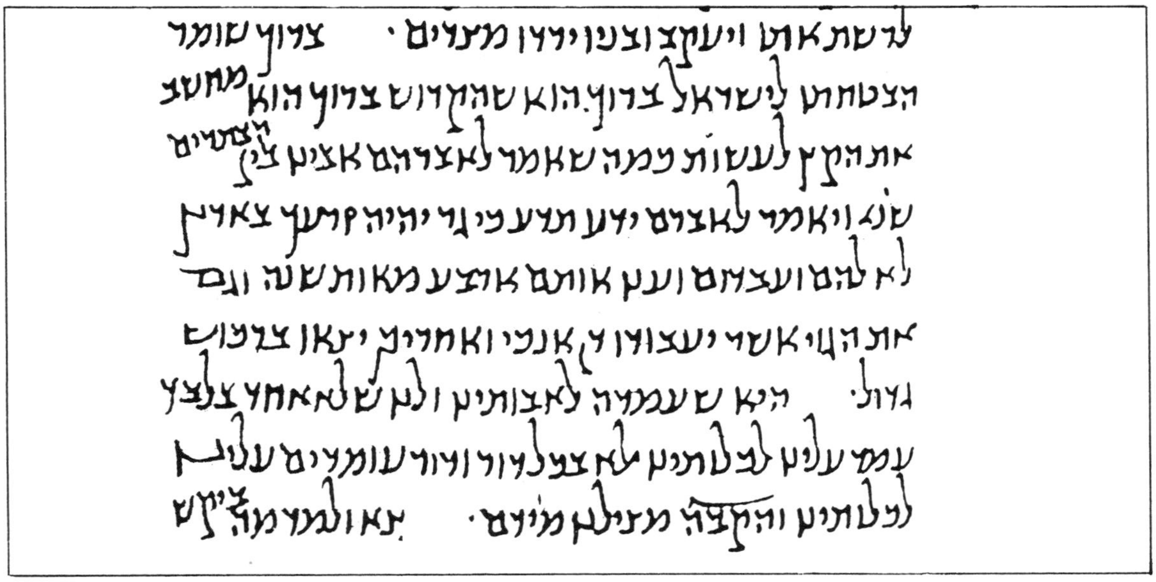

Fig. 121. A semi-cursive 'Eastern' script in a Passover Haggadah dating from 1203 (Oxford, Bodleian Library Ms. Poc. 262)

CHAPTER THREE: PRINTED HEBREW SCRIPT

A. THE BEGINNINGS

The imprinting of isolated letters or words on clay or other soft materials was an ancient practice. The letters were engraved in stone or some other hard material in a reverse position and order, so that the impression would come out in the right direction. In Mesopotamia many cylinder-seals were found carrying script and pictures as well. The Chinese were perhaps the first to print from woodblocks. The earliest known printed paper scroll from China dates from 868. In the 11th century, movable clay types were produced in China. Printing of cards and pictures of saints from woodblocks started in Europe in 1370. They were sometimes accompanied by inscriptions. In Strassburg in ca. 1440, Johann Gensfleisch, otherwise known as Gutenberg (ca. 1397-1468), who came from Mainz, invented a

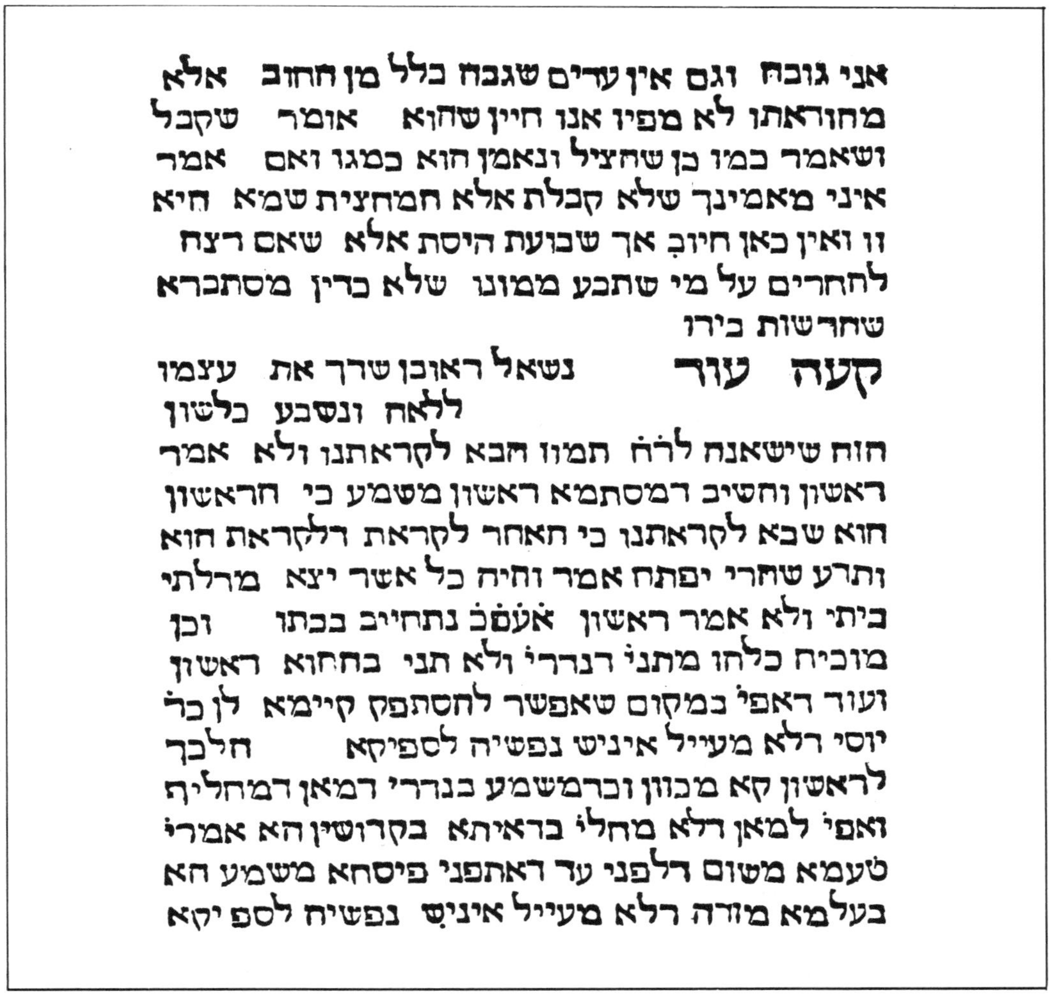

אני גוכח וגם אין עדים שגבה כלל מן החוב אלא
מהוראתו לא מפיו אנו חיין שהוא אומר שקבל
ושאמר כמו כן שהציל ונאמן הוא כמגו ואם אמר
איני מאמינך שלא קבלת אלא המחצית שמא היא
זו ואין כאן חיוב אך שבועת היסת אלא שאם רצה
לחחרים על מי שתבע ממונו שלא כדין מסתברא
שחדשות בירו
קעה עוד נשאל ראובן שרך את עצמו
ללאה ונשבע כלשון
הזה שישאנה לרח תמוז הבא לקראתנו ולא אמר
ראשון והשיב רמסתמא ראשון משמע כי הראשון
הוא שבא לקראתנו כי תאחר לקראת דלקראת הוא
ותרע שהרי יפתח אמר והיה כל אשר יצא מדלתי
ביתי ולא אמר ראשון אעפ״כ נתחייב בבתו וכן
מוכיח כלהו מתני׳ רנדרי׳ ולא תני בהחוא ראשון
ועוד דאפי׳ במקום שאפשר לחסתפק קיימא לן כר׳
יוסי דלא מעייל איניש נפשיה לספיקא הלכך
לראשון קא מכוון וכדמשמע בנדרי דמאן דמחליף
ואפי׳ למאן דלא מחלי׳ בראיתא בקרושין הא אמרי׳
טעמא משום דלפני עד דאתפני פיסחא משמע הא
בעלמא מודה דלא מעייל איניש נפשיה לספיקא

Fig. 122. Detail of a printed page from *Teshuvot She'eloth le-HaRashba'*, Rome, ca. 1470 press for the printing of movable types. In 1445 he printed alphabetic charts and abridgements from Donatus' Grammar, and in 1455/6 he printed the Bible with movable types in Mainz. The first dated printed book was the Catholicon with a colophon of 1460 declaring that Gutenberg was the inventor of printing. After 1470, printing was already practiced in several cities in Europe. The printers were also the publishers and booksellers. They ordered letter-types from designers and engravers. The first prints resembled manuscripts and the types were designed to resemble the handwritten letter-forms.

The exact date when Hebrew printing began is not known, as many of the early printed books are not dated. The earliest information we have about metallic Hebrew types is from Avignon: in 1444, a goldsmith named Prokopp Waldvogel from Prague taught the Jew Davin (Davinius? David?) de Caderousse the practice of printing Hebrew types. Hebrew printing apparently began in Italy. The first printer of books with Hebrew letters was probably Abraham, son of Solomon Conat of Mantua, who had formerly been a copyist of books. His early books were not dated. He printed books with square letters in the Ashkenazi script-style and semi-cursive letters in the Italian script-style. There are scholars who argue that the first printed Hebrew books were not those produced by Conat but books printed in Rome with square Ashkenazi letters (fig. 122), but there is no decisive evidence of that. At any rate, Hebrew printing began about 1470. The first dated Hebrew printed book was Rashi's commentary to the Pentateuch printed in Reggio di Calabria in 1475 by Abraham son of Garton (fig. 123).

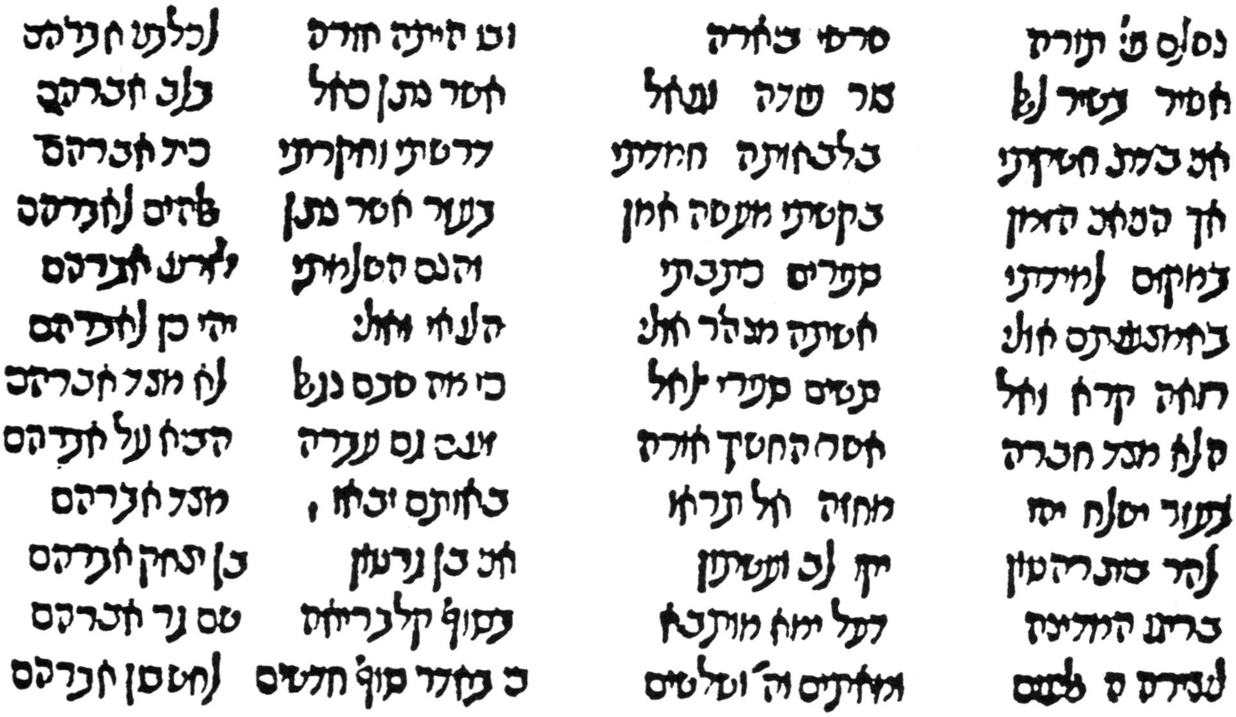

Fig. 123. The colophon in the first dated printed Hebrew book, Rashi's commentary on the Bible, printed in a semi-cursive 'Sephardi' typeface, at the press of Abraham son of Garton son of Isaac, Reggio di Calabria, 1475

In the seventies of the 15th century, Italy became the main centre of book printing. At that period, a group of Jewish printers also began their activity there. The types were first designed on the basis of Ashkenazi letter-signs, and later the Sephardi script-style prevailed but was influenced by the Ashkenazi forms (fig. 124). This is reflected mainly in the 'thickening' of the horizontal strokes, which was later to become a prominent feature of Ashkenazi Hebrew types, and has remained so until today. In the early stages of Hebrew printing, various types were designed on the basis of different script-styles used in manuscripts.

As mentioned above, Rashi's commentary on the Pentateuch was printed with types imitating the semi-cursive Sephardi letter-signs. In Spain and Portugal print also imitated manuscripts in Sephardi square and semi-cursive scripts. In 1492, the expulsion of the Jews from Spain stopped the activity of Hebrew printers there. In Italy, which was the main centre of incunabula, types were cast on the basis of square and semi-cursive Sephardi script-styles.

An early Hebrew text with vowelization signs is Rabbi David Kimhi's commentary to the book of Psalms printed in Bologna in 1477. In that same year, a commentary on Job by Rabbi Levi ben Gershom and Jacob ben Asher's *Tur Yoreh Deʿah* were printed in Ferrara in the press of Abraham ben Hayyim. From 1487 onwards, the first page was decorated, and it eventually became the title page. In the first 27 years of printing, Hebrew books were printed in 12 printing houses in various cities of Italy. The most famous printers of Hebrew books at that time were Abraham Conat (mentioned above), Meshullam Cusi, Joseph Gunzenhauser and his son ʿAzriel, and the Ashkenazi printers Yehoshuʿa, Solomon and Gershom in Soncino near Milan. The Soncino family printed the first complete Bible in 1488. In 1491 the most beautiful edition of the printed Bible came out in Naples, with vowelization and accentuation marks. Gershom Soncino continued to print Hebrew books after 1500 (from 1503 onwards; from 1498 to 1503 no Hebrew book was published, probably because of the difficult times).

Books printed before 1500 are called incunabula. Out of 50,000 incunabula, about 175 in Hebrew characters have survived. In the 15th century, 22 centres of Hebrew printing were active – twelve in Italy, nine in Spain and one in Constantinople. The following is a list of towns and cities in which Hebrew books were printed before 1500: Rome (about 1470), Reggio di Calabria (1475), Piove di Sacco (1475), Mantua (1476), Guadalajara (1476), Bologna (1482), Ferrara (1477), Soncino (1483), Hijar (1485), Casalmaggiore (1486), Naples (1487), Faro (1487), Samora (1487), Lisbon (1489), Brescia (1491), and Barco (1496). Hebrew incunabula are located in various places throughout the world, 65 of them in the National Library in Jerusalem and about the same number in the Hebrew Union College in Cincinnati in the United States. The largest number (about 150) are in the Jewish Theological Seminary in New York.

יהודה בן

תימא אומ׳ הוי עז כנמר

וקל כנשר ורץ כצבי וגבור

כארי לעשות רצון אביך

שבשמים

Fig. 124. A 15th century typeface based on Ashkenazi letter-forms in Italy: *Ṭur ʾOraḥ Ḥayyim*, press of Abraham Conat, Mantua 1476; *ʾArbaʿah Ṭurim*, Piove di Sacco 1475

לא טוב היות האדם

לבדו אעשה לו עזר

כנגדו

אילו נתן לנו את השבת ולא קרבנו לפני הר סיני דיינו
אילו קרבנו לפני הר סיני ולא נתן לנו את התורה דיינו
אילו נתן לנו את התורה ולא הכניסנו לארץ ישראל דיינו
אילו הכניסנו לארץ ישראל ולא בנה לנו את בית המקדש דיינו
אילו בנה לנו את בית המקדש ולא בנה לנו את בית הבחירה דיינו
על אחת כמה וכמה טובה כפולה ומכופלת למקום עלינו

הוציאנו ממצרים עשה בהם שפטים עשה דין באלהיהם הרג את בכוריהם נתן לנו את ממונם קרע לנו את הים העבירנו בתוכו בחרבה שקע צרינו בתוכו ספק צרכנו במדבר ארבעים שנה האכילנו את המן נתן לנו את השבת קרבנו לפני הר סיני נתן לנו את התורה הכניסנו לארץ ישראל בנה לנו את בית המקדש בנה לנו את בית הבחירה לכפרה על כל עונותינו: רבן גמליאל היה אומר כל שלא אמר שלשה דברים אילו בפסח לא יצא ידי חובתו פסח מצה ומרורים · פסח שהיו אבותינו אוכלין בזמן שבית המקדש קיים על שום מה · על שום שפסח המקום על בתי אבותינו במצרים שנאמר ואמרתם זבח פסח הוא לי״י אשר פסח על בתי בני ישראל במצרים בנגפו את מצרים ואת בתינו הציל ויקד העם וישתחוו

ואוחז מצה בידו ואומר

זו שאנו אוכלין על שום מה על שום שלא הספיק בצקן של אבותינו להחמיץ עד שנגלה עליהם מלך מלכי המלכים הקב״ה וגאלם שנאמר ויאפו את הבצק אשר הוציאו ממצרים עוגות מצות כי לא חמץ כי גורשו ממצרים ולא יכלו להתמהמה וגם צדה לא עשו להם··

ואוחז מרור בידו ואומר

מרור זה שאנו אוכלין על שום מה על שום שמררו המצריים את חיי אבותינו במצרים שנאמר וימררו את חייהם בעבודה קשה בחומר ובלבנים ובכל עבודה בשדה את כל עבודתם אשר עבדו בהם בפרך·· בכל דור ודור חייב אדם לראות את עצמו כאילו הוא יצא ממצרים שלא את אבותינו בלבד גאל הקב״ה

Fig. 125. A page from the Soncino Haggadah printed in 1486

Fig. 126. A 15th century typeface based on Sephardi letter-forms with an Ashkenazi influence, in the book *Måshal Ha-Kadmoni*, printed at the Gershom Soncino press, Brescia, ca. 1491

שפטים

ושטרים תתן לך
בכל שעריך אשר
יהוה אלהיך נתן לך לשבטיך ושפטו
את העם משפט צדק: לא תטה משפט
לא תכיר פנים ולא תקח שחד כי
השחד יעור עיני חכמים ויסלף דברי

Fig. 127. Detail of a printed page from Deuteronomy, Naples 1492

B. THE SIXTEENTH CENTURY

The 16th century was the golden age of Hebrew printing. The earliest Hebrew book in the 16th century was a prayerbook printed in 1503 by Gershom Soncino in Fano, Italy. In 1527 Gershom went with his son to Salonica and Constantinople. After Gershom's death, his son Eliʿezer continued printing books until 1547. Eliʿezer's son, Gershom, went to Egypt where he printed two books in 1557. Through the influence of the Soncino press, types in the Sephardi script-style were prevalent in Italy (fig. 125). In northern Italy, the printers imitated the Ashkenazi Gothic script-style (fig. 128). The Venetian printer Daniel Bomberg, a Christian who was to become the most important publisher of Hebrew books, and Aldus Manutius, gradually took the place of the Soncino printers. Daniel Bomberg came to Venice in about 1513 and founded a press there. The first Hebrew book he printed in Venice in 1517 on the basis of manuscripts was the Pentateuch with the five scrolls and Haftarot. In 1524/5 Bomberg printed a second edition of *Miqraʾot Gedolot* edited by Yaʿakov ben Ḥayyim, which became the authorised text of the Bible until the end of the 19th century. The quality and the number of Bomberg's productions excelled those of Soncino. Bomberg was the first person to print the entire Babylonian and Jerusalem Talmuds. The layout was already fixed at the Soncino press and became the standard form of the Talmud until today (fig. 129). Bomberg's press existed until 1549. He printed on paper as well as parchment. Bomberg's types, based on those of Soncino, determined the form of the Hebrew square types for a long time to come. The types designed by Guillaume le Bé of Troix (1525-1598), one of the most famous Hebrew type-cutters (see below), were also based on Bomberg's types. Bomberg's types were also used for Plantin's Bible printed in 1566.

From approximately 1512, Hebrew books were also printed in Prague, among them several books in an elaborated Ashkenazi Gothic style printed at the press of Gershom ben Solomon haKohen. These types were later also used in Germany and Poland. In 1530, the brothers Shmuʾel, Asher and Eliyakim Helitz founded a Hebrew press in Cracow, using types which they apparently got from Prague. From 1530 onwards, Ḥayyim Shaḥor printed Hebrew books in Ilsa, Augsburg (1533), Ichenhausen (1544/5) and Heddernheim (1546). In 1547 he founded a Hebrew press in Lublin. His work there was continued by his son, and his son-in-law Joseph ben Yakar. The Ashkenazi square and semi-cursive script-styles were gradually abandoned in favour of Sephardic styles. Ashkenazi semi-cursive was used mainly for popular books such as *Zʾenna u'Rʾenna*, as a result of which it was called *ZUR* letters.

In the 16th century Hebrew books were printed in various cities in Italy, such as Bologna, Verona, Treine, Mantua, Sabbioneta, Padua, Ferrara, Cremona, Rome and Riva di Trento. Until 1542, when the Inquisition was founded in Rome, the Jewish printers enjoyed considerable liberty. Among the Jews who emigrated to Italy from Spain and Portugal, and among the Marranos who came to Italy from Germany, were several skilled printers.

Lo soprascritto alphabetto e hebraico formato & li hebrei di
ce che la sua ragione, e che la lettera o, esser uno quadrato de
penna & la lettera mezza o, esser mezzo quadrato adon
que la longhezza & la larghezza uol esser longhe larghe
tanti quadrati di penna come tu uedi.

Fig. 128. The letters of the alphabet in Ashkenazi script of the Gothic style in the 1530 edition of Giovanantonio Tagliente's *Lo presente libro Insegna* first printed in 1524, perhaps in Venice (*Three Classics of Italian Calligraphy*, New York 1953)

In 1545/6 Guillaume le Bé designed his first Hebrew typeface for the Venetian printer Maria Antonio Giustiniani, calling it 'Texte du Talmuth' (fig. 132). Le Bé cut a large number of Hebrew types, in various square and cursive styles, first in Venice and later in Paris, where he designed Hebrew letters in the 'Venetian Style'. His types were most beautiful and were used mainly for books printed for Christians, while some of them were not used for printing at all. Guillaume le Bé was one of the most skilled type-cutters of Hebrew letters. Some 'specimens' of his designs have survived. He also collected types cut by others. In the Bibliothèque Nationale in Paris, there are two albums with 'specimens' from his

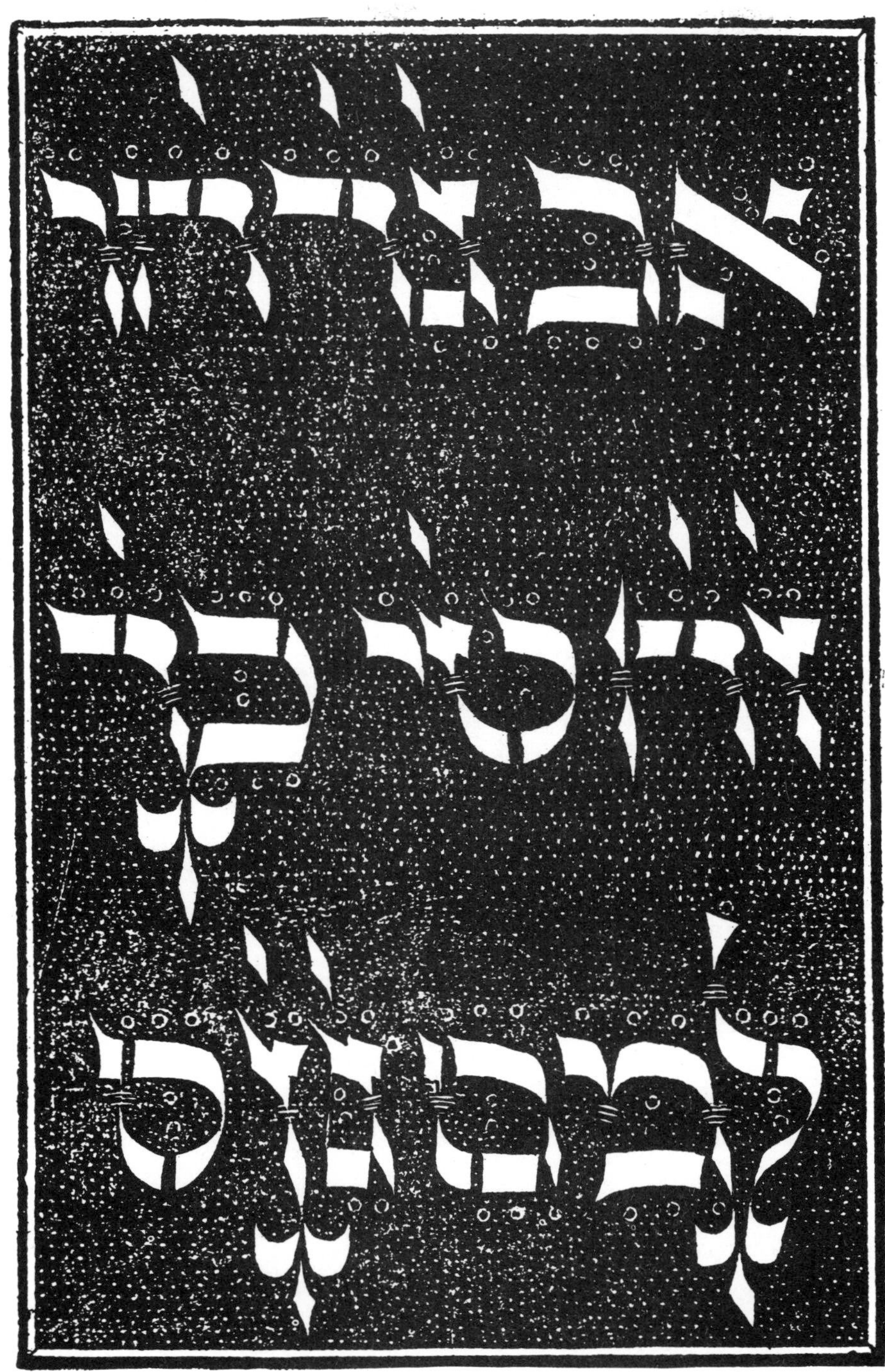

collection. Some are his own creations, and others are by Jean Arnoul, and there are types from Bomberg's and Giustiniani's publishing houses and from the printers in Constantinople. The second album includes 19 different typefaces he designed in Venice and Paris, among them 'Rashi' letters and square letters with vowelization marks. His typefaces vary in size and width. In the margins, he wrote notes concerning his designs. In 1573 he prepared enlarged models of his types to be cut in wood, and he commented that these were designed according to the Jewish and Hebrew tradition in Venice. Following a quarrel between two Christian printers who published Maimonides' *Mishneh Torah* in 1550, an edict was issued in

Fig. 129. A page from the Bombergian Talmud

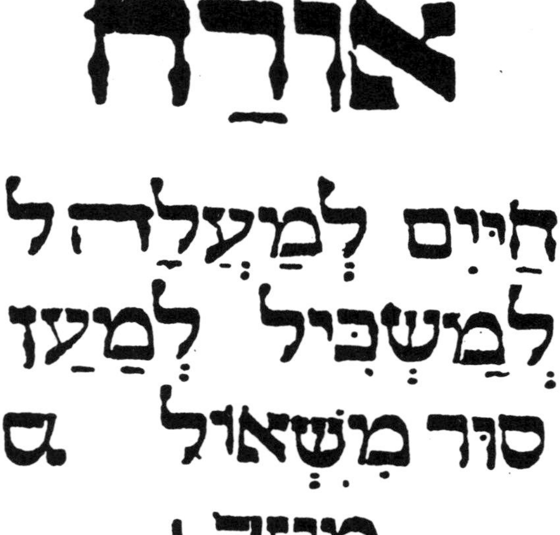

Fig. 130. A detail of a text printed in 'Prague' letters representing an elaborated Ashkenazi script of Gothic style (the Cracow press, 1534-6)

פודה · צדיק · קדוש · רחום

שדי · תקיף ·

אלמעכטיגר גוט בויא דיין טעמפל שירי אלזו שיר אין אונזרן טג
טאגן שירי יא שירי · בארמהערציגר גוט גרעבטר גוט
דעמטיגר גוט דובער גוט ווירדגר גוט
זעבפטר גוט חענטר גוט טרויסטר גוט
יודן גוט ברפטיגר גוט לעבדיגר גוט
מעכטיגר גוט באמהפטיגר גוט עביגר גוט
פארכטצומר גוט צארטר גוט קויגליבר גוט
דייבר גוט שטרקר גוט דובישט גוט
אוב נימנט מער אוב בויא דיין טעמפל שירי אלזו שיר אין אונזרן
טאגן שירי יא שירי ·

אני גרשם כהן · לא שבח נותן · ובתשואות חן חן · אשר דר לו ניר רה ·
נעימה אח נאה · בבתים ארבעה · מלאכתו נודעה · עשויה כשו רה ·
וזה לכבוד יוצרי · אשר היה עזרי · בהחילי ובגמרי · מלאכתי בשר רה ·
והם האגדות · הלא עם כל אורות · יקרות והמודות · סליקו בהד רה ·

בהדרת סליקו · והמלאכה נגמרת · נחקקה פה בקק פראג קהלה
המפוארת · בעט ברזל ועופרת בתכלית היופי מהודרת · גם בפירוש
נעים נסתרת · בסדור רב מסודרת · בציור נאה מצוירת · נערים
משנתם מעוררת · ואף לזקנים מישרת · לחוות לשונם בעט סופר
ממהרת · כי ביורש אנוש מבוארת · וירץ בה הקורא העומד לשרת ·
לשפוך שיח את פני אשר לו האמונה והאדרת · ותהי השלמות הם
המלאכה בפרשה אשר אום נאוה ושחרחורת · ארבע גאולות נתבשרת
והוצאתי וגאלתי ולקחתי והבאתי אתכם אל הארץ · ביום א כו
לחדש טבת שנת עזרי מעם יי עושה שמים וארץ · ובאשר קים
הבטחתו בגאולות שלשה · ככה ברביעית מעשירו ימהר יחישה ·
לפדות עמו ישרא מכובד גלותם ושאונם · וימחול עונם פשעם
וזדונם · ויעביר דמעה מעל כל פנים ינחמם וישמחם מיגונם · כה
מתחנן המחקק גרשם בן שלמה הכהן · בשתוף אחיו גרונם כץ
בני ר שלמה הכהן זל

אמן ואמן סלה

אדוננו מלכנו נחמנו · ו תביאנו ארצנו מ קדשנו נהלנו · ש יחתינו ל עתיד הראש

Fig. 131. A page of the Prague Haggadah printed 1526 at the press of Gershom haKohen and his brother, with Hebrew letters of Ashkenazi style

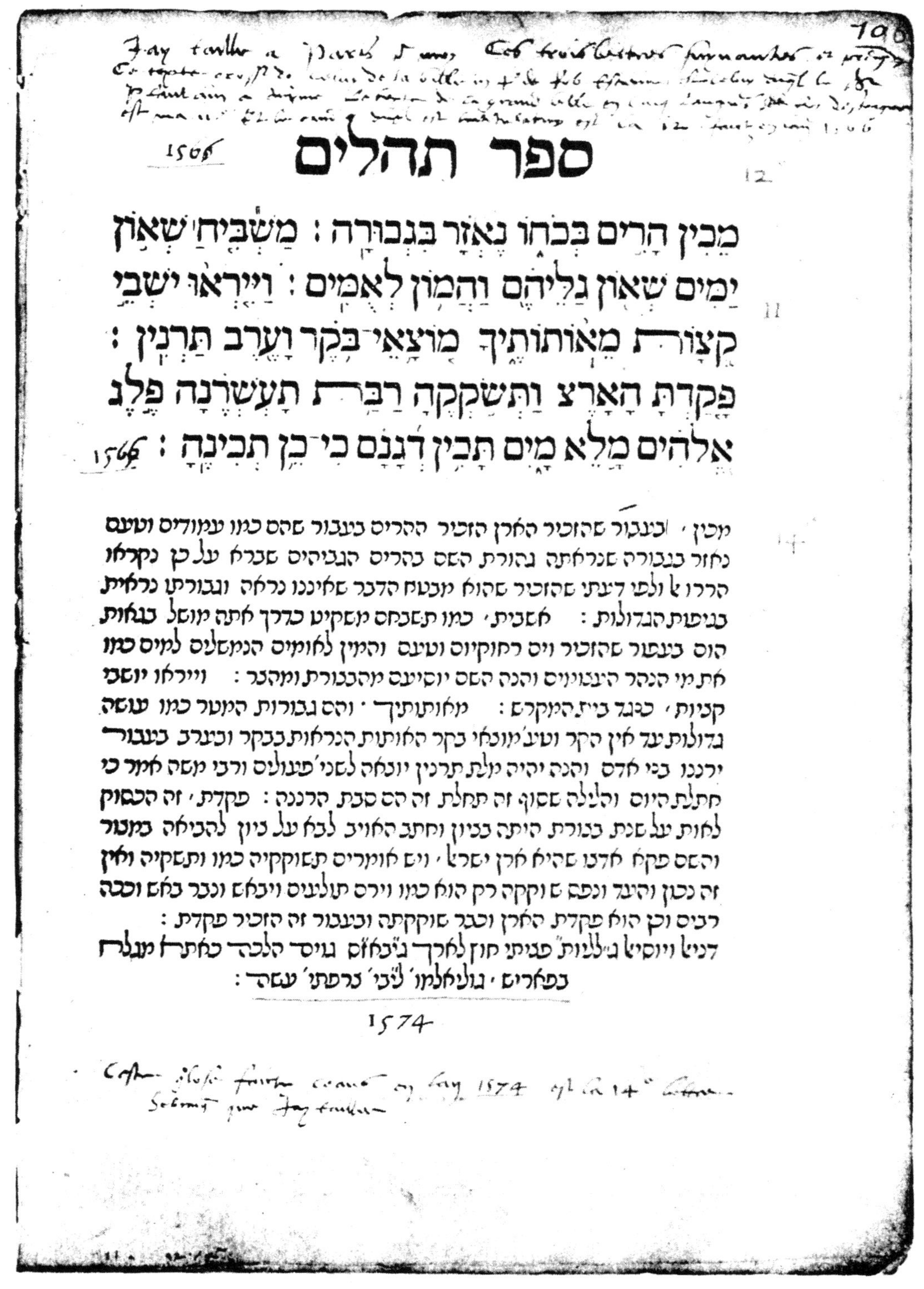

ספר תהלים

מכין הרים בכחו נאזר בגבורה : משביח שאון
ימים שאון גליהם והמון לאמים : וייראו ישבי
קצות מאותותיך מוצאי בקר וערב תרנין :
פקדת הארץ ותשקקה רבת תעשרנה פלג
אלהים מלא מים תכין דגנם כי כן תכינה :

מכין · בעבור שהזכיר הארץ הזכיר ההרים בעבור שהם כמו עמודים וטעם
נאזר בגבורה שנראתה גבורת השם בהרים הגבוהים שברא על כן נקראו
הררי אל ולפי דעתי שהזכיר שהוא מבטח הדבר שאיננו נראה וגבורתו נראית
בגיסות הגדולות : משביח · כמו תשבחם משקיט כדרך אתה מושל בגאות
הים בעבור שהזכיר ויש רחוקים וטעם והמון לאומים הנמשלים למים כמו
את מי הנהר העצומים והנה השם יושיעם מהגבורות ומהכר : ויראו יושבי
קצות · כנגד בית המקדש : מאותותיך · והם גבורות המטר כמו עושה
גדולות עד אין חקר וטע' מוצאי בקר האותות הנראות בבקר ובערב בעבור
ירננו בני אדם והנה יהיה מלת תרנין יוצאה לשני פעולים ורבי משה אמר כי
תחלת היום והלילה שסוף זה תחלת זה הם סבת הרננה : פקדת · זה הפסוק
לאות על שנת בצורת היתה בציון וחשב האויב לבא על ציון להביאה במטר
והשם פקד ארצו שהיא ארץ ישראל · ויש אומרים תשוקקיה כמו ותשקיה ואין
זה נכון והעד ונפש שוקקה רק הוא כמו וירם תולעים ויבאש ונכר באש ורבה
רבים וכן הוא פקדת הארץ ובכר שוקקתה ובעבור זה הזכיר פקדת :
דניאל וויסיאל ב׳ללנות״ פניתי חוץ לארץ ג״בלאזס גויסד הלכה כאתרא מגלח
בפאריס · גולאלמו׳ לבי׳ גרפתי׳ עשה :

Fig. 132. A printed page with Le Bé's 'Texte di Talmuth' letters cut in 1566

1553/4 ordering the burning of the Talmud and prohibiting Hebrew printing in Venice. That prohibition lasted for about 9 years. About the same time, Paul IV (1555-1559) published an Index of books to be censored, thus limiting the activity of Hebrew printers. The Jews set up a body, supported by rabbis, to protect the books from censorship. The harsh actions and edicts caused the decline of the Hebrew-printing centres in Venice and Prague. Other cities took their place, particularly Antwerp. Large printing centres also arose in the 16th century in France and Switzerland. It was the age of humanism and of erudite printers. In France, Italy, Germany and Switzerland, Hebrew printing remained in the hands of Christian humanists.

In 1555 Plantin founded his printing press in Antwerp, which at that time was a major port in western Europe, and in the second half of the 16th century took the place of Venice as the main European trading centre. Although the humanistic spirit did not prevail in Antwerp, Plantin succeeded in creating a kind of humanistic court. He became the leading printer in Antwerp and managed to continue his activities in spite of political and religious struggles. Plantin acquired typefaces from the most important type-cutters at that time. He had 21 kinds of Hebrew letters including those of Guillaume le Bé, as well as vowelization and accentuation marks. Most of the typefaces were of the Italian square letter type, earlier designed for the Soncino press and later improved for Daniel

Fig. 133. Guillaume le Bé's 'Very bold Hebrew' typeface, cut in 1559 on the basis of the Sephardi 'rounded' style

Bomberg's press in Venice. These typefaces were based on the Sephardi letters but showed the influence of the thick horizontal strokes of the Ashkenazi letters (fig. 133). In 1564-1567 Plantin printed three editions of the Hebrew Bible. Some of the books were sent to the book fair in Frankfurt and others exported to Morocco. These editions were for Jews. Plantin printed other editions of the Bible for Christians. In 1571, Philip II appointed Plantin chief printer of the Netherlands. In 1568-1573 Plantin undertook the printing of the Polyglot Bible, which was the largest printing enterprise of the 16th century and was known as the 'Biblia Réal' (Royal Bible). Plantin also printed books in the sphere of linguistics, mainly dictionaries. Among these books were *Leshon Limmudim* by Isaac Levite (a Hebrew grammar in Latin) printed in Hebrew types designed by Guillaume le Bé, and *Otsar Leshon haKodesh* by Sanctus Paninnus, the rubrics of which were set with le Bé's *Paragnon* typeface.

Plantin's press was the largest in Europe until the industrial revolution in the late 18th century. It was called 'the Golden Compasses'. The press moved to the building which now houses the Plantin Moretus Museum. During the war of the Netherlands against Spain, Plantin founded a press in Leyden, Holland. When he returned to Antwerp in 1585, his press passed into the hands of his son-in-law, Johannes Mortentorf (Jan Moretus). Moretus' descendants continued to run it until 1876.

In approximately 34 years Plantin printed about 2,400 publications. In Leyden, his son-in-law, Franciscus Raphelengius, inherited his press. He was a teacher of Oriental languages at the University of Leyden and an expert in Hebrew, printing the first books in Hebrew and Arabic to be published in Holland.

In 1577 a Hebrew press was founded in Safed by the printers Abraham and ʾEliʿezer, who came to Palestine via Lublin and Constantinople. They printed six books in Safed. In 1593-1598, Dona Reina, daughter of Hanna Grazia Mendes, printed Hebrew books in Constantinople. About 4,000 Hebrew books were printed altogether in the 16th century.

לא ימוש ספר התורה הזה מפיך והגית בו

יומם ולילה למען תשמר

לעשות ככל הכתוב בו כי אז תצליח

את דרכך ואז תשכיל:

כל ארחות יי'
חסד ואמת

חמשה חומשי תורה

נדפס עם רב העיון על ידי כריסט̈ופורו
פלנ̈טין במצות הסר בומב̈ירגי
יכ̈ו בשנת שכ̈ו לפ̈ק פה
העיר המהוללה

אנוירשה

Fig. 134. The title page of the Pentateuch printed 1566 by Plantin in Antwerp

C. FROM THE SEVENTEENTH TO THE END OF THE NINETEENTH CENTURY

In the 17th and 18th centuries the art of printing developed and spread. The types cut in Holland in the 17th century and especially those of Christofel van Dyke were partly influenced by the form of le Bé's faces. Christofel van Dyke worked in the sixteen-sixties for the press of Joseph Atiash, and cut types based on le Bé's patterns, while being influenced by the Latin typefaces of his time. At that time, Amsterdam became a prominent Jewish printing centre. The first Hebrew book was printed there in 1627 at Daniel de Ponaska's press. That same year, Menashe ben Yisrael founded a press at his home in Amsterdam. His typefaces, known by the name of 'Amsterdam letters' (fig. 135), spread from Holland to Germany and Eastern Europe.

In the 17th century the first Yiddish newspaper appeared, with the name *Currantin*. One of the earliest Hebrew newspapers, named *Qohelet Mussar*, appeared in Berlin in 1750. In 1783 the Hebrew periodical named *HaMe'assef* was founded in Königsberg. In the 17th and 18th centuries several editions of the Hebrew Bible were printed. The Connecticut edition (Oxford 1776-1780) was based on 600 manuscripts and on earlier editions.

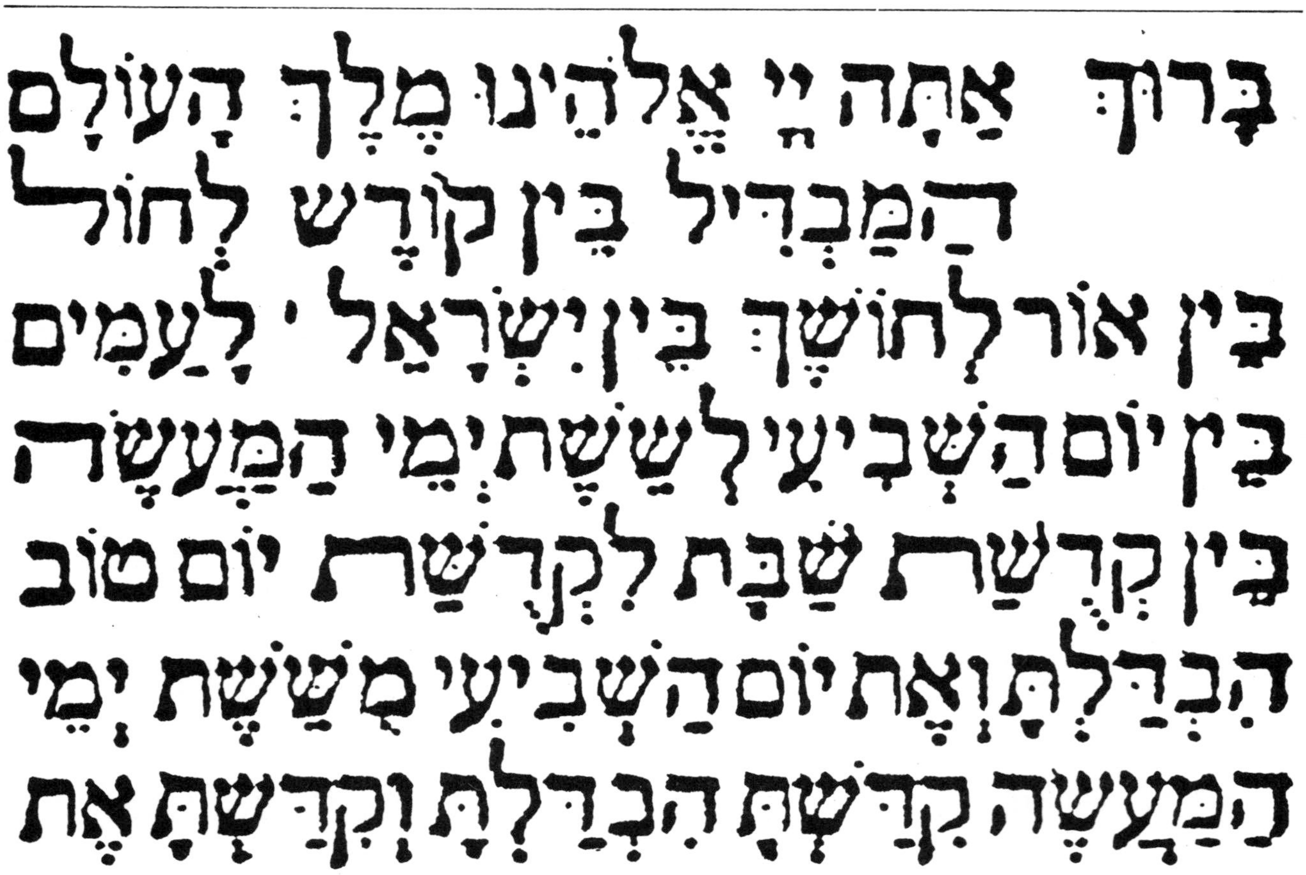

בָּרוּךְ אַתָּה יְיָ אֱלֹהֵינוּ מֶלֶךְ הָעוֹלָם
הַמַּבְדִּיל בֵּין קוֹדֶשׁ לְחוֹל
בֵּין אוֹר לְחוֹשֶׁךְ בֵּין יִשְׂרָאֵל לָעַמִּים
בֵּין יוֹם הַשְּׁבִיעִי לְשֵׁשֶׁת יְמֵי הַמַּעֲשֶׂה
בֵּין קְדֻשַּׁת שַׁבָּת לִקְדֻשַּׁת יוֹם טוֹב
הִבְדַּלְתָּ וְאֶת יוֹם הַשְּׁבִיעִי מִשֵּׁשֶׁת יְמֵי
הַמַּעֲשֶׂה קִדַּשְׁתָּ הִבְדַּלְתָּ וְקִדַּשְׁתָּ אֶת

Fig. 135. A text in 'Amsterdam' letters designed by Christofel van Dyke

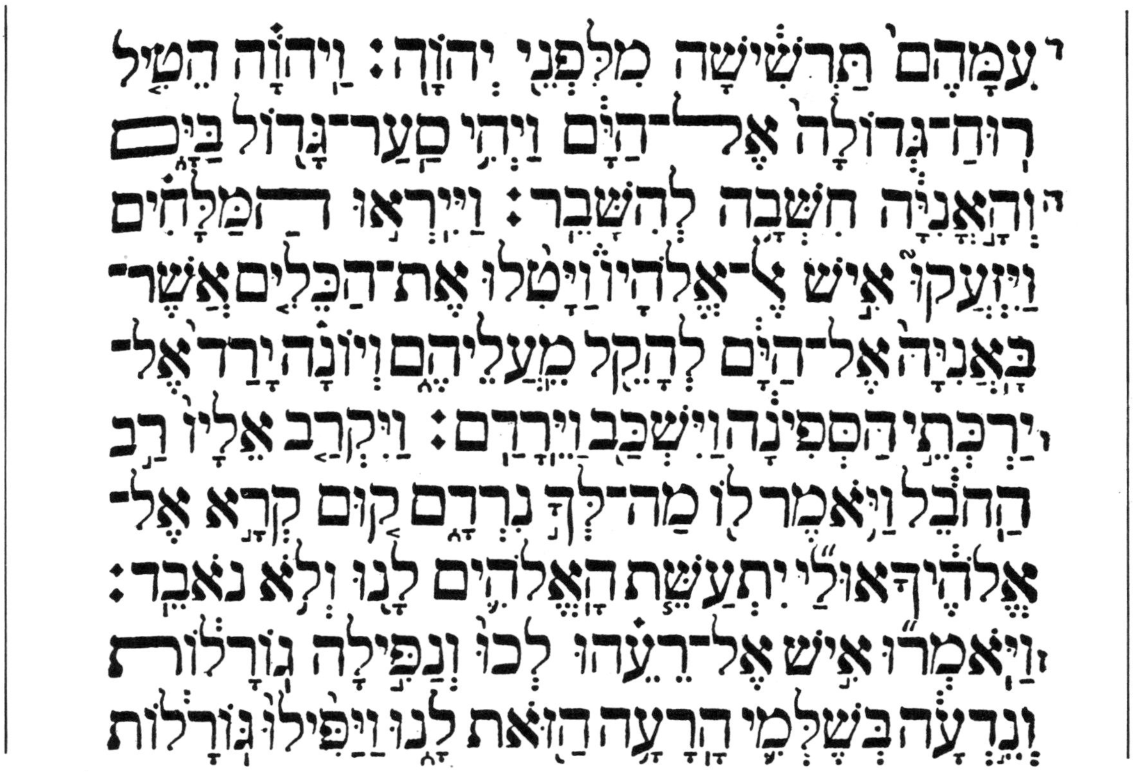

יֹ עִמָּהֶם֙ תַּרְשִׁ֔ישָׁה מִלִּפְנֵ֖י יְהֹוָֽה׃ וַֽיהֹוָ֗ה הֵטִ֤יל
רֽוּחַ־גְּדוֹלָה֙ אֶל־הַיָּ֔ם וַיְהִ֥י סַֽעַר־גָּד֖וֹל בַּיָּ֑ם
יְוָֽהָֽאֳנִיָּ֔ה חִשְּׁבָ֖ה לְהִשָּׁבֵֽר׃ וַיִּֽירְא֣וּ הַמַּלָּחִ֗ים
וַיִּזְעֲקוּ֮ אִ֣ישׁ אֶל־אֱלֹהָיו֒ וַיָּטִ֨לוּ אֶת־הַכֵּלִ֜ים אֲשֶׁ֣ר
בָּֽאֳנִיָּה֙ אֶל־הַיָּ֔ם לְהָקֵ֖ל מֵֽעֲלֵיהֶ֑ם וְיוֹנָ֗ה יָרַד֙ אֶל־
יְרַכְּתֵ֣י הַסְּפִינָ֔ה וַיִּשְׁכַּ֖ב וַיֵּֽרָדַֽם׃ וַיִּקְרַ֤ב אֵלָיו֙ רַ֣ב
הַֽחֹבֵ֔ל וַיֹּ֥אמֶר ל֖וֹ מַה־לְּךָ֣ נִרְדָּ֑ם ק֚וּם קְרָ֣א אֶל־
אֱלֹהֶ֔יךָ אוּלַ֞י יִתְעַשֵּׁ֧ת הָאֱלֹהִ֛ים לָ֖נוּ וְלֹ֥א נֹאבֵֽד׃
יְוַיֹּאמְר֞וּ אִ֣ישׁ אֶל־רֵעֵ֗הוּ לְכוּ֙ וְנַפִּ֣ילָה גֽוֹרָל֔וֹת
וְנֵ֣דְעָ֔ה בְּשֶׁלְּמִ֛י הָרָעָ֥ה הַזֹּ֖את לָ֑נוּ וַיַּפִּ֙ילוּ֙ גּֽוֹרָל֔וֹת

Fig. 136. Roedelheim typeface in a printed *Mahzor*, Heidenheim press, Roedelheim 1832

In the years 1732-1744, Raphael Hayyim's edition of the Bible was printed in Mantua on the basis of the critical Masoretic commentary *Minhat Shai* written by Solomon Yedidiyah of Norzi and completed in 1626. That edition, in turn, was the basis of the Heidenheim Torah (published in Roedelheim in 1918), which was considered the most accurate version of the Bible.

In the 18th century, most Hebrew printing took place in Eastern Europe. There were no major changes in the form of the typefaces. Experiments were made to improve the forms of the Hebrew typefaces on the basis of Giambattista Bodoni's typefaces, but they exaggerated the differences between the thick horizontal strokes and the thin vertical strokes of the letters. By the end of the 18th century about 16,250 Hebrew books had been printed altogether. In the late 18th century, following the rise of the Hassidic movement, independent Hassidic printing houses were established, the largest of which was that of Rabbi Pinhas of Slavutta, founded in 1792, which printed the first Hassidic Talmud in 1813. In the 19th century, there was little activity in the creation of new Hebrew typefaces. In the first half of the 19th century, Lithuania became the centre of Hebrew printing and the largest Jewish printing-house, called 'The Widow and Brothers Raam', was in Vilna. When Warsaw became the largest Jewish centre in Poland in the second half of the 19th century, many Jewish printing-houses were opened there. It became the main centre of Jewish printing after World War I and remained so until the beginning of World War II.

D. FROM THE END OF THE NINETEENTH CENTURY UNTIL TODAY

At the end of the 19th century, typographers and graphic-artists influenced by the revival of the Hebrew language and inspired by modern art, conceived the ambition of designing a modern Hebrew typeface. In the early 20th century several new Hebrew typefaces were created, based on Ashkenazi or Sephardi letter-forms appearing in manuscripts. The Drugulin press in Leipzig used the Drugulin Hebrew typeface, which was based on a square Ashkenazi face created in the 19th century under the influence of ancient Latin manuscripts. Frank and Rühl, in turn, created a new typeface which was named after them. Their design was influenced by the Art Nouveau prevailing in Europe at that time. They restored the balance between the horizontal and vertical strokes of the letters. They paid much attention to legibility and to the clear and balanced design of the letters, without neglecting the traditional forms. In a book published in Germany by Rafael Frank (R. Frank, *Über hebräische Typen und Schriftarten*, Berlin 1926) he writes (in German), "I tried to base my alphabet on the *ductus* of the early prints, particularly the Venetian ones, and I interfered only for pedagogic reasons, to differentiate between letter-signs similar in form. When asked by Christian or rabbinic scholars about a certain deviation ... I was able, as a qualified scribe, to justify my lines and convince the learned masters. Although I say that Frank-Rühl is a salutary reform, I do not overlook the fact that I have not still achieved my aim of inserting vowelization marks into the lines. The instructions for this are already to be found in classical literature, the letters *ʾhwy* serving as vowels. It could also have been possible, as in Ethiopic, to combine the vowelization mark with the letter sign. In this context I also thought of the diacritical points of Shin and Sin .... The calm and stability of my typeface are also the result of the straight tops of the letters. Each letter was designed as a closed unit, each individual part of which had a similar weight." Frank-Rühl's typeface (fig. 137) is still one of the most popular. The 'Peninim' typeface (fig. 138) designed in recent years was based on it.

עצירתה הפתאומית של המכונה באמצע מהלכה מקורה בליקוי
מיכני או בפעולה בלתי נכונה של הסדר. רובם של המעצורים
המובאים ברשימה זו אינם קורים אצל סדר מנוסה; ידיעתו את
המכונה וכושרו למנוע תקלות עוזרים למכונה לעבוד ללא הפרעה.
יש לשמור על שני כללים כדי למנוע הפרעות ממין זה: (א) הנעה

Fig. 137. Frank-Rühl typeface

אבגדהוזחטיכךלמםנן
סעפףצץקרשת

Fig. 138. 'Peninim' typeface

ספר חדש יצא לאור ונתקבל למכירה
אגרות דוד פרישמן עם תמונתו ועצם
כתב ידו נערכו בצרוף מבוא הקדמות
והערות

ועמד כלם צדיקים

Fig. 139. Bertholdt 'Stam' typeface, designed by Franzisca Baruch

ייחודו של רב סעדיה גאון כפייטן לא הגיע מעולם לתודעתם של חוקרים· הללו
ראו בו בראש וראשונה את בעל 'אמונות ודעות', את הפילוסוף היהודי הראשון
שפתח תקופה חדשה בתולדות המחשבה היהודית ויצר אסכולה פילוסופית
בישראל· עם המשך החקירות וגילויי הגניזה הקהירית נתגבשה ונתבלטה לעינינו
דמות פלאים של אישיות רבת-פנים ורבת-כוחות: נתגלה ה'גאון' במשמעו החדש,
שאינו רק תואר לבעל משרה מסויימת, אלא מציין את הכשרון המעולה, הכולל
והמקיף; הבא לשדד מערכות מתוך תחושה של שליחות עליונה· מלחמתו
ההרפתקנית בגאון הירושלמי (בן מאיר) בשאלת הלוח העברי; מרידתו בראש
הגולה - זה שהעלהו למעלת גאון - על פי צו מצפונו המוסרי; התכתשותו עם
הקראים ושאר כל המינים שבאו לפגוע בכבודה של היהדות, אמונת תורת חז"ל;
תרגום התנ"ך ללשון המדוברת, לערבית, וחיבור ספרים בתורת הלשון העברית
והשירה העברית; חיבור תפילות ופיוטים למאות, ומתן 'סידור' 'מדעי' ראשון
לקהילות ישראל - כל אלה אינם אלא צדדים שונים של דמות אשכולית אחת,
שנטלה על עצמה לנסח מחדש את תורת היהדות, על כלל כל המדעים שבדורו,
ולהיות 'ראש המדברים בכל מקום'·

Fig. 140. 'Schocken' typeface, designed by Franzisca Baruch

Before World War II, Berthold's 'Stam' typeface was created (fig. 139), designed by Franzisca Baruch. Other types, such as those of Markus Böhmer, were also cast on the basis of Ashkenazi letter-forms. During World War II, Franzisca Baruch designed the 'Schocken' typeface (fig. 140) on the basis of Soncino's and Bomberg's faces. After the war new modern typefaces were created such as 'Ḥayyim' (fig. 141) designed by Jan Le Witt, and 'Aharoni' (fig. 142) designed by Tuvia Aharoni. Both typefaces differ from handwritten letters in that their strokes are straight, simple and uniform in thickness, with no additional ornaments. 'Stam' types were cast at the same time, mainly for captions. In the Rockefeller Museum of Antiquities in Jerusalem, letters created by the sculptor Eric Gill were engraved in stone on walls and pillars. He also designed types

ויהי היום, באחד מערבי הקיץ היה
מעשה, ואני טוביה עובר עם סוסי ועגלתי
ביער וחוזר לביתי. ראשי נבט לארץ וב־
לבי חושך ושממון. מחשבות נוגות מבל־
בלות את מוחי - אני מעלה בזכרוני את
ביתי-אוי ואבוי לי! בית זה חושך ואפלה
בו; התינוקות, יחיו ויאריכו ימים, ערומים
ויחפים, כולם מציצים מן החלון ומחכים
עד־בוש לאבא שלהם, לחדל־אישים זה,
אולי ירחם ויביא פת לחם חם או עוגת־
סולת להחיות נפשם היבשה.

Fig. 141. ‘Hayyim’ typeface, designed by Jan Le Witt

for printing (fig. 143) but their use was limited. The 'Bezalel' face (fig. 144), designed by Harry Carter on the basis of Sephardi letters, was also used only for a short period. With the establishment of the State of Israel, graphic artists and typographers created several modern Hebrew typefaces on the basis of the traditional forms. The elegant 'Koren' face (fig. 145), designed by Eliahu Korngold-Koren, is based on Sephardi letter-forms. According to him, the design of the letter-forms was influenced by early Hebrew printing as well as ancient manuscripts; special attention was given to the modern design and legibility of the letters as well as the vowelization and accentuation marks which he designed especially for the Koren Bible. The 'Hadassah' typeface (fig. 146), created by Henri Friedländer, is one of the most popular Hebrew typefaces today. According to him, its design was mainly influenced by Ashkenazi letter-forms in manuscripts from about 1800, as well as semi-cursive 15th century Italian letters. Work on the 'Hadassah' letters continued for about

העקרונות של מס הכנסה באנגליה
נבדלים בהרבה מעקרונות פקודת מס
הכנסה שלנו: לכן לא תהיה תועלת
רבה להשוות את הפקודה עם החוק
האנגלי. הדרך היחידה הנכונה תהיה
לפרש באופן מילולי את הפקודה שלנו.
כשעושים זאת יש להשתמש בעיקרים
מתאימים לפירוש חוקי והם: א) לתת
פירוש בהיר, צודק ומתקבל על ללשון
הסעיפים, בלי נטיה לצד אחד או השני.

Fig. 142. ‘Aharoni’ typeface, designed by Tuvia Aharoni

thirty years until they were finally cast in 1958. The popular 'David' typeface (fig. 147) was created by Isamr David by the initiation of Dr. Moshe Spitzer, a scholar of ancient languages and scripts and a master of book printing and production. Spitzer was also involved with the production of another typeface, called 'Hazvi', which was derived from a basic design by Zvi Hausman (fig. 148). Both typefaces aimed at reviving letter-forms which appear in ancient manuscripts. In these typefaces, the individual letter-signs differ from each other in their basic strokes, have no additional ornaments, and the thickness of their strokes is almost uniform.

באות זו ניתן בידי בעל המקצוע כלי חדש המעשיר את מערכת אותיות הרפוס

This new Hebrew type face is one of the last ripe achievements of the late Eric Gill,

העבריות בתוספת רבת־חן ועזת־אופי. יתרו של הכתב, המפתיע בסגולותיו המיוחדות

the distinguished British sculptor and letter-artist. While living for some time

ובקוי־האופי החדשים שלו, הוא אֶרִיק גיל, הפסל ואמן־האות הבריטי הנודע,

in Jerusalem, Gill was attracted to the problems of Hebrew lettering, and as a result

הוא אשר קנה לו שם בראש מחדשי אותיות הרפוס בדור זה של חידוש ותיקון

of his studies he cut, in 1937, a Hebrew alphabet in stone from which the present

למלאכת הספר בעולם. בשעת שבתו בירושלים נמשך אריק גיל לחקור

fount is derived. He introduced some surprising features into his Hebrew alphabet, by adding

בצורות הכתב העברי ובבעיותיו. פרי מאמציו הניח אחריו אלף־בית עברי

to the letters distinct and unusual serifs, and investing them

חקוק על לוח אבן, והוא ששימש יסוד לגופן חרש זה. צביון אות חקוקה

with an inscriptional character, unprecedented in the history of Hebrew printing.

ששיוה הפסל לאלף־בית שלו, צביון שאין לו תקדים בתולדות הרפוס העברי.

As a type unusual in some of its featdres, GILL HEBREW *will be eminently suitable*

הוא הנותן לאות החדשה יחוד משלה המשנה אותה משאר כל האותיות.

for the setting of a solemn page and for the wide range of high grade display work

מפני שוני זה תצלח אות גיל ביותר לסידור עמוד חגיגי ולכל מטרה אחרת

where a 'different' and refined letter is called for.

שיפה לה כתב מיוחד במינו, עשיר־צורות ומרהיב־עין.

Fig. 143. 'Gill' typeface, designed by the sculptor Eric Gill

רבן גמליאל בנו של רבי יהודה
הנשיא אומר: יפה תלמוד תורה
עם דרך ארץ שיגיעת שניהם
משכחת עון וכל תורה שאין עמה
מלאכה סופה בטלה וגוררת עון:

Fig. 144. 'Bezalel' typeface, designed by Harry Carter

ט וַיֹּאמֶר אֱלֹהִים יִקָּווּ הַמַּיִם מִתַּחַת הַשָּׁמַיִם אֶל־מָקוֹם אֶחָד
י וְתֵרָאֶה הַיַּבָּשָׁה וַיְהִי־כֵן׃ וַיִּקְרָא אֱלֹהִים ׀ לַיַּבָּשָׁה אֶרֶץ וּלְמִקְוֵה
יא הַמַּיִם קָרָא יַמִּים וַיַּרְא אֱלֹהִים כִּי־טוֹב׃ וַיֹּאמֶר אֱלֹהִים תַּדְשֵׁא
הָאָרֶץ דֶּשֶׁא עֵשֶׂב מַזְרִיעַ זֶרַע עֵץ פְּרִי עֹשֶׂה פְּרִי לְמִינוֹ אֲשֶׁר
יב זַרְעוֹ־בוֹ עַל־הָאָרֶץ וַיְהִי־כֵן׃ וַתּוֹצֵא הָאָרֶץ דֶּשֶׁא עֵשֶׂב מַזְרִיעַ
זֶרַע לְמִינֵהוּ וְעֵץ עֹשֶׂה־פְּרִי אֲשֶׁר זַרְעוֹ־בוֹ לְמִינֵהוּ וַיַּרְא אֱלֹהִים
יג כִּי־טוֹב׃ וַיְהִי־עֶרֶב וַיְהִי־בֹקֶר יוֹם שְׁלִישִׁי׃

Fig. 145. 'Koren' typeface, designed by Eliyahu Korngold-Koren

עצירתה הפתאומית של המכונה באמצע מהלכה, מקורה בליקוי
מיכני או בפעולה בלתי נכונה של הסדר. רובם של המעצורים
המובאים ברשימה זו אינם קורים אצל סדר מנוסה; ידיעתו את
המכונה וכושרו למנוע תקלות עוזרים למכונה לעבוד ללא הפ-
רעה. יש לשמור על שני כללים כדי למנוע הפרעות ממין זה:
(א) הנעה סדירה של המכונה היא הטיפול הטוב ביותר. כשמ-
כונה זוכה לטיפול נכון — הרי במידה שגובר השימוש בה עולה

Fig. 146. 'Hadassah' typeface, designed by Henri Friedländer

עצירתה הפתאומית של המכונה באמצע מהלכה, מקורה
בליקוי מיכני או בפעולה בלתי נכונה של הסדר. רובם של
המעצורים המובאים ברשימה זו אינם קורים אצל סדר
מנוסה; ידיעתו את המכונה וכושרו למנוע תקלות עוזרים
למכונה לעבוד ללא הפרעה. יש לשמור על שני כללים כדי
למנוע הפרעות ממין זה: (א) הנעה סדירה של המכונה היא
הטיפול הטוב ביותר: כשמכונה זוכה לטיפול נכון — הרי

Fig. 147. 'David' typeface, designed by Ismar David

אבגדהוזחטיכ
דלמםנןסעפף
צץקרשת

Fig. 148. 'Hazvi' typeface, designed by Zvi Hausman

אבגדהווזחטיךכללםמןנסעףפץצקרשתשש

נרקיס תם

אין הדפוס צריך לסבול
את הגרוע ואף לא את הבינוני,
מאחר ומחיר יציקתן
של אותיות גרועות
זהה למחיר יציקתן של אלו
כלילות השלמות.

פייר סימון פורניה

נרקיס חדש

אלפביתין חדשים אינם יכולים להיות
אלא פיתוחים הגיוניים של
צורות קיימות, כשהם מעוצבים
בהתאמה לטכנולוגיות החדשות
וכביטוי לתקופה בה אנו חיים.

הרמן צאפף

נרקיסים שמן

במאה החמש עשרה
הכל השתנה,
החשיבה האנושית גילתה אמצעי
להנציח את עצמה...
המצאת הדפוס היא המאורע
החשוב ביותר בהיסטוריה.

ויקטור הוגו

נרקיסים

מכל ההמצאות והגילויים
במדע ובאמנות,
הדפוס הנו התוצר היחיד
של הציביליזציה
ההכרחי לקיום חירות האדם.

צ׳ארלס דיקנס

Fig. 149. 'Narkiss' and 'Narkissim' typefaces, designed by Zvi Narkiss

אות עברית זאת,הראשונה שעוצבה
בארבעה משקלות,הותאמה במיוחד.
לשימוש עם סדרת יוניברס הלטינית.
זאת הפעם הראשונה שאות עברית
הותאמה לאותיות הקטנות באלף בית לטיני
כך שיתאימו במיוחד, זו בצד זו, לטקסטים
דו לשוניים ארוכים, בהם השימוש באותיות
הגדולות (caps) בלבד יפגע מאוד בקריאות

Fig. 150. 'Oron' typeface, designed by Asher Oron

בספר זה ניתן לו לקורא להכיר את יצירותיו של פיטן העומד בראש תקופה ומשמש מופת לדורות· הצורה הספרותית והאמנותית שצר ינאי בפיוטיו, היא אם כל הצורות בספרות הפיוט וגולת הכותרת בסוגי הפיוט המורכבים שיש בהם שיטה ותכנית· הקדמון בסוגים אלה היא הקרובה, והראשון במחברי קרובות הידועים לנו בשמם הוא ינאי· כל עצמה של קרובה אינה אלא נוסח של תפלת העמידה, שהיה החזן הנקרא בארמית "קרובא" (האטימולוגיא של המלה שנויה במחלוקת) מנסח לו מדי פעם בפעם לפי המסורת שבידו, בזמן שלא היה עדיין נוסח קבוע ומקובל שאין לשנות ממטבעותיו· בכוח ההרגל ובתוקף המסורת החיה, שלפיה "צריך לחדש בה (בתפלה) דבר בכל יום" (ירו' ברכות ד ה"ד), הוסיפו חזני ארץ ישראל, ראשוני הפיטנים, לחדש דברים בתפלתם אף לאחר שנקבע נוסח של חובה· אלא שמעכשיו לא היה בחידושי הפיטנים משום ניסוח גופה של תפלה, אלא משום הרחבה וקישוט לנוסח קיים· וכך נולד סוג פיוטי, סוג הקרובה, שדרכי התפתחותו אינם נהירים לנו עדיין, אבל צורתו הסופית חתומה בחותמו של ינאי· ובזה חשיבותם היתרה של פיוטי ינאי לחקר צורות הפיוט· עד כאן לא ידענו בעצם צורה מקורית של קרובה מהי· עם גילוים של פיוטי ינאי ניתן לנו פרוטוטיפוס של הקרובה שהונח יסוד לקרובותיהם של פיטני כל הדורות·

Fig. 151. 'Drugulin' typeface

בראשית ברא אלקים
את השמים ואת הארץ:

Fig. 152. 'Margalit' typeface

הגרפיקה השימושית, ככל אמנות
אחרת, אינה תלויה על בלימה.
שרשיה נעוצים בקרקע הקובעת
את פרצופה. הקרקע וכל אשר
עליה הם חומר בידה, ואין לתאר
אף הישג אחד בשדה הגרפיקה
בלי שורש זה, כי למי פונה

Fig. 153. 'Miriam' typeface

קשה לתאר עד כמה היה ההר חשוף, חרב
ושמם. החריץ שהשתרע על פניו אולי
נתמלא מים לזמן־מה בעת ירידת הגשמים,
אבל בעת לא נראתה אף טפת מים בכל
המקום מסביב, שמש הקיץ יבשה את הרטי־
בות עד תמה וכל שיח, כל אות חיים לא
נראה מסביב. סלע הסיד הלבן, החשוף

Fig. 154. Modern 'Stam' typeface

In the nineteen-sixties, Zvi Narkiss designed the Narkiss face in several variations, and it was followed by the typeface called Narkissim (fig. 149). The 'Oron' sans-serif face was designed by Asher Oron for photographic printing (fig. 150) to go with the Latin 'Univers' typeface. Among other typefaces which are used in modern printing are 'Margalit', (fig. 152), 'Miriam' (fig. 153) and 'Ada' (fig. 155). A modern 'Stam' typeface is also used in print (fig. 154). Most of the above-mentioned typefaces are available in different weights and sizes.

For a number of years, numerous additional modern typefaces have been designed and adapted for computers, which have caused a revolution in the field of printing. In fact, almost anyone today can design typefaces for printing in accordance with his skill and taste, provided he possesses the means and knowledge to handle the computer. The computers as well as the graphic programs for computers are improving rapidly. However, the aesthetic rules depending on our eyes and senses remain unchanged. Our visual impressions are still dominated by our sense of balance and symmetry, and our feeling for harmony. These will be discussed further on, in Part 4 dealing with calligraphy and the design of typefaces.

אמתסהג אמתסהג אמתסהג
טחפקסע טחפקסע טחפקסע
בדכרלדז בדכרלדז בדכרלדז
ףצץנווייש ףצץנווייש ףצץנווייש

בָּרוּךְ אַתָּה יי
אֱלֹהֵינוּ
מֶלֶךְ הָעוֹלָם
שֶׁהֶחֱיָנוּ
וְקִיְּמָנוּ
וְהִגִּיעָנוּ לַזְּמַן הַזֶּה

אבגדהוזץ
חטיכלמנ
סעפצקר
שתדסוף

Fig. 155. 'Ada', 'Dafna' (bottom, right) and 'Repha'el' (bottom, left) typefaces

אבגדהו שעטנז
זחטיכד גצזץחי
למסנזס אפףול
עפףצץ רבדהכך
קרשת ממסתק

Part 2

HEBREW PALAEOGRAPHY

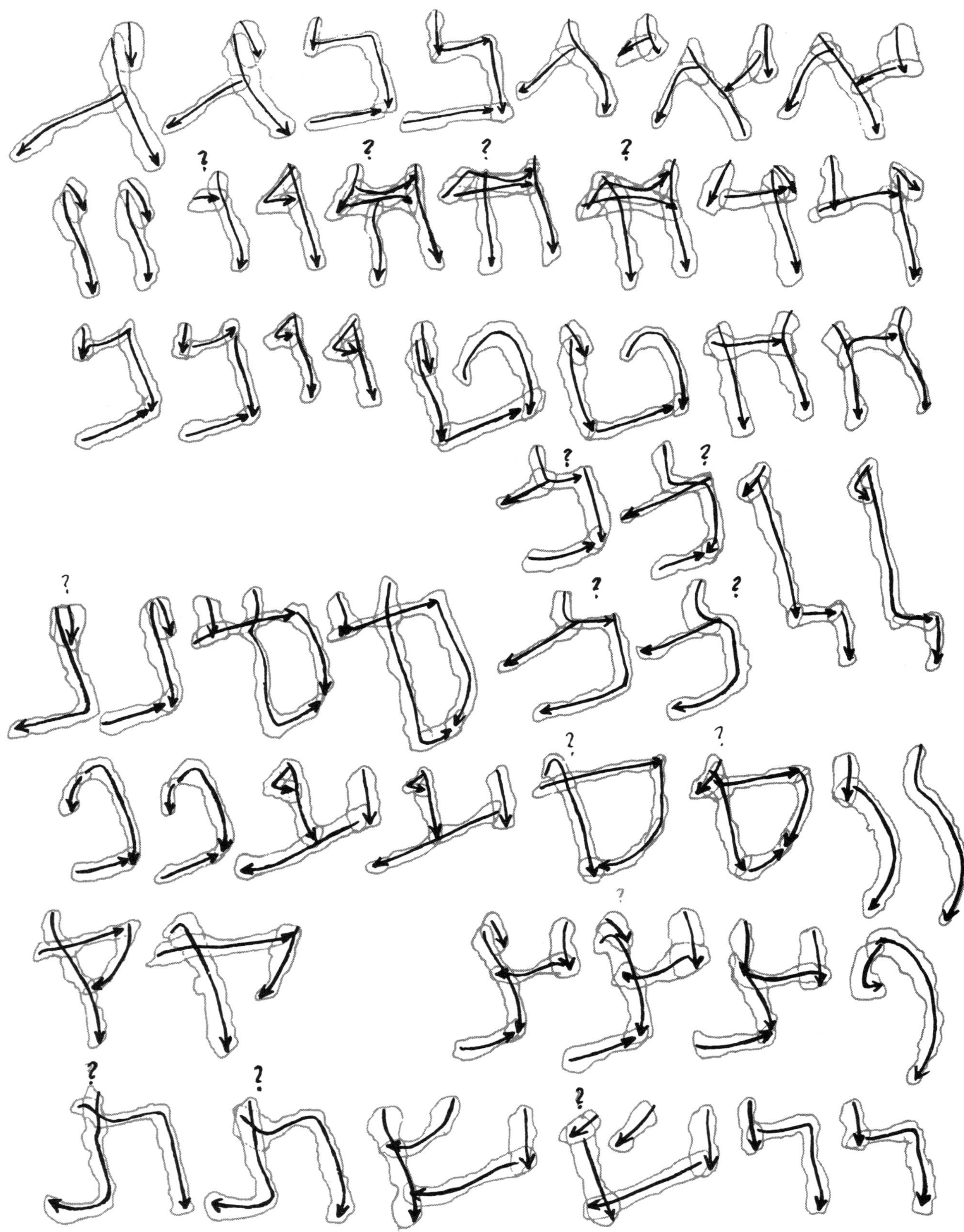

Fig. 156. Analysis of enlarged letter-forms taken from the Psalms scroll from Qumran (11QPs). The arrows designate the directions of the strokes

CHAPTER ONE: THE GRAPHIC ELEMENTS OF THE HEBREW LETTER AND THE BASIC RULES OF HEBREW PALAEOGRAPHY

A. THE STATE OF HEBREW PALAEOGRAPHY STUDIES

Two great discoveries of the modern era, the discovery of the Hebrew Genizah in Cairo and that of the Dead Sea Scrolls, gave an impetus to research into the Hebrew script. Yet, in both cases, most of the early finds do not carry dates. If it were not for the need for deciphering ancient scripts and dating undated texts, the interest in the Hebrew letter-signs would probably have remained restricted to the areas of typography and calligraphy. However, Hebrew palaeography has become an independent field of research and several works in this field have been published in recent decades, some of which shall be mentioned here (see also the bibliography).

The palaeography of the early material, especially the Dead Sea Scrolls, has been dealt with in some detailed scholarly works, the most important of which are those by Frank Moore Cross Jr. and by Naḥman Avigad. The evolution of the Hebrew script has been treated in a few articles, one of the most important being an article in Hebrew by Moshe Spitzer, as well as in some comprehensive surveys published in various encyclopaedias.

A collection of inscriptions and manuscripts accompanied by alphabetical charts was published by S.A. Birnbaum in his two volume work *The Hebrew Scripts*. The twenty-ninth volume of *Torah Shlema* by A. Kasher deals with the Hebrew script and with the literary sources of the scribal rules for the writing of the Sacred Scriptures. Colette Sirat has published books and articles on the methodology of the analysis of letters. Malachi Beit-Arié has also published some books and articles on manuscripts, in which he dealt with palaeographic issues. In the Israeli Laboratory of Physics an attempt was made to classify manuscripts by enlarging letter-signs and measuring various features of the letters and summarizing the results with the help of a computer. This experiment gave rise to an impressive scheme for classifying manuscripts according to geographical areas. Articles are occasionally published on individual inscriptions or manuscripts, including drawings and comparative alphabetical charts, mostly for dating the manuscripts on palaeographic grounds. Books and articles in the field of palaeography in general, including Hebrew palaeography, are also published occasionally, and congresses are held for the discussion of palaeographic matters where various methods are proposed for palaeographical research. All these works have encouraged scholarship in the field of Hebrew script. However, so far no method was proposed which has been generally accepted. Scholars agree that an objective 'scientific' method should be aimed at, which will use modern technological means for examining scripts and avoid the subjective judgement of the human eye. Several methods have been proposed, such as measuring and comparing the sizes and patterns of the letters, highly-developed photographical methods, holography, copying letters on the screen of the computer, etc. It is true that in the age of the computer palaeography should be assisted by the sophisticated means existing today. Many fields in the humanities make use of computers, and palaeography will also eventually be assisted by them.

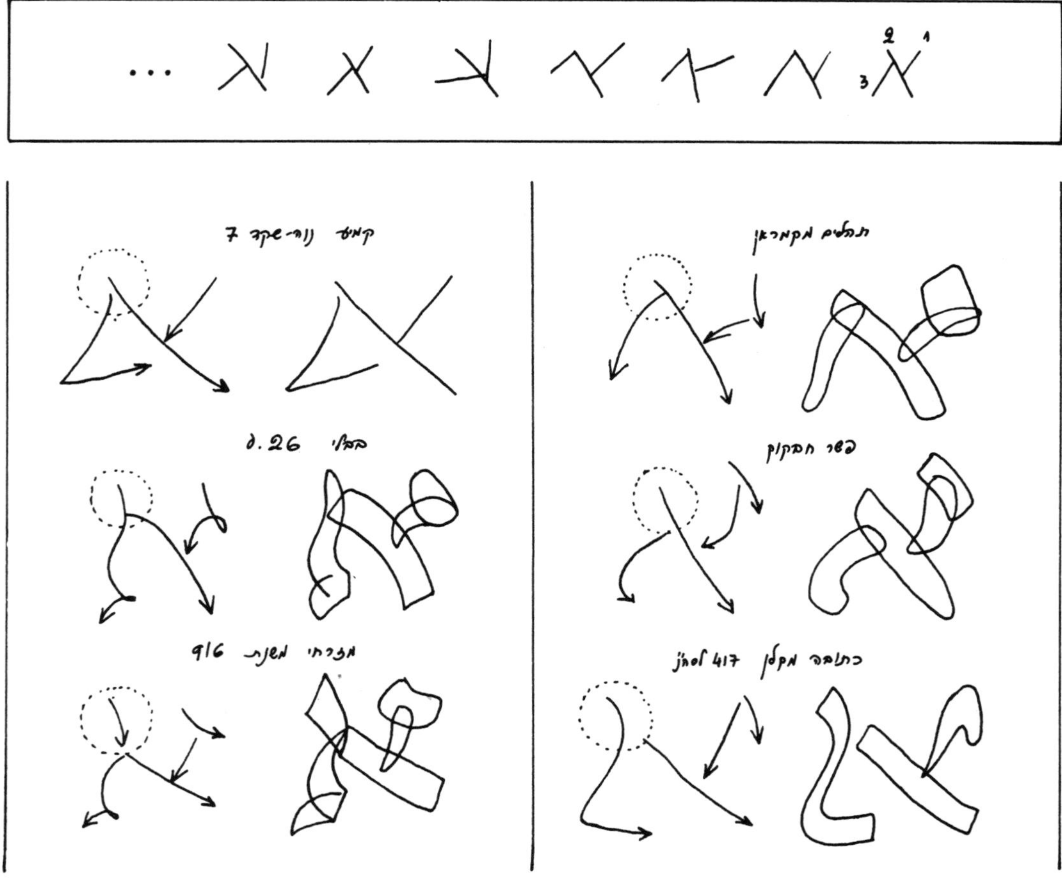

Fig. 157. An illustration of the schematic form of the 'root' and of the skeletons of Alef in different script styles

B. TOWARDS A 'GRAMMAR' OF THE HEBREW SCRIPT

An examination of Hebrew manuscripts of different periods reveals differences in the letter-forms – differences which our eyes can perceive. We are able to see that one script differs from another and that, for example, the letters in one are larger or smaller or thicker or thinner than in another, or that they are square or round, elegant or carelessly made, etc. However, we are usually unable to define the differences more precisely because we lack the means to do so.

In order to understand what we see we have to learn how to examine the letter-signs and their strokes and to analyze the components of the letter-forms. We should regard the letter-sign as an amalgam of several components.

The analysis of letters, in addition to other criteria, such as the archaeological context, historical events or names mentioned in the text, the linguistic features and vocabulary, the artistic style, etc., may also assist in the dating of undated epigraphical material. Palaeographers, however, are also interested in the pure letter-form and its development, and that is a field of research in itself. On one hand it relates to the field of art, as it deals with forms, and on the other hand it is also connected to linguistics, as writing is the systematic transmission of a language. Speech and script are both definite structure-systems rather than unrelated sequences of sounds or signs. Speech is composed of limited systems of consonants and vowels, each language having its own system. Script is composed of limited systems of signs, each language having its own system of letters. It is impossible to define the structure of a language or dialect without analyzing them grammatically (grammar is understood here in its traditional sense as phonology, morphology, syntax, etc.). In order to do this, one has to acquire the means: i.e., the basic principles and elements composing a given language. Thus, for example, in Semitic languages one has to learn to identify the roots of the verbs and distinguish them from the prefixes, affixes and infixes, to learn the verbal structure and the paradigms, the syntax, the accent and vowel shifts and the rules of assimilation and dissimilation, etc. In short, one cannot analyze a language unless one has acquired a knowledge of all the details concerning that language. Only then is one able to create a data base and to benefit in one's research from the assistance of a computer.

A similar situation exists in the field of palaeography. Before allowing the computer to do its work of evaluating statistics, one has to know all the details concerning the letter-signs, their structure in different script-styles, the phases of development and the factors influencing the changes in the forms. The use of the computer to find the common features of a script-style (i.e., a style with particular characteristics, used in a certain scribal school which was active in a certain place and a certain period) or to discover the features that distinguish one scribe from another, could be compared to using the computer to classify dialects or languages according to their individual characteristics. It is essential to feed the computer with the exact information about these characteristics, or else the work cannot be done. However, it is only in the last stages of the research and not at its beginning that one has acquired the knowledge that enables one to feed the computer with that information.

In the study of the Hebrew script, unlike the study of the Hebrew language, there is still no 'grammar' accepted by scholars. The field is open to experimentation, and there is still no terminology for defining the various components of the letter-forms and the factors influencing their formal development. Thus we may say that research is still in its early stages. To be able to define the script one has to study the structure of the system and its details. Before feeding the information into the computer, we have to construct a 'grammar' of the different script-styles: we have to familiarize ourselves with the 'roots' of the letter-forms and the additional ornaments in the various script-styles and discover the rules which determine the changes in writing over the course of time and in different places. We have to create a method for examining the components of the letter-forms and their evolution, and to define them for the use of scholars. We have to develop a 'study of letter-strokes' and a 'study of the morphology of letter-signs' in the Hebrew script.

Such a study needs time and painstaking work. Intuitive impressions of the differences between one script and another are not sufficient. Just as it is difficult to recognize the elements of words without having studied the grammar of a language, so the components of letters cannot be perceived at a glance. With the letter-forms, moreover, there is the additional difficulty that the personal features of handwritings sometimes obscure the basic structure of the letters.

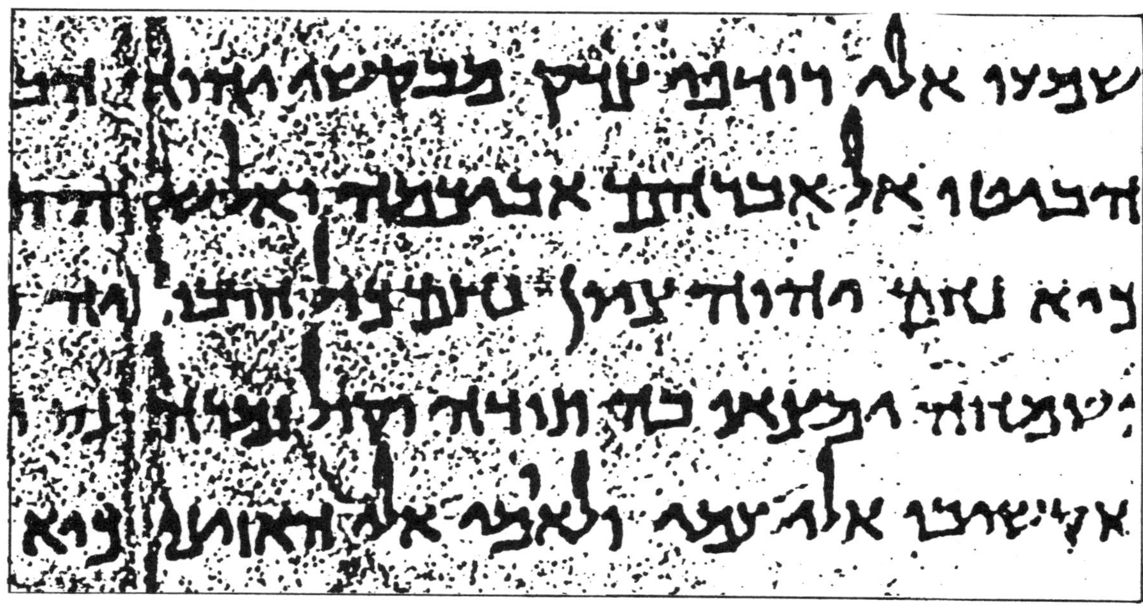

Fig. 158. Detail of the Isaiah scroll from Qumran (1QIsa[a]; enlarged)

C. THE STUDY OF SCRIPT-STYLES AS AGAINST THE STUDY OF DIFFERENT FORMATIONS OF A SINGLE STYLE

The 'square' Hebrew script has been in use from the time of the Second Temple until today, so that if we know the modern Hebrew script we are able to read any text in the ancient square script almost without difficulty. However, anyone with a sharp eye will see that there are differences between the scripts in manuscripts from the different times and places (in cursive and semi-cursive handwritings the differences are more striking, as the letters underwent extreme changes of form and their evolution was faster). The differences may be classified according to stylistic or personal characteristics.

It is essential to emphasize the difference between the two classifications. The study of styles can help to date manuscripts according to the phase of evolution of the script and the differences between the local styles. The study of personal hands seeks to define the differences between writers in the formation of the letter-signs in one and the same style. The two kinds of research use different means and methods.The different formations of one letter-sign in various handwritings may be compared to different pronunciations of one consonant by different people.

> In the study of script-styles we compare various manuscripts written by different scribes of the same place and period in order to find the points in common.
>
> In the study of personal handwritings we look for differences between individual scribes while defining their personal characteristics.

No two handwritings are identical, even though they may look very similar, as may be the case, for example, with forgers or with skilled calligraphers. Yet, in order to define styles of script, we have to ignore personal characteristics and look for the common features of different scribes of the same place and the same period of time. The differences between script-styles are not so much quantitative as differences of form or structure. They may consequently be defined in terms of form rather than by measuring.

The more a handwriting resembles a certain script-style and is executed by a skilled hand, the less personal features it displays. We should consequently begin our study with an examination of manuscripts written by skilled scribes.

A style may be defined in two ways – chronologically and geographically: that is, according to the development of forms in a certain place over a period of time, or according to the differences between letter-forms in various places at the same time.

D. THE BASIC RULES OF HEBREW PALAEOGRAPHY

The first step in the study of the letter-forms is the examination of the strokes. For that purpose one should imagine the abstract basic forms of the letters. This will enable us to perceive the changes they passed through as well as the changes which occurred in the forms of the ornamental additions. There are certain rules by which we may be guided:

1) Each letter in the alphabet is composed of a limited number of basic strokes – the 'root' of the letter, which distinguishes it from other letter-signs in the alphabet.

The 'root' of the letter is the basic, stripped, abstract form of the letter as against the 'skeleton', which is the central line running through the strokes of the actual existing form. In certain script-styles, the forms are composed of the 'root' together with the additional ornaments in the various stages of their evolution (fig. 157). The 'root' is an abstract form which exists only in the imagination. Many letters in the Hebrew script have in fact more than one 'root'. This is because the Hebrew script evolved from the Aramaic script, which already had a long history of formal changes that created variant forms of several letter-signs. These variants continued to exist in the Hebrew script. To reconstruct the 'roots' of the letter-forms one has to examine the ancient written material and trace the evolution of the letter-forms in their different stages.

What are the common features which characterize all the forms of ʾAlef in the square Hebrew script? An examination of ancient inscriptions, scrolls and manuscripts will reveal that in most of them ʾAlef is composed of three basic strokes. That is the minimal number of strokes of ʾAlef in the square Hebrew script (there is also an ʾAlef consisting of two strokes in the cursive script which resulted from a different line of development). The three strokes were inherited from the Aramaic script which in turn inherited them from the Phoenician script. In the square Hebrew script the three strokes constitute a certain structure that differs, for example, from the structure of the three strokes of Bet. The difference is in the direction of the strokes and in their meeting-points. This represents the minimal difference between the individual letters of the alphabet.

2) The basic difference between the individual letter-forms in the Hebrew alphabet is the difference in the direction of the strokes and in their meeting-points.

We shall now try to reconstruct a stripped form of the 'root' of ʾAlef. We shall begin by marking the central line that descends to the right: $^{2}\backslash$. That line already existed in ʾAlef in the Phoenician script as well as in the Aramaic and the Jewish scripts. We shall mark it with the figure 2 (the figures designate the estimated order of the strokes based on the formal evolution of the letter; although the order may occasionally have changed, the figures will remain, in order to prevent confusion). The line on the right which will be marked with the figure 1 may join line 2 at various points, from a point near the top of line 2 to a point near its bottom. The angle between the two lines may change but the top of line 1 is never lower than the meeting-point of its bottom with line 2.

3) There may be changes in the direction of the letter-strokes and in the position of their meeting-points. When the changes become systematic in several handwritings at a certain time and place they may be described as stylistic changes.

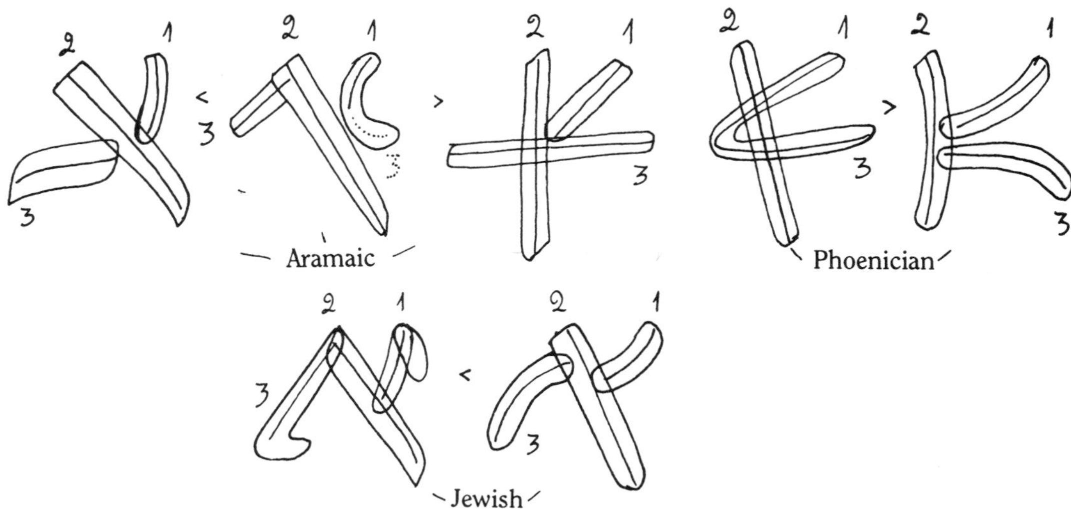

Fig. 159. The three basic strokes of Alef in the Phoenician, Aramaic and Jewish scripts

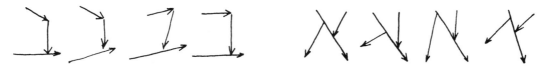

Fig. 160. The three basic strokes of Alef and Bet differing in their directions and in their meeting-points

Fig. 161. Alef in the 12th century cursive 'Eastern' script resembling modern cursive Mem: different forms of different letters sometimes become similar in the course of their evolution

Until now, we have been dealing with forms composed of a minimal number of straight lines. But, as we said, the 'root' of the letter is an abstract form existing only in our imagination. When examining the letter-forms in inscriptions or manuscripts we try to reconstruct the 'skeletons'. Letters that have been incised with a sharp implement often reflect their 'skeletons' more clearly than letters written with paint or ink, in which the thickness of the strokes hides their central lines.

The basic strokes of the letters are liable to various changes: lines may become round or wavy, shorter or longer, they may break or join together or disappear completely. When the changes become systematic they may be described as stylistic changes. A number of script-styles may exist

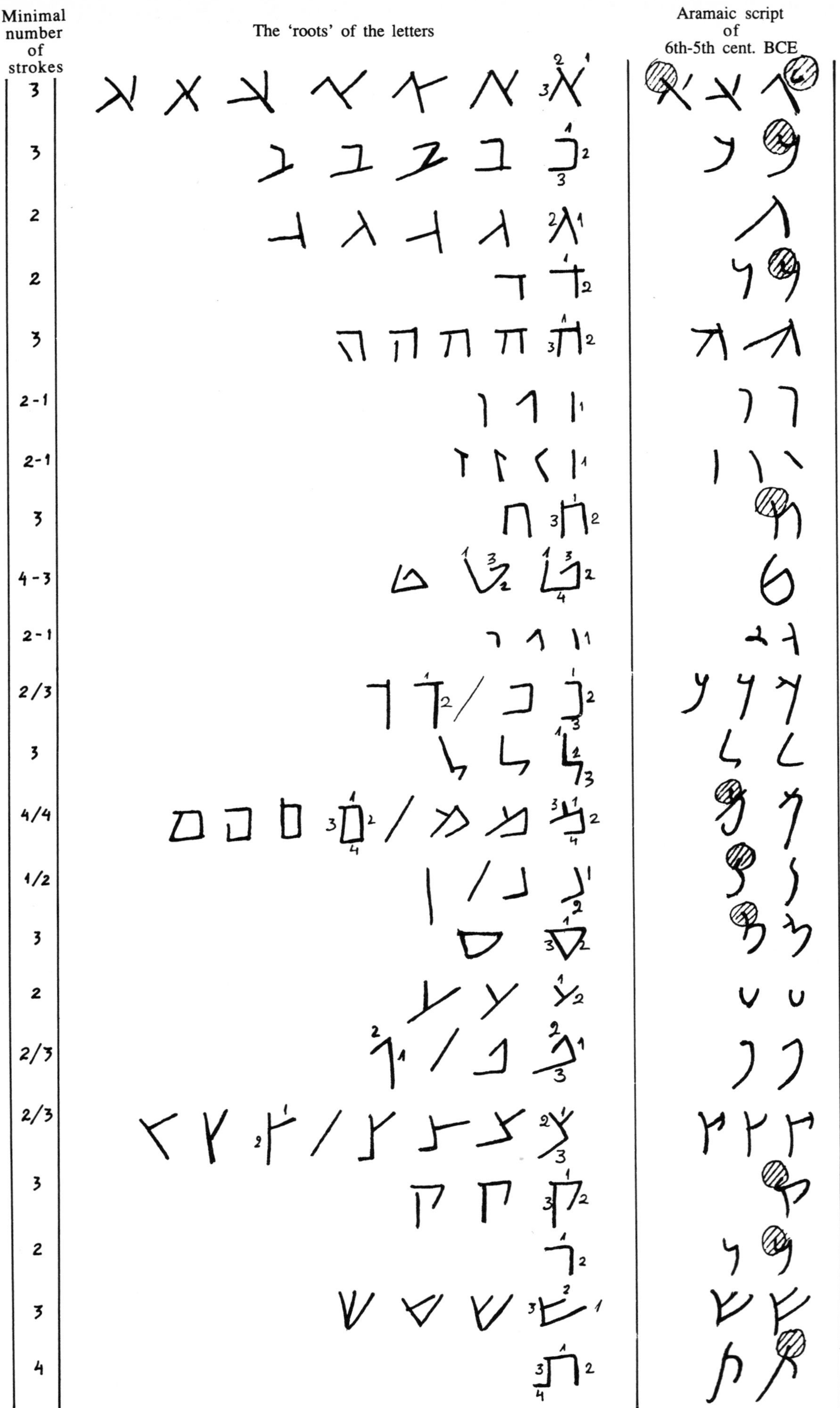

Fig. 162. A chart of the 'roots' of the Hebrew letters

simultaneously and one style may persist longer than another. A handwriting should not be dated by the form of individual letters but by a comparison of all the letters of the alphabet.

4) Each letter-form in the alphabet has its own rate of development.

The letter-signs of the alphabet do not change at one and the same time. Thus early and late forms may occasionally appear together in one inscription or manuscript.

5) Different letters of the alphabet may become similar in form in different script-styles and at different periods as a result of a different history of the form.

As an example we could mention ʾAlef in the cursive 'Eastern' Hebrew script-style that at a certain stage of its evolution had a form somewhat similar to the modern cursive Mem. The history of the two forms, however, is completely different.

Various components are added to the 'root' of the letter-form which play an essential role in characterizing the script-styles, because they are more liable to change than the basic lines. Some of the additional components were inherited from the Aramaic letters (fig. 162) and others evolved independently within the Jewish script in the course of time.

In different handwritings groups of letters may be classified according to similar graphic components. The letter-signs in those groups have one or more components which are formed in a similar way, such as the 'roofs' or the downstrokes or an additional ornament. Thus, for example, scribes at a certain period added serifs to certain letter-signs in analogy to others which already possessed serifs. In this way they enlarged the group of letters adorned with serifs. A recognition of the existence of this phenomenon helps us in distinguishing between different script-styles.

Occasionally a letter may have a similar form in two script-styles; however, the styles always differ in the grouping of letter-signs with similar stylistic components. Fig 164 shows letter-signs drawn from the mosaic inscription discovered in the synagogue of Reḥov dating from the late Byzantine period. The artist, using the technique of mosaic, tried to

Fig. 163. Ornamental additions in letters of one of the Meroth synagogue mosaic inscriptions

Fig. 164. Ornamental additions in letters of the alphabet taken from the Reḥov synagogue mosaic inscription

imitate the letter-forms written with paint. Similar components of the letter-forms appear in mosaic inscriptions from the synagogue of Meroth dating from approximately the same period (fig. 163): see, for example, the letters Zayin, Ṭet and Nun. At the tops of the letters the artist placed four stones – a square one at the centre and three triangular stones on three of its sides. That form was an imitation of the ornament written in ink with a flat implement, which consists of an extra stroke at the top of those letters. The seven letters *šʿṭnzgṣ* form a particularly important group. These letters, embellished with a similar ornament, already formed a group at the time when the scribal rules were fixed for transmitting the Sacred Scriptures.

6) In most of the Hebrew script-styles there are groups of letter-signs which have similar graphic components.

7) There is a limited number of components in the individual letter-signs of the different script-styles. Some of them may be similar in several letters of the same script-style.

8) The stylistic changes are caused by a variety of factors, of which the following are the most important: time and place, the writing materials and implements, the speed of writing, and the influence or imitation of other scripts.

a. Time. A script, like a language, changes in the course of time, even when a tradition is strictly followed. A minimal change may develop a dynamic of its own and gather momentum in a certain direction, thus influencing the evolution of the script. Sometimes a change in the letter-forms is temporary, leaving no trace in the script's subsequent development, as in the case of a certain mode or fashion, or in the case of the idiosyncracy of a certain scribe. Changes that become systematic are, as we said, stylistic changes. One of the major changes in a script – one which develops slowly – is the change in the relative sizes of the letters of the alphabet. Thus, for example, there is a difference in the relative size of the letter-signs in the script of the early scroll fragments from Qumran and the script used in manuscripts two centuries later (quite apart from other formal changes in the script). Rapid changes in the letter-forms are generally due to fluent writing with ink. Scripts of different degrees of cursiveness may sometimes be used for different purposes, such as writing official documents as against private letters. Script-styles constantly change and the situation is never static.

b. The nature of writing materials and writing implements. Letters of one and the same script-style will have a different appearance when written with different instruments on different surfaces. There is a difference between writing in ink on a soft surface and inscribing letters on a hard material. The writing implement, whether a brush, a reed-pen, a quill, a chisel, etc., and the way the implement is cut and held, also influence the form of the letters. A careful examination of their inner structure will reveal the common features of the letter-forms. On the other hand, the use

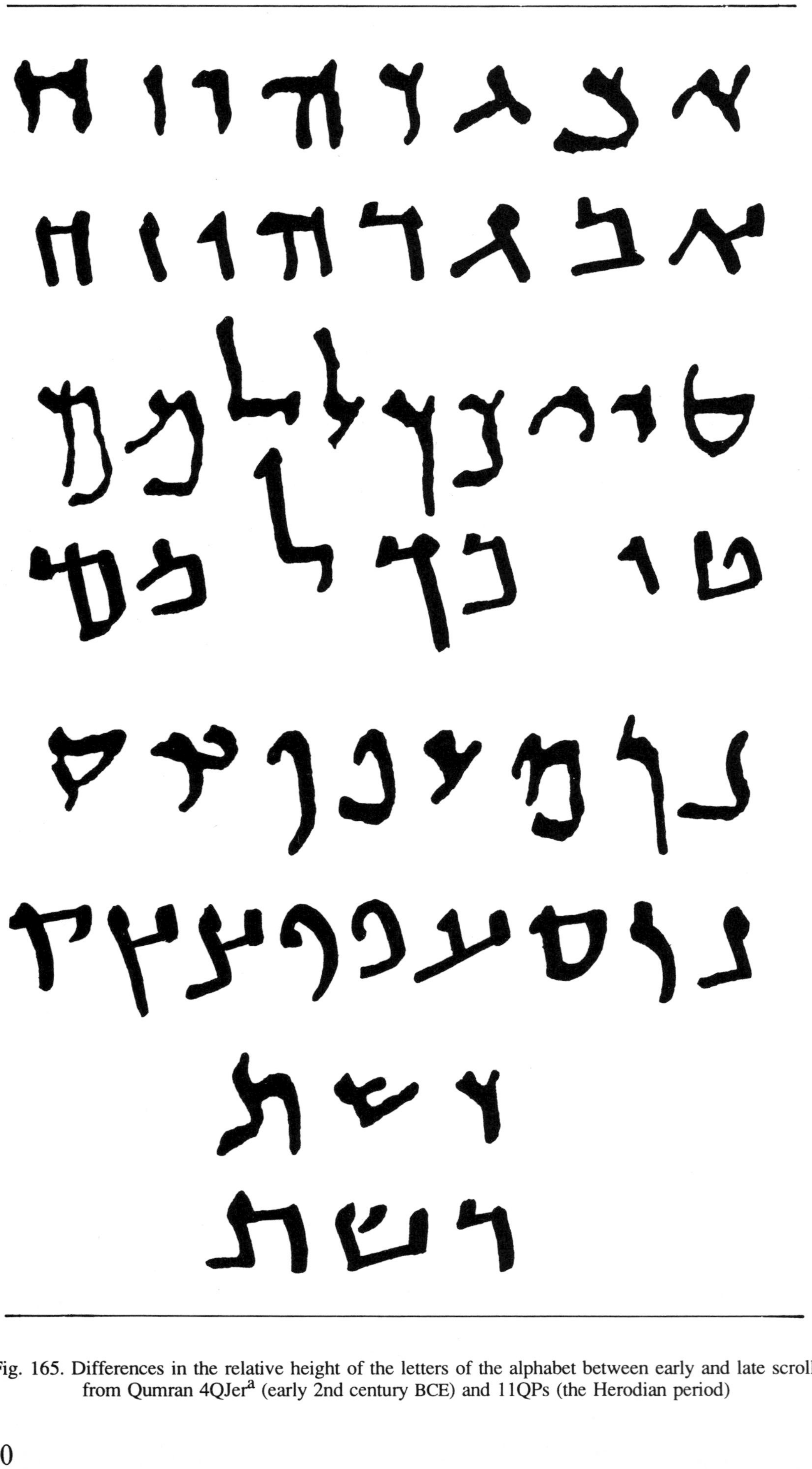

Fig. 165. Differences in the relative height of the letters of the alphabet between early and late scrolls from Qumran 4QJer[a] (early 2nd century BCE) and 11QPs (the Herodian period)

Fig. 166. Differences in the forms of the letter-strokes between the Hebrew Ashkenazi script written with a quill-pen and the Hebrew Sephardi script written with a reed-pen

of different implements and materials can result in formal changes in the script which can become stylistic. Thus, for example, it is difficult to draw horizontal strokes from right to left or vertical strokes in an upwards direction with a flat writing implement held in the right hand, while such strokes are easily made with a sharp or round writing implement. A flat pen, unlike a sharp or round pen, can be used for writing letters with thick and thin strokes and ornaments, which may become stylistic features of that particular script.

c. The speed of writing. Writing on a soft surface, unlike writing on a hard material, usually encourages flowing movements which may cause rapid changes in the form of the letters. Already in ancient times, a reed-pen or brush was used for writing in ink. As a result of this fluent writing, the forms of the letter-strokes as well as their meeting-points and the forms of their joints underwent fundamental changes. The lapidary script usually continued to exist together with the cursive hands and there was a mutual influence on their letter-forms; cursive forms found their way into the lapidary script and vice versa. This process gave rise to a large variety of letter-forms of different degrees of cursiveness, and cursive and semi-cursive script-styles emerged which were sometimes used concurrently for different purposes.

d. The geographical factor and the influence or imitation of other scripts. The Jewish script, and the later Hebrew script, evolved many styles due to contacts with foreign scripts. Already before the dispersion of the Jews throughout the world, the Jewish script came into contact with the Greek and Latin scripts as well as the Nabatean script. In later times many new script-styles evolved among the Jewish communities in the different countries, with the influence of the foreign scripts as well as the use of different writing implements and materials. The changes in the letter-forms were sometimes due to deliberate imitation and they sometimes occurred unintentionally, mainly because the continual use of foreign scripts together with the Hebrew script occasionally caused changes in the hand-movements of bilingual scribes. Thus the Hebrew scripts in the Islamic countries show affinities with the Arabic script while the Hebrew script-styles in Christian Europe show affinities with the Latin script-styles used in the different countries.

Fig. 167. Resemblance in the appearance of a Hebrew Ashkenazi semi-cursive script of Gothic style in a manuscript from 1224 and a Latin Gothic script in a manuscript from England dating from the late 13th century

The more strict the scribal tradition was, the less recognizable were the changes. Thus, for instance, in the calligraphic square Hebrew script which was used for the writing of sacred texts from the 9th century onwards,

Fig. 168. Simple ornamental additions and joints of strokes in book-hand letters from the post-Herodian period in contrast to the elaborated and complex ones in book-hand letters from the 10th century

minimal changes occurred in the course of time, while the cursive and semi-cursive script-styles, which evolved at about the same time, show considerable changes in the form of the letter-signs. However, even the calligraphic square scripts used for sacred purposes underwent stylistic changes. Thus the number of ornamental additions increased as well as the variety of forms of the joints between the letter-strokes.

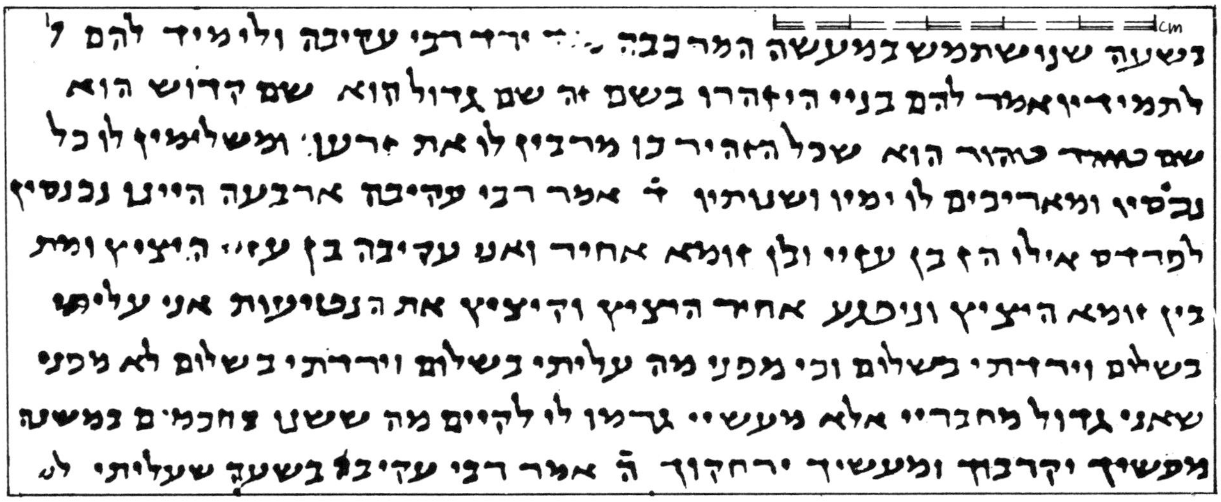

Fig. 169. Detail of an early Genizah manuscript of the 8th or 9th century (T-S K 21/95)

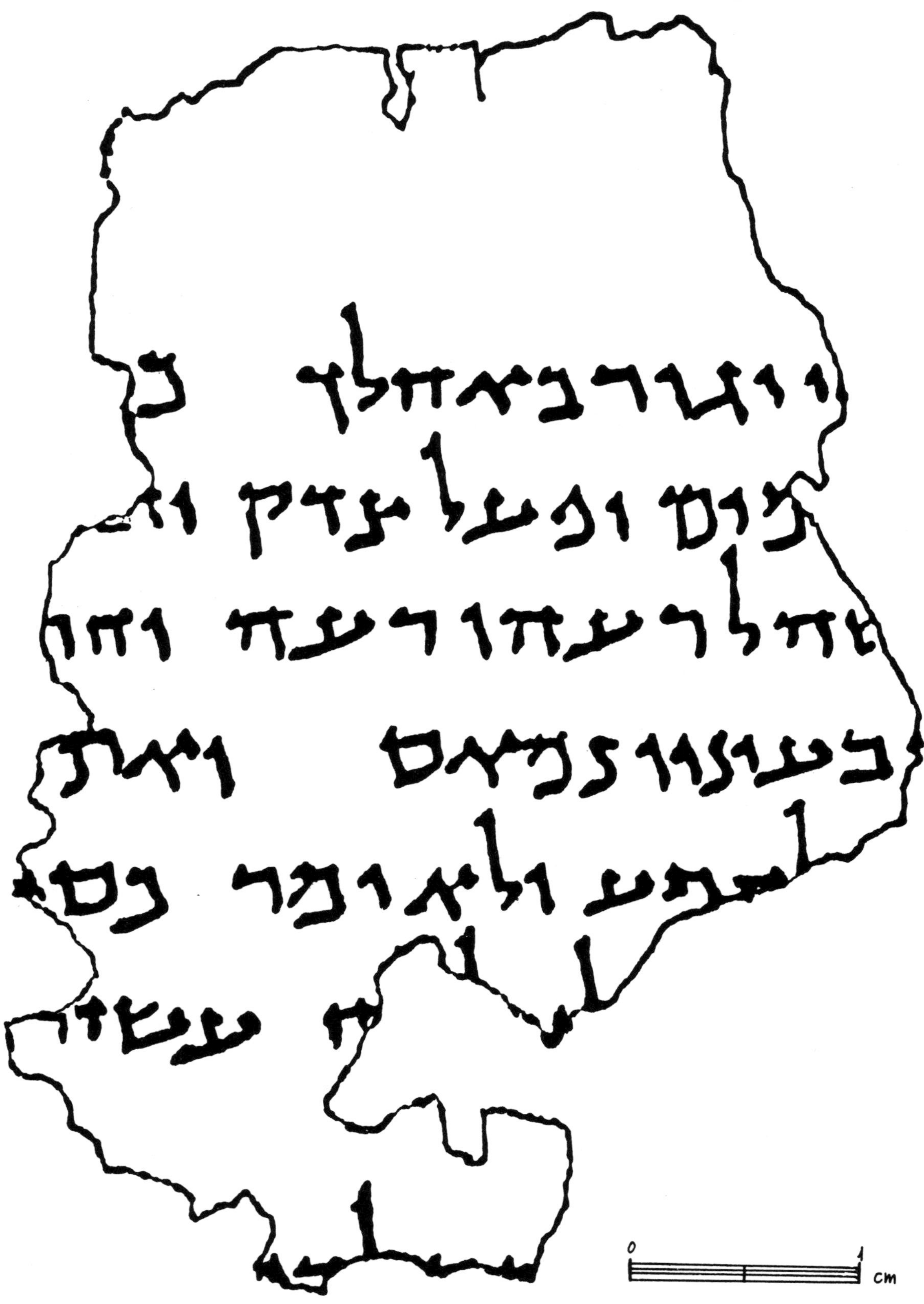

Fig. 170. A fragment of a Psalms scroll from Naḥal Ḥever (NḤ 41; enlarged)

E. THE PALAEOGRAPHIC ANALYSIS OF THE HEBREW LETTER-SIGNS

In order to demonstrate the analysis of the letter-forms, we shall examine the ʾAlef appearing four times in a fragment of a Psalms scroll dating from the early 2nd century (fig. 170).

Stroke No. 2 is the stroke slanting to the right. It is thick because it was drawn with a flat calamus held at an angle of about 45 degrees to the guideline (the thin lines are those which slant to the left).

What are the components of ʾAlef in this handwriting? Stroke No. 1 has a thick ornamental addition on its top right-hand side  , which projects to the right  . Stroke No. 1 touches stroke No. 2 at a point near its centre and a little above it  . Stroke No. 1 is also somewhat concavely curved. Stroke No. 1 and its ornament could be drawn with a flat calamus (reed-pen) in two movements without raising the implement from the surface. The form obtained will be similar to the form of ʾAlef in line 1

What is the origin of the ornament? If we look at the Aramaic ʾAlef of the 6th and early 5th centuries BCE, we shall see that stroke No. 1 occasionally resembled a crescent  . But there is no evidence of the survival of that element in later periods. It is therefore doubtful if there is a direct relation between the two forms, and it probably evolved independently within the Jewish script, at a stage when stroke No. 1 had an angular shape. At any rate, this element has continued to exist in the Hebrew book-hand from the second century until today.

Stroke No. 3 has a compound form also. First, we may notice that it touches stroke No. 2 at a point somewhat below its top. It then slants to the left and terminates above the imaginary base-line  .

An additional short stroke drawn to the right and appearing at its bottom is also an extra ornament which evolved in the course of time.

Now we may draw a synthetic form of ʾAlef in this handwriting.

A somewhat similar form of ʾAlef, but without the additional ornament in stroke 3, appears in the Psalms scroll from Qumran. That form is one of several variant forms of ʾAlef appearing in the scrolls of that period. We shall not deal at this point with the development of the letter-form because that is only possible after examining all the variant forms in the entire corpus of the epigraphical material.

In an undated papyrus fragment, now in the Bodleian Library in Oxford (Ms. Heb. f.114 (P); Fig. 94), the ʾAlef-sign seems to display similar elements, although a careful examination will reveal slight differences; stroke No. 2 slants to the right but is somewhat curved while stroke No. 1 joins it a little below its centre. The additional stroke at the top of stroke No. 1 is made independently and not in a to-and-fro movement. Stroke No. 3 starts above the top of stroke No. 2 rather than below it. It descends almost vertically, then turns at its bottom to the right and back to the left and downwards (lines 6, 8 and 10).

An ᵓAlef in which stroke No. 1 protrudes to the right in a similar way also appears in undated Genizah fragments of about the 9th century (they contain no reference to their provenance either). The tradition of writing that form of ᵓAlef should be examined, as it may point to an isogloss between scribal traditions.

The changes in the strokes of the letter-signs may be classified under a number of headings, as follows:

a. Changes in the form of the basic strokes:

1. Curving – a straight line may curve and become convex or concave, for example, the curving of stroke 2 in ᵓAlef.
2. Straightening – a curved line may become straight.
3. Lengthening – for example, the lengthening of stroke 1 in ᵓAlef.
4. Shortening – for example, the shortening of stroke 2 in ᵓAlef. This in fact is a change in the relative length of the strokes.
5. Undulating – a stroke may assume an undulating or wavy form: e.g., strokes 2 and 3 in He. 
6. Angulation – e.g., the creation of an angle in stroke 2 of ᶜAyin.
7. Thickening – total, partial or gradual: e.g., the thickening of stroke 2 of ᵓAlef.
8. Narrowing – total, partial or gradual: e.g., the narrowing of stroke 2 of ᵓAlef.

b. The omission of strokes (rare in the square script).

c. Changes in the direction of the strokes: e.g., stroke 1 of ᵓAlef.

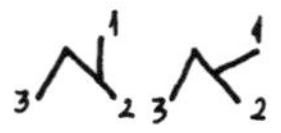

d. Changes in the meeting-points of the strokes: e.g., the meeting-point between strokes 1 and 2 of ᵓAlef.

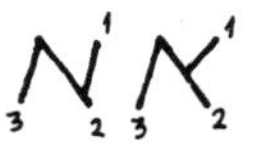

e. Changes in the additional ornaments (which come about in a similar way to the changes in the basic strokes).

f. Changes by way of analogy: e.g., an additional stroke at the top of Gimel by way of analogy to the additional stroke of Nun.

g. Changes in the grouping of letter-signs according to similar stylistic components: e.g., in certain script-styles, the change in the form of the top stroke of Waw, Gimel and Nun caused a change in the grouping of the letters. The group Zayin, Gimel and Nun, which had a similar ornament in the form of an additional stroke drawn to the right of their top, split into two groups: Zayin kept the original ornament whereas the ornament changed in Gimel and in Nun. Later, the top stroke of

Waw became similar to the top strokes of Gimel and Nun, so that Waw became part of the same group.

h. Changes in the relative sizes of the letters of the alphabet: e.g., Gimel extended below the imaginary base-line, thus becoming longer than other letters which terminated at the base-line.

i. Changes resulting from differences in the way of holding or the way of cutting the writing implement:

1. The main forms of strokes drawn in different directions with a right-angled flat instrument.

2. The main forms of strokes drawn in different directions with an obliquely-cut instrument.

j. The merging together of strokes or of stroke-segments or of strokes with ornaments: e.g., the merging together of the serif with the 'roof' of Bet, creating one concave stroke; the merging together of stroke 3 of Mem with a segment of stroke 1.

The creation of a new script-style is usually characterized by several changes in the form of the letter-strokes. In certain script-styles it may be difficult to identify the basic strokes of the letter-forms, in which case it may be helpful to define the different stages in the development of each stroke. It should be pointed out that the structure of the letter-forms does not usually depend on their actual size or their arrangement on the writing surface, except in the case of very small letters which often lack the additional ornaments.

In principle, the scribe's intention was to imitate the traditional letter-forms he had learned on a hard or a soft surface, but the technique he employed influenced the resulting forms. Thus, for example, when looking at certain inscribed Hebrew letters of the Byzantine period, one may get the impression that there is a thickening of the tops, which in fact is only the shadow resulting from a certain technique of engraving used mainly in inscriptions in Latin letters. In that technique, the strokes were engraved from their central line outwards.

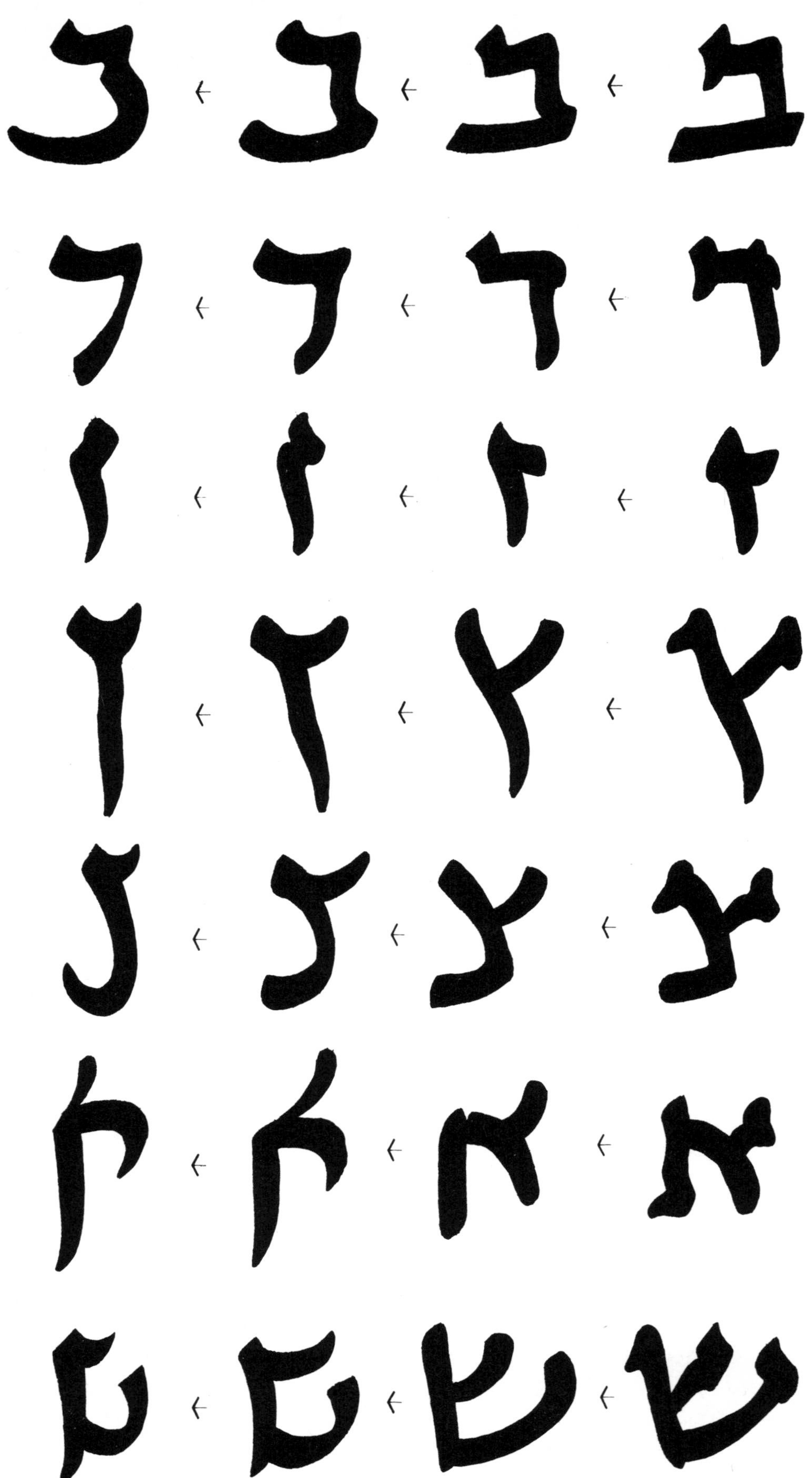

Fig. 171. The main stages in the evolution of letter-forms of the 'Eastern' book-hand into the semi-cursive Sephardi script

F. THE PALAEOGRAPHIC DESCRIPTION OF A SCRIPT-STYLE

In order to describe similar components of letter-forms in a certain script-style it is necessary to use a suitable terminology. Already in the Jewish literary sources dealing with scribal rules, a number of terms are used to describe the forms and components of the letters, some of which can still serve for that purpose, while new ones may be added.

Listed below are some terms which may be used for palaeographic descriptions of the components of the Hebrew letter-signs:
'arm' – the left or right downstroke in letters without a 'roof'. ע ש
'base'– the lower horizontal stroke: e.g. stroke 3 in Bet, Kaf, etc. ב כ
'foot'– the additional stroke at the bottom of stroke 3 in ʾAlef, Pe, Taw. א, פ, ת
'heel' – the lower part of the right downstroke in Gimel. ג
'horn' – stroke 3 in Mem. מ
'leg' – the left or right downstroke in letters without a 'base'. ה ח
'mast' – stroke 3 in Lamed. A 'flag' is sometimes attached to it. ל
'nose' – the left downstroke of Pe when curved or bent inwards. פ
'roof' – the upper horizontal stroke: e.g. stroke 1 in Bet, Dalet, etc. ב ד
'sting'/serif – a short stroke added to the basic strokes of the letters in different directions, or the projection of a stroke beyond its meeting-point with another stroke: e.g. the 'sting' at the left end of the 'roof' of Bet or at the bottom of Ṭet, etc. ב ט
'tail' – the projection at the lower right corner of Bet. ב

Forms of joints between strokes:
angular 
curved 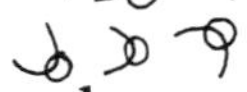
cross-shaped
extending beyond the meeting-point 
joint-like 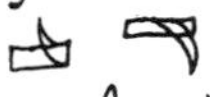
loop-shaped 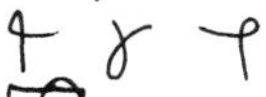
neck-shaped 
nail-shaped

In order to describe a script-style, we shall draw up a list in four parts:
a) A general description of the inscription or the manuscript.
b) A general description of the script.
c) A description of the similar graphic components in the letter-groups.
d) A description of the letter-signs in the form of an analysis and synthesis.

Each detail in the list will be marked in a way that will permit a classification with the help of a computer.

a) The general description of the inscription or the manuscript:
1. The provenance: the place where it was written or found.
2. The kind of item: burial inscription, votive inscription, stele, gravestone, seal, seal-impression, inscribed or painted ostracon, letter, manuscript of a literary text, list, graffiti, deed, book, scroll, amulet, etc.
3. The materials and techniques:
Engraving in stone, ivory, wood, clay, gypsum, metal (copper, silver, gold), etc.

Relief in stone, clay, gypsum, wood, etc.
Mosaic
Paint or ink on stone, plaster, clay, ostracon, papyrus, leather, paper, etc.
4. Writing implements (known or presumed): stylus, chisel, reed-pen, brush, calamus, quill-pen, etc.

b) The general description of the script.

1. The nature of the script: calligraphic, accomplished, free, fluent, regular, careless, vulgar, clumsy, etc.; square, ornamented, formal, semi-formal, semi-cursive, cursive, extreme cursive, etc.
2. The distinction between thick and thin strokes: no distinction, thick, thin or medium strokes; a slight distinction; a clear distinction.
3. The form of the writing implement: sharp, flat, broad, narrow, frayed, etc., and the way it was held.
Cut at a right angle and held parallel to the guideline.
Cut at a right angle and held perpendicularly to the guideline.
Cut obliquely and held parallel to the guideline.
Cut obliquely and held perpendicularly to the guideline.
Held at an angle to the guideline.
Held in one and the same direction.
Held in varying directions.
4. The general inclination of the script (reflected mainly in the direction of the downstrokes and occasionally also in the 'roofs' and 'bases'): leaning backwards; leaning forwards; upright.
5. The relative width of the letters: the width greater than the height; square; the height greater than the width.
6. The degree of uniformity: homogeneous; few variations in the forms of the letters; many variations in the forms of the letters.
7. Ornamental additions: yes; no (description).
8. The relative size of the letters of the alphabet (description).
9. Irregular forms and features.

c) Similar components in groups of letters: a description of the form of the basic strokes as well as the ornaments. The description of the individual strokes may include the following: the form of the stroke – straight, curved, or wavy; the direction of the stroke – horizontal, vertical, or slanting, and to what degree; the thickness of the stroke – uniform or changing; how it changes; a description of additional strokes and ornaments (as in the description of the basic strokes). The form of the joints between the basic strokes as well as the ornaments.

d) The description of the individual letters on the basis of analysis and synthesis. Certain letters in the alphabet have unique features, such as the 'mast' of Lamed or the diagonal of ʾAlef and of Ṣadi. Each letter needs to be described separately. In accordance with the detailed description, schematic or synthetic forms of the letters in a certain handwriting will be constructed in order to facilitate comparison with the letter-forms in other handwritings. For that purpose, the letter-forms of the handwriting will be placed inside rectangles of identical height, the width of which will be determined by the broadest letter in the handwriting. This should permit a comparative analysis of the structure of the letters. Each rectangle will have a register of coordinates dividing it into smaller rectangles, all of identical size. Sixteen rectangles will suffice for our purpose.

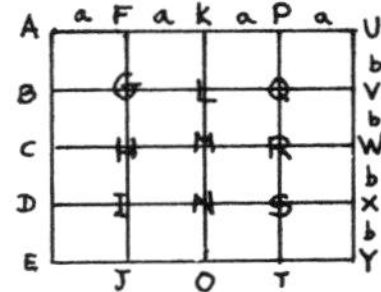

The meeting-points of the coordinates will be marked with letters. The individual letter-signs will be placed on enlarged rectangles for an analysis of the directions of the strokes and their relative sizes. It is recommended that small letter-signs should be enlarged so that details can be seen more clearly. The rectangle should be enlarged proportionally. The segments of the letter-strokes extending beyond the sides of the rectangle may be analyzed by adding as many small rectangular units as needed in each direction.

In the case of bold letter-strokes, we may have to trace the central line of each stroke: i.e., the 'skeleton' of the letter-form. When the 'skeletons' of the letter-forms are drawn on the rectangles, we shall mark the starting-point and the point of termination of each stroke, as well as a few transition-points, as in the following example:

Starting point: F; transition-points: L. Ma(+), S; terminating point: Ta(-).

The meeting-points of the strokes may be described by dividing each basic stroke into a number of segments (e.g. four), and marking them with identifying marks. To facilitate comparison, the division should be the same for each stroke, whether long or short:

s3 and s2: Aa s1 and s2 D(-)

In order to compare the different handwritings it is recommended to increase or reduce the size of the letter-signs until they attain the same height, so that the differences between the rectangles will be in the width alone. In an advanced stage of the work it will be sufficient to examine the 'skeleton' alone, while the thickness of the strokes is determined by the width of the writing implement and the angle at which it is held, as well as the relation between the width of the writing implement and the height of the letter, and other general factors. A comparison of the 'skeletons' of the letters will reveal all the changes and differences in the directions of the strokes and the additional ornaments, as well as their length, their form,

Various forms of ʾAlef

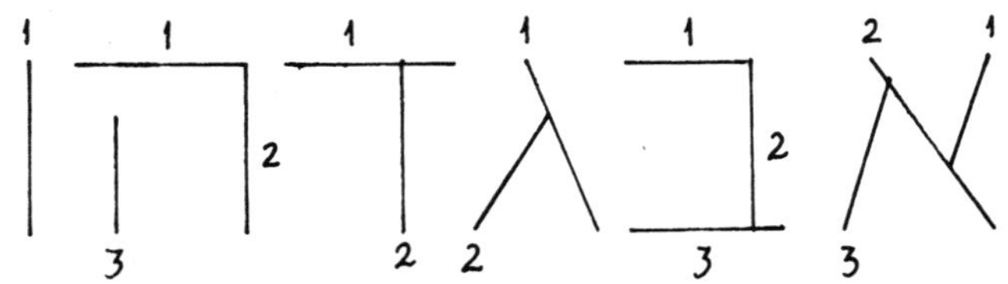

The basic strokes in different letters

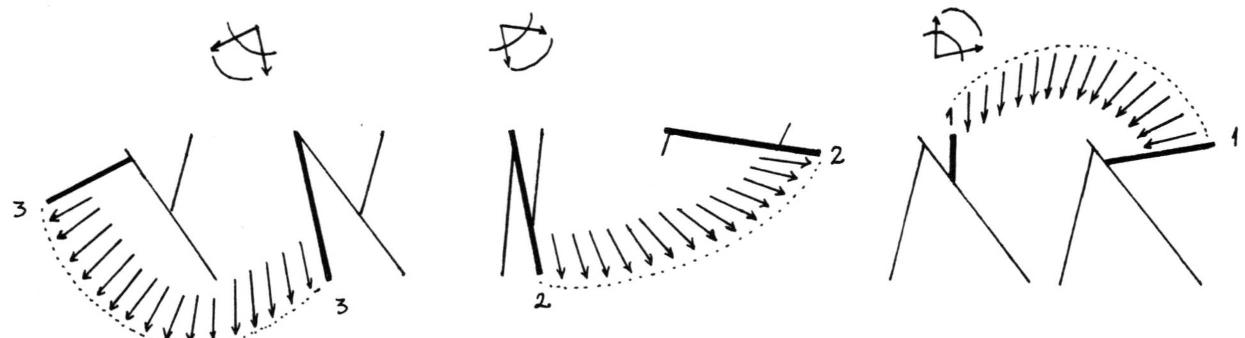

The range of directions of the three basic strokes of ʾAlef

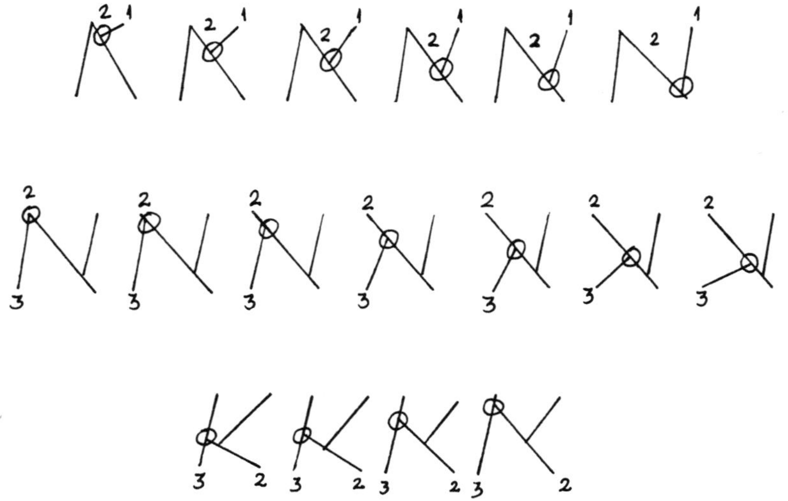

The meeting-points of the three basic strokes of ʾAlef

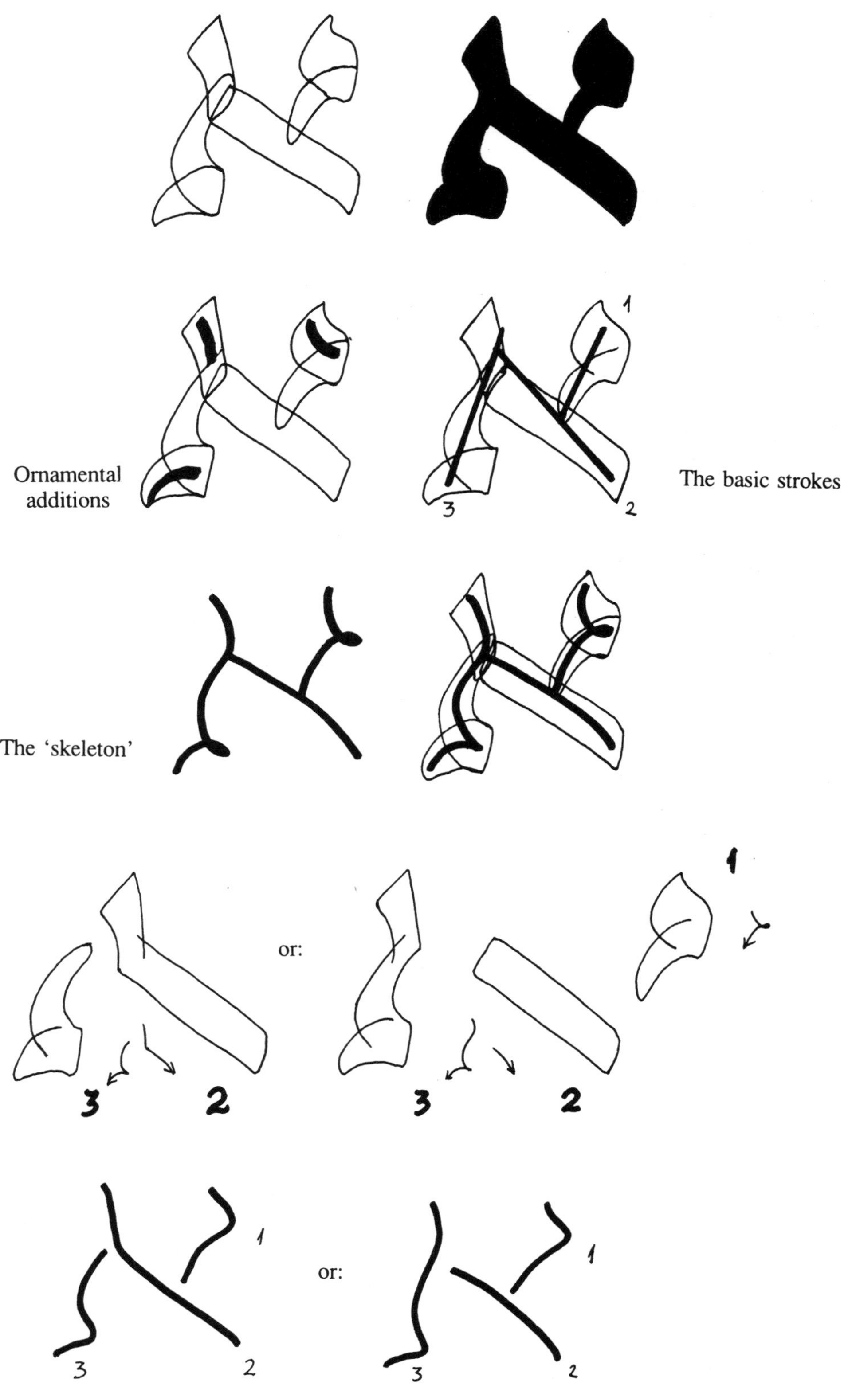

The order of the strokes

their joints with one another, the groupings of letters according to similar graphic components and the changes in the relative sizes of the letters as well as the strokes of the individual letter-forms.

In order to describe the graphic components of the letter-signs we shall compile a short list of the main components which appear in different handwritings in different script-styles. There will be no classification according to the different styles in that list, because such a classification is possible only after making an analysis and a detailed description of each letter-form in the different handwritings, as suggested above.
Listed below are some characteristics that should be observed in each basic stroke as well as in each ornamental addition:

a) The form and direction of the stroke:
transversal stroke: horizontal, straight —, slanting, descending to the left
descending to the right
downstroke: vertical, straight |, slanting, descending to the left //,
descending to the right \\
transversal stroke: curved, convex ⌒, concave ◡
downstroke: curved, open to the left), open to the right (
changing directions (description of the changes);
thick, of medium thickness, thin (definition according to the width of the writing implement, the form in which it was cut [at a right angle, oblique, upwards to the left or upwards to the right], and its angle to the guideline);
changing thickness (e.g., becoming narrow at its centre);
transversal stroke: bent or curved at one side (right, left, upwards, downwards);
downstroke: bent or curved at one side (top, bottom, leftwards, rightwards);
wavy ~, curved inwards at its centre, sharp at its end,
rhomboid ◇, forming two rhombuses, angular ⟨ ⟩, etc.

b) Form and direction of ornamental additions: serif: thin, thick, of medium thickness, made with a flat, sharp or frayed implement, cut at a right angle or obliquely (downwards to the right or to the left); held parallel, perpendicularly or obliquely to the guideline;
drawn in the form of a horn; hook; rhombus ◇; loop: triangular, round, drawn to the left, to the right ; shaped like a comma:
sharp at the top or at the bottom ; tangential ; angular:
open to the left, right, upwards, downwards ; drawn in the form of a crown: with 2,3,4 'stings' ; made with a to-and-fro stroke: left and right, right and left, downwards and upwards, etc.
shaped like a hammer; a cross; a flag; a cone; a square □;
a circle ○ ; undulating ; etc.

The various graphic components may be given identifying marks. After registering all the details of the letter-signs in a certain handwriting, we may feed the computer with the information for a statistical comparison. The use of the computer will thus be the last stage of the palaeographic research and not its beginning. As we said, one first has to study all the components and characteristics of the letter-signs in the various script-

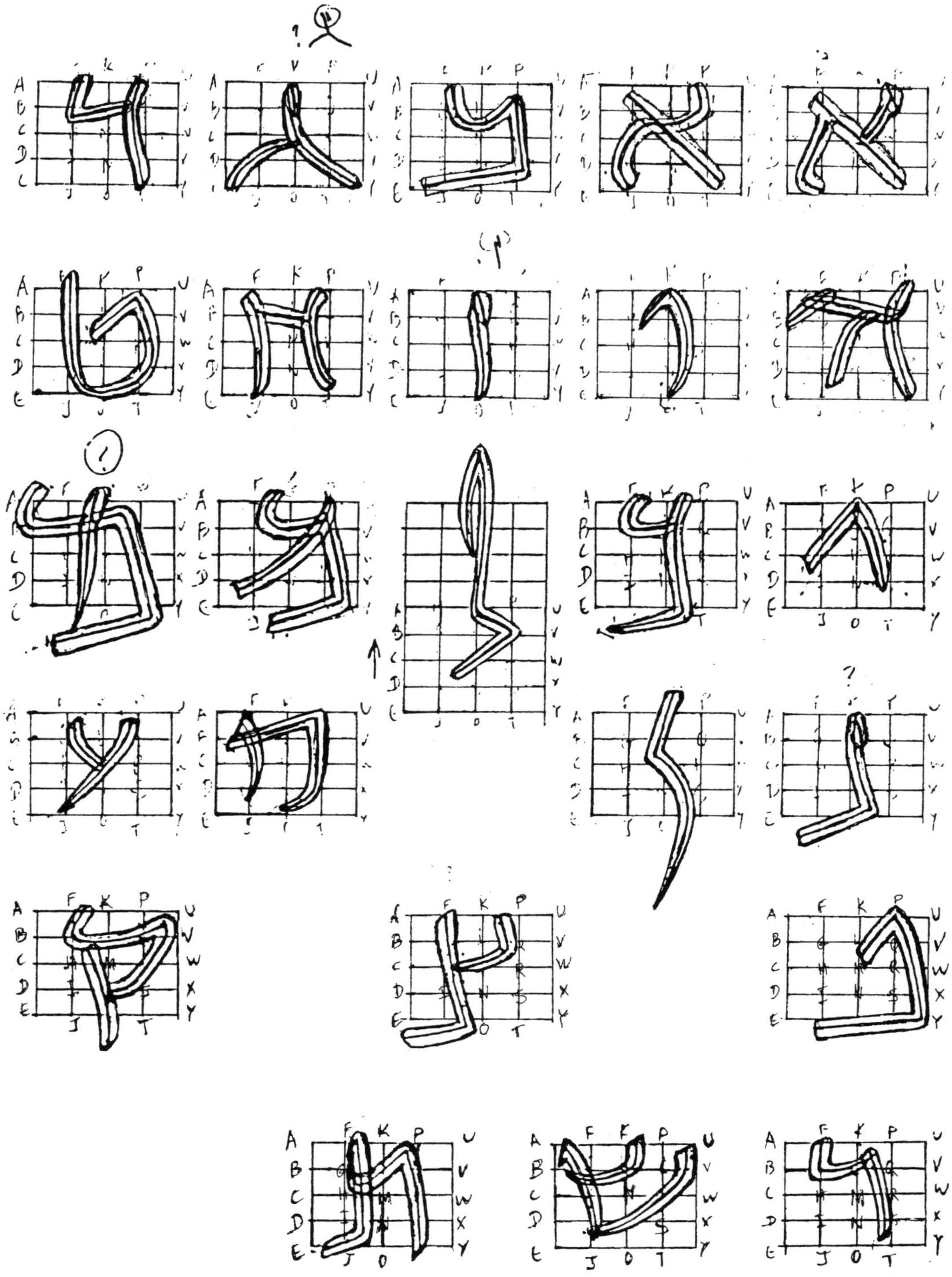

Fig. 172. Synthetic, average forms of the letters of 1QIsa[a], col. XLII, enlarged and placed on rectangles for a palaeographic description

styles carefully and in detail. Only then will one be able to compare them and draw conclusions about the dating of undated inscriptions or manuscripts, as well as about their provenance if it is unknown, and about the relationships between various handwritings. The stages of evolution of the individual strokes and ornamental additions, as well as of their meeting-points, can be discerned through a diachronic examination, while the differences between local script-styles can be revealed through a synchronic examination of inscriptions and manuscripts from different places at a given period.

In this chapter, we have proposed a method for the study of letter-strokes and their components and for a detailed description of handwritings. This method is meant to be a basis for the examination of letter-forms and for the definition of handwritings through a systematic analysis of the letter-signs rather than through intuition alone. The study of the letter-strokes and the morphology of the letter-forms will help to provide an understanding of the letters' structure, as well as assist in their classification into different script-styles and their dating. It will be of benefit to scholars of Hebrew palaeography on the one hand and, on the other hand, to calligraphers and graphic artists who design Hebrew typefaces on the basis of the rich material appearing in inscriptions and manuscripts from the various periods in the history of the Hebrew script. We have made the experiment of creating a system of 'roots' and terms to assist in the understanding of the structure of the letter-forms as well as their evolution, and in the classification of the different Hebrew script-styles according to their formal characteristics. As each letter-sign is composed of a limited number of graphic components, it is not too difficult to describe and compare them in order to learn the characteristic features of each script-style. We shall find the 'root' of the letter-sign and distinguish the 'root' from the ornaments and other components, and discover the changes that occurred in the individual components. We shall examine the grouping of the letter-signs according to similar graphic components and distinguish between the different stages in the evolution of the forms. We shall then be in a position to construct a 'grammar' of the different script-styles and lay the foundations of the palaeography of the Hebrew script.

* A detailed description of the method and an analysis of a number of manuscripts appear in my work 'The Palaeographic Elements of the Hebrew Script' (a copy of this unpublished work is located in the Hebrew Palaeographical Project, the Jewish National and University Library, Givʿat Ram, Jerusalem).

CHAPTER TWO: THE HAND MOVEMENTS AND THE DIRECTIONS OF THE STROKES IN HEBREW WRITING

The general direction of Hebrew writing is from right to left, as in all the West-Semitic scripts, including its ancestors – the Phoenician and Aramaic scripts – as well as the Arabic scripts. However, the strokes of the individual letters are executed in various directions. There are several basic hand movements in Hebrew writing: the general movement of the line from right to left, and the movements of the hand in making the individual strokes, some of which go from left to right and others of which go downwards or on a slant. One may ask whether there are any strokes which are drawn from right to left or upwards.

When using a writing implement with a sharp or a round end, like a pencil or a ball-pen, there is no difficulty in drawing the lines in every direction. However, with an implement with a flat end there may be difficulty in drawing lines in an upwards direction, or from right to left with the right hand or from left to right with the left hand. The writing implement is stopped by the writing surface unless it is held in an unnatural way. Usually, we learn to grip the writing implement in our right hand between the index finger and the thumb while it leans on the upper phalanx of the third finger on one hand and on the membrane joining the index finger and the thumb, or the lower phalanx of the index finger, on the other. The way one grips the implement also depends on its size as well as the size of the hand and length of the fingers. Thus, there are people who lean the writing implement on the middle or even the lower phalanx of the finger or grip it between the third finger and the ring finger.

In calligraphy we exert more energy with our fingers than in ordinary writing to stabilize the instrument at the desired angle. For this purpose, the instrument may be held near its nib with the tops of the thumb and of two fingers. This enables one to control the angle between the writing implement and the guideline.

Fig. 173. Relaxed holding of a writing implement resting on the finger's lower phalanx

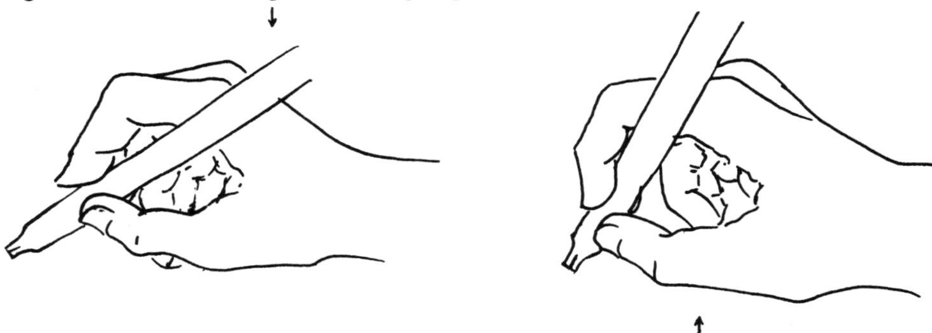

Fig. 174. Stabilizing the writing implement by holding it between the tops of the thumb, the index finger and the third finger

In any case, the drawing of strokes in a vertically upwards direction with a flat implement is almost impossible unless its end is worn out and the writing surface is smooth. But this gives poor results.

The question concerning strokes in a contrary direction in the Hebrew script arises because of the difference between thick horizontal strokes and thin downstrokes which usually characterizes certain square script-styles. Did that difference exist in all stages of the Hebrew script?

If we examine the early manuscripts we realize that the answer is No. As we said, the square Hebrew script evolved from the Aramaic clerical script of the 5th and 4th centuries BCE. In the 5th century BCE, most letters had rounded and oblique strokes, the thickness of which varied according to their direction. The thickest parts of the strokes were at an angle of about 45 degrees to the guideline and the thick strokes were those which descended obliquely from left to right. The writing implement was a rush pen, the end of which was formed into a flat brush. The writing of almost every letter began on the left-hand side at the top and then moved to the right or downwards. Several letters, such as Gimel, He, Ḥet, Ṭet, Ṣadi and Shin, contained oblique strokes descending to the left.

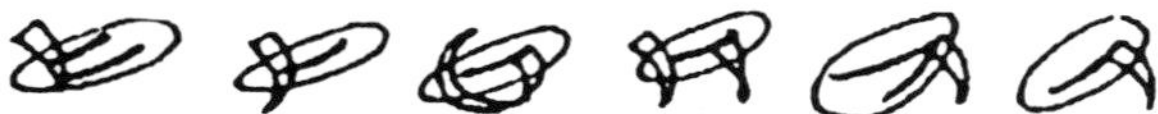

In the 5th century BCE the Aramaic letters did not have thick base-strokes with the exception of Bet, which was sometimes drawn from left to right. In that case, its left extremity was thicker than the right.

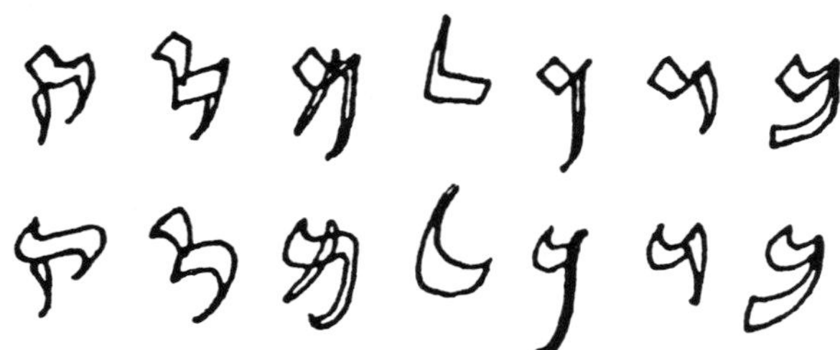

Most of the 'roofs' were concave. The tendency to include straight horizontal strokes in the writing of some letters already began in the early 5th century BCE, particularly in the case of the 'roof' of He and the base of Bet. That tendency continued in the 4th century and, as a result, the letter-signs developed thick horizontal strokes and thin downstrokes. The 'roof' of He became extremely thick.

In early manuscripts from Qumran, dating to the late 3rd and early 2nd centuries BCE, the script still resembles 4th century Aramaic calligraphy. In Aramaic documents of the Hellenistic period, when the reed brush was replaced by a thin calamus (reed pen), the thickness of the strokes is more uniform, as it is also in most of the scrolls in the Jewish script from Qumran dating to the 2nd and 1st centuries BCE. The calamus was less

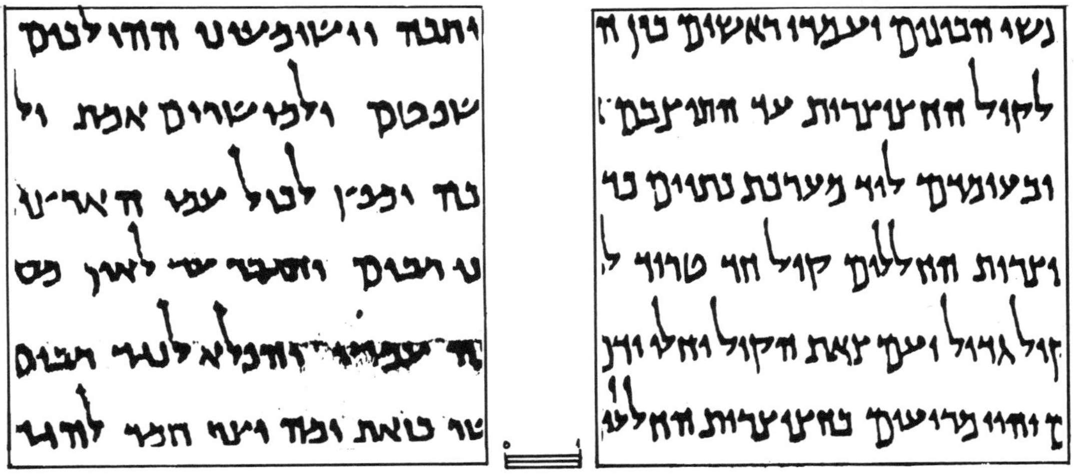

Fig. 175. Details of the text in the War scroll and in the Thanksgivings scroll from the Judean desert dating from the Herodian period. The letters are inclined forward

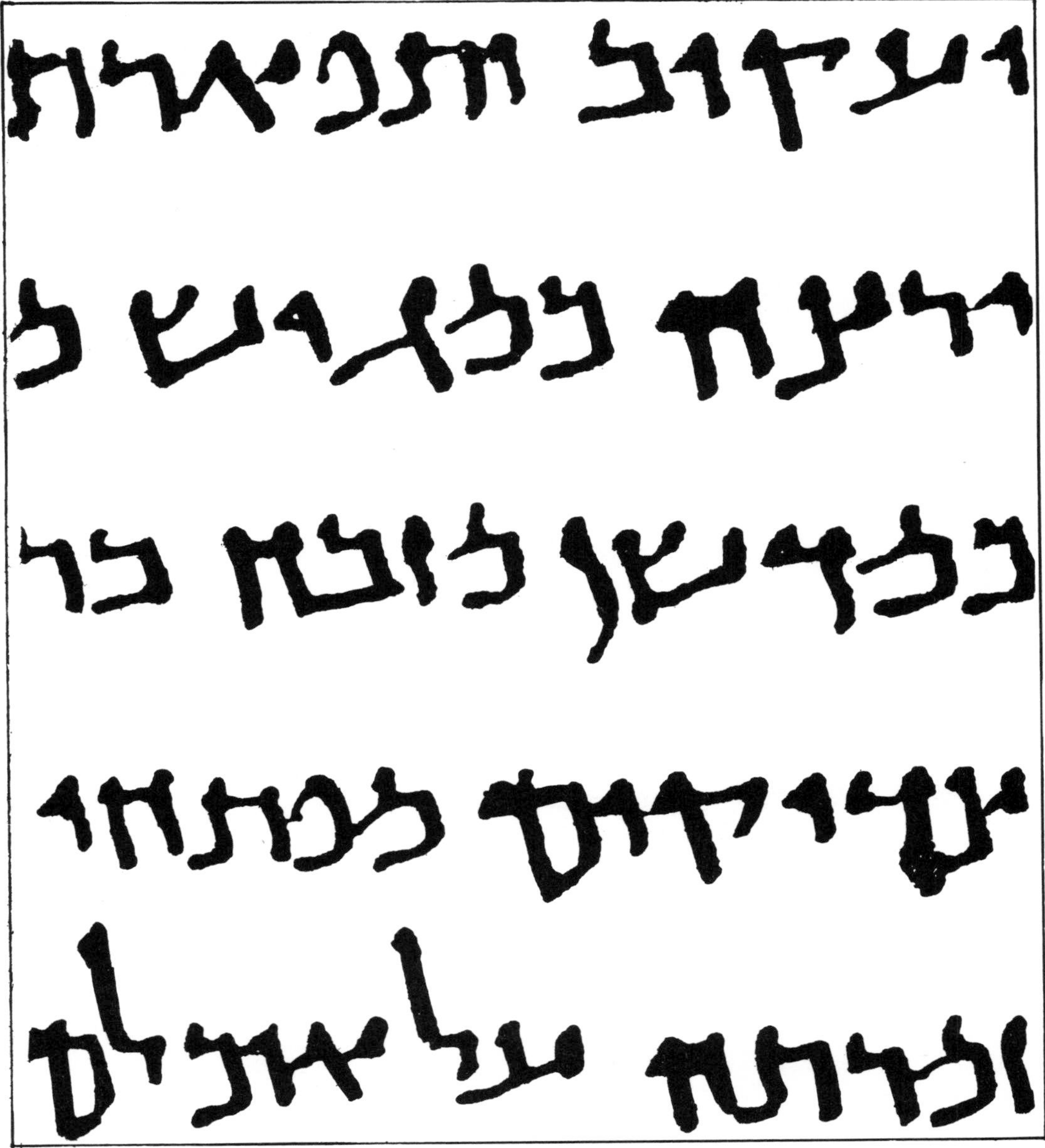

Fig. 176. Thick downstrokes and thin horizontal strokes in the Psalms scroll from Qumran (11QPs; the Herodian period)

flexible than the reed brush. This may have been the reason for the 'square' appearance of the Jewish script: i.e., the angular nature of the meeting-points between the strokes.

In the Herodian script many of the letters began to lean forward (fig. 175). This tendency increased in the Post-Herodian period. In some of the documents of the Herodian period the downstrokes of some letters are thicker than their 'roofs' (fig. 176).

The thickness of the strokes is the result of two main factors: 1) The way the writing implement is cut. A flat instrument cut at a right angle creates large differences in thickness between strokes drawn in different directions. 2) The angle that exists between the flat end of the instrument and the guideline. When using the right hand and holding a flat instrument at a sharp angle to the guideline, the thick strokes are those descending to the right.

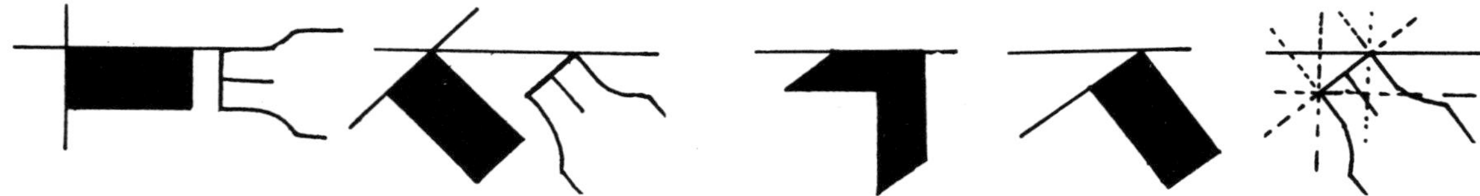

From about the 8th century onwards the 'roofs' and 'bases' of the Hebrew letters gradually became thick and almost horizontal, in contrast to the thin downstrokes. This feature dominated the 'square' Hebrew script until recent years.

When the hand, from the little finger to the wrist, is leaning on the writing surface, the movements of the fingers holding the writing implement are limited to stretching and contracting the fingers and to slight round movements of the hand.

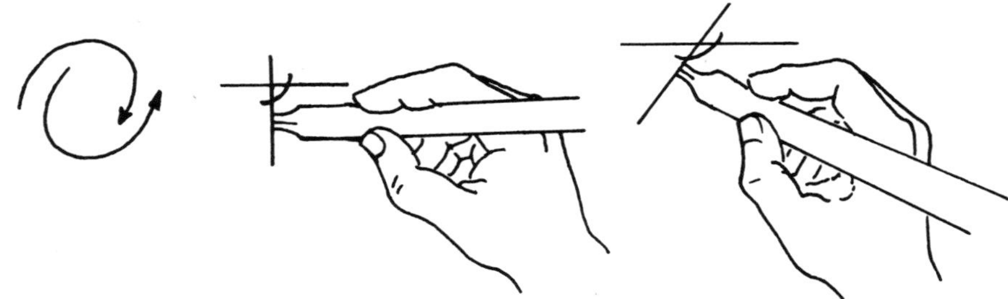

Fig. 177. Limited movements of the fingers stretching and contracting while the palm leans on its side, resting on the writing surface from the little finger to the wrist

When the hand is leaning on the upper phalanx of the little finger and on the outer bone of the wrist, the main movements may be concentrated in the top of the three fingers holding the instrument.

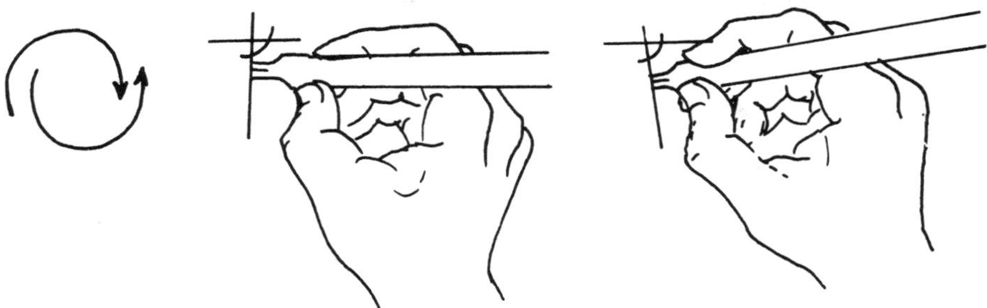

Fig. 178. Limited movements of the the fingers holding the writing implement (the thumb, the third and the index fingers) while the hand leans on the outer side of the wrist and on the distal phalanx of the little finger

The main directions of the strokes in square Hebrew writing with a flat implement may be described schematically, as in the following figure:

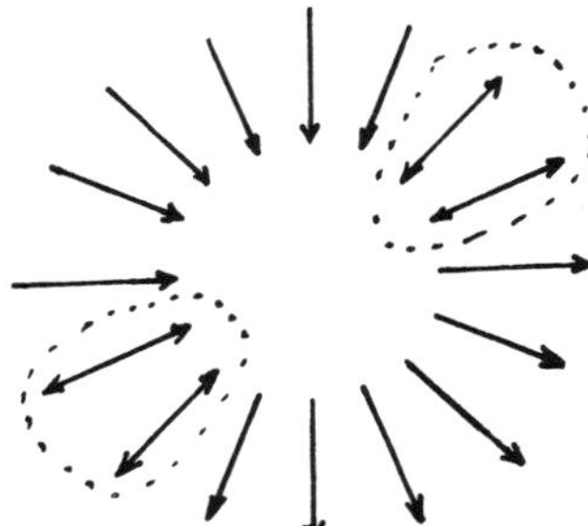

Fig. 179. The main directions of drawing the strokes in the Hebrew square letters with the flat end of the writing implement

Most of the strokes are drawn from left to right and from top to bottom, except for the oblique strokes descending to the left, which may be drawn in both directions. The rotation of the instrument for drawing strokes in various directions is facilitated by holding the writing implement in an erect position and increasing the pressure of the fingers on it. However, drawing strokes directly upwards or upwards to the left is difficult.

As letters are composed of a limited number of strokes, we may follow the development of each stroke in the individual letters of the different script-styles and determine the differences between those styles by the changes which occurred in the components of the letters (see above, chapter one). An examination of manuscripts of various periods in the square Hebrew script shows that toward the beginning of the 2nd millennium CE the letter-signs underwent considerable changes in the direction of the strokes and in their ornamental additions. In the early letters, the strokes were mostly drawn in three main directions: 1. The 'roofs' and 'bases' generally ascended to the right; 2. The downstrokes descended vertically or slanted to the right; 3. The diagonals descended to the left. The joints were simple. In the early Herodian period, independent ornamental additions developed and their number increased in the post-Herodian period, while the structure of the letters became more elaborate. In the later calligraphic square Hebrew script the number of the components in individual letters increased and the joints between the strokes became more elaborate. There were more wavy and curved strokes, as well as variations in the thickness of the strokes in individual letters. The joints were formed in various ways and various ornaments were added to the letters.

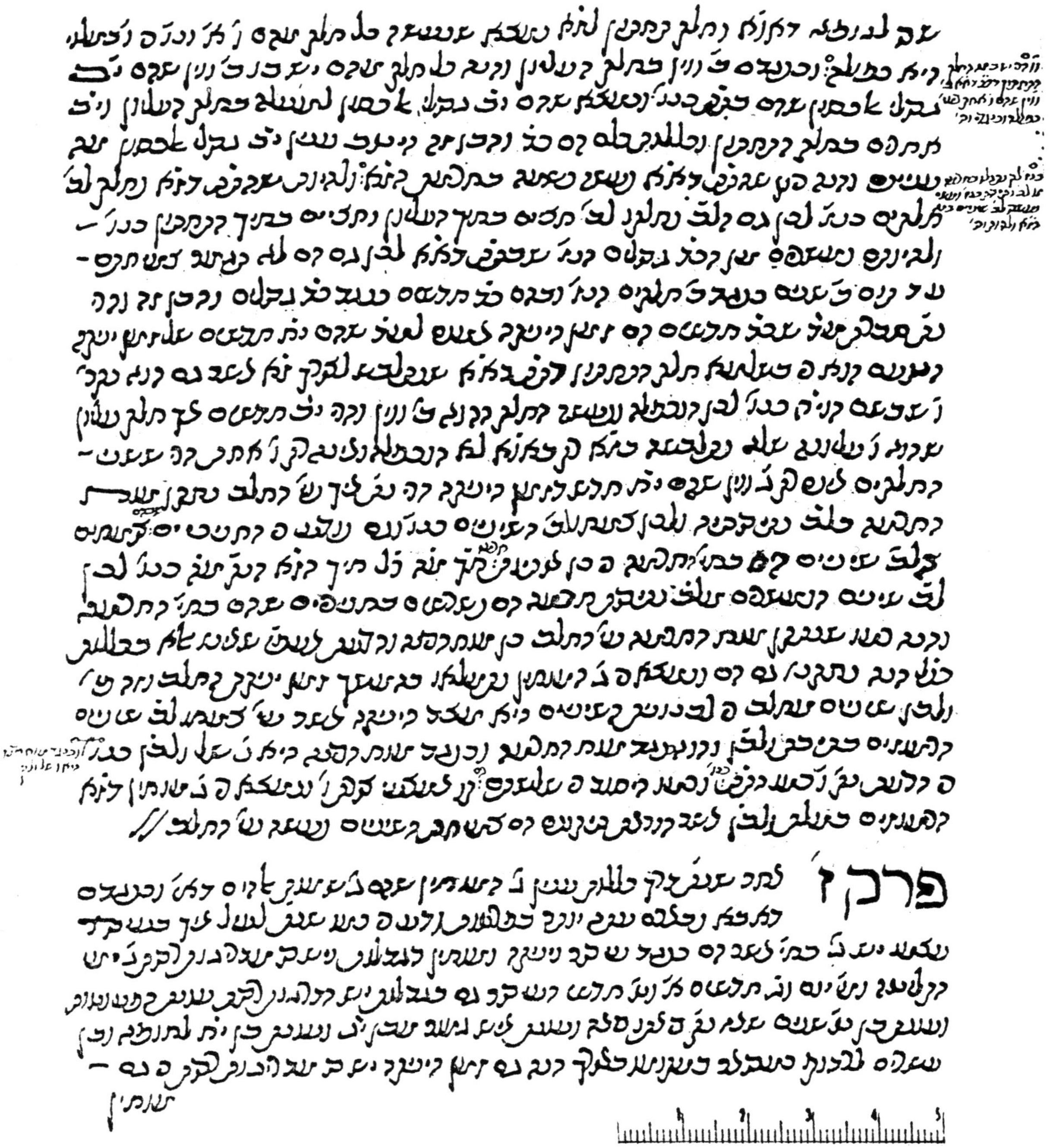

Fig. 180. A page of a manuscript in a late Sephardi semi-cursive script from North Africa, written 1761 in Marakesh (The Jewish National and University Library Jerusalem, 8º 1637, Fol. 113b. See a modern, cursive version of this script-style in chart 47)

Part 3

SCRIPT-STYLES AND SCRIPT CHARTS

In the long history of the Hebrew script, from about the 3rd century BCE until today, many changes occurred in the shapes of the letter-signs in different times and places. Among the many different forms, a number of script-styles may be discerned which differ from each other in the structure and ornamentation of the letters. These script-styles evolved as a result of various factors (see above, part 2). In this chapter, charts are shown of Hebrew script-styles of various periods accompanied by short descriptions of the main characteristics of each style.

1. THE EARLY JEWISH OR 'PRE-JEWISH' SCRIPT (CHARTS 1-2)

In Judea in about the late 3rd century BCE, a local script started to develop which differed in certain respects from the late Aramaic script used for a couple of centuries by the inhabitants of the region. The earliest documents in that script are biblical scroll fragments from Qumran (especially 4QSam^{b}, 4QJer^{a} and 4QEx^{f}; fig 51). In the early stages of its evolution, the Jewish script still greatly resembled the late Aramaic script found in documents of the 4th and 3rd centuries discovered in Egypt and Israel. Two major features are common to both scripts: 1. The relative size of the letters of the alphabet. 2. The calligraphic system: i.e., the use of a flat writing instrument causing differences in the thickness of the strokes drawn in different directions. The formal development of the letters is reflected, for example, in the straightening of curved strokes, resulting in the angular junctions which give the Jewish book-hand its square appearance. Another characteristic is the regularity of the writing, which is a result of the suspension of the letters on horizontal guidelines (not found in Aramaic documents written in ink).

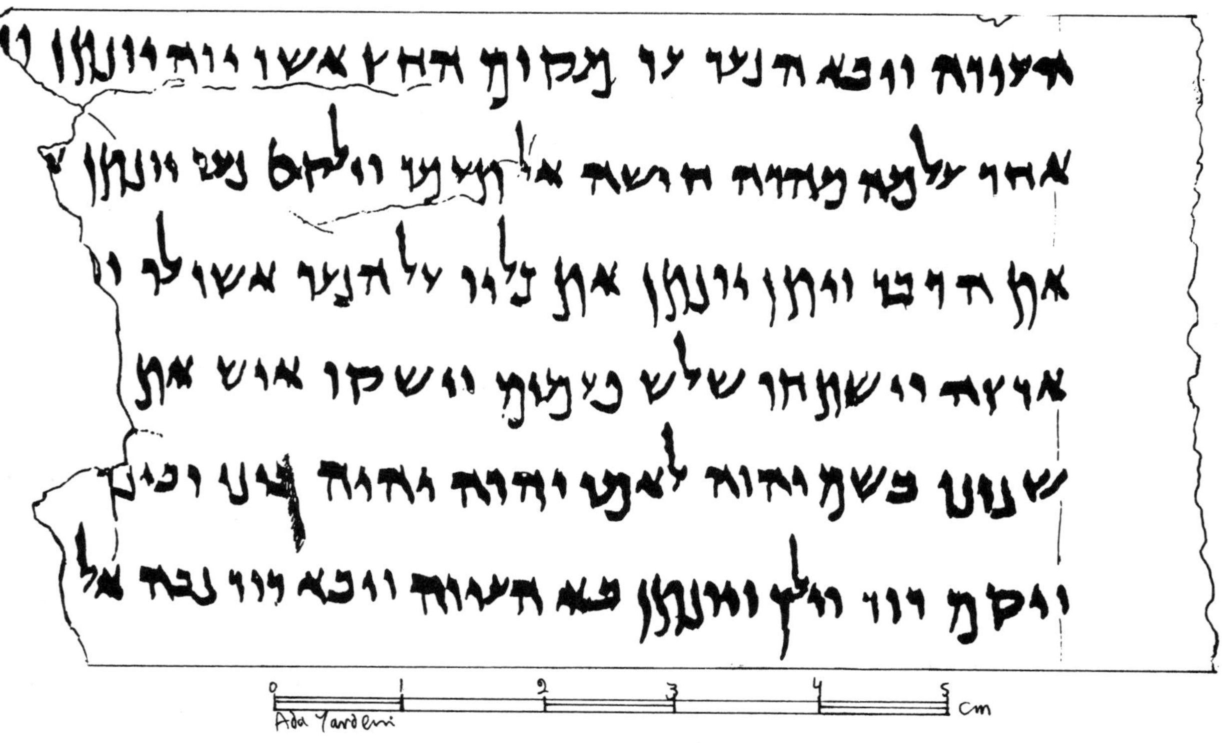

Fig. 181. Detail of 4QSam^{b} (enlarged)

Chart 1. The Proto-Jewish script of late 3rd century BCE: 4QSam^b

At this early stage of independent development, the letters of the Jewish script did not yet have ornamental additions, except for the inherited serifs in certain letters (Bet, Dalet, Kaf, Mem, Qof and Resh). At that period there is no evidence of a grouping of letters with similar graphic components; all the letters of the alphabet, with the exception of Dalet and Resh, differ from each other, so that each letter may be identified even if only remnants of it survive. The handwritings of the early scroll fragments from Qumran differ in their stylistic features which were inherited from different Aramaic script-styles. The scribe of 4QSam[b] used the official script-style found in 4th century Aramaic documents discovered in Israel (e.g. SP1; fig. 46), whereas the scribe of 4QJer[a] used a more cursive script-style, found, for example, in an Aramaic ostracon from Edfu (Aram. O 4; fig. 42). The calamus was apparently also cut differently. In 4QSam[b] a flat and relatively thick calamus was used, cut at a right angle, whereas the relatively thin calamus of 4QJer[a] was apparently cut obliquely. One should notice the very broad final Lamed appearing in both handwritings (in 4QJer[a] it appears regularly at the end of words). In 4QSam[b] there is a regular distinction between the medial and final forms of the letters Kaf, Mem, Nun, Pe and Ṣadi. In 4QJer[a] Ṣadi appears only in its medial form.

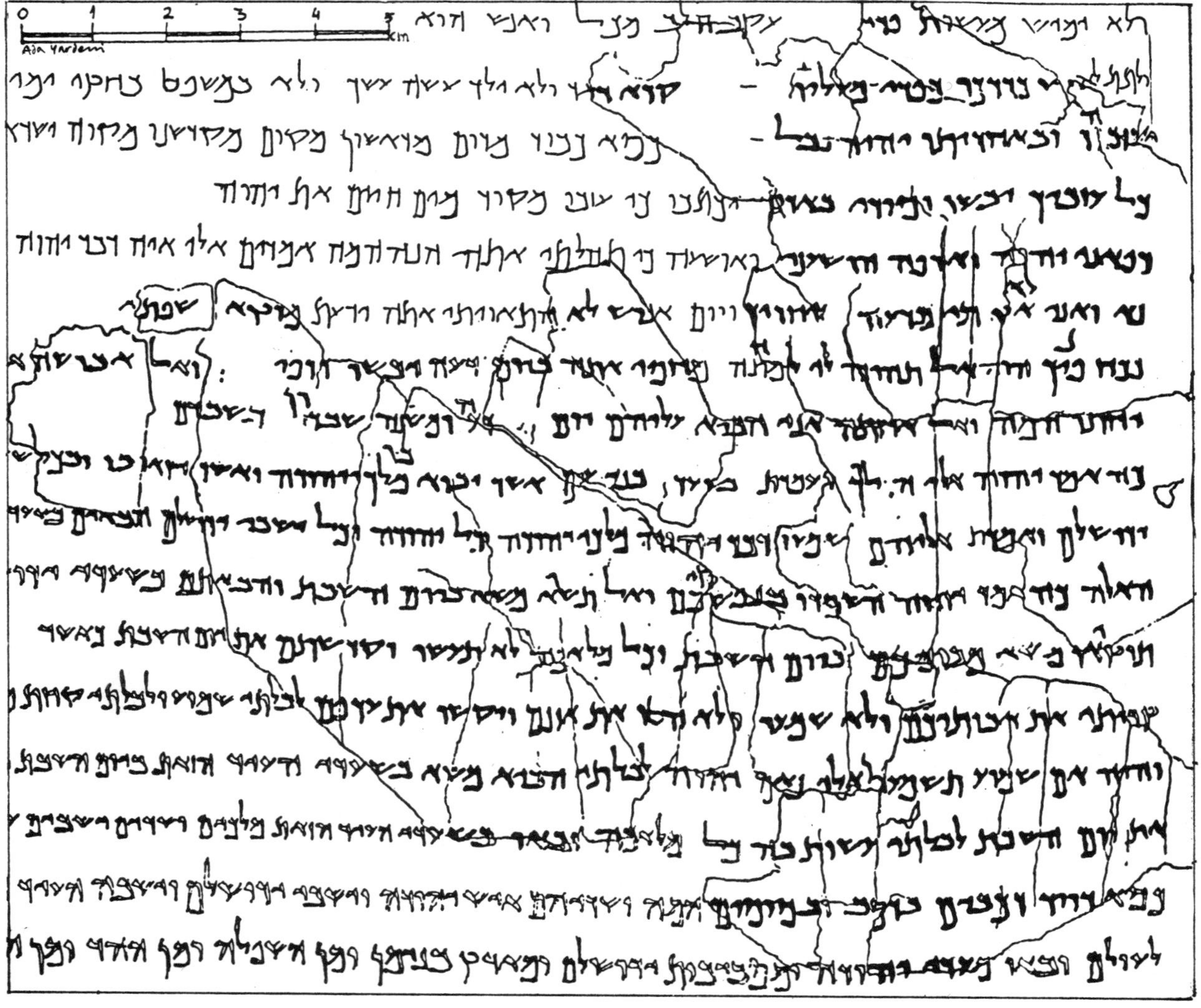

Fig. 182. Detail of 4QJer[a] (with text partly restored; real size)

Chart 2. The Proto-Jewish script of early 2nd century BCE: 4QJer[a]

2. A 'PRE-JEWISH' CURSIVE SCRIPT (CHART 3)

Fragments of an Exodus scroll from Qumran (fig. 51) are the only known examples of the cursive script used in the early stages of the evolution of the Jewish script. They date from approximately the late 3rd or early 2nd centuries BCE. The script on the fragments was damaged and the ink ate into the hide. In spite of this, it is possible to trace in them almost all the letter-forms of the alphabet (except Ṭet). The writing is irregular, and the individual letters are written with various degrees of fluency, although there are hardly any ligatures. It is difficult to define stylistic features in this script, and it is shown here only on account of its uniqueness.

These are some characteristics of the script in these fragments: there is no distinction between medial and final forms of the letters, and thus the system consists of 22 basic forms appearing in variant types and shapes. The inherited serifs of Bet, Dalet, Kaf, Qof and Resh are sometimes vertical and join the 'roofs' at a right angle.

These are some features of the individual letters: the downstroke of Dalet curves inwards. Waw and Yod are still distinguished from each other. Waw is composed of a downstroke and a short horizontal stroke which joins the downstroke below its top. Yod is relatively large, made with two strokes: a right stroke which slants downwards to the right and a left stroke which emerges from below the top of the right stroke and curves downwards to the left. Kaf has a broad 'roof' and a long downstroke curving to the left at its bottom. Mem appears in various degrees of cursiveness, occasionally without a base, usually at the end of words; its left stroke is mostly long while the inherited serif is indicated by the concave 'roof'. Samekh is open and Pe still has no 'nose'. Ṣadi appears in two main types – one with an angular right 'arm' that opens in an upwards direction and a wavy left downstroke; the other has a curved right 'arm' and the downstroke curves upwards at its bottom (both types are already to be found in the late Aramaic script). The most cursive letter-sign is Qof, which was made without lifting the calamus from the surface. Resh and Shin once appear with a ligature which prefigures the later cursive hands. Taw has a long, generally wavy left downstroke, occasionally bending to the left at its bottom, creating a short base-stroke. In general the order of the strokes resembles that in the book-hand.

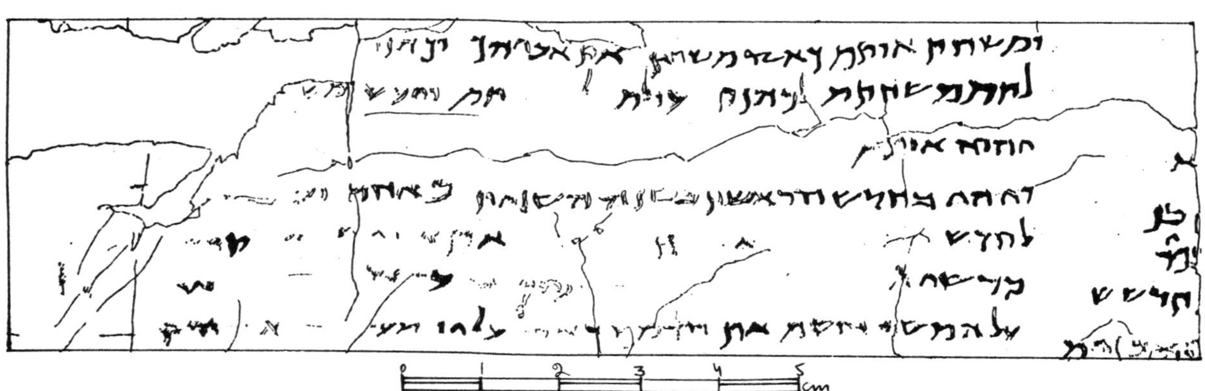

Fig. 183. Detail of 4QEx^{f} (real size)

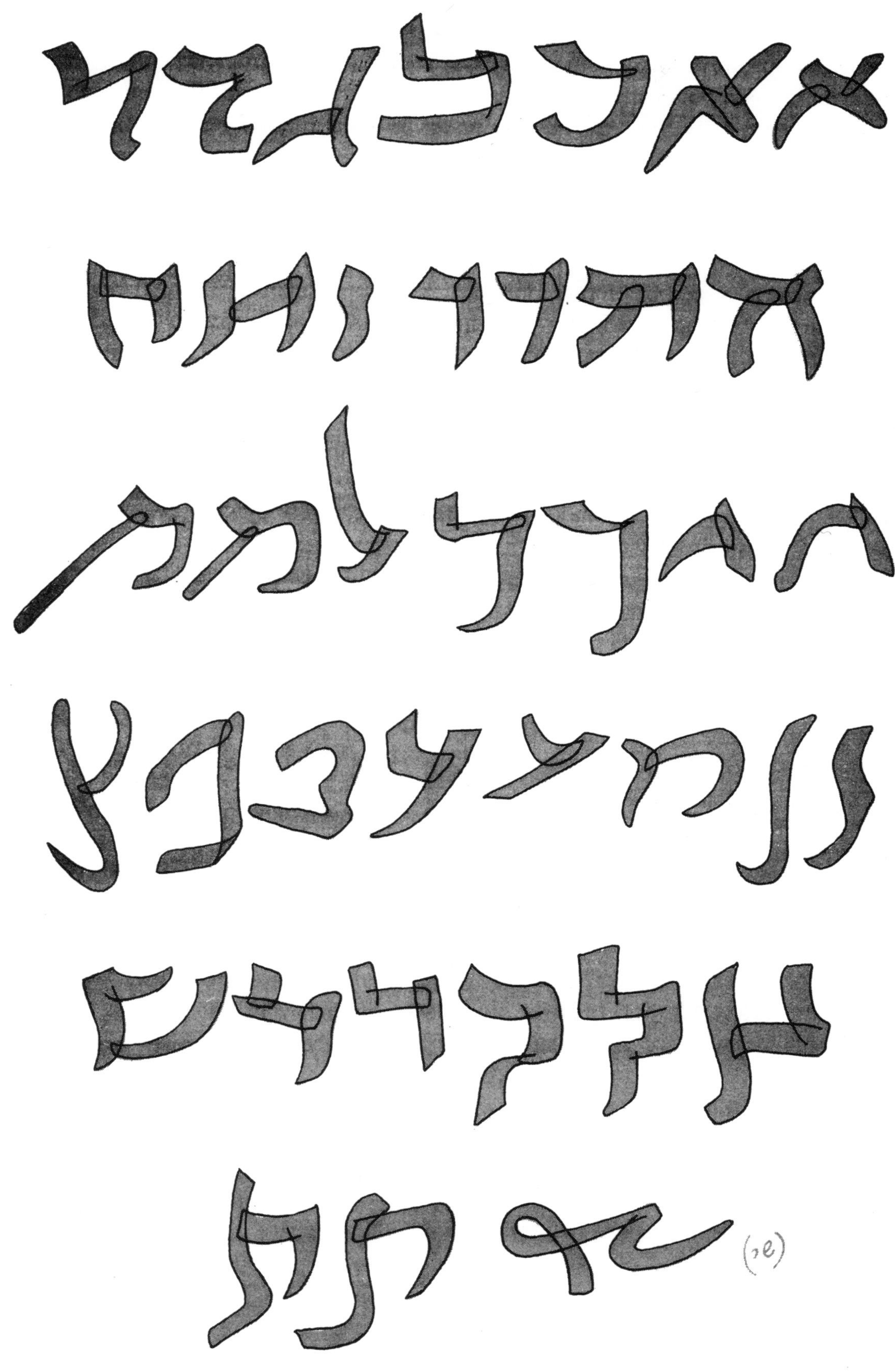

Chart 3. A pre-Jewish or early Jewish cursive script: 4QEx^{f}

3. THE EARLY HASMONEAN SCRIPT (CHART 4)

The Jewish script known from most of the Judean desert scrolls was crystallised in the second half of the 2nd century BCE. An Isaiah Scroll from Qumran (1QIsa[a]; fig. 53), representing an early stage in the crystallisation of the Jewish script, dates from that time: i.e., the Hasmonean period. It is written with a frayed calamus, all the letter-strokes being of almost the same thickness. Ornamental additions begin to appear, mainly in the form of vertical serifs (which, as we have seen, are inherited), in the letters Bet, Dalet, Kaf, Mem, Qof and Resh, as well as an additional stroke slanting downwards to the left on the left edge of He and occasionally of Taw and of final Mem. A large 'hook' curves downwards from the top of Lamed. The top of Gimel, Zayin, Nun and Ṣadi sometimes curves backwards, as the right downstroke of Dalet, Ḥet and Kaf also does occasionally. In 1QIsa[a] there is almost no distinction between medial and final forms of Kaf, Pe and Ṣadi, although that distinction already began to appear in the Aramaic script and is almost regular in the earlier 4QSam[b] and 4QJer[a]. This may be accounted for by a difference between scribal traditions or between levels of writing.

These are some major features of the letters in 1QIsa[a]: the letters Kaf, Mem, Nun, Pe and Ṣadi are still relatively long, extending below the imaginary base-line, while ʿAyin and Lamed are relatively short, ending above that imaginary line. The 'roofs' in Bet, Dalet, Ḥet, Kaf, Samekh and Resh are occasionally slanted or concave. Bet still has no 'tail' at the lower right corner. The 'base' of Kaf slants downwards to the left. Lamed has a very long 'hook'. Final Mem is very long; its 'roof' is emphasized and its 'base' extends beyond its meeting-point with the left downstroke, which occasionally terminates above the base. Samekh is open at its lower left corner. Qof is short and small. Taw has a high shoulder.

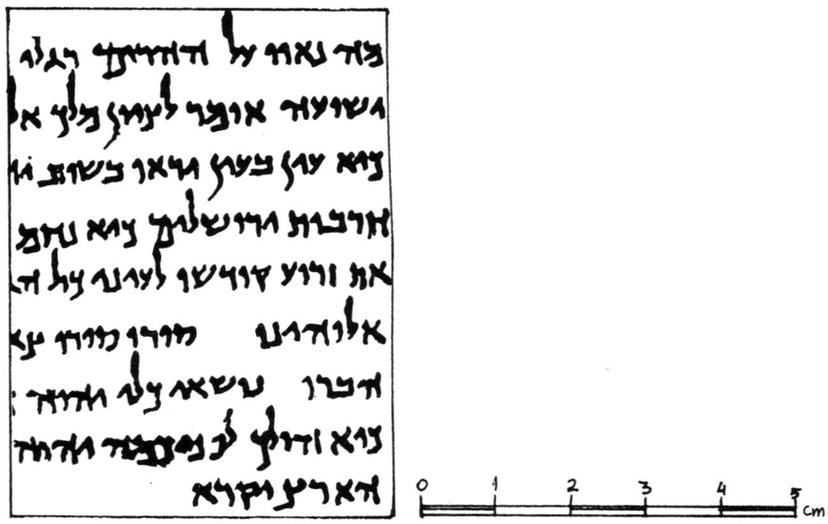

Fig. 184. Detail of 1QIsa[a] (real size)

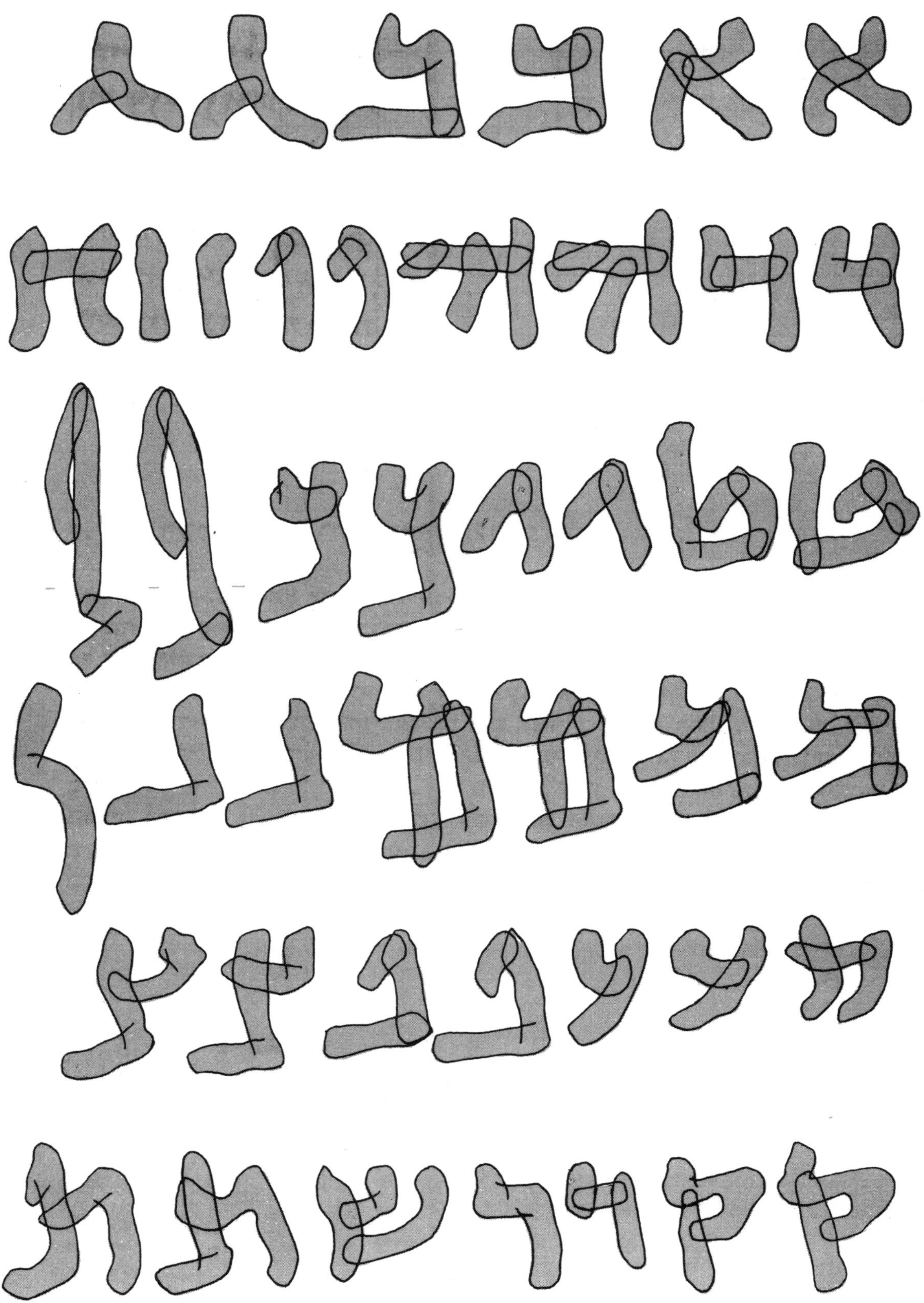

Chart 4. An early Hasmonean book-hand: 1QIsa[a]

4. A SEMI-CURSIVE MIXED HASMONEAN SCRIPT (CHART 5)

In the late 2nd century BCE, the Jewish cursive script-style had not yet been crystallised. Certain cursive forms of the late Aramaic script persisted in the Jewish script. Side by side with the elaboration of the Jewish book-hand, cursive letter-signs were used, which gradually evolved into a distinct script-style. The Jewish cursive script was not entirely stylized until about the 1st century CE. The Nash papyrus (fig. 52) represents an early stage in the evolution of the Jewish cursive script. On palaeographic grounds it may be dated to approximately the middle of the 2nd century BCE. Recently, a dated Idumean marriage contract on an ostracon written with Aramaic letters was discovered in Mareshah (fig. 48). Its date corresponds to the year 176 BCE. There is a similarity between many letter-forms in that ostracon and letters in the Nash papyrus, confirming the dating of the latter. These are the major cursive forms in the Nash papyrus related to those in the late Aramaic script: the 'looped' ʾAlef and Taw, the tripod-like He, the Ṭet resembling the numeral 6, the Yod made with a to-and-fro movement, and the Kaf resembling the numeral 3. There is a regular distinction between medial and final forms. There are no ornamental additions, except for the inherited serifs.

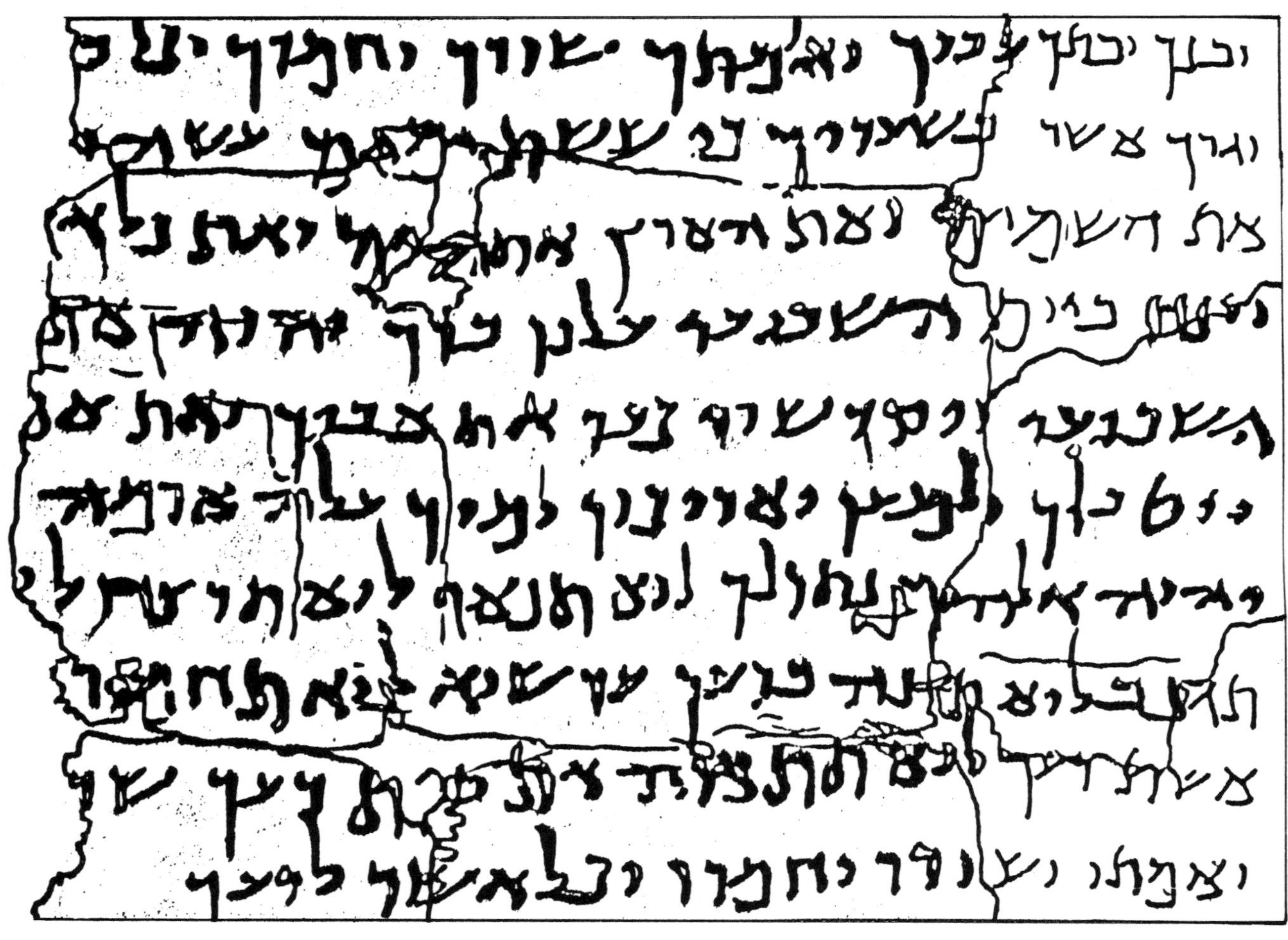

Fig. 185. Detail of the Nash Papyrus (enlarged)

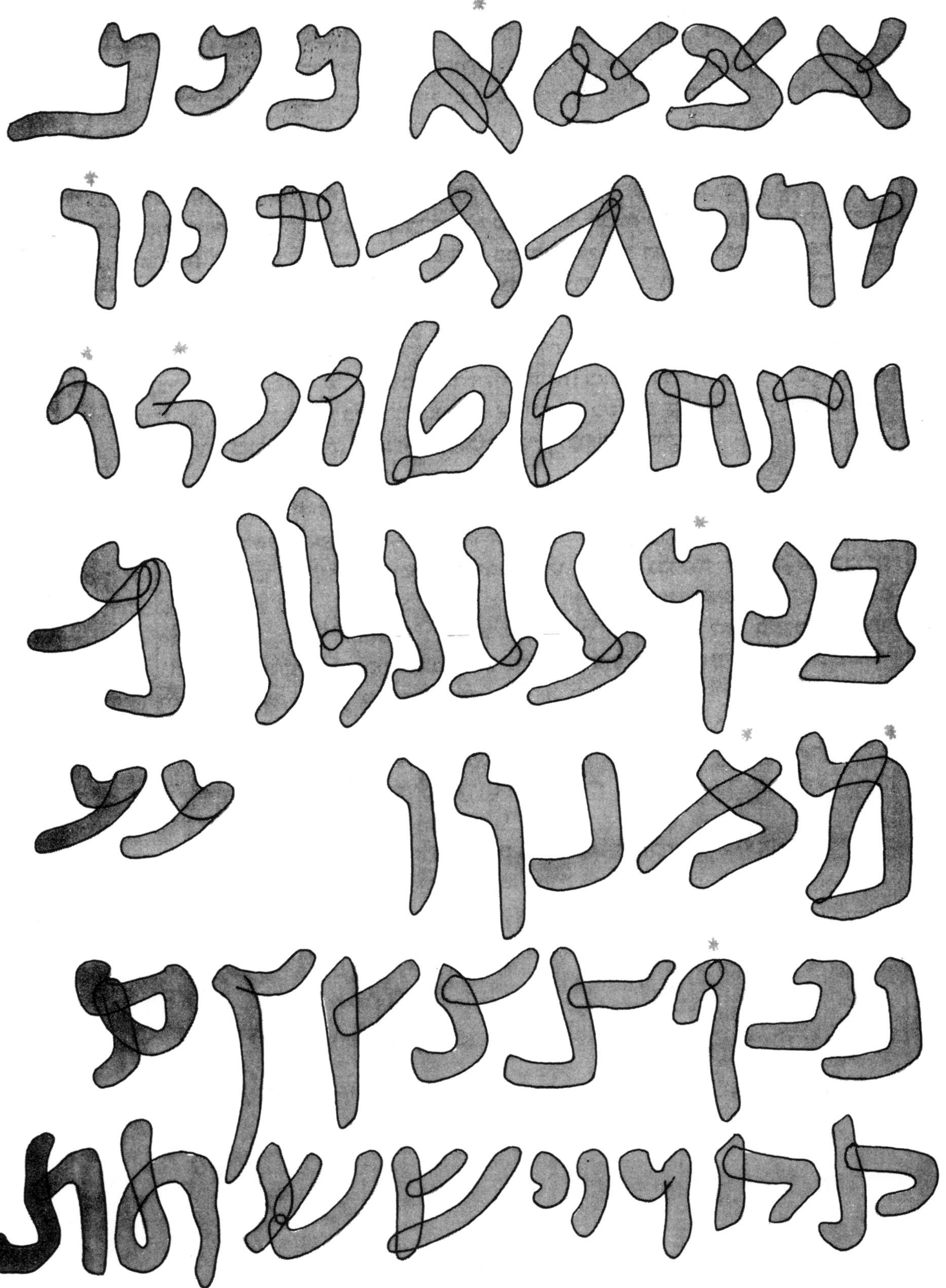

Chart 5. A mixed semi-cursive Hasmonean script: the Nash Papyrus

5. THE HERODIAN BOOK-HAND (CHARTS 6-7)

Not having any explicit dates, the Qumran scrolls are dated mainly through palaeographic criteria. Scholars discern three main phases in the evolution of the Jewish script: 1. The Hasmonean period (ca. 150-ca. 30 BCE); 2. The Herodian period (ca. 30 BCE-70 CE); 3. The post-Herodian period (ca. 70-135). The evolution of the Jewish script was in fact a continuous process, even though not all its stages are documented. The earlier Herodian book-hand is represented here by the War Scroll (fig. 186), whereas a later Herodian book-hand is exemplified by the Thanksgivings Scroll (fig. 187). A regular distinction between medial and final forms already exists in the early Herodian book-hand, and the medial letter-signs become somewhat shorter. The downstrokes generally slant downwards to the right while the 'roofs' usually slant upwards to the right but are still relatively small. The letters are often suspended on guidelines. During the Herodian period, the number of ornamental additions increased and groups of letter-signs with similar graphic elements came into being.

These are the main groups: ʾAlef and Ṣadi (medial and final forms) have an extra stroke at the right end of the right arm, later also appearing in ʿAyin and Shin. Bet, Dalet, Kaf, final Mem and Qof have a serif slanting downwards towards the left-hand extremity of their 'roof'. A horizontal base-stroke appears in Bet, Kaf, Mem (both medial and final), medial Nun, Pe, Ṣadi and Taw. Final Kaf, final Ṣadi and Qof have long vertical 'legs'. The left downstroke of He and Qof starts at the 'roof'. Waw and Yod, which became similar in their form, occasionally have a triangular loop to the left of their top. Zayin and Nun (and occasionally Gimel and Ṣadi) have a short additional stroke to the right of their top. The right arm of ʿAyin and Shin bends inwards.

These are the major features of individual letters: the left stroke of ʾAlef bends inwards. This part was later to become an independent stroke. In the later Herodian book-hand, the base-stroke of Bet extends beyond its

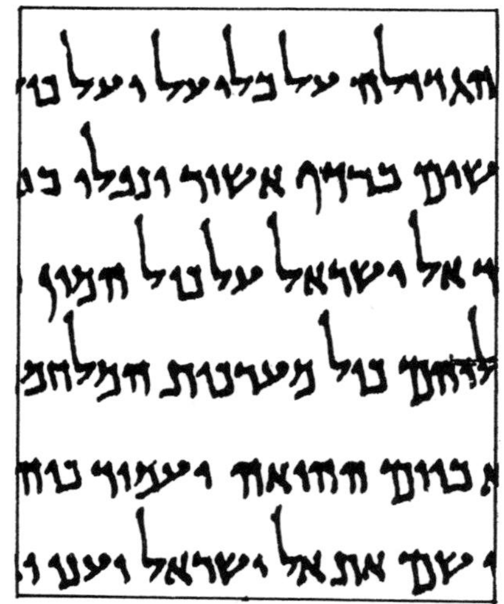

Fig. 186. Detail of the War Scroll from Qumran (real size)

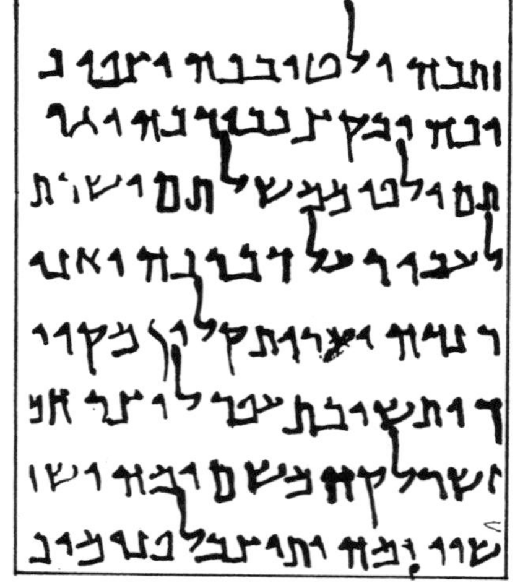

Fig. 187. Detail of the Thanksgivings Scroll from Qumran (real size)

Chart 6. An early Herodian book-hand: the Qumran War Scroll

meeting-point with the downstroke, thus forming a 'tail' in the lower right-hand corner. The downstroke of Dalet occasionally starts above the 'roof' (unlike that of Resh). He generally has a thick 'roof' made with two strokes. Ṭet gradually becomes broad, with a long base-stroke. The 'hook' of Lamed is usually short. The serif of medial Mem becomes an independent stroke. Final Mem occasionally has an additional short stroke at the centre of its 'roof' – the top of the left downstroke, which became an independent element. Final Nun is still represented by a wavy downstroke and final Pe is curved. ʿAyin gradually becomes larger.

Single letters on ostraca from Masada represent the late stage of the Herodian script (fig. 188).

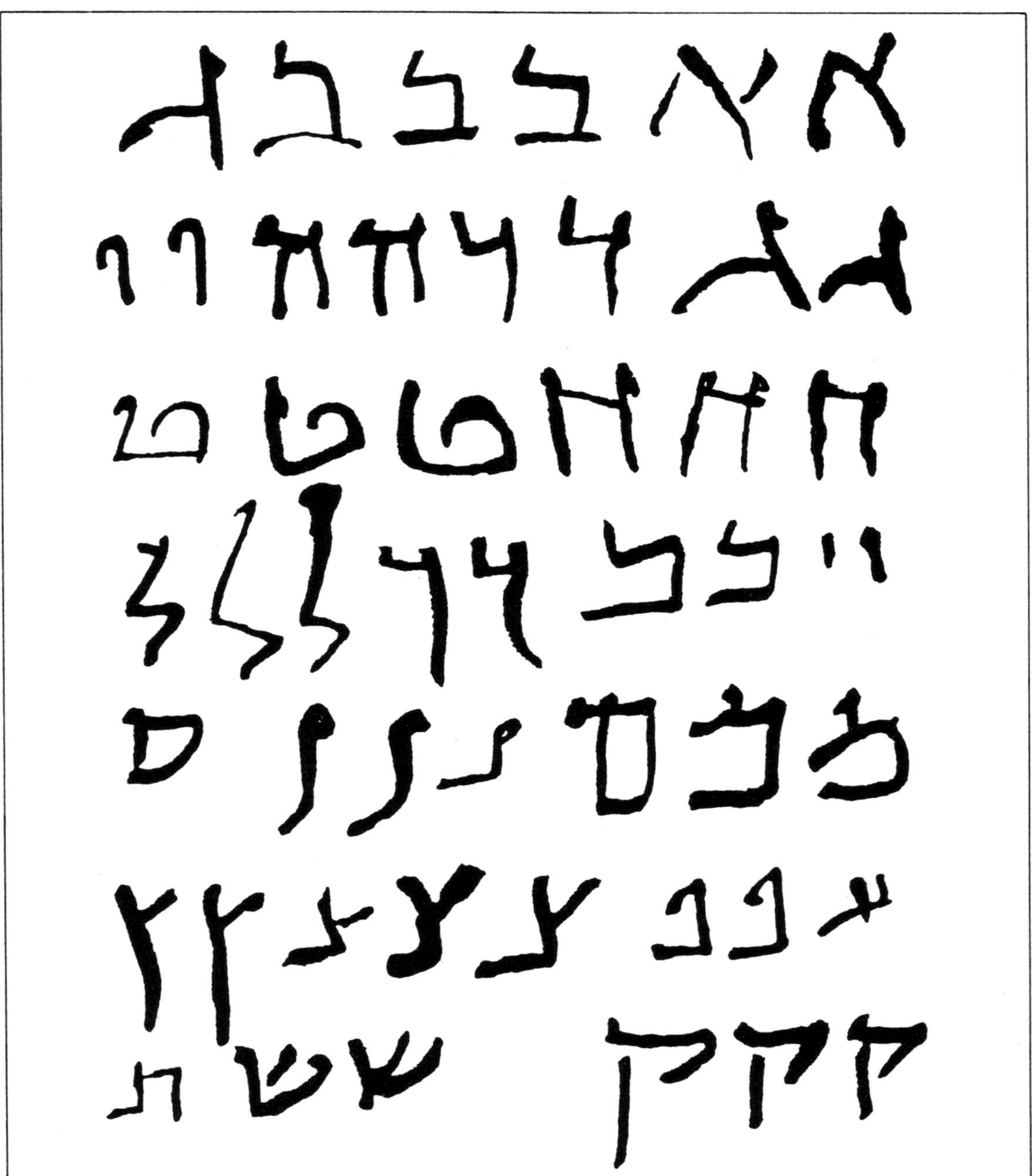

Fig. 188. Letters of the alphabet taken from clay 'notes' found in Masada (enlarged)

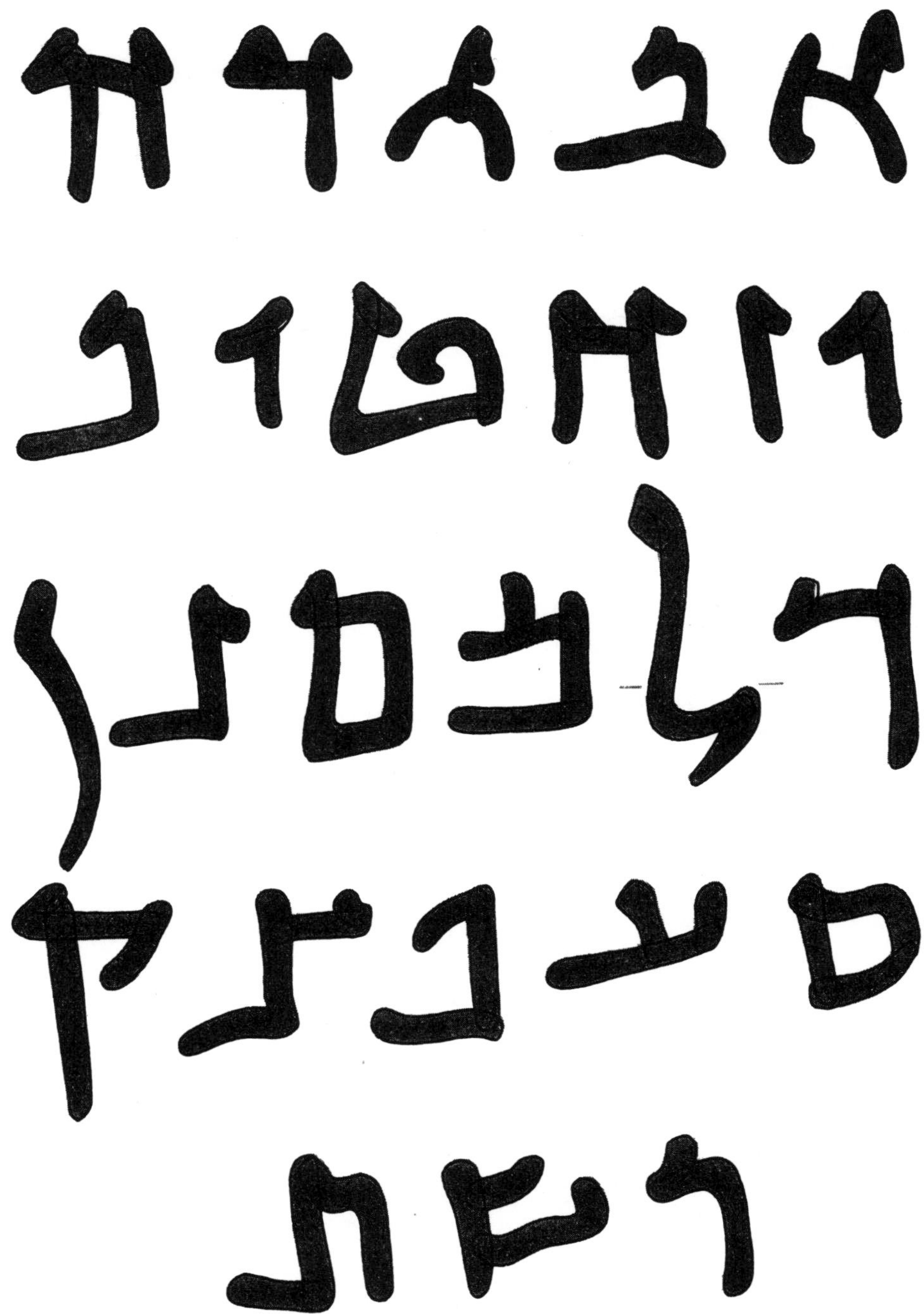

Chart 7. A late Herodian book-hand: the Qumran Thanksgivings scroll

6. THE 'LOOP MODE' IN HERODIAN OSSUARY INSCRIPTIONS (CHART 8)

Many of the ossuary inscriptions of the Herodian period were inscribed with a sharp instrument. The letters in these inscriptions appear in various degrees of elaboration. The main ornaments of the letters are triangular loops (fig. 189) which, in that fashionable script-style, replace the serifs and 'stings'. Although these ornamental elements often appear in contemporary inscriptions and manuscripts written in ink, they are emphasized in those ossuary inscriptions in which only the 'skeletons' of the letters appear. In Jewish literary sources of a later period dealing with scribal instructions for writing sacred texts, these letters are referred to as 'rolled' letters. The interpreters of these tractates in the Middle Ages and afterwards, trying to reconstruct the form of the letters on the basis of these descriptions but not possessing visual evidence of the early forms, created letter-forms which do not resemble the actual forms found in the ancient inscriptions and manuscripts.

We may observe some features of the script. The 'roofs' and 'bases' were usually drawn horizontally and the downstrokes were drawn vertically. The letters became wider and their height was evened out.

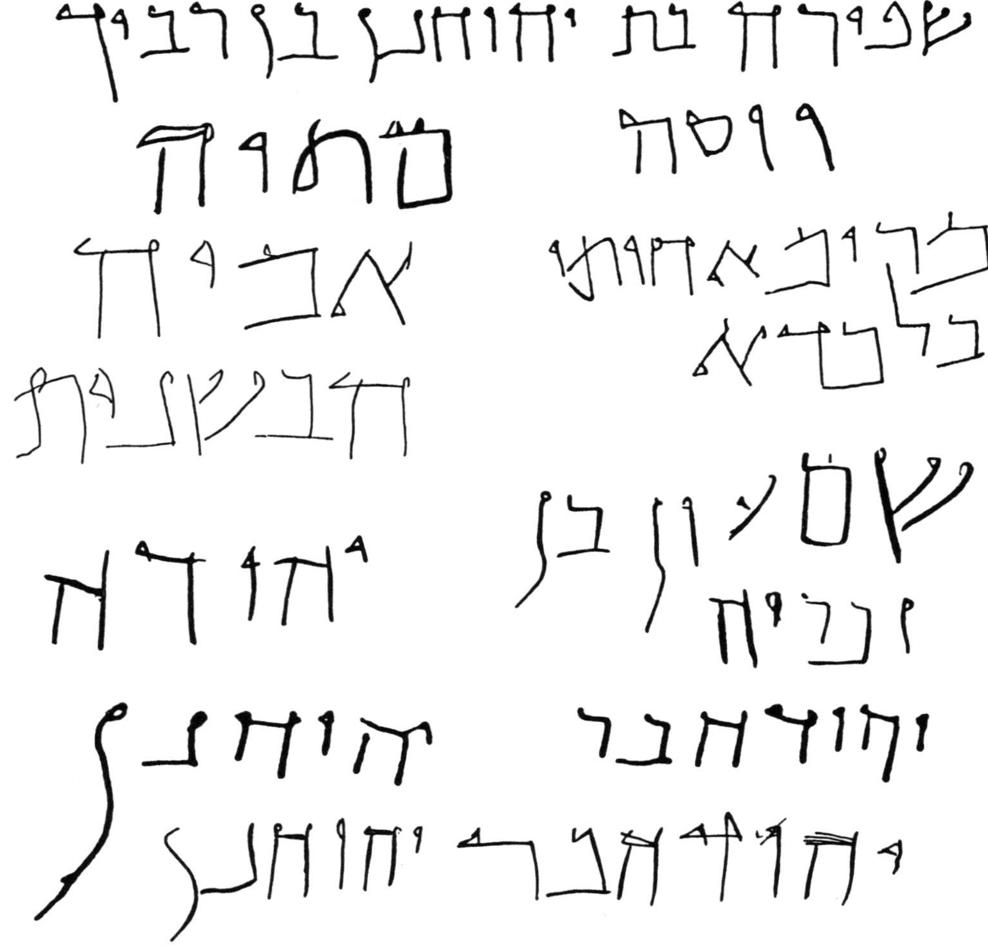

Fig. 189. Selected ossuary inscriptions from the Herodian period

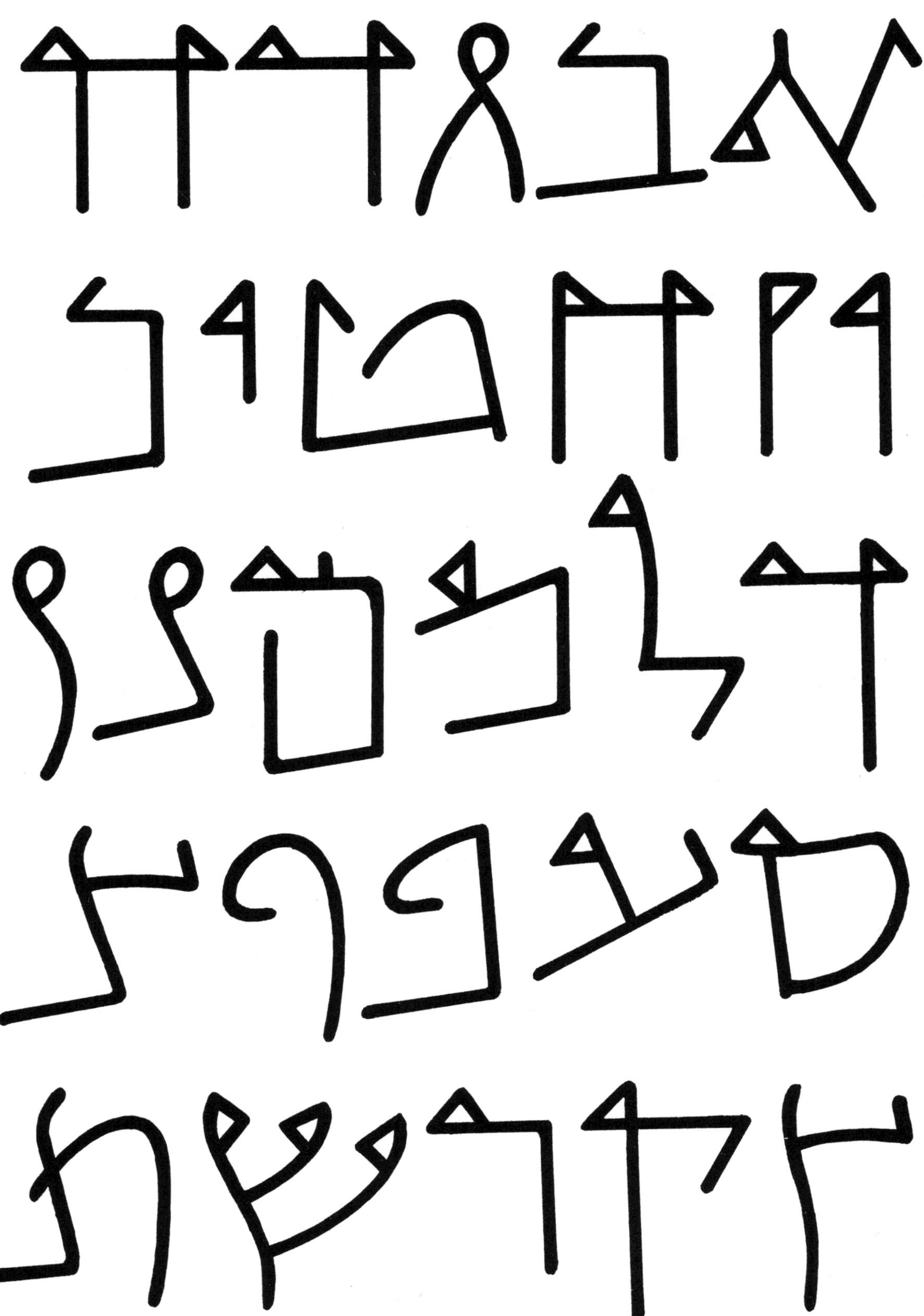

Chart 8. Stylized letter-forms based on the elaborate script of Herodian ossuary inscriptions

7. THE HERODIAN SEMI-CURSIVE SCRIPT (CHART 9)

In the early 1st century, the cursive Jewish script became stylized. Every script that is written rapidly tends to accelerate the process by reducing the number of hand movements as well as the number of interruptions between the individual strokes of the letter-signs. This tendency can sometimes cause the script to lose its clarity as a result of a distortion in the form of the letters. In extreme cases groups of letters become identical in form and the script is illegible. Each letter-sign usually has its own pace of formal evolution. If we compare the original forms and the extreme cursive forms, we see that the letters differ from each other in the number of stages of their formal evolution. Enoch^{g} from Qumran (4Q212; fig. 190) represents an early stage in the evolution of the Herodian cursive script-style (it is sometimes referred to as a semi-cursive hand).

These are some major features of this handwriting: ʾAlef still resembles the book-hand form of the letter made with three strokes. Bet has a convex base, drawn from left to right, occasionally meeting the downstroke above its bottom. Dalet and Resh as well as Waw and Yod, are clearly distinguished from each other. Ṭet is in an early stage of evolution towards its cursive form. Final Mem has a triangular shape while medial Mem is rounded. There is only a slight difference between the medial and final forms of Ṣadi. The right 'arms' of Shin curve in a concave manner towards the upper part of the left downstroke. The most cursive forms in this script are those of medial Mem, of Qof, which was often drawn without lifting the hand, and of the looped Taw.

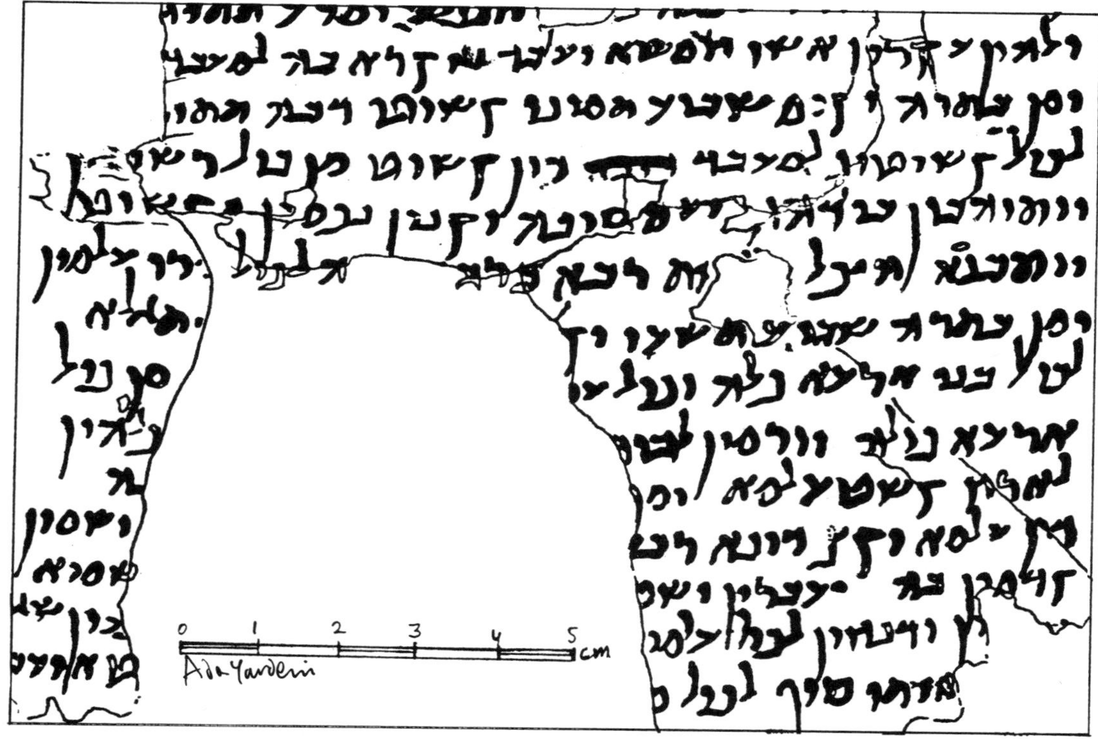

Fig. 190. Jewish semi-cursive script in the Enoch fragments from Qumran (En^{g}; 4Q212; real size)

Chart 9. A semi-cursive Herodian script: the Qumran Enoch^{g} manuscript (4Q212)

8. THE POST-HERODIAN BOOK-HAND (CHART 10)

Towards the end of the 1st century BCE, the post-Herodian book-hand was already an elaborate script-style characterized by its many ornaments and the even height of the letters (except for Lamed and the letters with long 'legs'). The scribal 'rules' for sacred writings appear to have been fixed at approximately that period. A few undated fragments of biblical scrolls in an elaborate Jewish book-hand of that period were discovered, including a small fragment of a Psalms scroll from Naḥal Ḥever (fig. 170), and fragments of a Genesis scroll and of an Exodus scroll from Wadi Murabbaʿat, both of which were written by one and the same scribe (fig. 191). A somewhat less elaborate book-hand appears in four deeds dating from the time of the Bar Kokhba revolt, three of them written by one scribe (NḤ 44-46) and the fourth (Mur. 24) written in a very similar script. The script represented here is that of the Genesis fragments from Wadi Murabbaʿat.

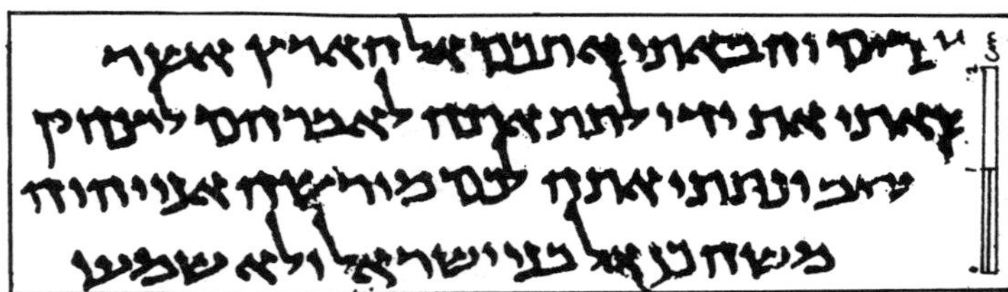

Fig. 191. Fragment of an Exodus scroll from Wadi Murabbaʿat (real size)

These are the main features of that script: the letters have become short and wide, in particular Shin and Ṭet (not represented here). The right downstrokes and most of the left ones slant downwards towards the right, while the 'roofs' and bases slant upwards to the right; thus the letters, except for ʾAlef, lean forward. Most of the letters are embellished with additional ornaments, and thus several groups of letters with similar ornaments may be discerned: ʾAlef and Ṣadi have a similar additional short stroke at the top of the right 'arm'. Bet, Dalet, Kaf, final Mem and Resh have an additional short stroke at the left end of the 'roof'. Dalet, He, Ḥet and final Kaf have an additional short stroke slanting downwards to the right towards the top of the right downstroke. Gimel, Zayin and Nun (as well as the left downstroke of Ṭet) have an additional short stroke slanting downwards from their top to the right. Waw and Yod have an additional stroke slanting downwards from their top to the left. A similar additional stroke or a triangular loop appears at the top of the left downstroke of ʿAyin, Ṣadi, Shin and Lamed. A triangular 'loop' also occasionally appears to the left of the 'horn' of medial Mem. The upper part of the right 'arm' of ʿAyin and of Shin bends inwards.

In addition to these groups, we may list some major characteristics of individual letters: the diagonal of ʾAlef starts below the top of the left stroke. The right downstroke of Bet starts above its meeting-point with the 'roof'. The letter He occasionally has an additional short stroke slanting leftwards at the left end of its 'roof'. The left stroke of medial Pe curves inwards while in final Pe it bends inwards in an angle. The additional ornaments at the left ends of the 'roofs' contribute to the balance of the letters which lean forwards. From that period onwards the ornamental additions were retained in various styles of the Hebrew book-hand.

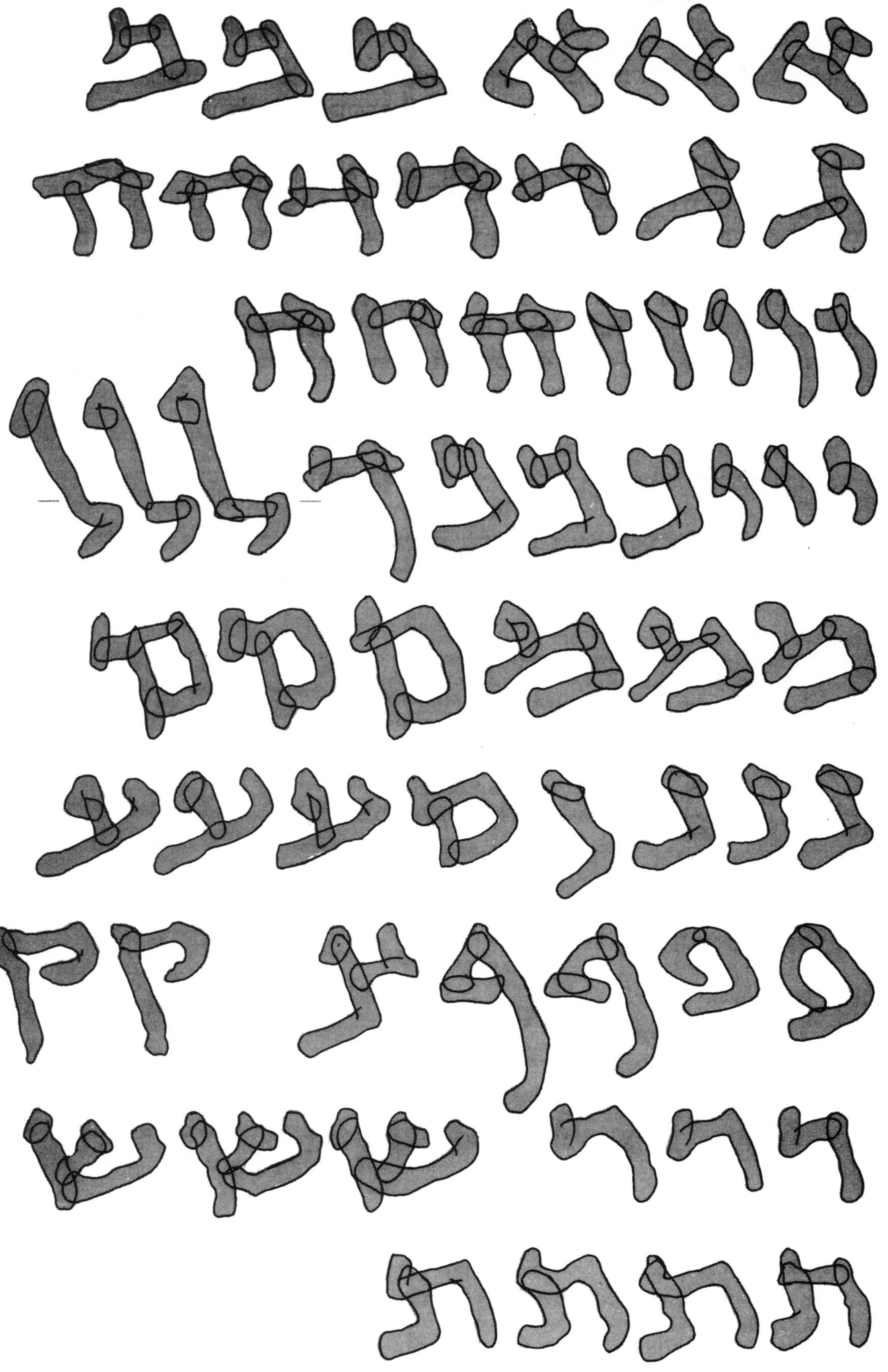

Chart 10. A post-Herodian book-hand: the Wadi Murabbaʿat Genesis fragments

9. THE POST-HERODIAN CURSIVE SCRIPT (CHARTS 11-12)

Fluent writing is one of the main factors that cause changes in the form of the letters in every script-style. This is a continuous process of evolution which creates new forms of the letter-signs and occasionally new script-styles. The Jewish cursive script is thus characterized by a large variety of letter-forms, the number of which constantly increased during the time of its existence, reaching its peak in the early 2nd century. Among the finds from the post-Herodian period, ending with the Bar Kokhba revolt, there are many documents in cursive script written by various hands which differ in the degree of fluency and personal characteristics of the writers. Despite the differences, however, these handwritings belong to a common script-style. The official documents written in that cursive script show that it was not only used for private purposes. Some of the differences between certain groups of handwritings are perhaps due to different scribal schools or traditions. These differences have not been defined so far because of the relatively small number of documents surviving from that period, and consequently the handwritings represented here do not reflect the variety of the cursive letter-forms. The deed of a gift from Naḥal Ḥever dating from the year 120 (fig. 192) represents only one of many cursive hands. It is a double document in which the text appears twice. The upper version is written in a small cursive script and the lower in a larger script; however, the forms of the letters in both versions are similar. In order to demonstrate the relationship between this cursive script and the Jewish book-hand, we will give a short description of the main stages in the evolution of certain letter-signs.

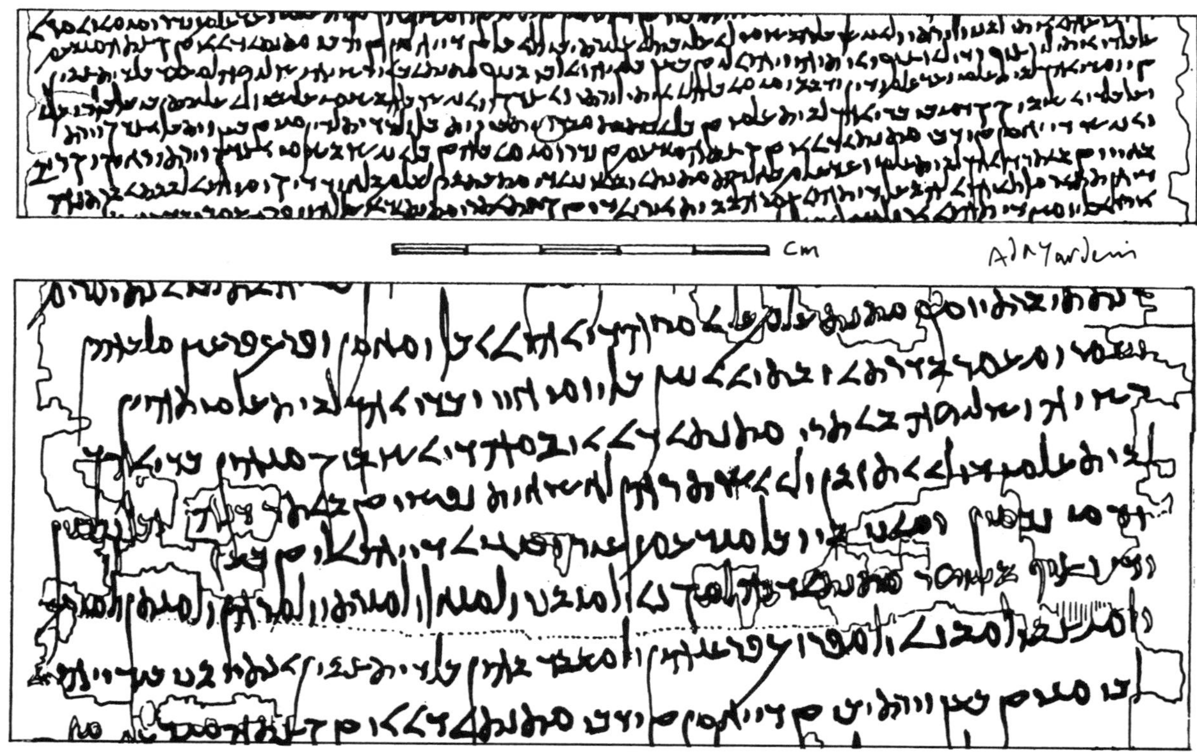

Fig. 192. Details of the upper and lower versions of a deed of gift from Naḥal Ḥever (NḤ 7; 120 CE; real size)

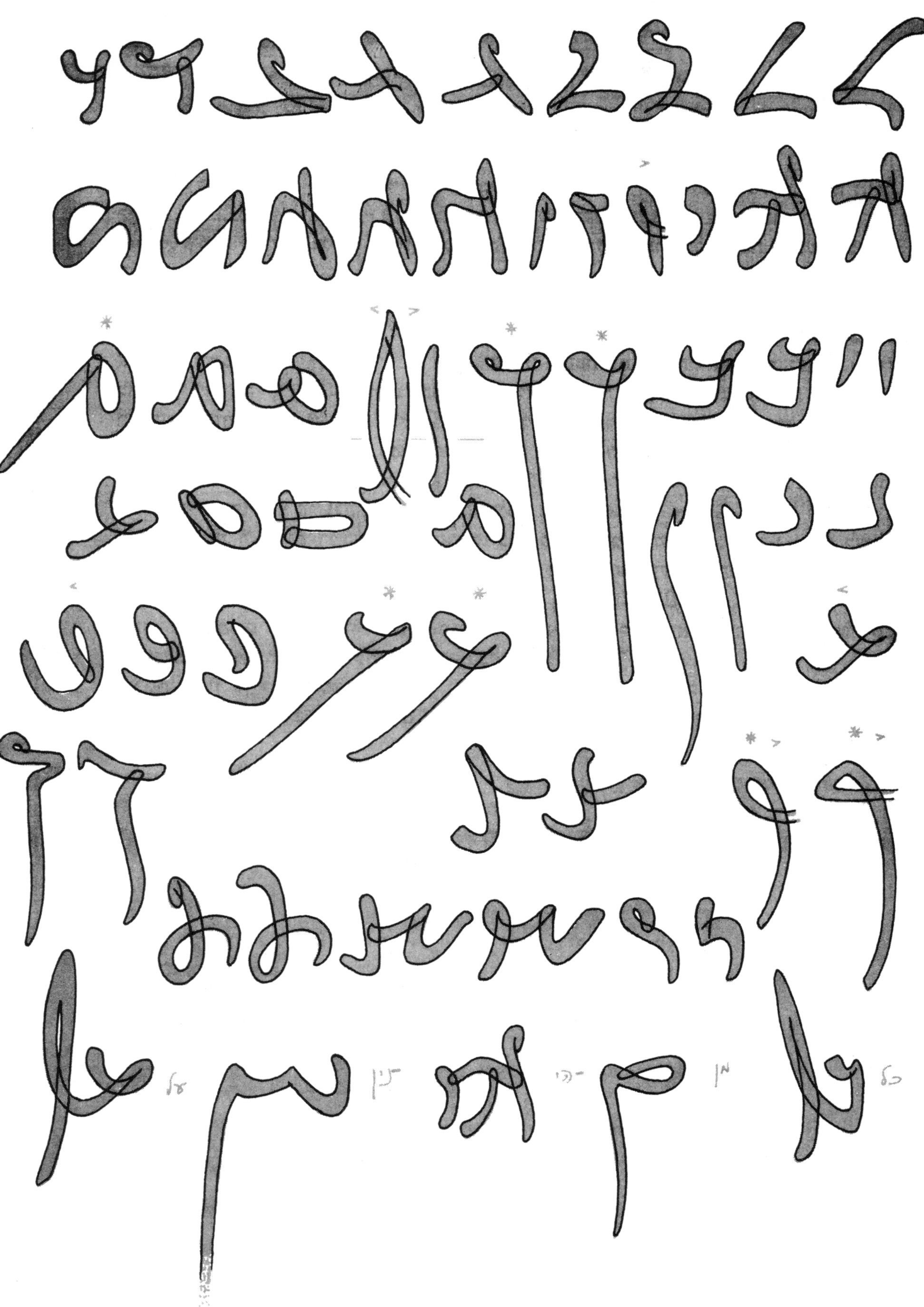

Chart 11. A post-Herodian cursive script: the deed gift from Naḥal Ḥever (NḤ 7)

An ᵓAlef written with two strokes already appears in certain Aramaic handwritings. However, there is no evidence of the existence of similar forms of ᵓAlef in the Jewish script before the Herodian period. Consequently no direct relationship can be shown between the Jewish and Aramaic forms of the two-stroke ᵓAlef. Another late Aramaic form, the looped ᵓAlef, evolved into one of the forms of the two-stroke ᵓAlef in the Jewish script – a form that usually appears at the beginning or in the middle of a word.

The final form apparently evolved from another type of ᵓAlef, in which the left stroke shortened until it vanished.

The cursive Bet evolved from the form with a 'base' that was drawn from left to right and extended beyond its meeting-point with the downstroke. The extreme cursive form without a 'tail' already appears in the Aramaic script.

The cursive Gimel evolved when its two strokes were drawn without lifting the hand.

Dalet was made with two strokes or with one stroke like Resh. In extreme cursive writing it occasionally resembles Waw or Yod.

He was drawn with three or two strokes.

The cursive Waw and Yod became a short downstroke drawn in various directions.

Zayin was occasionally written with its top bent backwards.

The cursive Ḥet evolved when its three strokes were drawn without lifting the hand.

Ṭet developed various cursive forms when its base-stroke joined the left edge of the right curve.

One of the cursive forms of Kaf resembles Bet with the 'base' drawn beyond its meeting-point with the downstroke. The extreme cursive form of Kaf is a short downstroke resembling the extreme cursive form of Bet, Nun, ᶜAyin, Waw, Yod and Zayin.

Lamed became a long downstroke (as was already to be found in the Aramaic script).

Mem was one of the letter-signs which developed a cursive form at an early stage of its evolution. Already in early scroll fragments from Qumran (4QEx^f) the letter was short and rounded. Cursive forms of Mem are found in the Hasmonean period. The stages of its evolution may be reconstructed as follows:

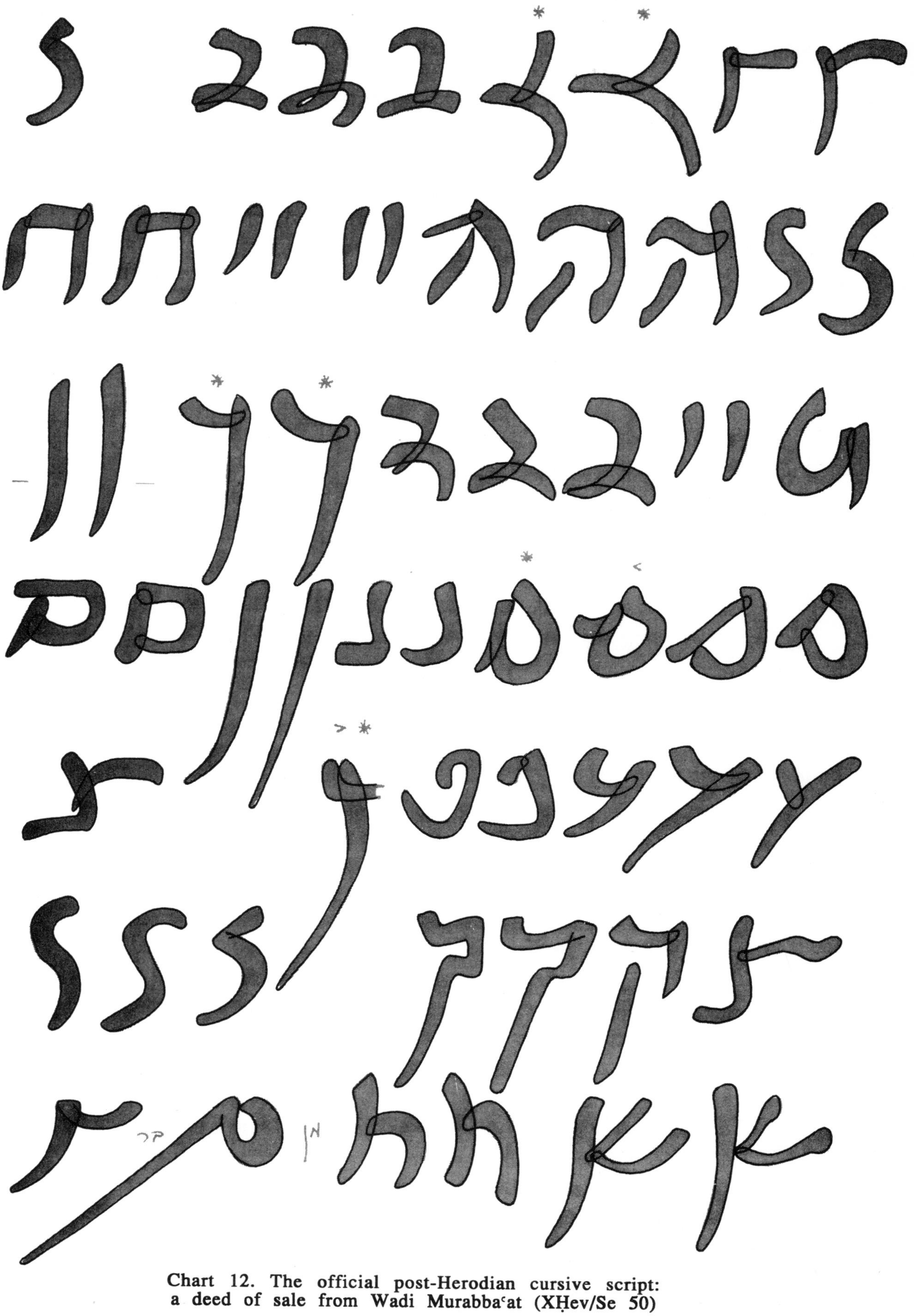

Chart 12. The official post-Herodian cursive script: a deed of sale from Wadi Murabbaʿat (XḤev/Se 50)

A unique, triangular form of Mem appears generally in a final position in the early Herodian period:

It is not found in the post-Herodian period. The final Mem of that period resembles the medial form, but its left stroke is occasionally longer.

The top of the cursive Nun sometimes bends backwards, while the extreme cursive form of Nun is a short downstroke shaped like a comma.

The final Nun is a wavy or straight downstroke which grew longer in the course of time.

Samekh became a closed letter during the second half of the Hasmonean period. The cursive Samekh occasionally resembles the cursive Mem but it usually has a horizontal 'roof' and a vertical left downstroke.

Extreme cursive forms of ʿAyin, usually seen in ligatures, appear as small downstrokes curving leftwards at their bottom.

The cursive Pe occasionally appears without its characteristic 'nose'. A rare form of the cursive Pe resembles the cursive Bet with a base-stroke drawn from left to right which continues beyond its meeting-point with the downstroke.

(2)

The cursive Ṣadi was occasionally written without lifting the hand between its two strokes. Extreme cursive forms of Ṣadi may be identified by their horizontal right 'arm'.

In the extreme cursive form of Qof all strokes were drawn continuously without lifting the hand; occasionally only the 'roof' and 'leg' remained.

The evolution of the cursive Resh resembles that of Dalet.

The cursive Shin appears in a variety of forms and postures. It was usually made with three basic strokes, sometimes drawn without lifting the hand. In the Herodian and post-Herodian periods there are extreme cursive forms, made with two strokes, occasionally resembling a cursive ʾAlef.

The evolution of the cursive Taw already began in the Aramaic script when both its strokes were drawn continuously, without lifting the hand, starting with the left stroke and creating a loop.

In the cursive Jewish hands there are many ligatures of entire words or of two or more successive letters. The words *br* (son of), *kl* (all), *ksp* (silver), *mn* (from), *ʿl* (on), and *zwzyn* (a monetary unit) often appear as ligatures.

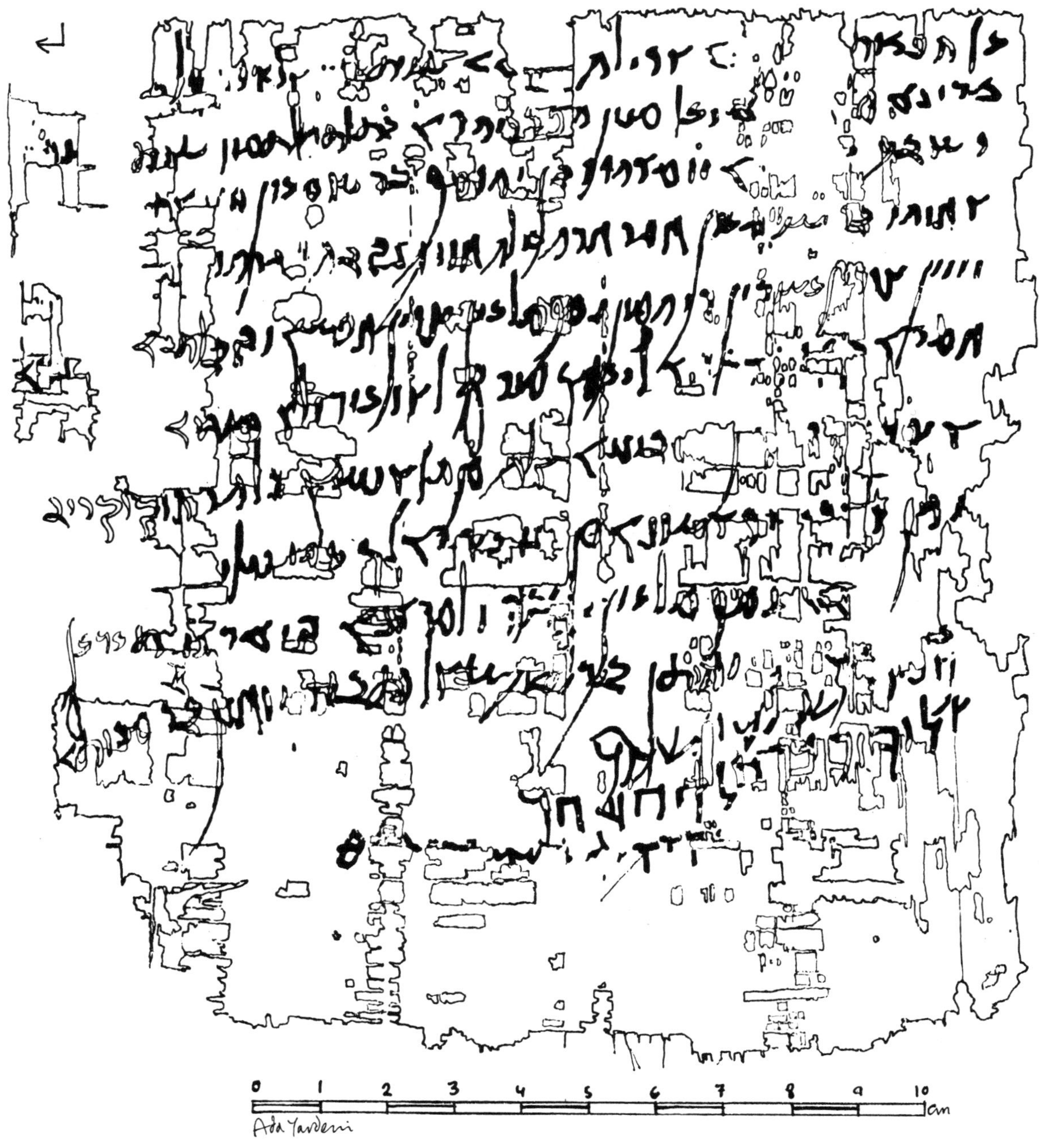

Fig. 193. The Jewish cursive script in a papyrus deed of sale from Naḥal Ḥever (NḤ 8), dating from Tamuz 3, 122 CE

10. THE POST-HERODIAN EXTREME CURSIVE SCRIPT (CHART 13)

The extreme Jewish cursive script reached its peak in the post-Herodian period. Almost all the documents in the Jewish extreme cursive hands found so far have been deciphered, although some of them only partially. This script is represented here by a Hebrew double deed from Wadi Murabbaʿat dating from the year 135 (Mur. 30; figs. 60, 194). The letter-signs in the chart were taken from the lower part of the document and represent only a small number of the many variants appearing in that document (the upper part is even more cursive and includes a large number of ligatures, the individual letters often being hard to distinguish).

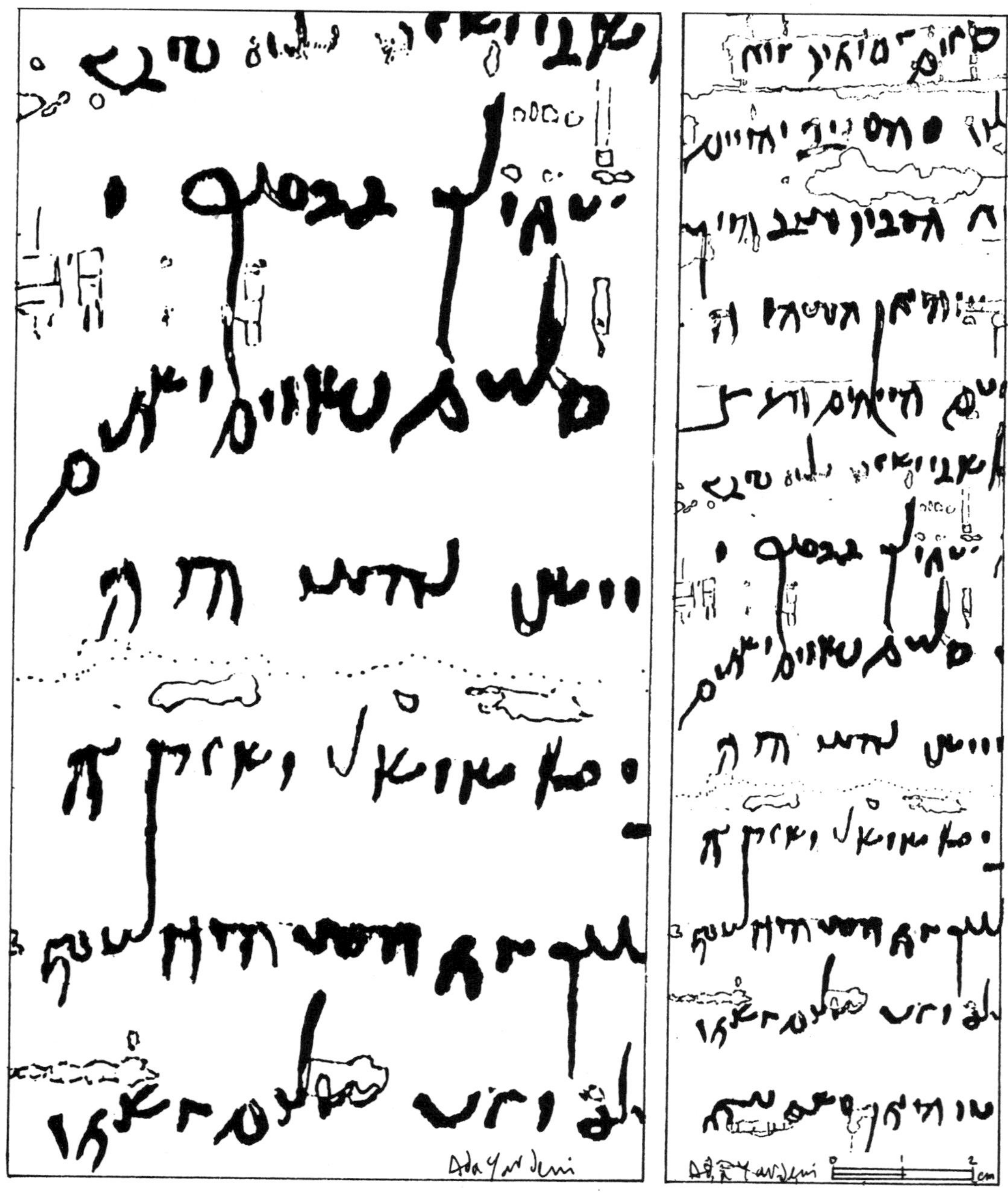

Fig. 194. Details of a Hebrew deed of sale from Wadi Murabbaʿat (Mur. 30; 135 CE) in an extreme cursive hand. Right: real size. Left: enlarged

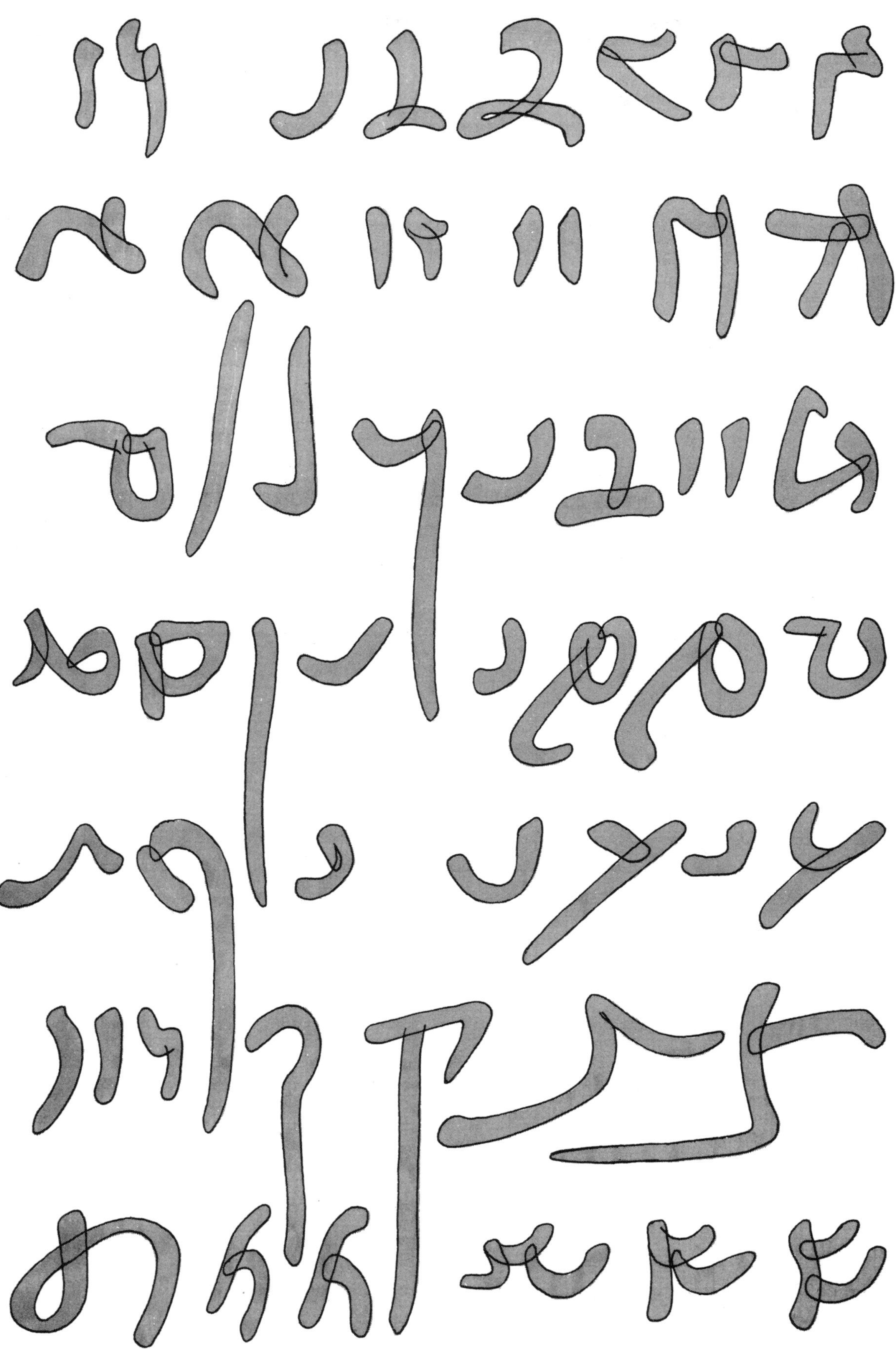

Chart 13. A post-Herodian extreme cursive script: a deed of sale from Wadi Murabbaʿat (Mur. 30)

11. A SEMI-CURSIVE SCRIPT OF THE LATE 2ND OR EARLY 3RD CENTURY (CHART 14)

There is no evidence of the survival of the local Jewish cursive script after the end of the Bar Kokhba revolt in the year 135. All cursive hands in later inscriptions and manuscripts evolved from later Hebrew script-styles. In some of the Bar Kokhba letters (fig. 61), however, a non-calligraphic formal hand appears that has some affinities with the script of a fragment discovered in the Dura-Europos synagogue (figs. 77, 195). As the synagogue was destroyed in the year 256, it may be assumed that that fragment was written before the destruction: i.e., in the first half of the 3rd century or perhaps earlier. The text is damaged, and although many letters can be identified, the nature of the document is unclear. The script may be described as semi-cursive. ʾAlef resembles the letter K; the diagonal became almost horizontal, starting at the centre of the vertical left downstroke. The right 'arm' slants downwards to the left and meets the horizontal stroke near its centre. The other letters are less cursive and some of them are adorned with serifs or additional short strokes slanting to the left from the left end of the 'roof', as in Bet, Dalet, He, Kaf, Samekh, Resh and occasionally Taw, or from the top, as in Gimel, Yod and Waw.

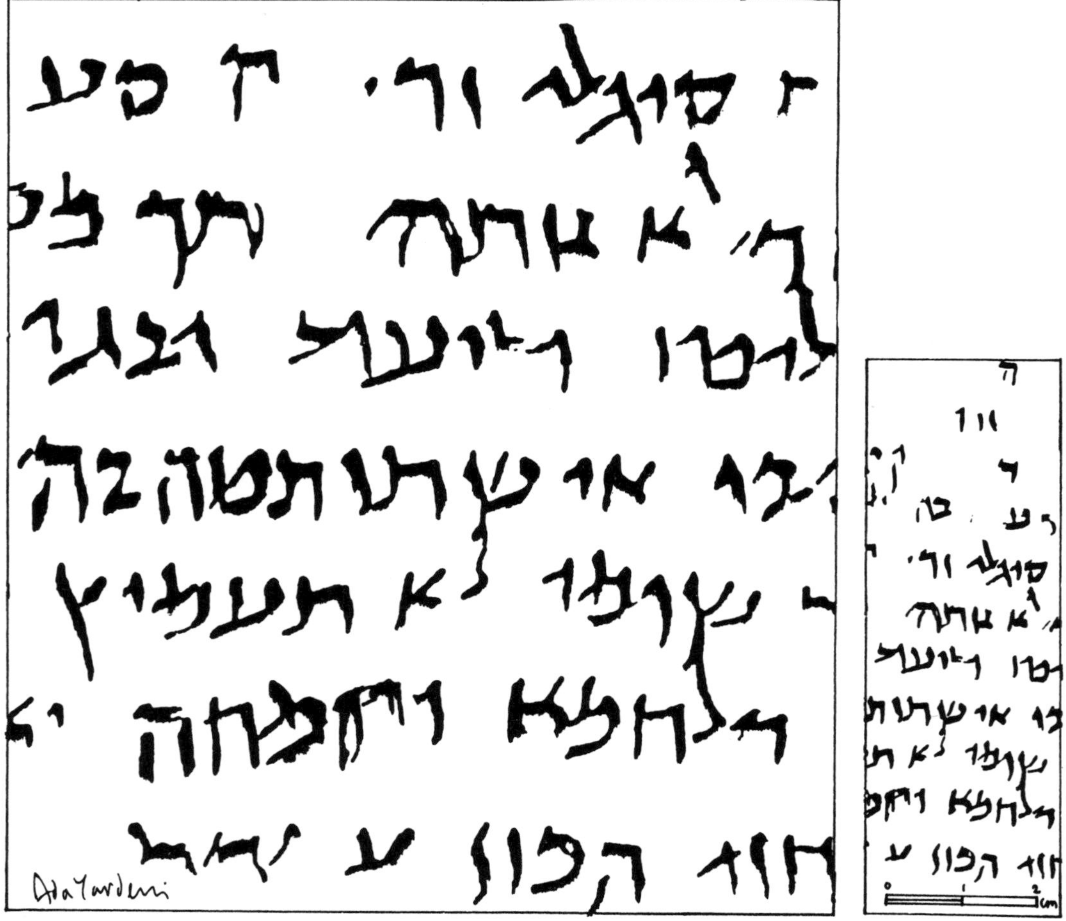

Fig. 195. Details of a document from Dura-Europos (see fig. 77). Right: real size. Left: enlarged

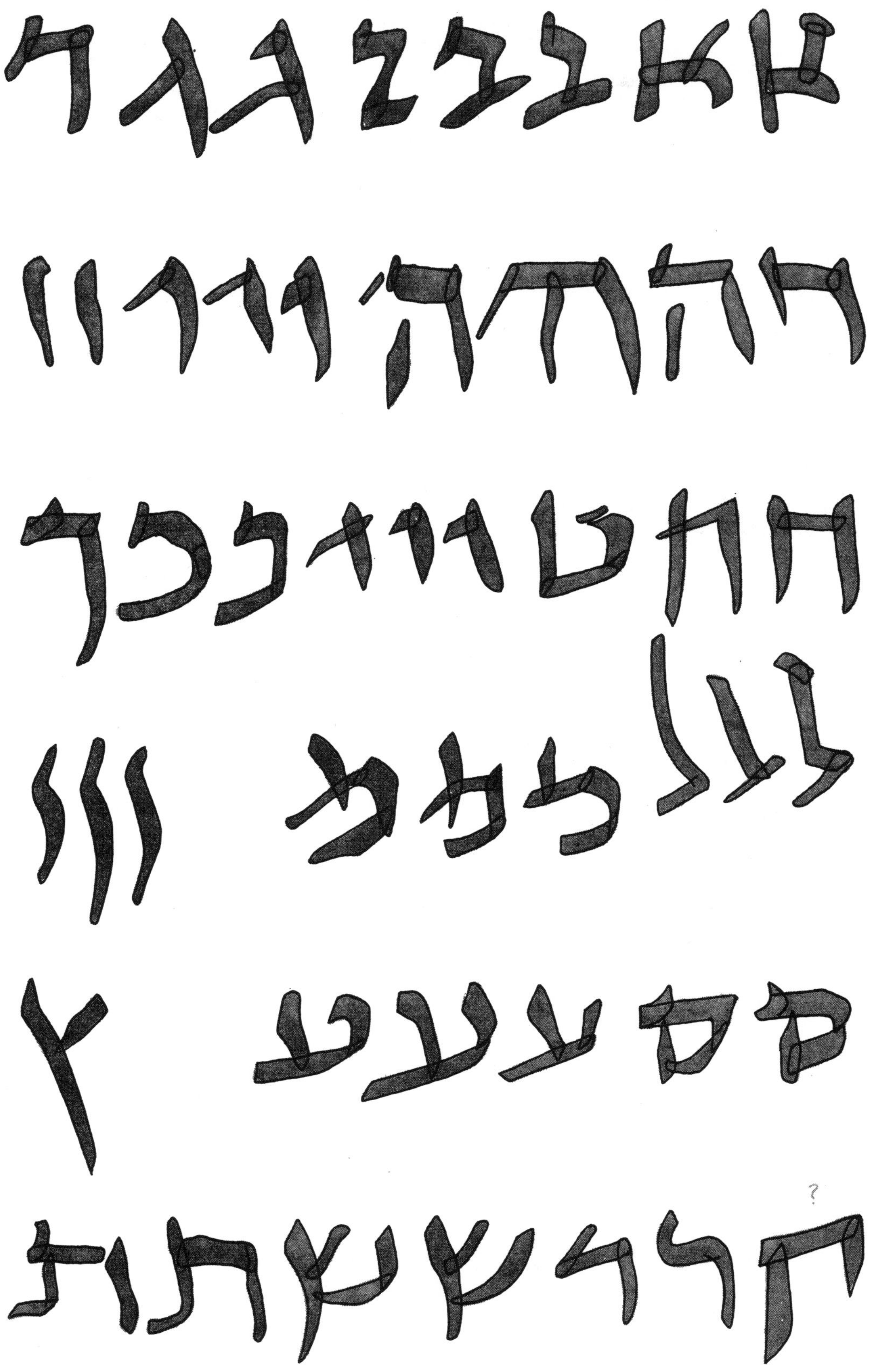

Chart 14. A semi-cursive script from the late 2nd or early 3rd century CE: a document from the Dura-Europos synagogue

12. BURIAL INSCRIPTIONS OF THE 3RD AND 4TH CENTURIES (CHART 15)

The script-style found in burial inscriptions of the 3rd and 4th centuries is represented here by the inscription on the lid of a coffin from Beit Sheᶜarim and other inscriptions in a similar script-style (the script in the chart is a modern design based on these inscriptions). The inscription is undated. However, the cemetery of Beit Sheᶜarim existed for about one and a half centuries, from the early 3rd century until its destruction during the rebellion against Gallus in 351. Most of the inscriptions in Beit Sheᶜarim are in Greek, whereas most of the inscriptions in caves 14 and 20 are in Hebrew letters. This script is particularly characterized by its square shapes and the spacious character of the letters. At that period it was a custom to fill the incised letters with red paint (remains of red paint are also to be found in the letters of an inscription from the synagogue in Meroth [fig. 80], the script of which is somewhat similar to that in the Beit Sheᶜarim inscriptions, and which may therefore also perhaps be dated to the 4th century).

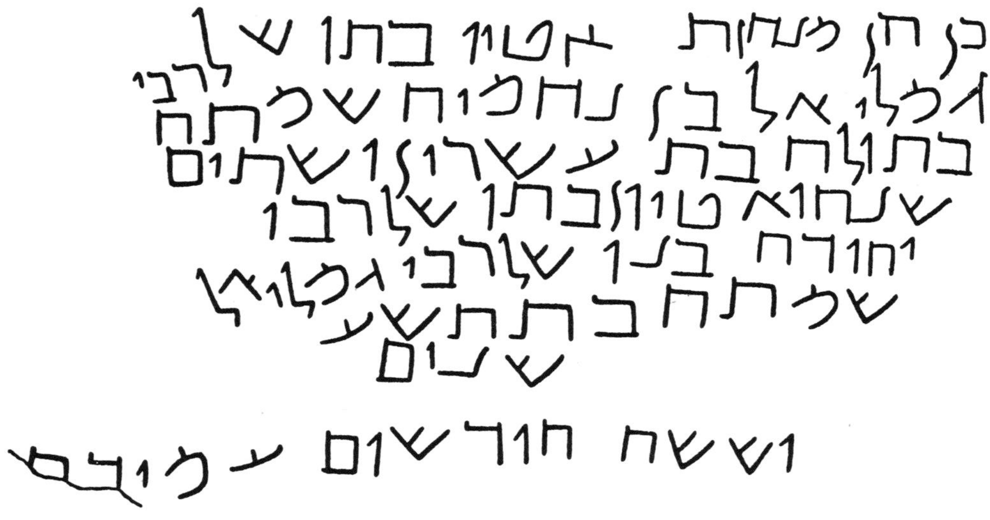

Fig. 196. A burial inscription from Beit Sheᶜarim

These are some of the main features of this script: the 'roofs' and base-strokes are horizontal and the downstrokes are of uniform thickness. Most strokes are straight except for the wavy final Nun. The letters Bet, Dalet, Kaf and Resh have a small vertical serif at the left end of the 'roof'. The tops of Gimel, Zayin and Nun bend backwards. He and Qof are closed. The left downstroke in He, Ḥet, final Mem, Qof and Taw (and perhaps also Samekh) starts either at the 'roof' or above it. He and Ḥet occasionally look almost identical, except for the right downstroke which starts above the 'roof' in Ḥet, while Waw and Yod differ mostly in their height, Yod being shorter. A short stroke slants downwards to the left from the top of Waw, Yod and Lamed. Ṭet, ᶜAyin and medial Mem usually have a curved right shoulder. Lamed has a short 'body' which often drops below the line.

Chart 15. Stylized letter-forms based on the Beit Sheʿarim burial inscriptions dating from the 3rd and 4th centuries CE

13. AN 'EASTERN' SCRIPT-STYLE ON PAPYRUS OF THE 5TH CENTURY (CHART 16)

A recently-published marriage contract (fig. 93) was written on a large sheet of papyrus (about 1 meter long) in Antinoupolis in Egypt. The main text is in Aramaic, but the opening lines (a fragmentary date formula) are in Greek written with Hebrew letters. The date in the Aramaic text appears to have been damaged. According to the publishers (Colette Sirat and Mordechai Friedman), the contract dates from 417. Thus, it is one of the very few dated inscriptions from that period (about 15 dated epitaphs of the 4th and 5th centuries were discovered in Zoʿar). In general, this script may be described as a semi-formal, non-calligraphic hand which appears to be distinct from the calligraphic book-hand. However, in the absence of dated manuscripts from that period, a precise classification is not possible.

These are the main features of this script: the downstrokes are somewhat wavy and the serifs are relatively large, slanting downwards to the left. Large serifs, characteristic of the script of the Byzantine period, already appear in signatures in a non-calligraphic book-hand on a deed from the time of Bar Kokhba (fig. 197). The horizontal and vertical strokes of the letter-forms are of an almost identical length and thickness, thus creating large spaces inside the letters. The downstrokes and base-strokes usually slant downwards to the left and the letters lean forwards. The downstrokes narrow to a point at the bottom.

These are some major features of individual letters: the diagonal in ʾAlef starts near the centre of the left downstroke (compare the ʾAlef of the Dura-Europos fragment, above). The left downstroke of ʾAlef and the left stroke of Pe bend to the right at their bottom. The 'roofs' of Bet, Dalet, He, Ḥet, Kaf, Samekh, Qof, Resh and Taw start with a large serif slanting downwards to the left. The tops of Gimel and Nun curve or bend backwards, while in Zayin an additional large stroke slants downwards to the right from its top. The left downstroke of He and Qof starts at the 'roof'; He resembles Ḥet. Ṭet is rounded and its left stroke starts high above the line. The additional short stroke in Lamed crosses the 'mast'. Final Mem is open.

↓ Fig. 197. Letters with large serifs in signatures on a deed from the time of the Bar Kokhba revolt (NḤ 42; 132 CE)

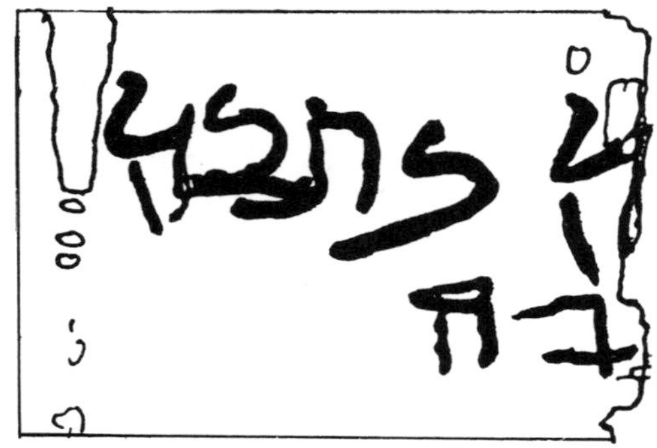

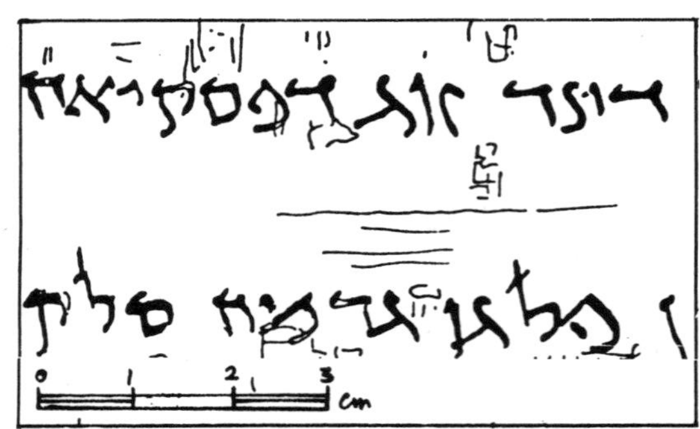

Fig. 198. Detail of the Antinoupolis *Ketubbah* dating from 417 CE (real size; see fig. 93) ↑

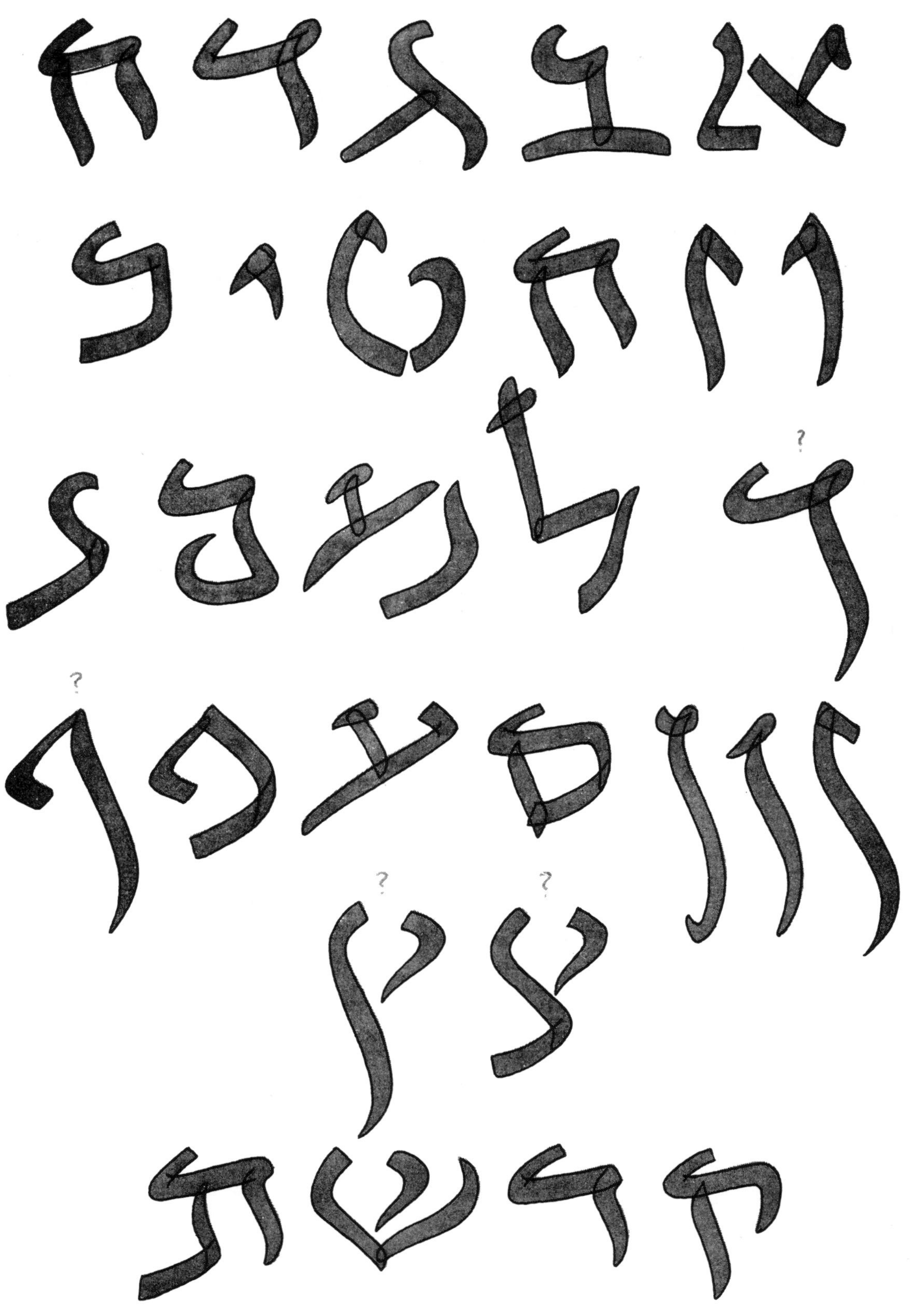

Chart 16. A 5th century CE 'Eastern' script:
the Antinoupolis papyrus marriage contract (417 CE)

14. THE BOOK-HAND ON PAPYRUS OF THE 3RD TO 6TH CENTURIES (CHART 17)

Among the hundred and fifty or so known papyrus fragments written with Hebrew letters, there are several belonging to the Byzantine period. Except for the marriage-contract of the year 417 mentioned above, none of them is dated. Some of them were discovered together with Greek material dating from the 3rd to 5th centuries. They include a small group of official letters in Hebrew found in Oxyrhynchus (fig. 92), mentioning persons bearing the title 'Rosh Ha-Knesset' (i.e., *Archisynagogus*, Head of the Synagogue), as well as another letter in Aramaic (fig. 94), the period and provenance of which are not known, and which may be somewhat later (perhaps dating from the 5th or 6th century). The Hebrew script on the fragments shows a clear affinity to the post-Herodian book-hand. The letters are wide, and the spaces within and around them are well-balanced. In the Aramaic letter mentioned above, the letters are embellished with elaborate ornamental additions.

These are the main features of its letter-forms: the script generally leans forward as a result of the downstrokes slanting downwards to the right. The 'roofs' are almost horizontal and are balanced through their ornaments. The base-strokes slant diagonally downwards to the left. The letter-group *šʿṭnzgṣ* is characterized by the ornament at the top of their left downstroke (the letters Zayin and ʿAyin are not found in the text but they apparently had the same ornament, made with a to-and-fro movement, sometimes resembling a cross). The 'roofs' of Bet, Dalet, He, Ḥet, Kaf, final Mem, Samekh, Qof, Resh and Taw start with a serif slanting downwards to the left. The left downstrokes of He and Qof, as well as of final Mem, are separated from the 'roofs'. Shin has a triangular form.

Fig. 199. Details of papyrus letters mentioning the title *Archisynagogus* (see fig. 93)

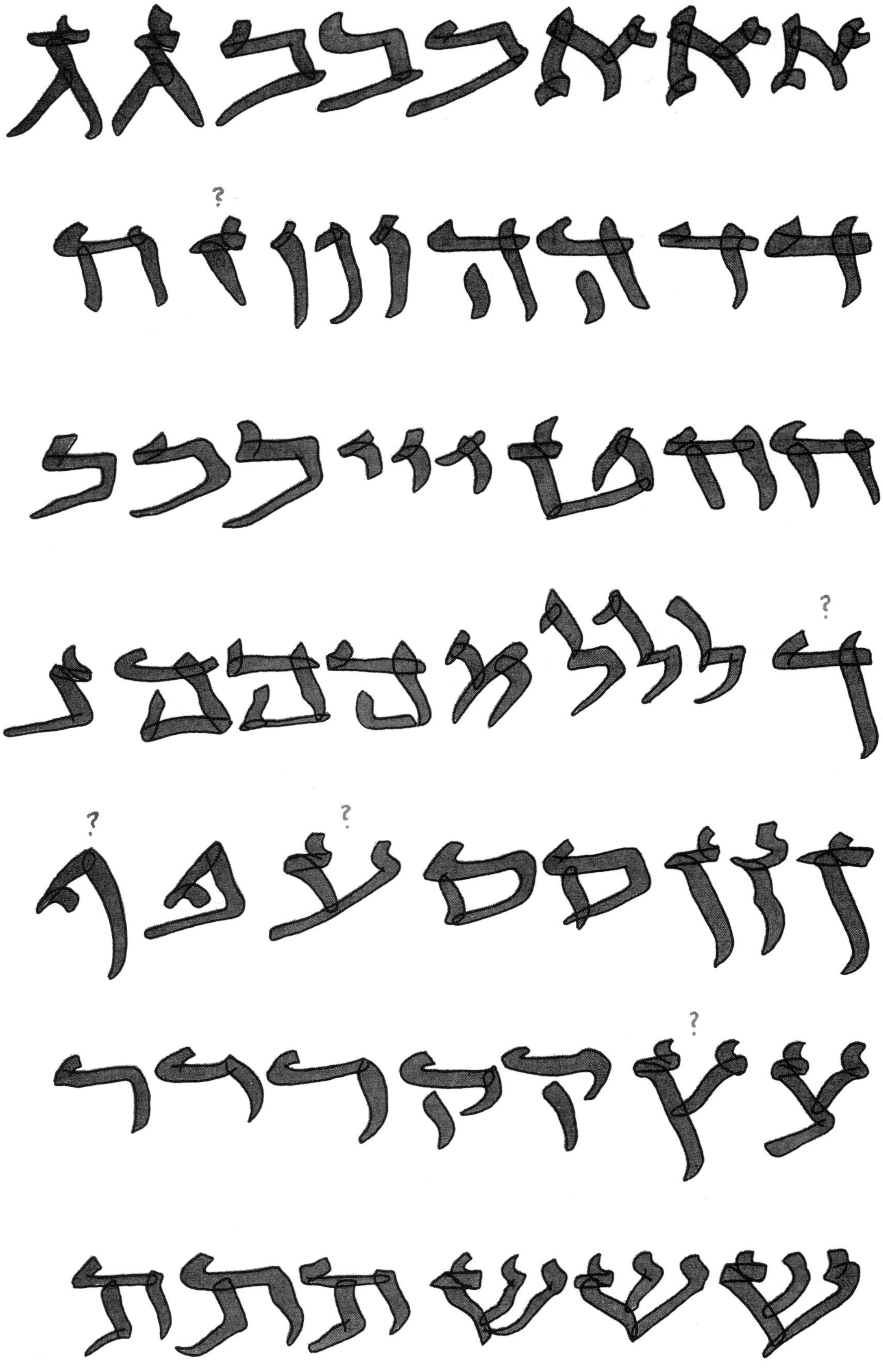

Chart 17. A 5th or 6th century elegant book-hand: a Hebrew papyrus letter (Ms. Heb. f.114)

15. THE SCRIPT ON MOSAICS OF ABOUT THE 6TH CENTURY (CHART 18)

The script which appears in scores of synagogue mosaic inscriptions dating from the 5th-6th centuries is represented here by the monumental Halachic inscription found in the Reḥov synagogue. The script in the mosaic inscriptions had not become stylized and they vary in the forms of their letters. However, some features in certain inscriptions show common stylistic traits which perhaps reflect the calligraphic book-hand of that period. The letters were composed of square and triangular stones with which the artists tried to imitate the forms of the letter-signs written with paint on the plaster underneath (see the collection of synagogue inscriptions in the book *On Mosaic and Stone* by J. Naveh [in Hebrew]). In the Reḥov inscription the letter-signs take a variety of forms. The general impression is of an elaborate script, some of the letters being embellished with elaborate ornamental additions. The average height of the letters is about 8 cm. and they are arranged in long lines. The letter-signs are broad, with large spaces inside and around them. The 'roofs' and the base-strokes are almost horizontal and the downstrokes mostly vertical or slanting downwards somewhat to the right or the left. The letters reflect the irregularity of the painted script underneath, which seems to have been written somewhat carelessly. In spite of the variety of letter-forms, several groups may be distinguished: although the seven letters Gimel, Zayin, Ṭet, Nun, ʿAyin, Ṣadi and Shin already seem to have constituted a group with similar ornaments, they appear in a variety of forms in the Reḥov inscription. The most complex one is the ornament that appears irregularly on top of Zayin, Ṭet, Nun and Shin, consisting of three triangular stones placed on three sides of a square stone. A 'serif' indicated by an additional square stone adorns the 'roofs' of Bet, Dalet, He, Kaf, final Mem, Samekh, Qof, Resh and Taw. A triangular stone represents the 'hook' of Waw, Yod, Lamed and medial Mem. ʾAlef, Pe and occasionally Gimel have an additional square stone to the right of the bottom of the left downstroke. The right 'arm' of ʾAlef has an additional triangular stone pointing downwards to the right. The diagonal and the left downstroke of ʾAlef meet at their top. The left downstroke of He is separated from the 'roof', whereas in Qof it touches the 'roof'. The right side of Ṭet curves inwards. The 'mast' of Lamed slants downwards to the right. Pe has a broad horizontal 'roof'. The left downstroke of Taw bends leftwards at its bottom in a right angle.

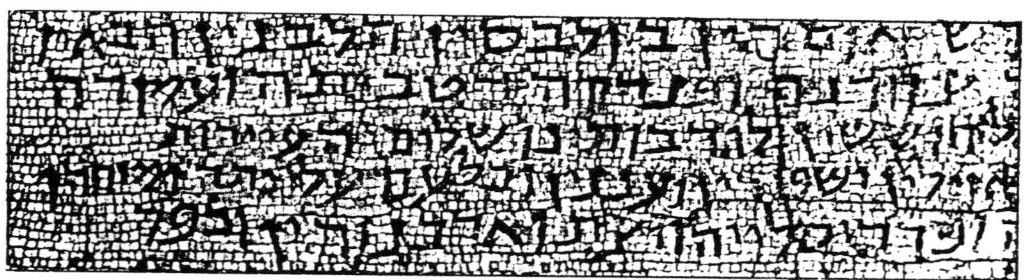

Fig. 200. Detail of the Halachic mosaic inscription from the Reḥov synagogue (the late Byzantine period; reduced)

Chart 18. A Byzantine period mosaic script from about the 6th century: the Reḥov synagogue inscription

16. THE SCRIPT ON AMULETS OF THE BYZANTINE PERIOD (CHARTS 19-20)

Over fifty amulets, incised or scratched on metal in a variety of handwritings, were found in various places, most of them in Israel. They were probably made between the 4th and the early 7th centuries. Only a few were inscribed by skilled hands. As the letters appear in their bare 'skeleton', the structure and components of the letters are clear. The major characteristics of the script are the large number of slanting strokes and the emphasized ornamental additions. Groups of letter-signs embellished with similar ornaments are common to most amulets, despite the large variety of letter-forms. The script of the amulets is represented here by two examples written in Aramaic. These amulets represent only their own script and are not characteristic of all the amulets (for other examples, see fig. 87 and the amulets published by J. Naveh and S. Shaked). The additional ornaments reflect their forms in manuscripts written in ink.

These are the main features of the script in chart 19 (Naveh-Shaked 7): the base-strokes of Bet, Ṭet and final Mem are straight, generally slanting upwards to the right, while the bases of Kaf and Pe are concave. Most of the 'roofs' are almost horizontal. The left downstroke of ʾAlef and Pe bends to the right at its bottom. The 'roofs' of Bet, Dalet, He, Ḥet, Kaf, final Mem, Samekh, Qof, Resh and Taw are adorned with serifs. Gimel, Zayin and Nun have a short 'roof' slanting upwards to the right on top of the downstroke. The downstrokes of He and Qof start at the 'roof'. A short stroke slants downwards to the left from the top of Waw and Yod, Lamed and medial Mem. Similar 'hooks' adorn the left stroke of ʿAyin and the right stroke of Ṭet. The right strokes of ʿAyin and Shin curve to the left in their upper part. Medial Mem has no 'base' while Ṭet has a broad one. The left downstroke of final Mem is separated from the 'roof'. Medial and final Nun are curved, as is the left downstroke of Taw. Final Pe and final Ṣadi do not appear in this amulet.

Fig. 201. Detail of an amulet from the Byzantine period (Naveh-Shaked 7; enlarged; see Fig. 202)

Chart 19. A 5th or 6th century incised script on an amulet: Naveh-Shaked 7

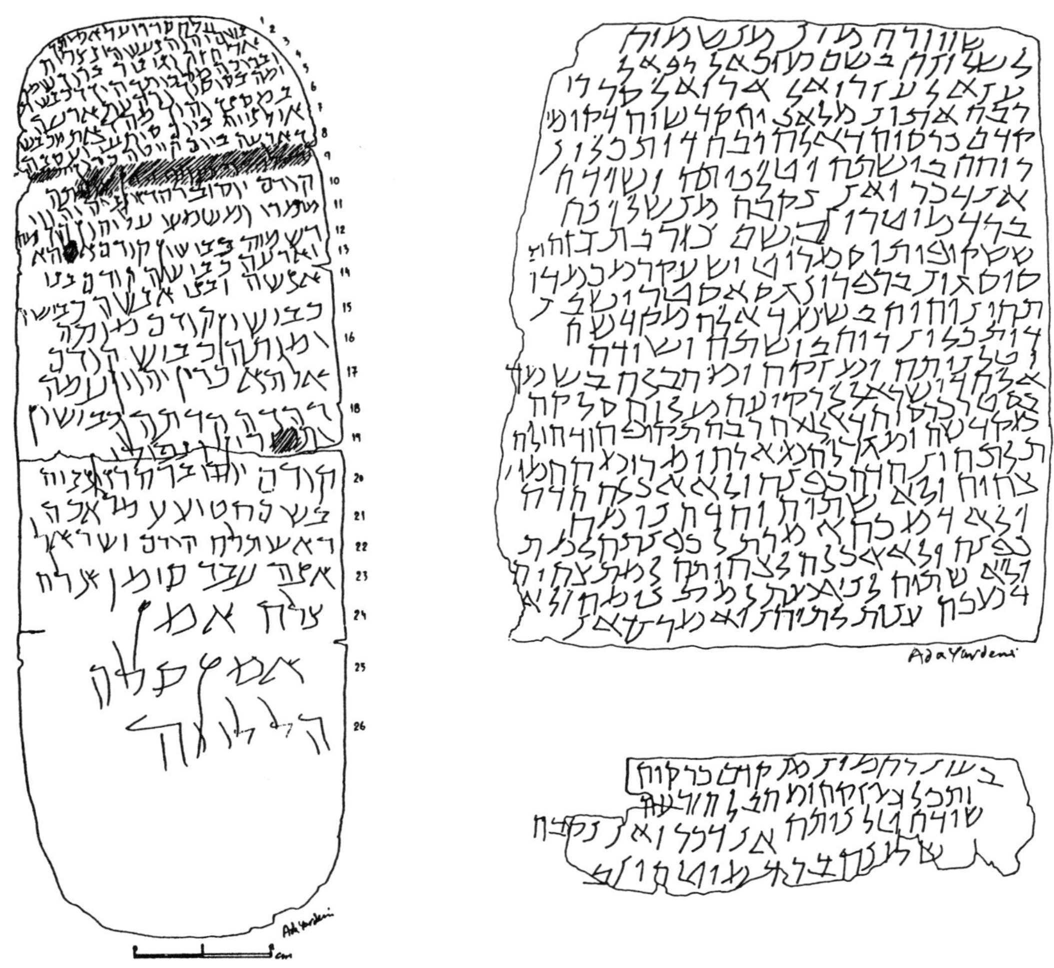

Fig. 202. An amulet from the Byzantine period (Naveh-Shaked 7; right; real size) and an amulet from the Meroth synagogue, dating from the 7th or 8th century (left; real size)

Another amulet, which seems to be somewhat later, was discovered in the synagogue of Meroth (chart 20).

These are the main features of its script: the base-strokes generally slant downwards to the left and the downstrokes slant downwards to the right. The right 'arm' of ʾAlef resembles a sharp angle and reflects the customary ornament appearing in the 'Eastern' book-hand (see, for example, charts 17 and 22). The loop in Zayin and Nun (and perhaps also in Gimel, which appears to have been drawn in a similar way) reflects a scribal tradition which groups these letters together. Most letters with broad 'roofs' (including Lamed) have large serifs slanting downwards to the left and joining the 'roofs' in a curve. A similar form of Lamed appears in fragments of a Genesis scroll from the Genizah (see chart 22). The downstrokes in He, Qof, and final Mem are separated from the 'roof' (in final Mem that stroke is extremely short and occasionally curves inwards). The upper part of the left downstroke of Ṭet and Ṣadi curves backwards. The 'mast' of Lamed slants downwards to the right.

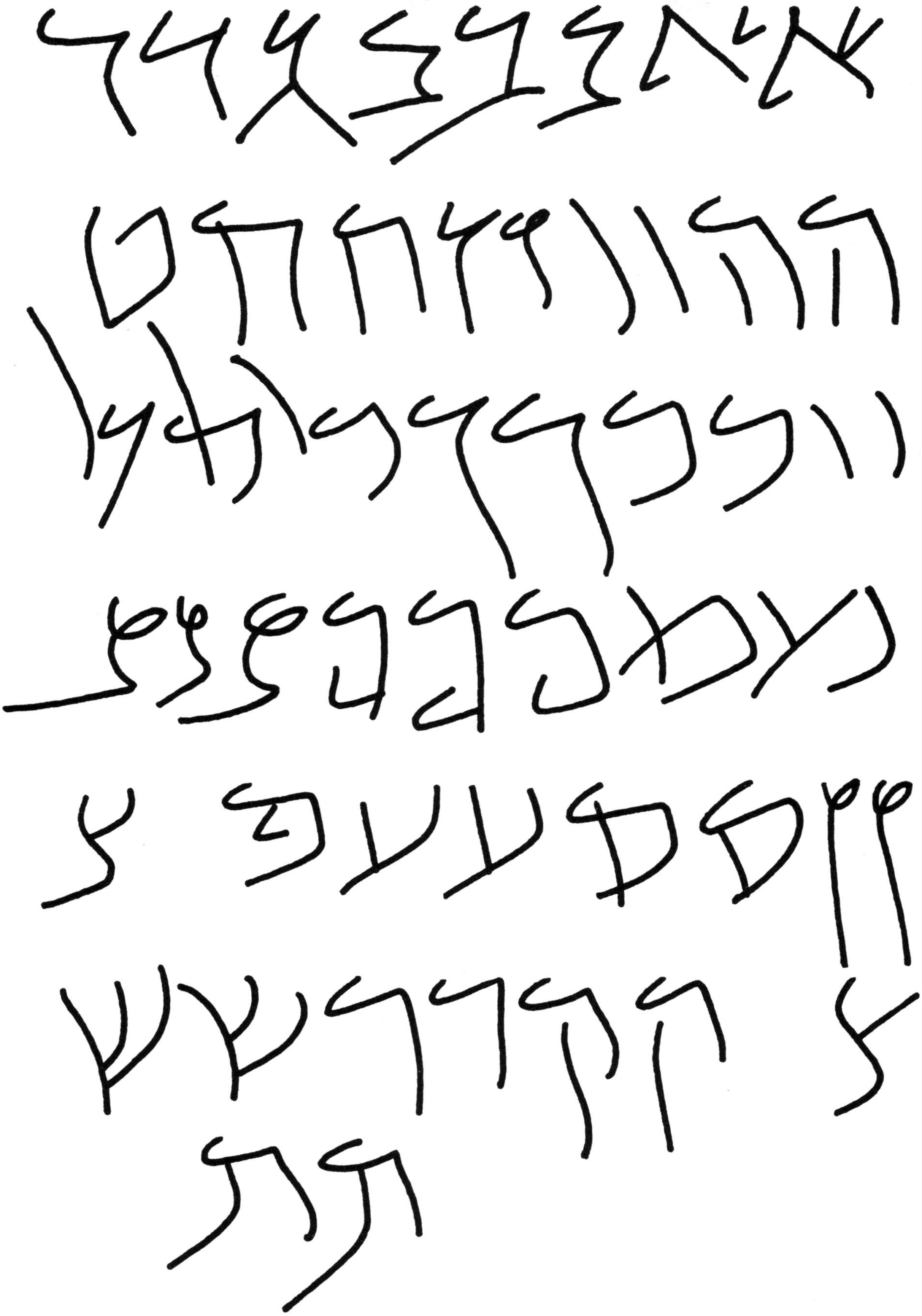

Chart 20. A 7th or 8th century incised script on an amulet:
the Meroth synagogue amulet

17. THE SCRIPT ON INCANTATION BOWLS FROM THE BYZANTINE PERIOD (CHART 21)

A large variety of handwritings appears on incantation bowls, none of which is dated. Most of the bowls were found in Iraq. They are made of clay and written on in ink. The text was written in concentric circles on the inside of the bowls. The letter-signs in most of the bowls have no ornamental additions and their strokes are uniform in their thickness. Only a few bowls were written in a script resembling the book-hand. The letters are generally short and square. As writing on a concave surface is extremely difficult, the forms of the letters are generally somewhat distorted. The script chosen for the chart is unique in that its downstrokes grow sharp at the bottom, giving it a certain elegance. The script in the chart is a stylized modern version of the script on the bowl.

These are some general features of the letters: the 'roofs' are more or less horizontal while the base-strokes slant downwards to the left. The letters are short and the script is quite spacious. The downstrokes, as well as the 'mast' of Lamed, slant downwards to the right and the script leans forward.

These are the major features of the main groups of letters with similar graphic components: the left downstroke of ᵓAlef and Pe curves or bends to the right at the bottom. The 'roofs' of Bet, Dalet, He, Kaf, final Mem, Samekh, Resh and Taw slant downwards to the right and curve upwards before joining the right downstrokes, which start a little above the 'roofs' and slant downwards to the right. An additional short horizontal stroke is drawn to the right of the top of Gimel and Nun, as well as of the left downstrokes of Ṭet, ᶜAyin, Ṣadi and Shin, while the almost vertical downstroke of Zayin descends from the centre of a similar short stroke. The left downstroke of He and Qof is sometimes separated from the 'roof' and occasionally starts at the 'roof'. Waw and Yod have a similar form, although Waw is sometimes longer; they have a convexly curved top with a serif that starts high above it. A similar serif occasionally adorns the 'horn' of Mem. Thick serifs (not represented in the chart) occasionally slant downwards in a leftwards direction at the left end of the broad 'roofs' of Bet, Dalet, He, Kaf, final Mem, Qof, Resh and Taw. The upper part of the right stroke of ᶜAyin and of Shin curves to the left.

Here are some features of individual letters: the diagonal of ᵓAlef starts at the centre of the left downstroke (compare the same feature in the Dura-Europos fragment [chart 11] and the marriage contract from Antinoupolis [chart 13]). Bet resembles Kaph; its 'tail' is occasionally indicated by the extension of the right downstroke beyond the base-stroke. Waw and Yod are curved. The 'body' of Lamed is small and triangular, while the short right downstroke in Qof is almost vertical. The middle stroke of the triangularly-shaped Shin sometimes does not touch the other strokes.

Chart 21. Stylized letter-forms based on an incantation bowl (Naveh-Shaked 6) dating from about the 6th century

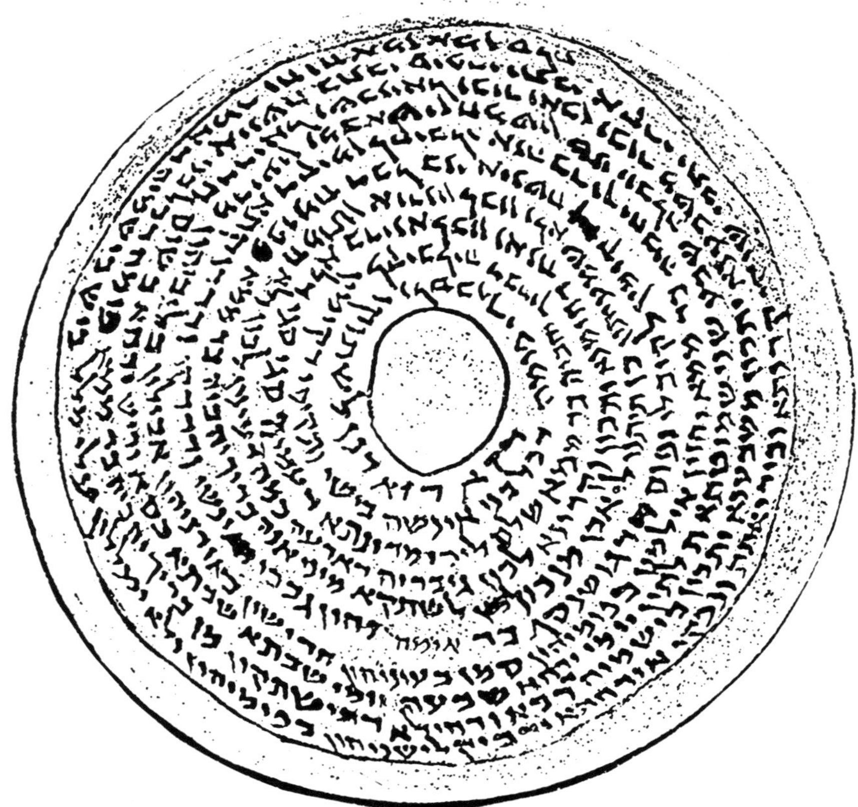

Fig. 203. An incantation bowl from the Byzantine period (Naveh-Shaked 6)

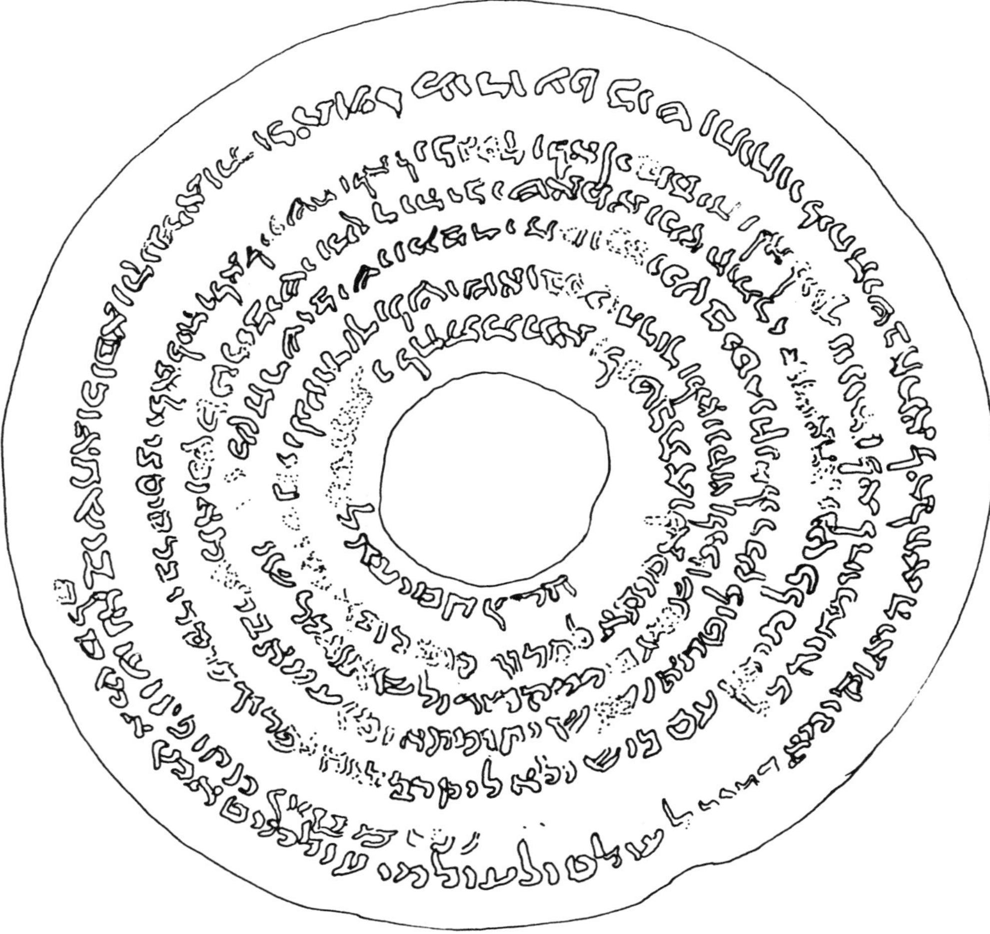

Fig. 204. Incantation bowl (Yale Babylonian Collection 2393)

18. THE 'EASTERN' BIBLICAL BOOK-HAND (CHARTS 22-24)

A space of more than five centuries separates the book-hand of the post-Herodian period (fig. 191) from the early biblical manuscripts discovered in the Cairo Genizah. As these manuscripts are not dated, palaeographic examination of the material can help in their chronological classification. The 'roots' of the book-hand letters as well as their basic structures continued to exist in the different script-styles which evolved over the years, but since the ornamental additions were generally subtly blended with the basic strokes, we are usually unable to define the exact differences between the handwritings and between the script-styles. Although a thorough examination of a large number of manuscripts may help us to develop a special sense for distinguishing between early and late manuscripts, only a systematic analysis of the different handwritings and letter-forms will enable us to arrive at an exact perception of the differences and of the formal evolution of the letter-forms. Such a perception requires a careful analysis of each stroke and of every component of the different letter-signs. This may also help in the dating of manuscripts according to the evolution of the letter-forms and their ornaments, despite the personal characteristics sometimes obscuring the stylistic features of the handwritings. In this way, we may discover that the 'Eastern' book-hand really continued the scribal tradition found in the elaborate script surviving in a few papyrus fragments and synagogue inscriptions of the Byzantine period. We will now provide a description of three manuscripts which can serve as indicators of the evolution of the letter-forms.

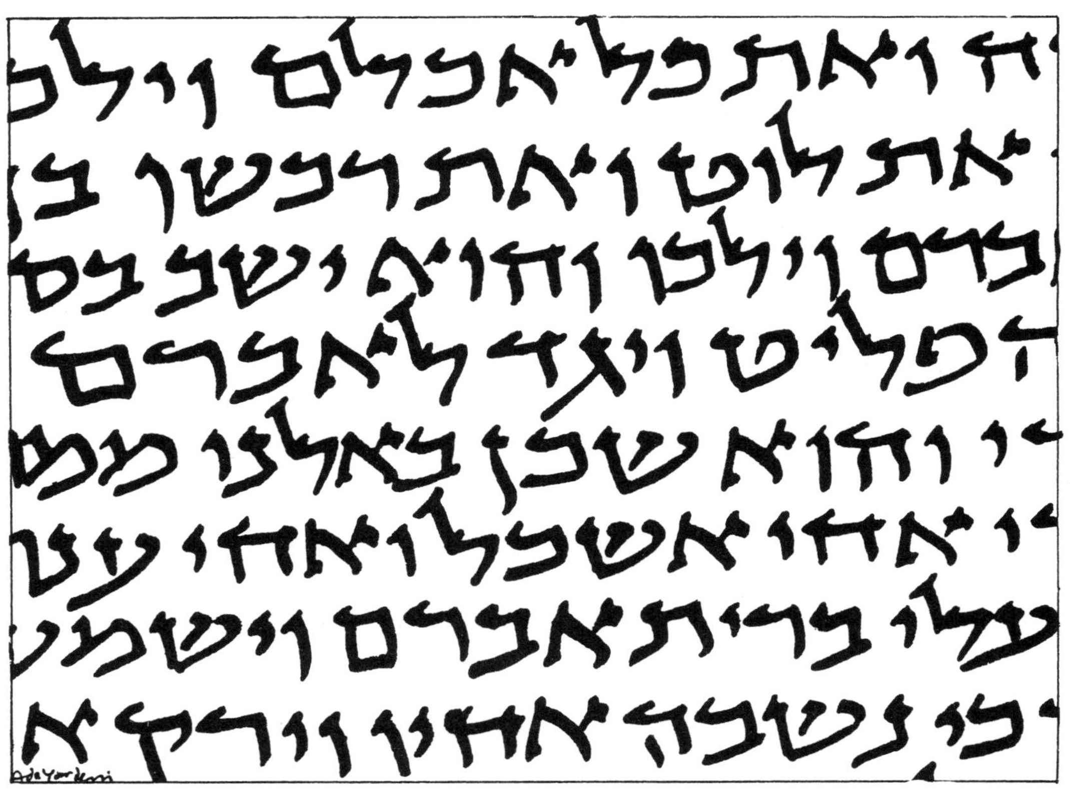

Fig. 205. Detail of a fragmentary Genesis scroll dating from about the 8th century (see fig. 97)

A. THE 'EASTERN' BIBLICAL BOOK-HAND OF THE 7TH OR 8TH CENTURY (CHART 22)

No dated manuscripts have been found from the period between the early 7th century and the end of the 9th century. The earliest manuscripts from the Genizah perhaps belong to the middle of that period. One of these consists of two large fragments of a Genesis Scroll. In the larger fragment, remains of five consecutive columns have survived. This manuscript is today in the Cambridge University Library (T-S NS 3.21; fig. 97). Its script, apparently written by a professional scribe, resembles that of certain papyrus fragments of the Byzantine period. It is a relatively elaborate script, embellished with all the ornamental additions used at that period for sacred writings, and relatively homogeneous, having almost no variations in the forms of the letters. Thus, this manuscript is an important piece of evidence of the 'Eastern' scribal practice in the writing of Torah scrolls in the early Islamic period. The earliest literary reference to the ornamental additions to the letters is to be found in the Babylonian Talmud, *Menaḥot* 29. It is said there of Rabbi ʿAqiva, son of Joseph, that he "will preach heaps and heaps of Halachot on each of the hooks of the letters". This rabbi lived in the late 1st and early 2nd centuries CE, but his sayings have not survived. In the same tractate another rabbi is mentioned, by the name of Rava. He was the head of the Meḥoza Yeshiva in the 4th century. He said: "Seven letters need three 'Zaynin' – *šʿṭnzgṣ* (Shin, ʿAyin, Ṭet, Nun, Zayin, Gimel, Ṣadi)". Other references to the structure of the letters appear in the tractate *Shabbat*. Thus, we may assume that the form of the letters reflected in the Halachot was their form in the 2nd to the 4th centuries. There were evidently some early writings dealing with the ornaments of the letter-signs and they were no doubt based on early scribal traditions. However, the earliest known composition dealing with that subject is *Sefer Tagei* ('The Book of Crowns'), mentioned in literary Jewish sources. This book was a kind of commentary discovered in the time of the Geʾonim (see Y.D. Eisenstein, *Otsar Dinim uMinhaggim*, New York 1917). Already in the time of the Geʾonim, the terms used for describing the forms of the letters in the Talmud were interpreted in different ways, and this was even more the case in later times. The tractate *Sofrim* ('Scribes'), although drawing on early sources, is a relatively late composition, dating from about the 8th century. The forms of the 'crowns' adorning the letters in modern Torah scrolls are relatively late. Similar ornaments adorning isolated letters appear in a manuscript from England dating from the year 1189 (Valmadonna MS 1; fig. 234).

One may ask what the original form of the crowns was. When we examine the letter-forms of the Genesis scroll fragments from the Genizah we see that the letters in the group *šʿṭnzgṣ* are adorned at the top of their left downstroke with an ornament in the form of an angle opening upwards to the right (compare chart 17). This ornament was sometimes shaped like a small cross. In the Mishnah there is no reference to the ornaments of the letters, whereas in the Talmud the group *šʿṭnzgṣ* is already mentioned. We may thus assume that the scribal tradition reflecting, inter alia, the forms of that letter-group, was consolidated between the canonisation of the

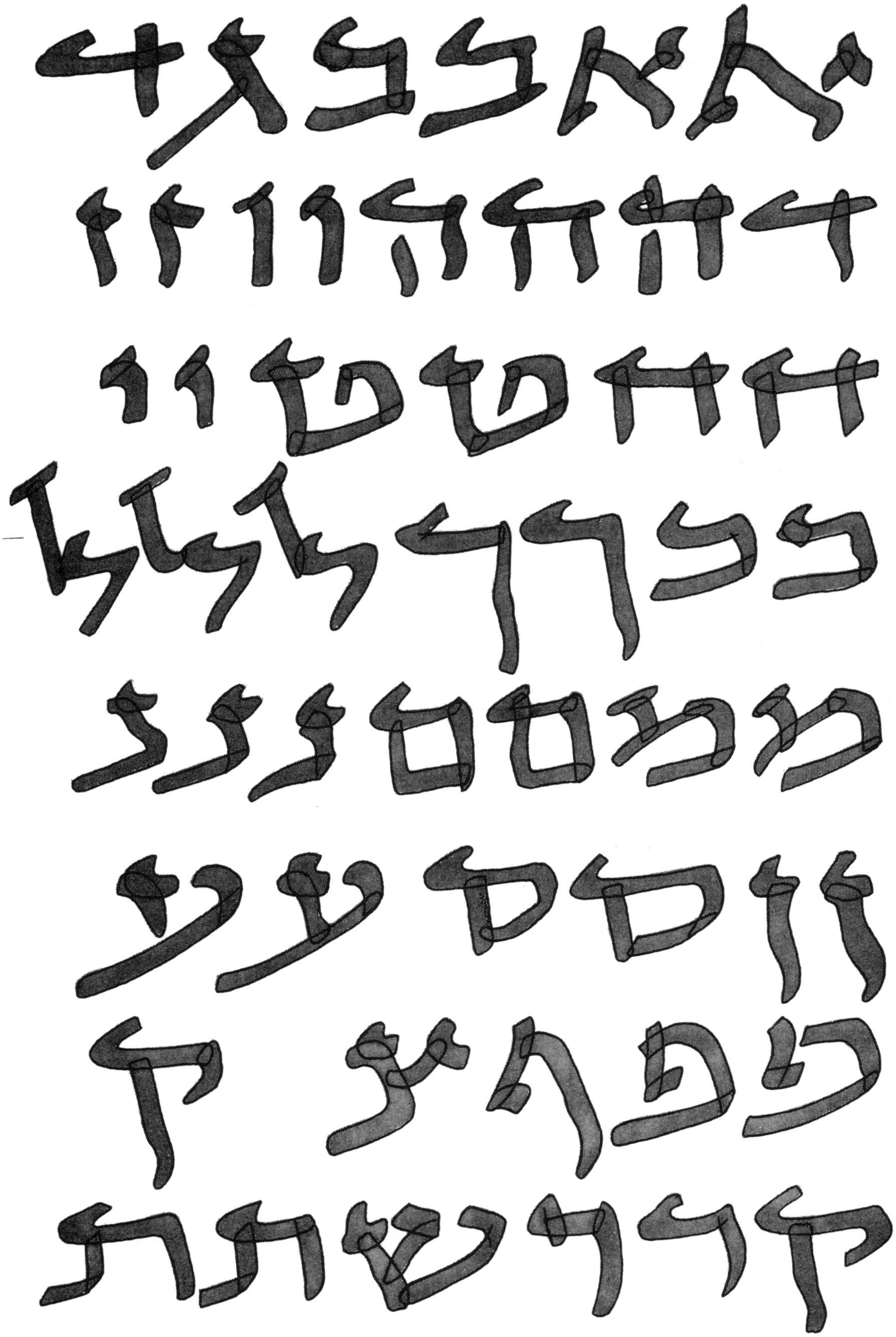

Chart 22. A 7th or 8th century 'Eastern' book-hand: fragments of an early Genesis scroll from the Cairo Genizah (T-S NS 3.21)

Mishnah and that of the Talmud. Parallel to the Masoretic effort to preserve the biblical text, there was an attempt, beginning at that time, to preserve the scribal tradition of the sacred writings. The written instructions concerning the forms of the letters, which were understood at the time, were misinterpreted in later periods.

As we have said, the letter-forms changed with time through a natural process of evolution, despite the relative conservatism of the tradition. The interpreters of the Talmud in later periods were responsible for the creation of the forms of the ornaments appearing in modern Torah scrolls, which do not resemble the ancient forms. In the Genesis scroll fragments, which appear to date from the 7th or 8th century, the letter-group *šʿṭnzgṣ* is fully represented, with the left downstroke of the characters formed like the letter Zayin and adorned with the authentic 'crown'.

These are some other major features of this handwriting: the bases and, to a lesser degree, the ‘roofs’, slant upwards to the right, while the downstrokes slant downwards to the right. The script thus leans forward, although this tendency is balanced to some degree by the long bases and the large serifs, which slant downwards to the left, and by the strokes which are drawn in the opposite direction, such as the right and the left strokes of ʾAlef, the left stroke of Gimel, the right stroke of Ṣadi, Lamed and Qof, and the right and middle strokes of Shin. The letters are broad and spacious, in the tradition of the post-Herodian and the Byzantine book-hands. Lamed is unique in that it has an extra serif at the left end of the horizontal stroke – a serif comparable to the serifs of other letters with broad 'roofs', such as Bet, Dalet, He, Ḥet, Kaf, final Mem, Samekh, Qof, Resh and Taw. A similar Lamed appears in the amulet from the synagogue of Meroth (chart 20 and fig. 202) which dates from approximately the 7th or the 8th century. Another prominent letter is Gimel, with a very long left stroke. Similar forms of Gimel appear in some papyrus fragments from Egypt that were found together with Greek material from the 3rd-5th centuries. There are other groups of letters with similar components: ʾAlef and Ṣadi have a similar ornament at the top of their right 'arm'. The bend backwards at the bottom of the left downstroke of ʾAlef occasionally resembles the 'nose' of Pe; however, there is also another form of ʾAlef drawn with a to-and-fro movement. Bet, Kaf, final Mem, Samekh, Qof, Resh and Taw have a high right 'shoulder'. In Dalet, He and Ḥet the right downstroke runs down across the 'roof'. The right downstroke in He and Ḥet is shorter than the left one. The left downstroke of He occasionally starts at the 'roof' in the same way as in Qof, but it is sometimes separated. Ṭet, medial Mem and Pe have a short, somewhat convex 'roof' which joins the right downstroke in a curve (the 'roof' of medial Pe is somewhat longer). In the group which includes final Mem, Samekh, Qof and Taw (and occasionally He), the upper left-hand 'corner' has a similar form, the left downstroke starting at the 'roof' opposite the top of the serif (the left downstroke of final Mem sometimes starts at the top of the serif and runs across the 'roof'); medial Nun and medial Ṣadi have similar base-strokes.

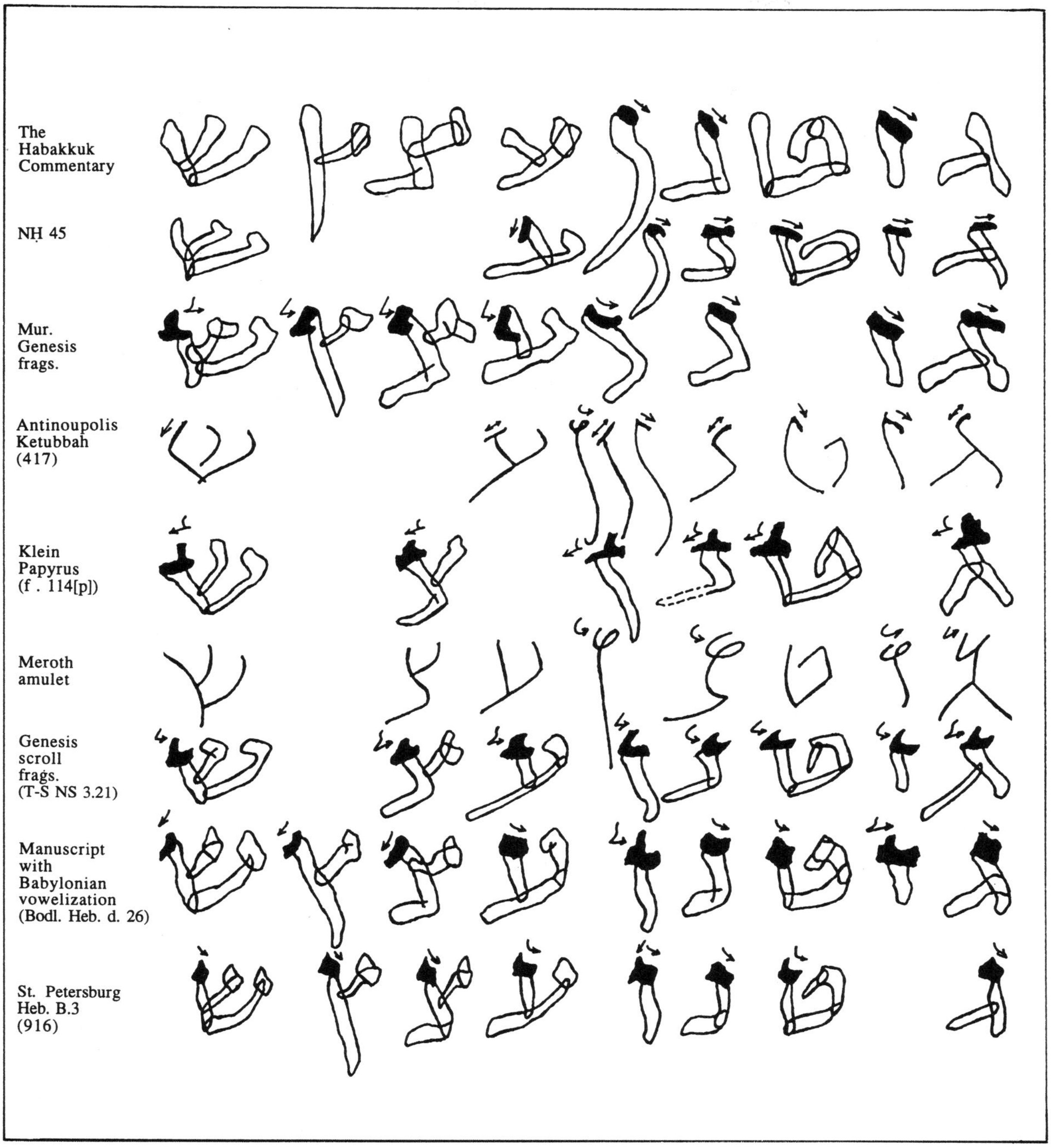

The Habakkuk Commentary

NḤ 45

Mur. Genesis frags.

Antinoupolis Ketubbah (417)

Klein Papyrus (f . 114[p])

Meroth amulet

Genesis scroll frags. (T-S NS 3.21)

Manuscript with Babylonian vowelization (Bodl. Heb. d. 26)

St. Petersburg Heb. B.3 (916)

Fig. 206. A comparative chart of the ornamental additions of the letter-group *š‘ṭnzgṣ*

B. THE 'EASTERN' BOOK-HAND OF THE 9TH CENTURY (CHART 23)

Among the early manuscripts from the Cairo Genizah there are several undated manuscripts with early Babylonian vowelization. The scholars who deal with the evolution of the Babylonian and Palestinian vowelization systems used before they were gradually superseded by the Masoretic system have distinguished certain stages in their development. This can help us in determining a relative chronology of undated manuscripts. A manuscript of the Bible with the Targum (Aramaic translation), now in the Bodleian Library in Oxford (Ms Heb. d.26; fig. 108) is one of the manuscripts with early Babylonian vowelization. It may perhaps be dated to the 9th century. The script has most of the special characteristics of the 'Eastern' script-style found in the elaborate biblical book-hand appearing in dated manuscripts from the end of the 9th century and which reached its peak in the 10th and 11th centuries (see below).

These are the main features of the letter-forms in that manuscript: the script is relatively small, and a distinction between thick horizontal strokes and thin vertical strokes begins to show. The base-strokes and some of the 'roofs' slant upwards slightly to the right and the downstrokes slant downwards to the right, with the result that the letters lean forward. If we examine the changes in the ornaments and in the grouping of the letters, we shall see that at that period the tradition had somewhat loosened its hold on the book-hand. For instance, the group *šʿṭnzgṣ* had split into three groups: 1. Gimel, Zayin, Ṭet, medial Nun and ʿAyin have on top of their left downstroke a rhomboid additional stroke made with the flat side of the calamus; this ornament, which was formerly drawn to the right of the stroke, has now moved to the left. 2. Zayin and final Nun resemble each other and the ornament at their top is shaped like a cross. 3. The ornament of Ṣadi and Shin is a short, thin stroke slanting downwards to the left from the top of the left downstroke, as in Waw and Yod. Other groups are as follows: ʾAlef and Ṣadi both have a right 'arm' made with a to-and-fro movement. ʾAlef and Pe have a similar ornament on their left downstroke. A comma-shaped short stroke adorns the left end of the 'roof' of Bet, Dalet, He, Kaf and Resh. The ‘roofs’ of final Mem, Samekh, Qof and Taw are formed in the same way, as are the the joins between the 'roof' and the left downstroke. The 'roofs' of medial Mem and Pe still form part of the curved right downstroke that sharpens gradually towards its bottom. The right 'arms' of ʿAyin and of Shin are occasionally shaped alike.

These are some major features of individual letters: the diagonal of ʾAlef is somewhat convex, starting far below the top of the wavy left downstroke (compare Pe). The left downstroke of Ḥet starts above the horizontal 'roof' and slants downwards to the right with a wavy movement. The short stroke adorning the 'mast' of Lamed starts below its top and slants downwards slightly to the left. The short final Nun is one of the significant features for dating manuscripts in the 'Eastern' book-hand.

Chart 23. An 8th or 9th century 'Eastern' book-hand: a manuscript with Babylonian vowelization (Ms. Heb. d.26)

C. THE ELABORATED 'EASTERN' HEBREW BOOK-HAND OF THE 10TH CENTURY (CHART 24)

In the 10th century, the Hebrew book-hand reached its height of elaboration. Its uniformity and elegance testify to a strong and authoritative scribal school. At that time of Gaonic activity and great Yeshivot, as well as close contacts between the Jewish communities of Babylonia, Egypt, North Africa and Palestine, the scribal tradition became crystallized. The letters in that book-hand are large and clear. Skilled scribes did a thorough job of shaping each individual letter and ornament. The 'Eastern' book-hand of the 10th century is represented here by a manuscript of the Bible with a mixed vowelization, belonging to the Firkowitch collection in St. Petersburg and dating from the year 916 (fig. 109). The place where it was written is not mentioned. In this script, the 'roofs' and 'bases' of the letters are a little thicker than the downstrokes. The flat writing implement was apparently cut somewhat obliquely and was held firmly, with only minimal changes in its angle in relation to the guideline. The letters are still spacious although their height is somewhat greater than their width, giving the letters an elegant appearance (compare the letters of this manuscript with the very broad letters of the Genesis fragments from the Genizah; chart 22). The spaces between the letters and between the words are reduced, so that the entire line appears to be a single graphic unit.

These are the main groups of letters with similar graphic components: the letters *š*ʿ*ṭnzgṣ* appear as a group, with a rhomboid additional stroke above their left downstroke, which starts with a narrow 'neck', created by the writing implement held at an oblique angle to the guideline. When the ornament and the downstroke were drawn without lifting the hand, the ornament 'moved' leftwards. This represented a transitional stage in the evolution of these ornaments, between the early stage in which the top of the left downstroke bent backwards, and the later stage when the ornament became a short 'roof', as in the Sephardi and Ashkenazi book-hands of the later Middle Ages.

The right 'arm' of ʾAlef and Ṣadi and the middle stroke of Shin are shaped alike. The lower part of the left stroke of ʾAlef and Pe is made with a to-and-fro movement. The emphasized curve of that stroke in ʾAlef is typical of the 'Eastern' book-hand of the 10th and 11th centuries, and in a different type (see, for instance, fig. 110) the upper part of the stroke is extremely thick. The upper right-hand corner of Bet, Kaf, Mem, Samekh, Qof, Resh and Taw is a right angle, whereas in Dalet, He, Ḥet and final Kaf the right downstroke is drawn across the 'roof'. A short upright stroke, shaped like a comma, adorns the left end of the 'roofs' of Bet, Dalet, He, Kaf and Resh. The right downstroke of He, Ḥet and Taw tends to be somewhat shorter than the left one (usually following a letter with a long base-stroke). The left downstroke of He starts at the 'roof', while in Qof it starts above the 'roof', as in Samekh, final Mem and Taw. Waw and Yod are shaped alike, although Yod is shorter. The long 'legs' of final Kaf, Pe, Ṣadi and Qof are straight downstrokes. The right downstroke of Lamed

Chart 24. An elaborate 10th century 'Eastern' book-hand: the St. Petersburg manuscript Heb. B.3 dating from 916

and Qof slants downwards to the right and then to the left, but in Lamed, unlike Qof, it again curves downwards. Medial Mem has a short 'roof' (in Pe the 'roof' is still undeveloped). The right 'arms' of ʿAyin and Shin resemble each other in their form.

These are some major features of individual letters: an upright stroke descends towards the meeting-point of the diagonal and the left stroke of ʾAlef; that stroke, which was formerly an integral part of the left downstroke, became a separate stroke at that stage of evolution, and part of the diagonal in the following stage. The base-stroke of Bet terminates with a 'tail' which has a sharp end turning upwards. The 'heel' of Gimel extends beyond the imaginary base-line, while the left stroke is long and slants downwards to the left. Zayin is extremely short in order to be distinguished from the short final Nun, which has a similar form. The straight left downstroke of Ḥet starts above the 'roof'. The right stroke of Ṭet starts with a convex curve and joins a broad, slanting base-stroke. Lamed has a straight, upright 'mast' with an extra stroke slanting downwards from its top to the left. Medial Mem has a thick 'horn' that joins the 'roof' at an obtuse angle; its left downstroke is thin and terminates above the base-stroke. The right-hand stroke of ʿAyin is very long. Ṣadi is long and narrow, extending beyond the imaginary base-line. Shin has a triangular shape.

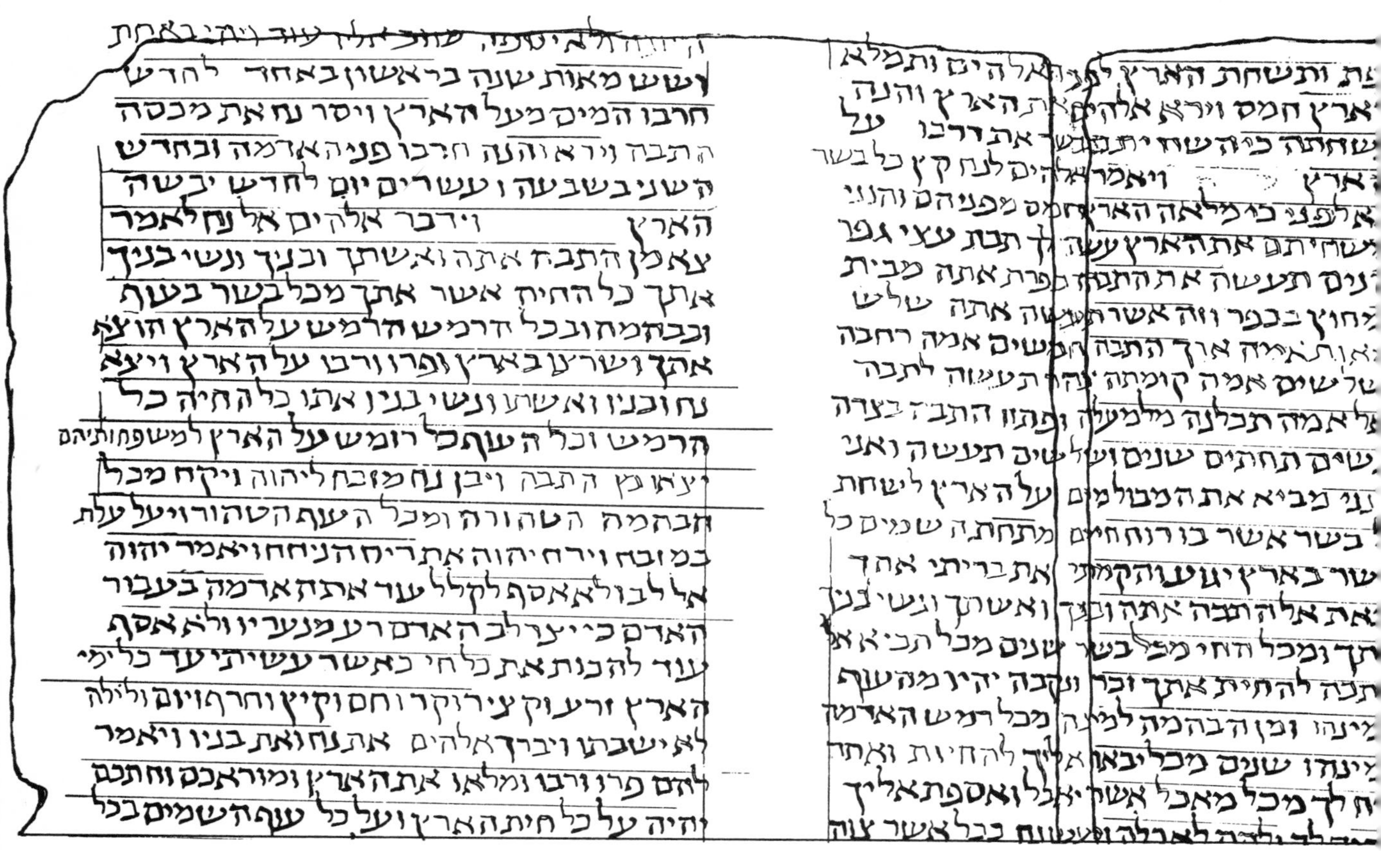

Fig. 207. Detail of an erased Genesis scroll cut and overwritten with a Greek text (not shown in the facsimile). (Florence, Biblioteca Medicea Laurenziana, Plut. LXXIV, cod. XVII)

Fig. 208. Detail of a page of the Aram-Zobah manuscript of the Bible written in the 'Eastern' elaborated book-hand, with Tiberian vowelization and with accentuation marks (enlarged)

19. A 12TH CENTURY SEMI-CURSIVE 'EASTERN' SCRIPT FROM EGYPT (CHART 25)

Together with the elaborated book-hand, several non-calligraphic Hebrew scripts of various degrees of cursiveness came into being. These have not become stylized. Owing to the lack of a strict scribal tradition due to the dispersion of Jewish communities in different countries, a large variety of letter-forms was created, as we observe from the manuscripts written in different places. A general characteristic of the non-calligraphic scripts is the irregularity of the letter-forms, the strokes of which appear in varying sizes and face different directions, creating a feeling of confusion and disorder.

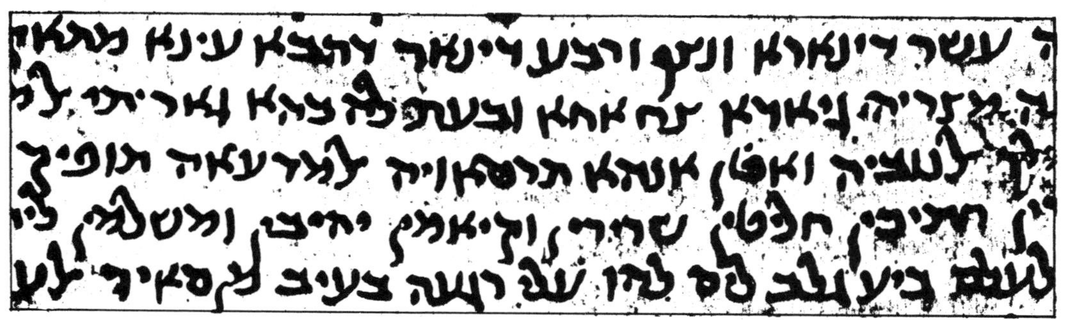

Fig. 209. Details of a manuscript from Fuṣṭāṭ (old Cairo) dating from 1100, written in the Arabic language and in a semi-cursive 'Eastern' script

A few manuscripts from Egypt, and especially from Fuṣṭāṭ (old Cairo), where a large Jewish community existed, show definite characteristics of a semi-cursive 'Eastern' hand. This script is represented here by a document from Fuṣṭaṭ dating from the year 1100, written with a flat calamus in the Arabic language and in Hebrew letters. Among the major features of this script are the concave or wavy 'roofs' of the letter-signs. Except for the group of letters with the characteristic 'roofs', the individual letters differ from one another, and no other groups can be distinguished. Each letter appears in several variant forms. There are no ornaments and almost no ligatures, except for that of ʾAlef and Lamed. A similar script appears in a book written in 1136 (fig. 210).

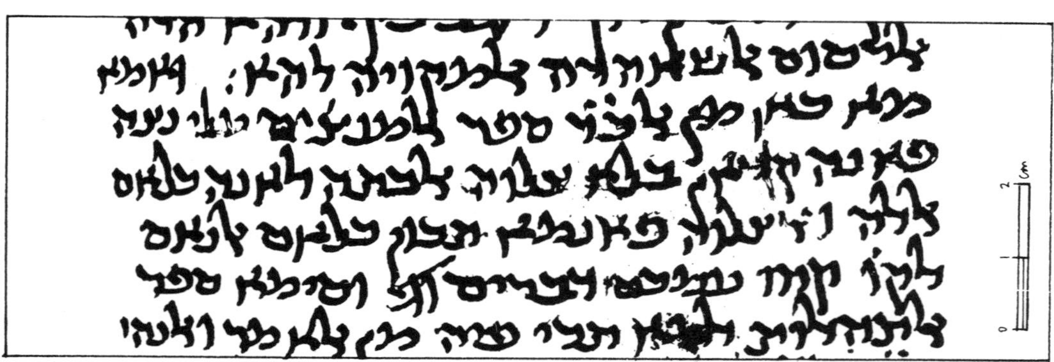

Fig. 210. A semi-cursive 'Eastern' script in a manuscript from Egypt from 1136 (Paris, the Jacques Musseri and Family collection, JNM II.1; real size)

Chart 25. A 12th century semi-cursive 'Eastern' script: a manuscript from Fuṣṭāṭ dating from 1100

20. THE 15TH CENTURY SEMI-CURSIVE 'EASTERN' SCRIPT FROM BUKHARA (CHART 26)

A book written in Bukhara in 1497 (fig. 211) represents another type of the semi-cursive 'Eastern' script. It is characterized by curved strokes and short and rounded letter-forms. Remnants of thin serifs, either upright or slanting downwards, appear at the left ends of the 'roofs' of Bet, He, Ḥet, Kaf, final Mem, Samekh, Qof, Resh and occasionally Taw. The thickness of the strokes varies according to their direction, the flat end of the calamus being held perpendicularly to the guideline. Most downstrokes gradually sharpen towards their bottom. Most of the base-strokes are concave while most of the 'roofs' are convex.

These are some letters which have a unique form: ʾAlef, the diagonal of which became a horizontal base-stroke while the right 'arm' took the shape of a semicircle open to the right. The upper part of Gimel is drawn in the form of a semicircle open to the left, while the 'heel' is drawn as a separate short and thin downstroke. The right downstroke of He occasionally starts above the 'roof', while the small left stroke is separated from the 'roof'. The top-stroke of Zayin is an emphasized concave stroke to the right of the vertical downstroke. The 'hook' and 'mast' of Lamed merged together, while its 'body' is rounded (Lamed resembles modern cursive Ṣadi). Final Nun has a concave base. The other letters have more or less regular forms.

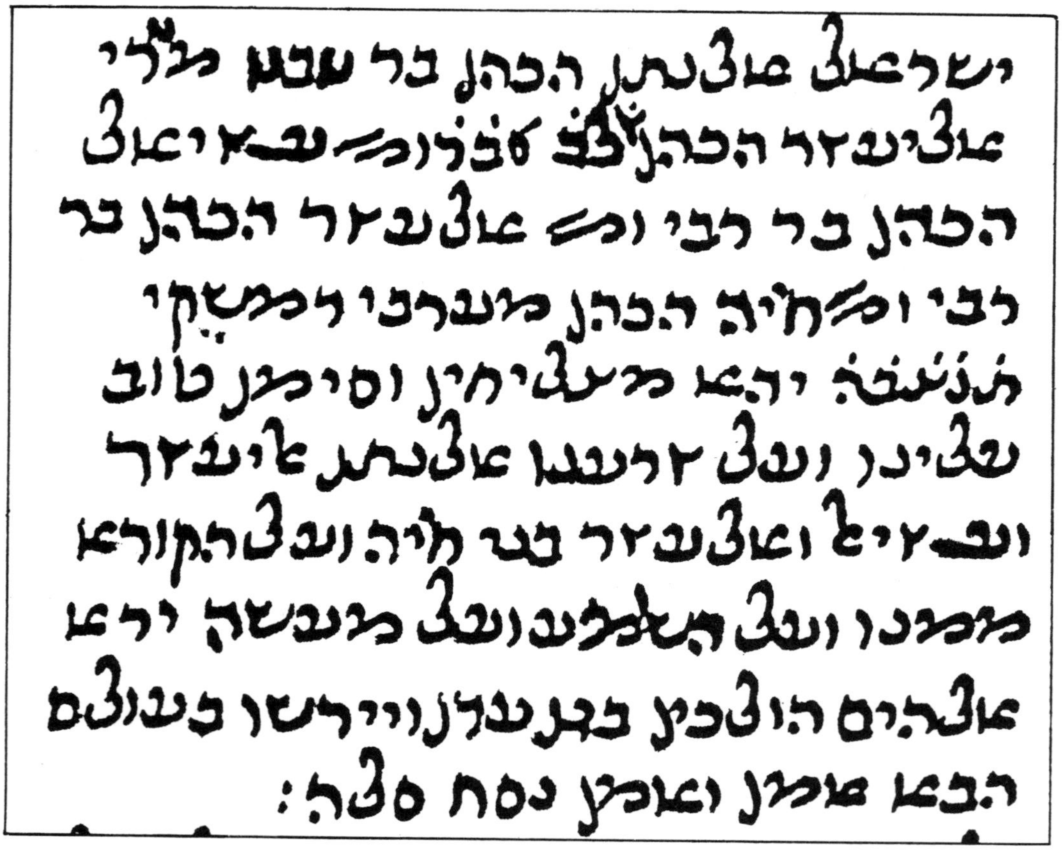

Fig. 211. A semi-cursive 'Eastern' script of Persian style in a manuscript from Bukhara

Chart 26. A local variant of the 15th century semi-cursive 'Eastern' script: a manuscript from Bukhara dating from 1497

21. THE ITALIAN BOOK-HAND OF THE 11TH OR 12TH CENTURY (CHART 27)

With the weakening of the contacts between the Jewish communities in Europe and those in the Middle East, several independent script-styles evolved in the Christian countries on one hand and in the Islamic countries on the other. All these styles originated from the common 'Eastern' style. An example of a beautiful handwriting from Italy, in which certain characteristics of the 'Eastern' style may still be distinguished, is to be found in the Kaufmann 50 A manuscript of the Mishnah (now located in Budapest). This is a Palestinian version of the Mishnah with Tiberian vowelization. The manuscript bears no date; however, it may perhaps on palaeographic grounds be dated to the 11th or the 12th century, although an earlier date is not impossible.

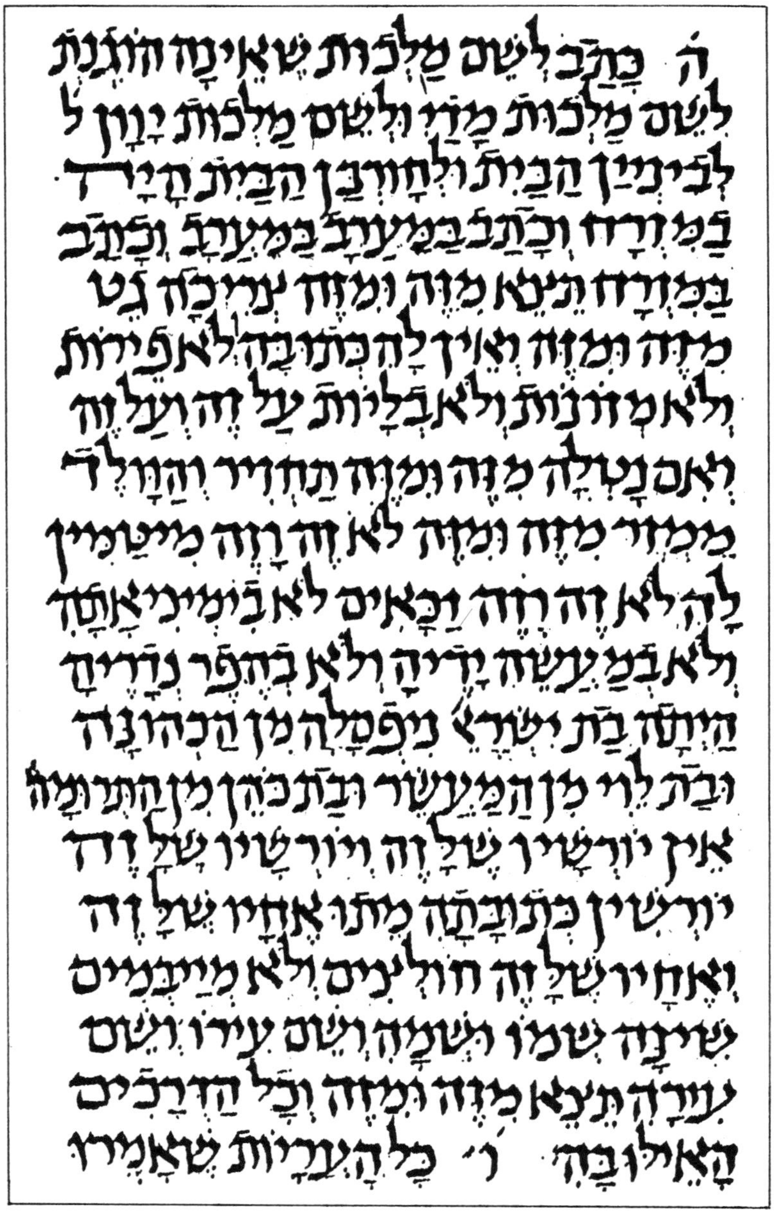

Fig. 212. Detail of a page of MS Kaufmann A 50 of the Mishnah written in an Italian book-hand of the 11th or 12th century

Chart 27. An 11th or 12th century Italian book-hand: the Kaufmann 50 A manuscript of the Mishnah

These are the main features of this handwriting: the delicate 'stings' and endings of the strokes perhaps indicate the use of a quill-pen which was used by scribes in Christian Europe. The horizontal strokes are only slightly thicker than the downstrokes, which sharpen to a point at the bottom. The script is spacious, like the 'Eastern' book-hand of the 10th century, and the letter-signs are large and some of them quite broad. The downstrokes which lean slightly forwards, are balanced by the long bases. An extra stroke adorning the 'roofs' of the individual letter-signs slants downwards towards the letter immediately following. Thus, each word, rather than each letter-form, appears as a separate graphic unit. Early features in the development of these letters are the curved upper part of Waw and Yod and the compound ornament in the letter-group *šʿṭnzgṣ*, which is drawn here with two short strokes, the right one partly covered by the left one, which terminates with a sharp end turning downwards. In contrast to the 'Eastern' book-hand, in this script-style the 'roofs' of the letter-forms are horizontal and the 'bases' also tend to horizontality because of the vowelization marks underneath. All the wide 'roofs' were made in the same way, and embellished with a thin 'sting' slanting downwards from their raised left end. Thus the letters Bet, Dalet, He, Ḥet, Kaf and Resh form one group together with final Mem, Samekh, Qof and Taw. The left downstroke of Qof is usually separated from the 'roof', while in He it occasionally starts at the 'roof'. The long 'legs' of the final forms of Kaf, Nun, Pe, Ṣadi and Qof are mostly wavy downstrokes terminating with a curve to the left. The right 'arm' of ʾAlef and Ṣadi and the middle stroke of Shin take the form of an angle rather than a to-and-fro stroke. The right stroke of ʿAyin and Shin slants downwards to the left and then bends at the bottom, forming the beginnings of a base. The left strokes of ʾAlef and final Pe (which has a peculiar form) are drawn in the same way, while in medial Pe, the 'nose' is different, curving to the right. Medial Mem still has no 'roof', whereas Pe has a short horizontal one.

These are some features of individual letters: ʾAlef is sometimes drawn without the left downstroke. When it exists, it descends vertically, and the short diagonal starts near its centre, sometimes without touching it. This form of ʾAlef is reminiscent of the form of ʾAlef in the marriage contract from Antinoupolis (see above, chart 16) and probably follows the same scribal tradition. It may thus be assumed that already at an early period different varieties of the 'Eastern' script emerged in different places, and later evolved into different styles. Bet has the typical raised 'tail'. The right stroke of Ṭet lacks a 'sting'. The 'body' of Lamed is small and has a short 'roof' and a curved right downstroke, while its 'flag' is in the form of a small triangle drawn below the top of the short 'mast'. The middle stroke of Shin is occasionally separated from the other strokes.

22. THE ASHKENAZI BOOK-HAND OF THE 13TH CENTURY (CHARTS 28-29)

The Ashkenazi script-style evolved out of an 'Eastern' script type which appears to have reached Europe by a northern route through Byzantium and Italy. In Christian Europe the quill-pen was the main scribal implement already in the early Middle Ages. No Ashkenazi manuscripts have survived from that period, however. The Hebrew letters which appear, for example, on epitaphs from southern Italy dating from the 9th century (fig. 88) still do not show the typical characteristics of the Ashkenazi book-hand appearing in manuscripts from the 12th century onwards. They seem, rather, to continue the scribal practices reflected in engraved inscriptions from the 3rd and 4th centuries, such as a third-century inscription from Palmyra (fig. 78) and burial inscriptions of the 3rd and 4th centuries from Palestine (see above, chart 15).

לחם חמץ יקריב קרבנו
על זבח תודת שלמיו:

Fig. 213. Ashkenazi book-hand in a manuscript from England dating from 1189 (Valmadonna Trust Library, MS. I; enlarged)

In the 13th century, the Gothic style prevailed in Christian Europe and found expression in calligraphy as well as the arts and architecture. The main characteristic of the Gothic Latin script is the 'broken' letters with the rhomboid or wavy strokes. The Hebrew book-hand was influenced by the new style, inasmuch as the horizontal strokes became very thick while the downstrokes became either very thin or 'broke' into two rhomboid strokes. Separate 'serifs' and ornaments were added with the sharp side of the flat end of the quill-pen or with another sharp pen. The attention given to the details of the letter-forms and the slow speed of writing prevented radical changes from taking place in the forms of the letters in that book-hand, and it continued to exist with minor local variations until the invention of printing in the 15th century.

The Ashkenazi book-hand is represented here by two manuscripts: one from 1272 (fig. 214), perhaps from Germany, and the other written in 1296 in France. The letters were drawn with a quill-pen, the flat end of which was held perpendicularly to the guideline, creating thick horizontal strokes. The downstrokes slant downwards to the right and the letters lean forward. The script is spacious and the letters are short. The following is a description of the script in both manuscripts.

A. THE MANUSCRIPT OF 1272 (CHART 28)

These are the main groups of letter-forms with similar graphic components: the group *šʿṭnzgṣ* is fully represented; each one of the letters in that group has an additional short concave stroke, drawn to the left, at the top of the left downstroke. A tiny, thin 'sting' curves downwards from the lower corner of that stroke. The downstroke consists of two parts. The upper one, which starts at the top-stroke, using the full width of the quill-pen, curves downwards and terminates in a sharp end. From that point, in Gimel, Zayin, Nun and Ṣadi, another short, rhomboid stroke slants downwards to the right. Ṭet, Shin and Samekh have a round 'base' instead, while the downstroke in ʿAyin has only one part. The ornament on the top of Lamed is somewhat similar to the ornament of that group, although much narrower. The pair of letters ʾAlef and Ṣadi have a right stroke shaped like a flag facing rightwards. Another pair is ʾAlef and Pe which have similar ornaments at the bottom of their left downstrokes. A new group consists of Waw, Zayin, Resh and Taw as well as the long-legged letters, except for Qof, in which the lower part of the right downstroke has the form of a narrow rhombus. The right downstrokes of Kaf and Pe occasionally also have a rhomboid form. The relatively short right downstrokes of Dalet, He and Ḥet start from inside the 'roof' with a fat, slightly curved top, and slant downwards to the right, sharpening towards the bottom. Another group consists of Bet, Mem and medial Nun, in which the right downstroke turns in its lower part to the right, creating a thick protrusion in the lower right-hand corner. The diagonal of Ṣadi is shaped in a similar way. The left downstroke of ʾAlef, Ḥet and Pe starts above the guideline. Waw and Yod have short, horizontal 'roofs', while the 'horn' of medial Mem resembles Yod.

These are some features of individual letters: Gimel has a long 'heel'; Ṭet has a horizontal 'roof' adorned with a tiny 'sting' pointing downwards. The right downstroke of Lamed slants downwards to the left. It is drawn in a downwards direction and is thin, unlike the right stroke of Qof which is drawn upwards in a curve and is therefore thick at its left end, while sharpening as it moves upwards, in the same way as the right stroke of ʿAyin and Shin. Medial Mem has a convex 'roof', while its left downstroke is very thin, descending vertically or slanting slightly to the left. The 'leg' of final Pe is very short. The 'leg' of Qof curves downwards to the right and becomes fat at the bottom.

טבורי היה משתיית ארץ וחוצות ובישת

תו ארץ וחוצות מחוקי אל חוק הארץ ח

וחוצות משתייתי אל משתיית ארץ וח

Fig. 214. 13th century Ashkenazi book-hand, perhaps from Germany, dating from 1272 (Jerusalem, The Jewish National and University Library, Heb. 4°781/1)

Chart 28. An elaborate 13th century Ashkenazi book-hand: a manuscript (Heb. 4°781/1), perhaps from Germany, dating from 1272

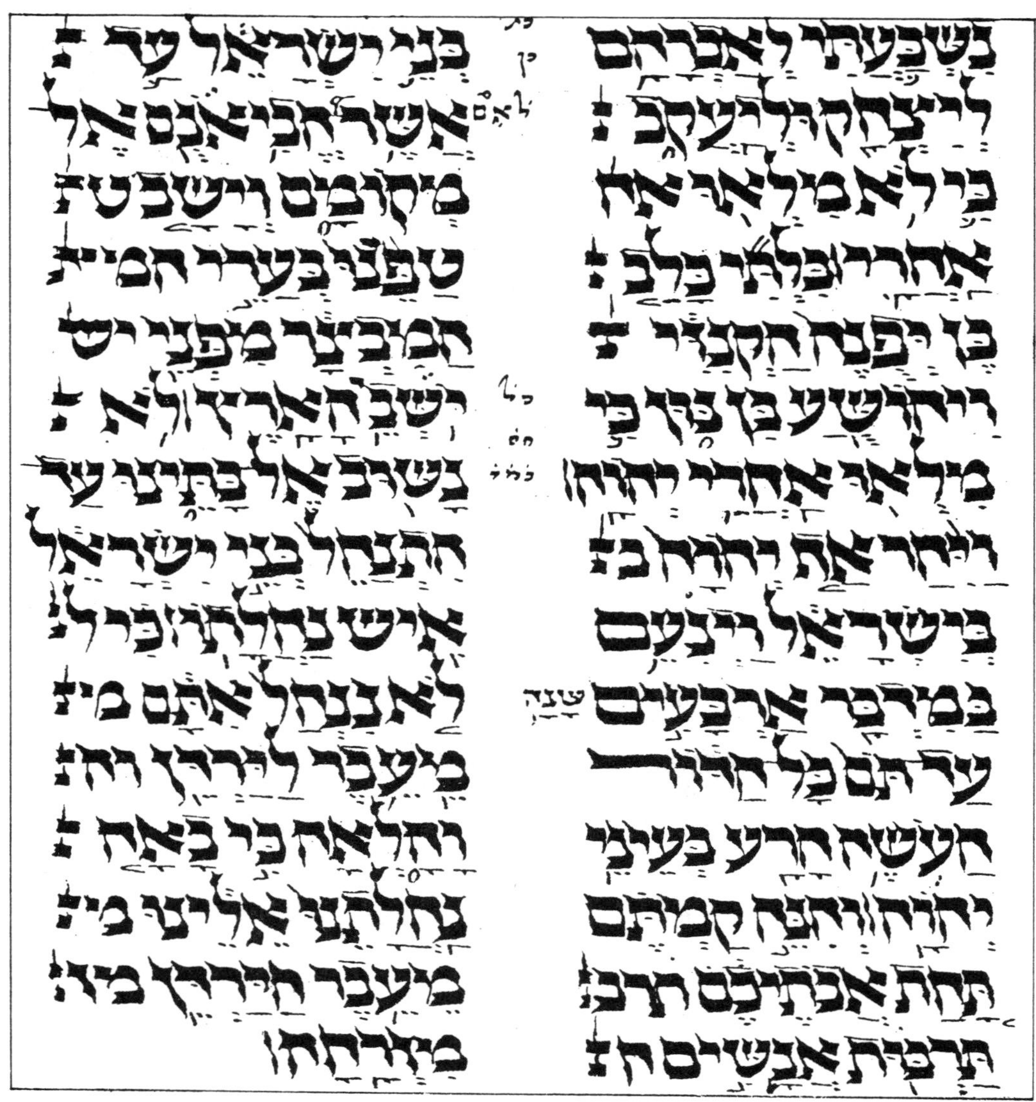

Fig. 215. Detail of a page of a biblical manuscript in an elegant Ashkenazi book-hand written 1303 in Paris by the scribe Abraham son of Jacob

B. THE MANUSCRIPT FROM FRANCE (CHART 29)

This manuscript generally resembles the one just described, with only minor differences. The pressure on the split, flat end of the flexible quill-pen often created a kind of 'fish-tail' at the beginning of fat strokes, which was deliberately emphasized in that script. A large group of letters with similar rhomboid right downstrokes is Gimel, Dalet, He, Waw, Zayin, Ḥet, Resh and Taw, as well as Bet, Mem, medial Nun, Pe and Ṣadi, the downstrokes of which extend into the right end of the horizontal bases. The 'long-legged' letters also have rhomboid downstrokes, which are relatively short. In ʾAlef, Ḥet and Pe, the left downstroke starts above the guideline and descends vertically, or slants slightly downwards to the right. In Pe it is extremely high. Another prominent feature is the elaborate 'mast' of Lamed, which curves at its bottom before joining the 'roof'.

Chart 29. Stylized letter-forms of an elaborate 13th century Ashkenazi book-hand, based on a manuscript from France dating from 1296

23. THE SEMI-CURSIVE ASHKENAZI GOTHIC SCRIPT-STYLE OF THE 14TH CENTURY (CHART 30)

The semi-cursive Ashkenazi script, which became stylized under the influence of the Latin Gothic style, is represented here by the Munich manuscript of the Talmud dating from 1343 (fig. 216). The outstanding characteristic of this script, as we said, is its 'broken' rhomboid strokes. As a result, in its semi-cursive form, the traditional shape of the letters is distorted and many letters are hardly recognizable, particularly when strokes of the individual letters are separated from each other and connected by ligatures to strokes of the letters immediately following. The similarity in the strokes of different letters often makes it difficult to identify the individual letters. However, through a careful examination, it is possible to perceive the characteristics of each letter-form and, with a little practice, to read the text.

Fig. 216. Detail of the Munich manuscript of the Talmud dating from 1343, written in a semi-cursive Ashkenazi script of Gothic style (Munich, Bayerische Staatsbibliothek, Cod. Heb. 95; enlarged)

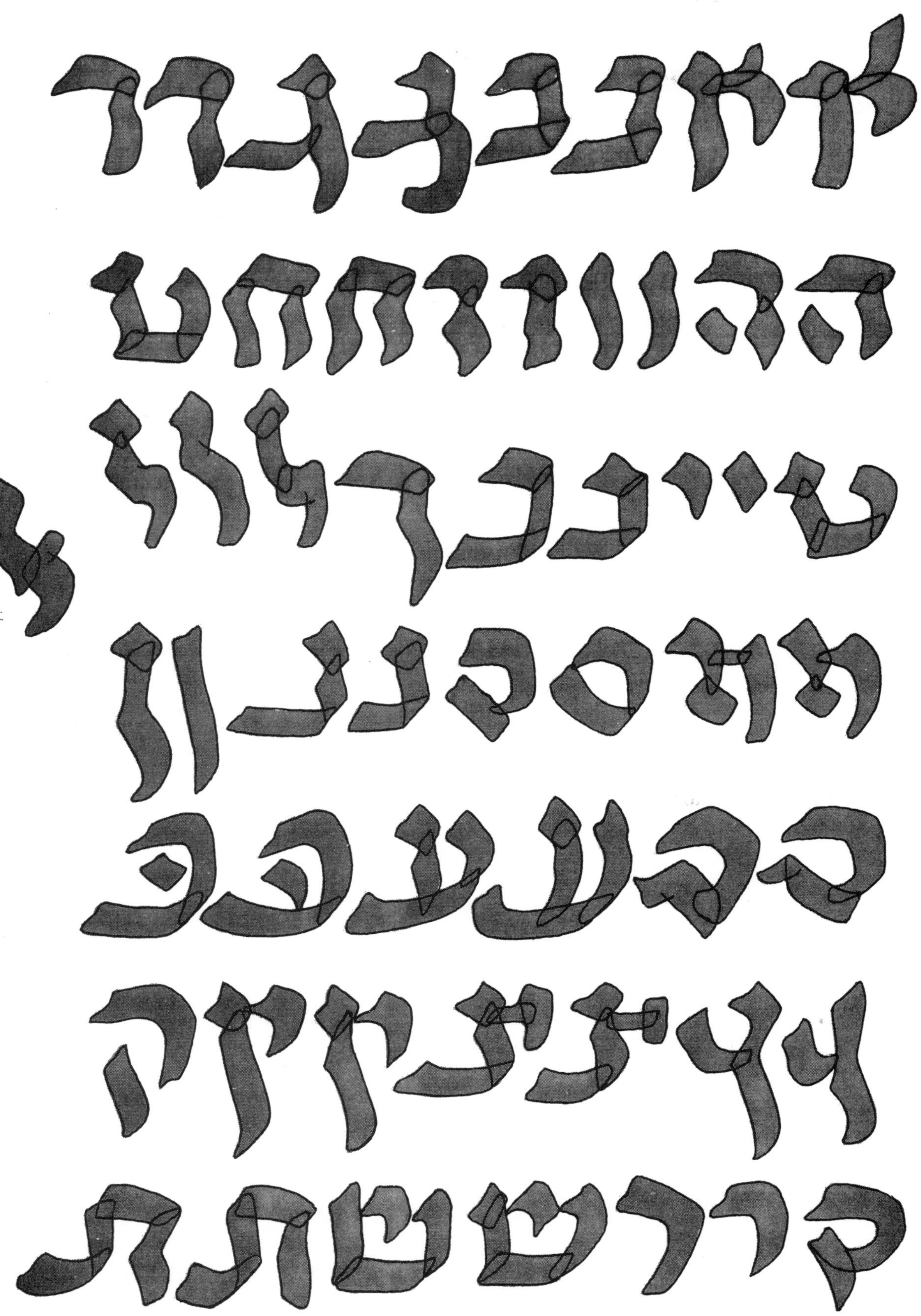

Chart 30. A 14th century semi-cursive Ashkenazi script of the Gothic style: the Munich manuscript of the Talmud dating from 1343

The semi-cursive Gothic Ashkenazi style is based on a cursive Ashkenazi script (see below) which evolved in the late Middle Ages and was used together with the book-hand. The semi-cursive Gothic hand is a spare script, lacking most of the additional ornaments which characterize the Ashkenazi book-hand, and the letters consist of a relatively small number of strokes. However, some of the ornaments became integral components of the letter-forms in that style, as in the case, for example, of the small square strokes at the top of ʾAlef, Gimel, Ṭet, Lamed, Nun, ʿAyin, Ṣadi, Qof and Shin.

The following is a description of the script in the manuscript from Munich (chart 30): the letters were written with a flat quill-pen, which was cut and held obliquely. The thin parts of the letter-forms are at the meeting points between the individual strokes. The base-strokes are mostly concave and emphasized.

These are the main groups with similar graphic components: Dalet, He, Ḥet, final Kaf and Taw have 'roofs' starting with the full width of the pen, which then slant downwards to the right, becoming thinner towards their right end. The rhomboid, somewhat wavy downstrokes meet the 'roofs' at their pointed ends, creating a thin 'neck'. The rhomboid left downstrokes of the letter-group *šʿṭnzgṣ* and ʾAlef have to the left of their pointed top a small square stroke, extended at its left 'corner' in order to join the 'roof' of the letter immediately following. The pointed end of the left downstroke of Ḥet and of Taw joins the higher 'corner' of the 'roof'. The 'roofs' of final Mem, Samekh, Pe and Qof are generally convex strokes.

These are the main features of individual letters: the right stroke of ʾAlef is made with a to-and-fro movement and it touches the low left downstroke above its centre. Bet differs from medial Kaf in that its lower right corner projects slightly to the right. Gimel has a high 'heel' extending below the imaginary base-line, while its left stroke is almost horizontal. He is like a Dalet with an additional small rhomboid left stroke. Waw is an almost vertical downstroke. Zayin resembles Dalet, with a short 'roof'. Yod is a small rhomboid stroke. Lamed has a small 'body' as well as a small 'mast' with a rhomboid stroke at its top. Medial Mem has no 'base' and its 'roof' is very thin and narrow. Its short left downstroke terminates in an additional rhomboid stroke turning inwards. Final Nun is like a long Waw or a long Zayin. Final Mem is almost round, made of two curved strokes. Samekh differs only a little from final Mem, having an additional short stroke slanting downwards to the left towards the letter immediately following. Pe has a separated short stroke turning inwards, representing its 'nose'. In final Pe the lower end of that stroke touches the long 'leg', while the 'roof' is missing. The 'leg' of Qof is relatively short and separated from the 'roof', but it occasionally touches the lower end of the right curved downstroke. The medial stroke of Shin starts at the left downstroke and terminates above the base-stroke without touching it.

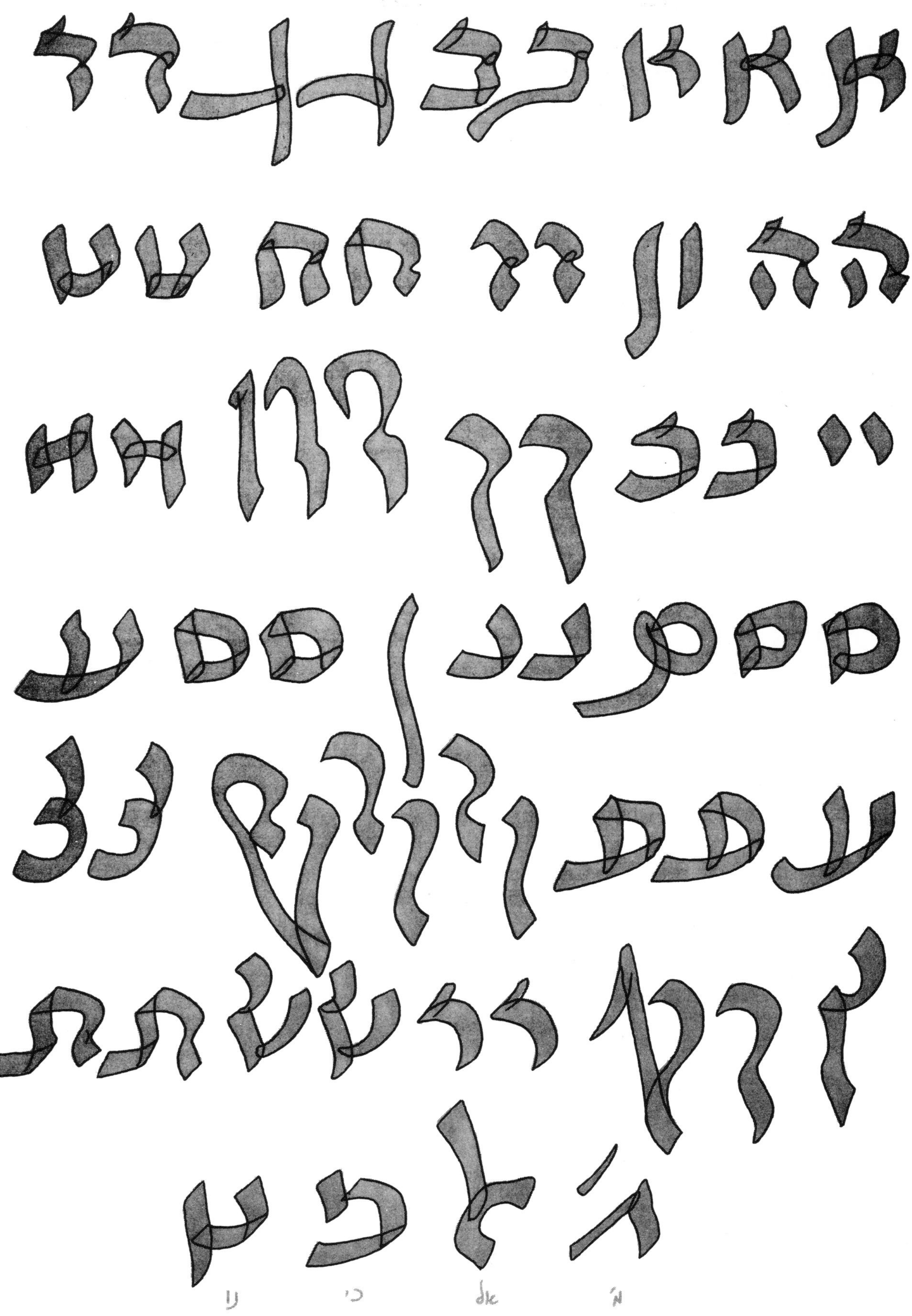

Chart 31. A 15th century cursive Ashkenazi script: the Parm. 2407 manuscript

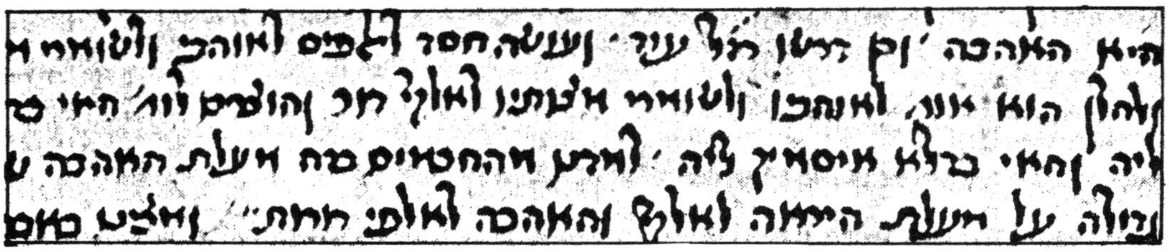

Fig. 217. Detail of a 15th century manuscript from Italy written in a cursive Ashkenazi script (MS Parm. 2407; De Rossi 484; enlarged)

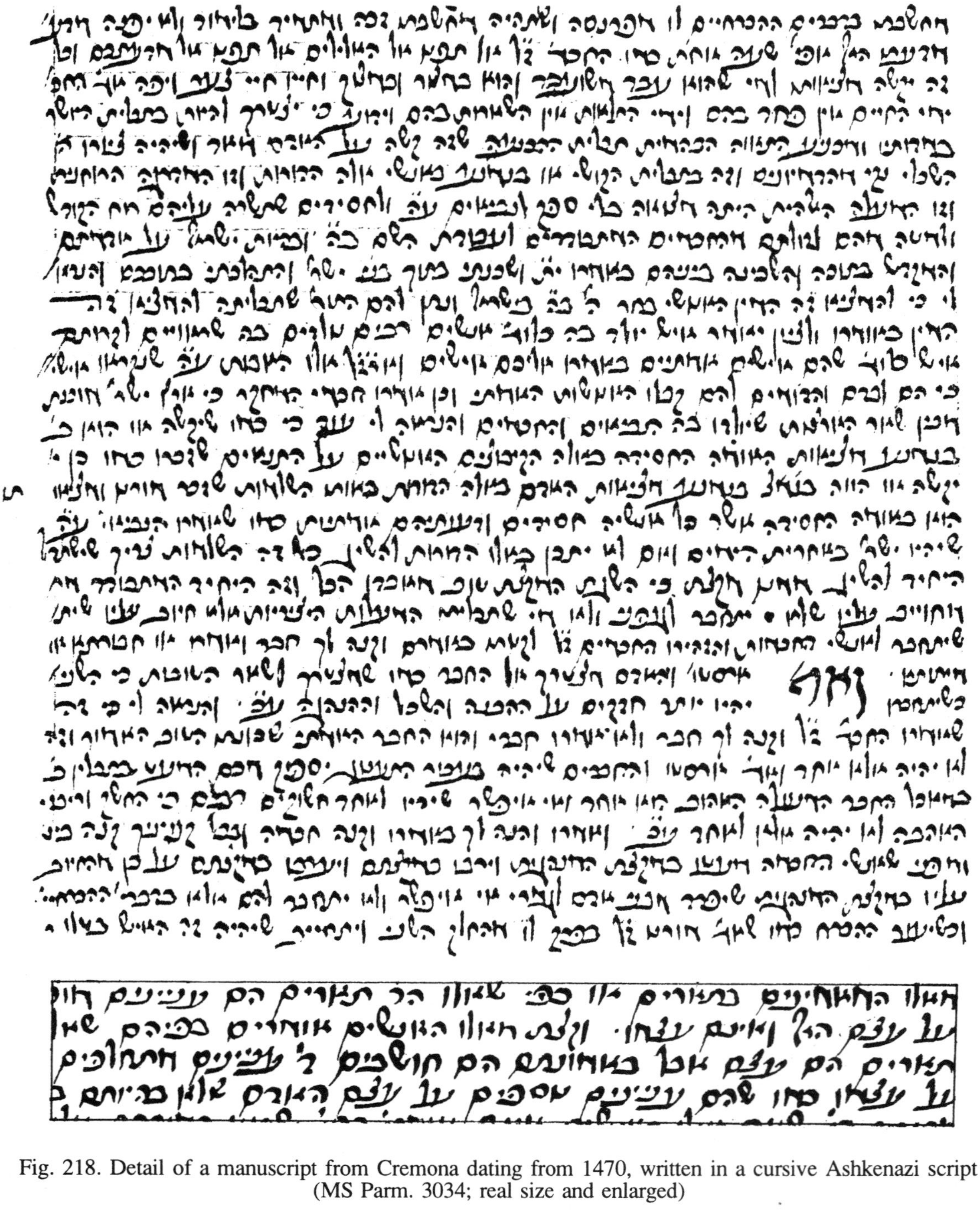

Fig. 218. Detail of a manuscript from Cremona dating from 1470, written in a cursive Ashkenazi script (MS Parm. 3034; real size and enlarged)

24. THE CURSIVE ASHKENAZI SCRIPT OF THE 15TH CENTURY (CHARTS 31-32)

Two contradictory phenomena usually influence the evolution of cursive letter-forms. On the one hand, a consequence of the fluent writing is that large groups of letters become identical in their form. On the other hand, the fluent writing creates many variant forms of each letter. These phenomena reduce the legibility of the script and as a result the characteristic features of the individual letter-forms are often deliberately emphasized. Manuscripts of Two books, which are now in the Palatine library in Parma, Italy (Nos. 2407 [fig. 217] and 3034 [fig. 218]), represent the cursive Ashkenazi script of the 15th century. In these manuscripts, the tendencies we have mentioned have not yet become extreme. Some of the rhomboid strokes of the Ashkenazi semi-cursive Gothic hand also appear in the cursive, as in the downstrokes of Bet, Dalet, He, Zayin, Ḥet and Taw, for instance. Unlike the semi-cursive Ashkenazi Gothic script, which was essentially an elegant calligraphic hand, the cursive hand had no such pretensions. It is therefore interesting to note that the small serifs which occasionally adorn the 'roofs' of Bet, Dalet, He, Kaf and Resh in the cursive style do not appear in the semi-cursive Gothic hand. The 15th century manuscripts in that script-style which have survived do not show extreme idiosyncrasies in the letter-forms, and despite the differences between that script and the modern cursive script which evolved from it, it is easy, after a little practice, to identify the individual letters. An examination of the letter-forms in the De Rossi manuscript of 1470 shows a remarkable affinity between some of these forms and the modern forms of those letters. A comparison between the letter-forms in the two manuscripts shows that those in the second one are rather more fluent than in the first. This fluency is mainly expressed in the ligatures between the strokes and in the curved joints of the 'roofs' with the right downstrokes.

A. MS PARM. 2407 (CHART 31)

MS Parm. 2407 was written with a quill-pen, which was cut obliquely and held at an angle of about 45 degrees to the guideline. Most of the base-strokes are somewhat concave and occasionally long.

These are the main groups of letter-signs with similar graphic components: in Dalet, He, Ḥet, final Kaf and Taw, and occasionally Bet, the 'roof' starts with the full width of the flat end of the quill-pen, curving downwards at its right end, while growing sharper towards its join with the rhomboid downstroke. The left downstroke in Ḥet, final Mem, Samekh, medial Pe and Taw starts at the left end of the 'roof' and descends vertically.

These are the main features of the individual letters: in ʾAlef, the right and middle strokes were made in a to-and-fro movement, touching the left, vertical and long downstroke near its centre. Bet somewhat resembles the numeral 3, but with a fat or long base. Gimel has a high 'heel' extending downwards below the base-line and sometimes curving leftwards at the bottom. Its left leg is a long, almost horizontal stroke, drawn close to the base-line. He has a short, separated, rhomboid left stroke, slanting downwards to the right. Waw is a vertical stroke. Zayin resembles Dalet with a short 'roof' and without the extra serif. The right stroke of Ṭet lacks the convex additional stroke at its top. Yod is a tiny rhomboid stroke. Final Kaf resembles a very large Zayin. Lamed occasionally has a short 'mast' with a large convex top and its lower part is an almost vertical downstroke. Medial Mem has a peculiar form made of two vertical downstrokes and a cross-bar – a transitional stage toward its modern N form. Final Mem is composed of a semicircle and a vertical left downstroke, or a closed circle with a long left downstroke, sometimes curving leftwards at the bottom. Samekh resembles medial Mem. The left stroke of medial Pe descends vertically and terminates at the long base-stroke. Final Pe has a peculiar form in which the additional ornament is emphasized and, together with the left part, forms a separate wavy stroke. It is occasionally joined by a ligature to the right downstroke. Medial Ṣadi already resembles its modern cursive form. The final form of Ṣadi differs from the medial form in that its lower part is a vertical, somewhat wavy downstroke. Qof resembles final Kaf, but occasionally has an extra stroke to the left of its 'roof'. Resh is a curved stroke with a serif. The medial stroke of Shin starts high above the guideline and at the bottom it joins the top of the left downstroke.

B. MS PARM. 3034 (CHART 32)

ʾAlef resembles a Latin K form, Bet has a convex 'roof', drawn together with a slanting downstroke, which curves rightwards at the bottom. Its 'base' is a long horizontal stroke. The form of Gimel prefigures its modern cursive form, its large left stroke gradually becoming the prominent part of the letter-form. Dalet appears in two forms, one of which already resembles its modern cursive form of two curves – a large one surmounting a smaller one – but still retains the small serif at its top. The letter He likewise resembles the modern cursive He, apart from the serif at its top. Waw is a straight vertical downstroke. Zayin resembles a narrow Dalet. Ḥet resembles the modern cursive form of the letter. Ṭet is very small and is made with two strokes: a right downstroke, curving at the bottom, and joining a vertical downstroke. Yod and Kaf resemble their modern cursive forms. Lamed appears in two forms, one of which is a high downstroke with a large 'hook'. Medial Mem is at a late stage of evolution toward its N form, while final Mem resembles its modern cursive form. Samekh consists of a circle and a left downstroke. ʿAyin has a long base. The 'nose' of medial Pe is a separated small stroke inside the letter, while final Pe has a complex form in which the left stroke resembles a large Zayin. Medial Ṣadi resembles its modern cursive form and so do Qof (which is close to a certain type of modern Qof), Resh, Shin and Taw. The ligatures which appear most often in this handwriting are those of ʾAlef with Lamed and of Nun with Waw.

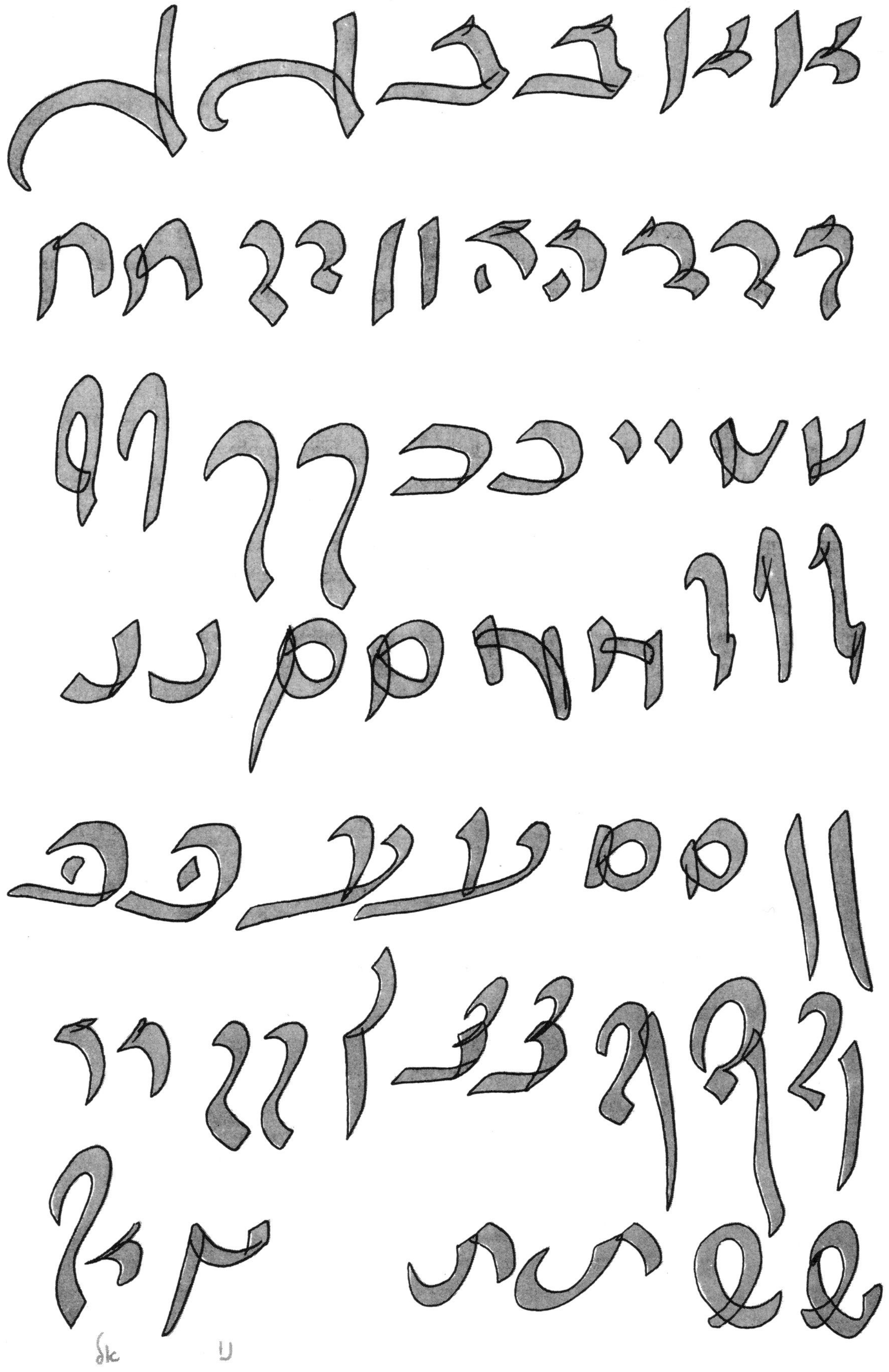

Chart 32. A 15th century cursive Ashkenazi script: the Parm. 3034 manuscript dating from 1470

25. THE SEPHARDI BOOK-HAND OF THE 13TH CENTURY (CHART 33)

In the 13th century, the Sephardi book-hand had already developed characteristics which distinguished it from both the 'Eastern' and the Ashkenazi hands. The calamus used by the Sephardi scribes was less flexible and less sharp than the quill-pen used by the Ashkenasi scribes. The calamus was usually cut obliquely and held at a sharp angle to the guideline and there is consequently only a small difference in the thickness of the horizontal and vertical strokes. The thick strokes are those which slant downwards to the right and the thin strokes are those which slant downwards to the left. Already at an early stage of the development of the Sephardi style, the curved right stroke of ῾Ayin and Shin became angular, and it was later drawn as two strokes – a right downstroke and a base-stroke. In the Ashkenazi style it remained a single curved stroke. The Sephardi book-hand is represented here by a biblical manuscript from Toledo dating from 1241. The strokes of the letter-forms in this script are simple, unlike the flamboyant Ashkenazi letter-forms of that period. There are almost no ornamental additions except for those which had already become integral parts of the letter-forms in the 'Eastern' script: for instance the additional ornament on the left stroke of ᾽Alef and Pe, or the ornament on the letter-group *š῾ṭnzgṣ* which evolved into a short square stroke on top of the downstrokes, connected to them by a thin 'neck' and giving the letters an elegant appearance. The downstrokes are mostly vertical and the 'roofs' are generally horizontal, with the remnant of a serif at their left end. The rhythmical effect of the script is somewhat diminished by the oblique strokes in some of the letters, such as ᾽Alef, Ṣadi, ῾Ayin and Shin, Lamed and Qof and some curved strokes such as the 'roofs' of Ṭet, Mem and Pe and the left strokes of ᾽Alef, Pe and Taw.

These are the main groups of letter-signs with similar graphic components: the lower parts of the left strokes of ᾽Alef and Pe are shaped alike. The right 'arm' of ᾽Alef resembles the right 'arm' of Ṣadi as well as the middle stroke of Shin, which is somewhat longer. The 'roof' of Bet, medial Kaf, final Mem, Samekh, Resh and Taw is joined to the right downstroke at a right angle. The 'roof' of Dalet, He, Ḥet and final Kaf slants downwards at its right extremity and extends beyond its meeting-point with the right downstroke. The left downstroke of Ḥet, final Mem, Samekh and Taw and occasionally Qof (when starting at the 'roof') starts with a narrow 'neck' to the right of the left end of the 'roof'. The 'body' of Lamed and the right part of Qof are drawn in the same way. As we have pointed out above, in the letter-group *š῾ṭnzgṣ*, a short, square stroke slants downwards to the right, meeting the narrow 'neck' of the left downstroke.

These are some major features of the individual letter-forms: ᾽Alef stands upright, leaning on its left 'leg' and supported by the diagonal which extends to the base-line; the right 'arm' meets the diagonal below its centre, while the left downstroke starts below its top. Gimel is narrow and resembles Nun, except for its small 'heel'. The left downstroke of He starts very near its 'roof' and only a tiny space between the leg and the 'roof'

Chart 33. The 13th century Sephardi book-hand: a manuscript from Toledo dating from 1241

דבר

אחר ביד חזקה שתים ובזרוע

נטויה שתים ובמורא גדול שתים

ובאותות שתים ובמופתים שתים

אלו עשר מכות שהביא הקב"ה

על המצרים במצרים אלו הן

דם צפרדע כנים ערוב דבר

שחין ברד ארבה חשך מכת

Fig. 219. 14th century Sephardi book-hand in the Sarajevo Haggadah

distinguishes He from Ḥet. Waw has a short 'roof' slanting downwards to the right and joining the narrow 'neck' of the downstroke. The right stroke of Ṭet starts with a convex curve and has an additional 'hook' slanting downwards to the left into the space within the letter. Yod is made in the form of a right angle leaning backwards. The 'flag' at the top of Lamed resembles the short 'roof' of Waw, while the 'mast' curves at its bottom before joining the horizontal stroke. Medial Mem, as well as Pe, still have a convex top. The left downstroke of medial Mem starts at the 'roof' and slants downwards to the left, terminating near the base-line; the 'horn' is a short, slanting stroke. Final Mem resembles Samekh but its 'base' is somewhat wider and more horizontal. Final Nun is shaped like a long Zayin. ʿAyin is a long letter, its base-stroke slanting downwards to the left and continuing below the base-line. Pe has an extra serif at its upper left-hand corner. Medial Ṣadi has a short base-stroke. The left downstroke of Qof sometimes starts at the 'roof'. The medial stroke of Shin terminates at the meeting-point of the left downstroke with the base. The upper parts of the final forms of Nun, Pe and Ṣadi resemble those of the medial forms.

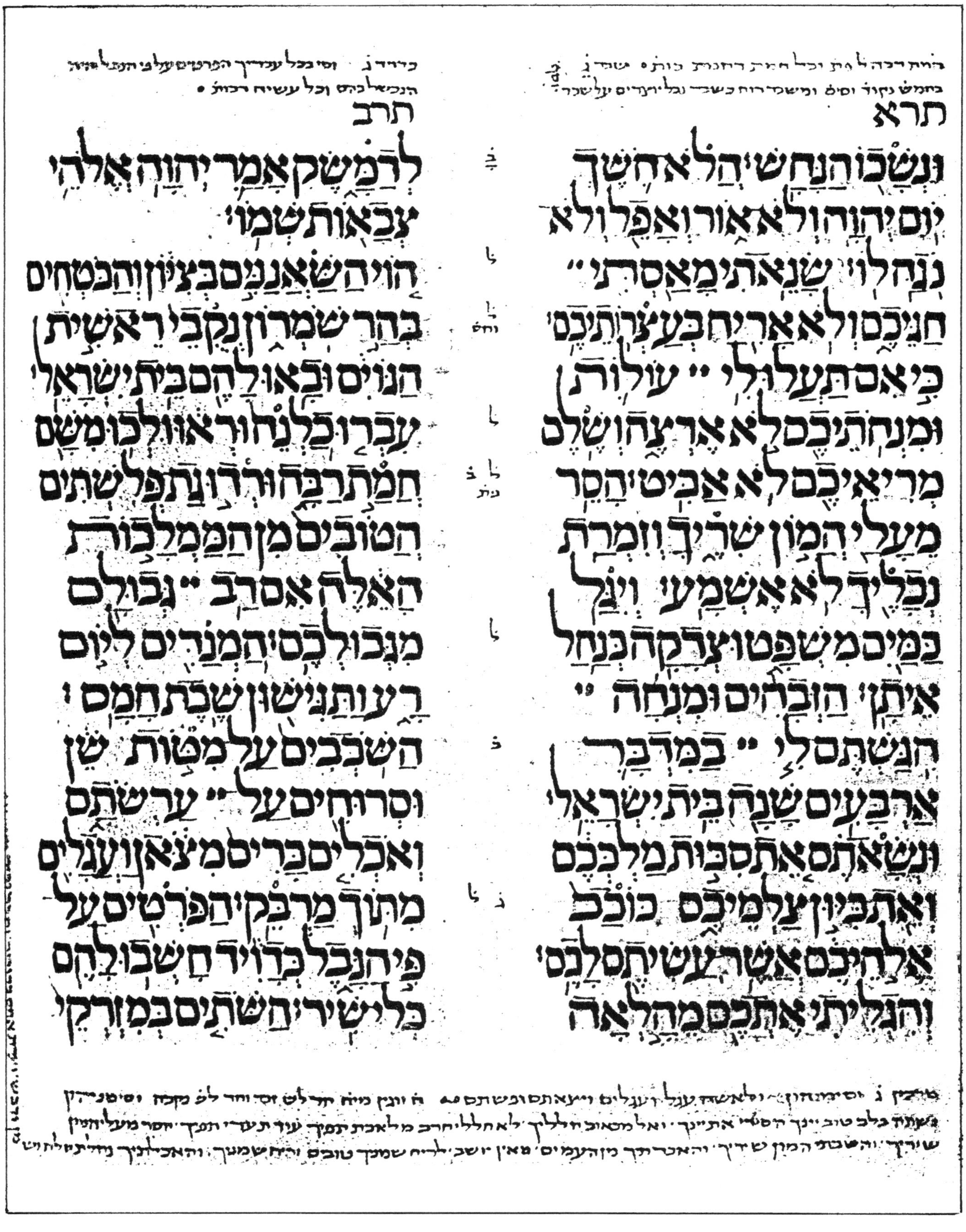
תרא

ונשכו הנחש׃ הלא חשך
יום יהוה ולא אור ואפל ולא
נגה לו׃ שנאתי מאסתי
חגיכם ולא אריח בעצרתיכם׃
כי אם תעלו לי ״ עלות
ומנחתיכם לא ארצה ושלם
מריאיכם לא אביט׃ הסר
מעלי המון שריך וזמרת
נבליך לא אשמע׃ ויגל
כמים משפט וצדקה כנחל
איתן׃ הזבחים ומנחה ״
הגשתם לי ״ במדבר
ארבעים שנה בית ישראל׃
ונשאתם את סכות מלככם
ואת כיון צלמיכם כוכב
אלהיכם אשר עשיתם לכם׃
והגליתי אתכם מהלאה

תרב

לדמשק אמר יהוה אלהי
צבאות שמו׃
הוי השאננים בציון והבטחים
בהר שמרון נקבי ראשית
הגוים ובאו להם בית ישראל׃
עברו כלנה וראו ולכו משם
חמת רבה ורדו גת פלשתים
הטובים מן הממלכות
האלה אם רב ״ גבולם
מגבולכם׃ המנדים ליום
רע ותגישון שבת חמס׃
השכבים על מטות שן
וסרחים על ״ ערשתם
ואכלים כרים מצאן ועגלים
מתוך מרבק׃ הפרטים על
פי הנבל כדויד חשבו להם
כלי שיר׃ השתים במזרקי

Fig. 220. A page of a biblical manuscript from Toledo dating from 1222, written in a Sephardi book-hand (Oxford Bodleian Library, Kennicot 7 [2331])

26. THE SEPHARDI SEMI-CURSIVE SCRIPT OF THE 15TH CENTURY (CHARTS 34-35)

Together with the 'square' Sephardi book-hand, there were semi-cursive and cursive script-styles, which apparently derived from an 'Eastern' cursive script influenced by the Arabic cursive script. (The Arabic script evolved from the Nabatean cursive script, retaining the cursive characteristics of the letter-signs, i.e., the curving strokes and the numerous ligatures.) Under the influence of Arabic calligraphy, elaborate, calligraphic styles of the Sephardi Hebrew cursive and semi-cursive hands evolved; they are to be found in several different kinds of manuscript.

Following the colophon of a Torah manuscript (MS Parm. 2018), Don Moshe son of Shemuʾel al-Tortos, signed his name in three different Sephardi script styles, and explained (in Hebrew): “A man should always write his name on his book lest someone else will come from the market and say: ‘This is mine’, even though it is not. Therefore I wrote and signed my name here in the Assyrian script [i.e., the ‘square’ script] and in the *Māshiq* script [an Arabic term designating the model semi-cursive script] and in the *Moʿāʾliq* script [an Arabic term designating the cursive script in which the letters are connected to each other in ligatures]”.

אני יוסף
כתבתי החומש
הזה עם הפטרות וששה
מגלות בנקוד ובמסרת אל הגביר
דון משה בר׳ שמואל נ״ע אל טורטוש וסיימתיו
בעזרת האל יתעלה בחדש ניסן:
פרשת ויעש כאשר צוה
יי׳ את משה שנת
כי ביום הזה
יכפר עליכם
לטהר אתכם
מכל חטאתיכם
לפני יי׳ תטהרו:

ממני זה הספר משה אלטורטוש

לעולם יכתוב אדם שמו על ספרו פן יבא אחר מן השוק ויאמר שלי הוא. ולא יהה כן
על כן כתבתי וחתמתי שמי פה בכתב אשורי׳
ובכתב מאשק ובכתב מועאליק
משה בר׳ דון שמואל נ״ע אל טורטוש – משה בר׳ דון שמואל נע׳ אלטורטוש –

Fig. 221. The colophon of MS Parma 2018, with the signatures of Moshe al-Tortos in three Sephardi script-styles (real size)

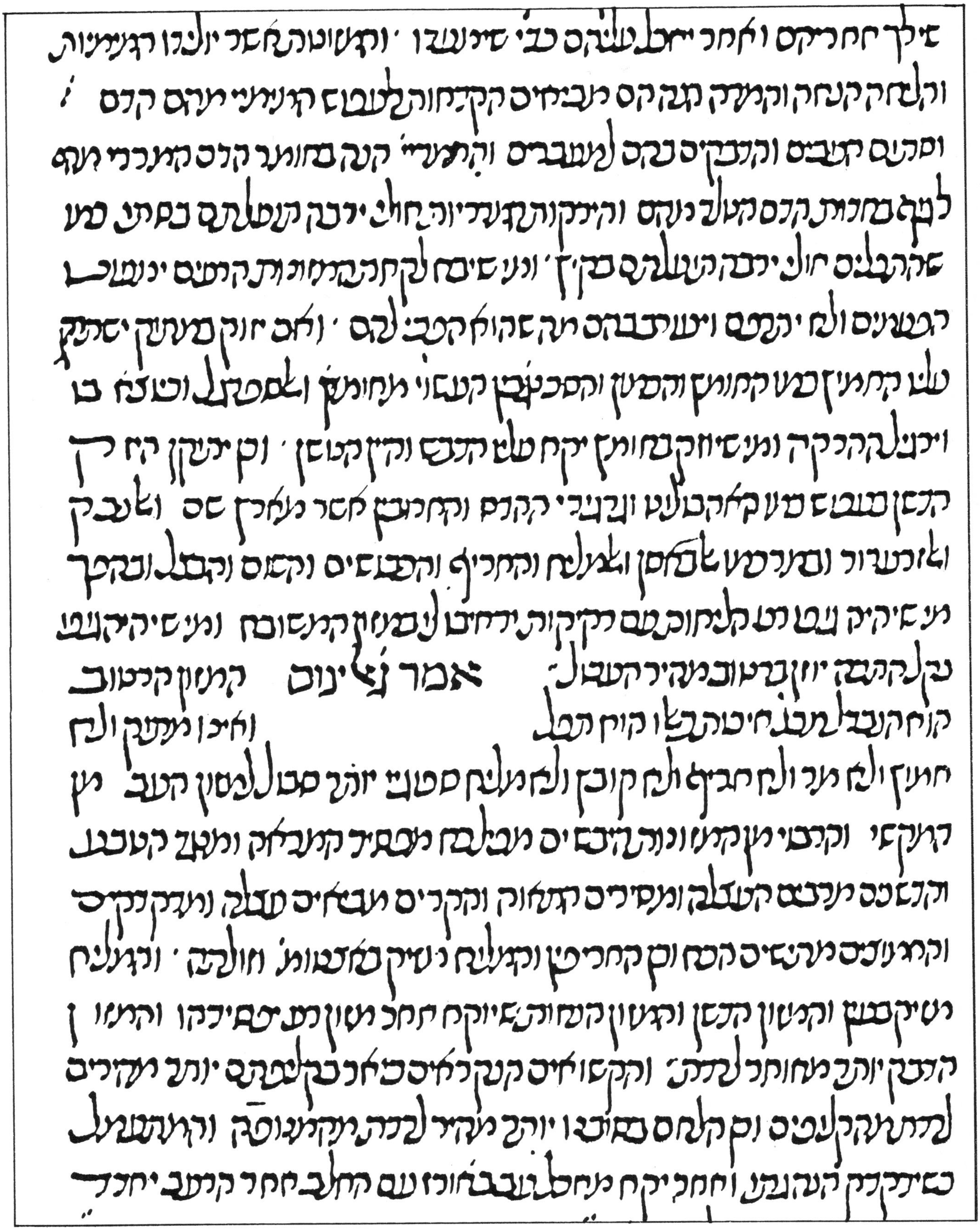

Fig. 222. A semi-cursive Sephardi script in a manuscript from Villalón dating from 1480 (Munich, Bayerische Staatsbibliothek, Cod. Heb. 373; enlarged)

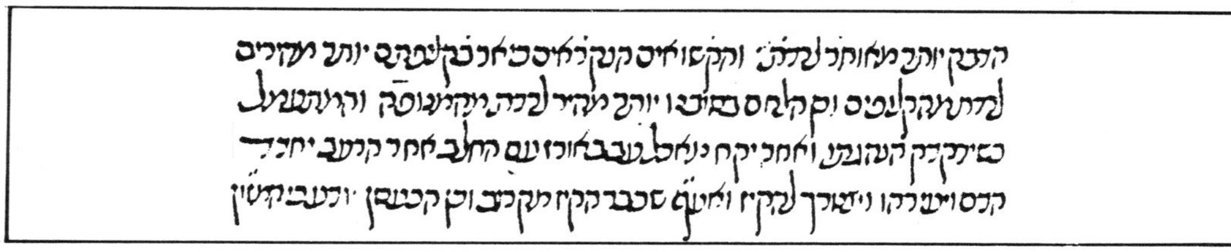

Fig. 223. Detail of the manuscript from Villalón (real size)

The best known of these styles is the semi-cursive Sephardi 'rabbinic' script-style which served as the model for the letter-types in which Rashi's commentary to the Bible and Talmud was printed in 1475. It is consequently known as 'Rashi script'.

The major feature of the script is its 'rounded' appearance, due to the curved strokes. The script was written with a thin, flat calamus, cut obliquely. The thickness of the strokes changes according to their direction. There are almost no ornamental additions to the letters and the number of strokes in many letter-forms is smaller than in the 'square' script. Despite the relatively slow speed of writing caused by the raising of the hand between the individual strokes, the long base-strokes of many of the letter-forms touch the letters immediately following. The letter-forms are narrow and tightly packed.

The script is represented here by two manuscripts from Spain – one written in Villalón de Campos in 1480, and the other written in Toledo in 1477. There are slight differences between the forms of the letters in the two manuscripts.

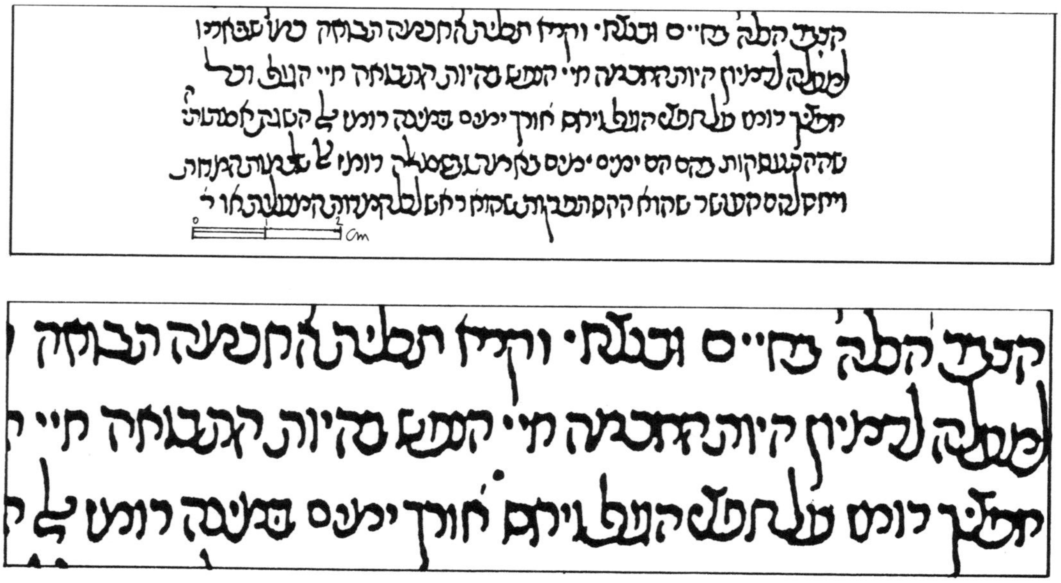

Fig. 224. A semi-cursive Sephardi script in a manuscript from Toledo dating from 1477. Above: real size. Below: enlarged

Chart 34. The 15th century semi-cursive Sephardi 'Rabbinic' script: a manuscript from Villalón dating from 1480

A. THE MANUSCRIPT FROM VILLALÓN (CHART 34)

These are the main groups of letter-signs with similar graphic components: ʾAlef and Ḥet have a similar appearance apart from the extra stroke on the top of ʾAlef. Bet, Dalet, He, Kaf, Samekh, final Mem, Qof, Resh and Taw have a similarly-shaped concave 'roof'. Bet, Kaf, Lamed, ʿAyin and medial Pe have long concave base-strokes. The right downstrokes of Dalet, He, Ḥet, Qof, Resh and Taw curve leftwards at the bottom.

These are some features of the individual letter-signs: the thin right 'arm' of ʾAlef starts high above the line and slants downwards to the left, towards the left end of the horizontal 'roof', which in fact is the upper part of the former diagonal stroke. The downstroke of Bet curves at its bottom to the right, creating a projection at the lower right corner of the letter. The left stroke of Gimel becomes a wavy horizontal base-stroke. The left downstroke of He drops below the 'base' line. The top of Zayin is made with a to-and-fro movement. The left downstroke of Ṭet extends beyond its meeting-point with the base. Lamed has a long, concave 'base'. The 'horn' and part of the left stroke of medial Mem form one long stroke, which curves at its bottom to the left. Samekh has a long left downstroke which extends beyond its meeting-point with the base. ʿAyin has two parallel downstrokes, the right one having a convex top which occasionally touches the left one. Medial Pe has a short, vertical left downstroke, unlike final Pe which has a curved 'nose' and an additional ornament at its top in the form of a thin, vertical stroke. The former right 'arm' of Ṣadi becomes an almost horizontal stroke at the top of the downstroke. The 'leg' of Qof is separated from its 'body'. The former medial stroke of Shin becomes a horizontal stroke joining the top of the left downstroke. The left downstroke of Taw is separated from its 'body' and it has a large and low base-stroke, curving to the left.

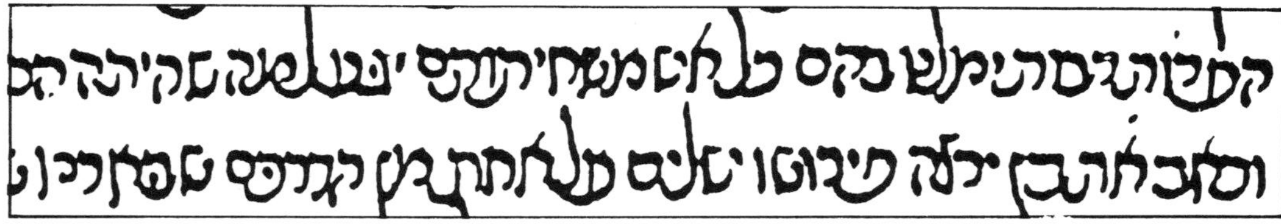

B. THE MANUSCRIPT FROM TOLEDO (CHART 35)

The script of the manuscript from Toledo (fig. 111) differs slightly from that of the Villalón manuscript in the form of some of its letters, the most prominent of which are listed below: Yod often appears as a small rhomboid stroke inside the immediately preceding letter. The final form of Pe resembles its medial form, but has an additional vertical stroke on its top, and its 'nose' is curved. Ṣadi is very high.

Chart 35 .A 15th century semi-cursive Sephardi 'Rabbinic' script: a manuscript from Toledo dating from 1477

27. A VARIANT STYLE OF THE SEMI-CURSIVE SEPHARDI SCRIPT OF THE 14TH CENTURY (CHART 36)

The semi-cursive Sephardi script appears in two variants, which differ from each other in the formation of the individual letter-strokes but resemble each other in the basic structure of the letter-forms. They appear to have emerged in different localities or different scribal schools. The less common of the two styles is represented here by a manuscript from Fez dating from the year 1332 (fig. 112), now located in the Bodleian Library in Oxford. The script was written with a thin calamus, the flat and somewhat frayed end of which was held perpendicularly to the guideline. The horizontal strokes are thus thicker than the vertical. Most of the letters lean backwards. The downstrokes of the 'long-legged' letters, however, are long vertical strokes. The major feature of the script is the curved, thick ends of the downstrokes. The 'roofs' are horizontal. The top of Zayin and of final Nun is shaped identically, as is the right stroke of Ṣadi and the middle stroke of Shin. The bases of Dalet, He, Ḥet, Resh and Taw appear to be drawn from left to right.

These are the main features of the individual letter-signs: the form of ʾAlef is of the K-type, with a very long left downstroke that curves downwards to the left, continuing below the imaginary base-line. Bet has a high right shoulder and a projection at its lower right-hand corner. Gimel is long and has a wavy base-stroke and a very short 'heel'. The downstroke of Dalet slants downwards to the left and curves at the bottom. The right side of He resembles Dalet, and its wavy left downstroke is on a slant. Zayin has a short, thick stroke on top of the wavy downstroke. The left downstroke of Ṭet goes beyond its meeting-point with the curved 'base' and is very small. The 'base' of medial Kaf forms a continuity with the downstroke. Lamed has a vertical 'mast'. Medial Mem has no base. In final Mem the 'base' has merged with the right and left downstrokes. The left downstroke of Samekh continues below its meeting-point with the base. Final Pe has an extra stroke at its top, shaped like a horn, and a curved 'nose'. The right stroke of Ṣadi starts at the downstroke and is drawn upwards to the right. The long 'leg' of Qof starts in the left part of its 'roof'. The downstroke of Resh curves leftwards at the bottom. Resh differs somewhat from Dalet in the formation of its 'shoulder'. The left part of Shin resembles medial Ṣadi but the curve at its bottom is shorter. The left downstroke of Taw starts in the left part of the 'roof' and curves downwards to the left.

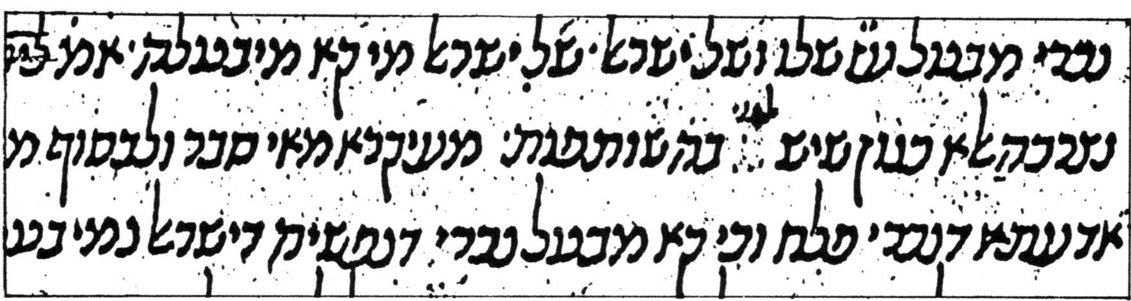

Fig. 225. Detail of a manuscript of the Talmud from Obide dating from 1290, written in a semi-cursive Sephardi variant script (New York, JTS 44830 R.15)

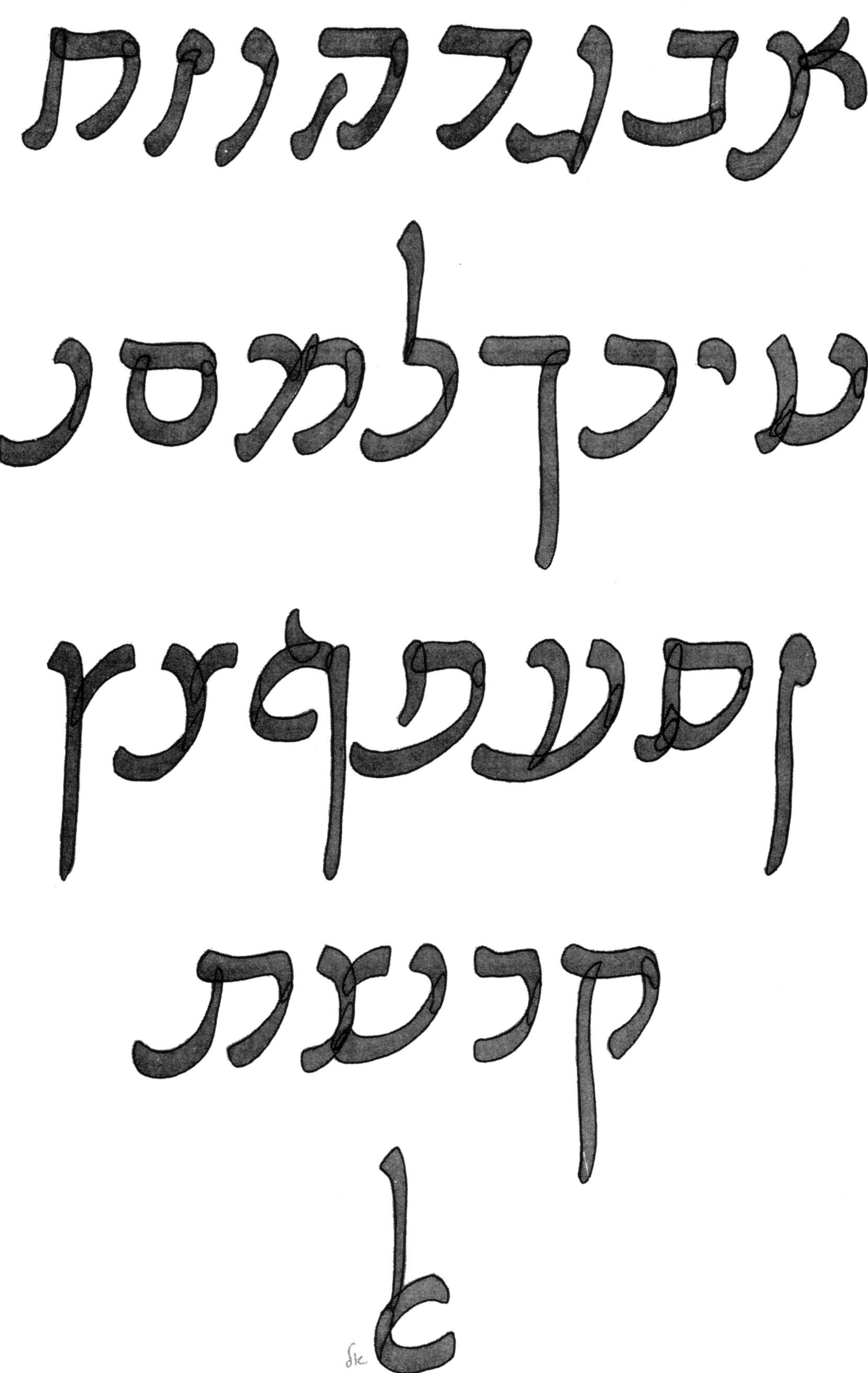

Chart 36. A 14th century variant of the semi-cursive Sephardi script: a manuscript from Fez dating from 1332

28. THE CURSIVE SEPHARDI SCRIPT OF THE 12TH AND 15TH CENTURIES (CHARTS 37-38)

The extreme cursive Sephardi script is already to be found in manuscripts dating from the early 12th century. It appears to have evolved from an 'Eastern' cursive script influenced by the Arabic cursive script, and was used together with the 'Eastern' book-hand. No evidence of the earliest stages of its evolution survives, however. A relatively early example of the extreme cursive Sephardi script (fig. 106) is an undated letter of Rabbi Yehudah Ha-Levi (died in 1140), which is represented here. Despite the personal features of the handwriting, it is possible to recognize in it the stylistic elements that appear later in the decorative cursive hand represented here by the script of a book on mathematics written in Qalaᶜat Aiyub in 1475 (fig. 113). The rather narrow letter-forms were drawn with a very thin calamus. In many letters, the basic strokes were merged together into one or two strokes which were drawn continuously. There are numerous ligatures of two or more letters. In order to identify the individual letter-signs we shall try to trace the basic strokes of each letter.

The following letter-signs were made without lifting the hand between the strokes: ʾAlef, Bet, Gimel, Dalet, He, Waw, Zayin, Ṭet, Yod, Kaf, final Mem, Nun, Samekh, (ᶜAyin), Ṣadi, Qof, Resh and Taw. The letter-signs that were formed with two strokes (which means the hand was lifted once) are Ḥet, Lamed, medial Mem, ᶜAyin, Pe and Shin.

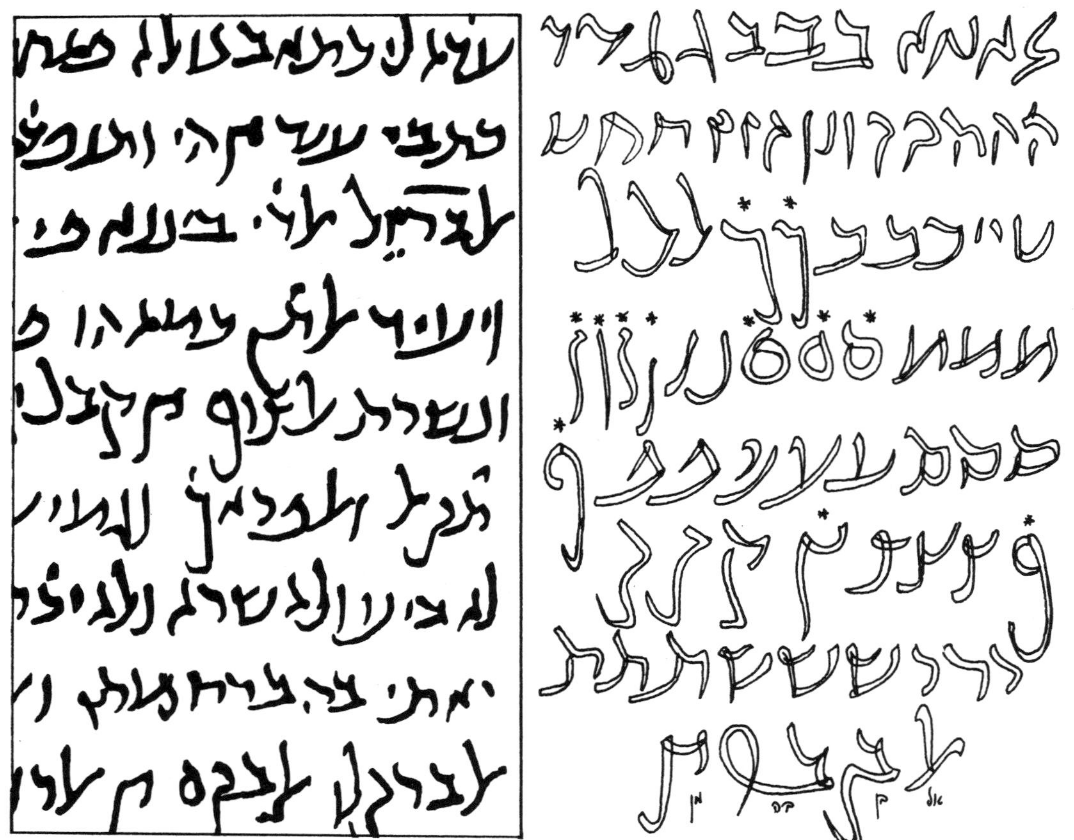

Fig. 226. Detail of a letter of Naharai son of Nissim written in an 11th century cursive Sephardi script from North Africa (Cambridge University LIbrary, T-S 13 J14.2; enlarged)

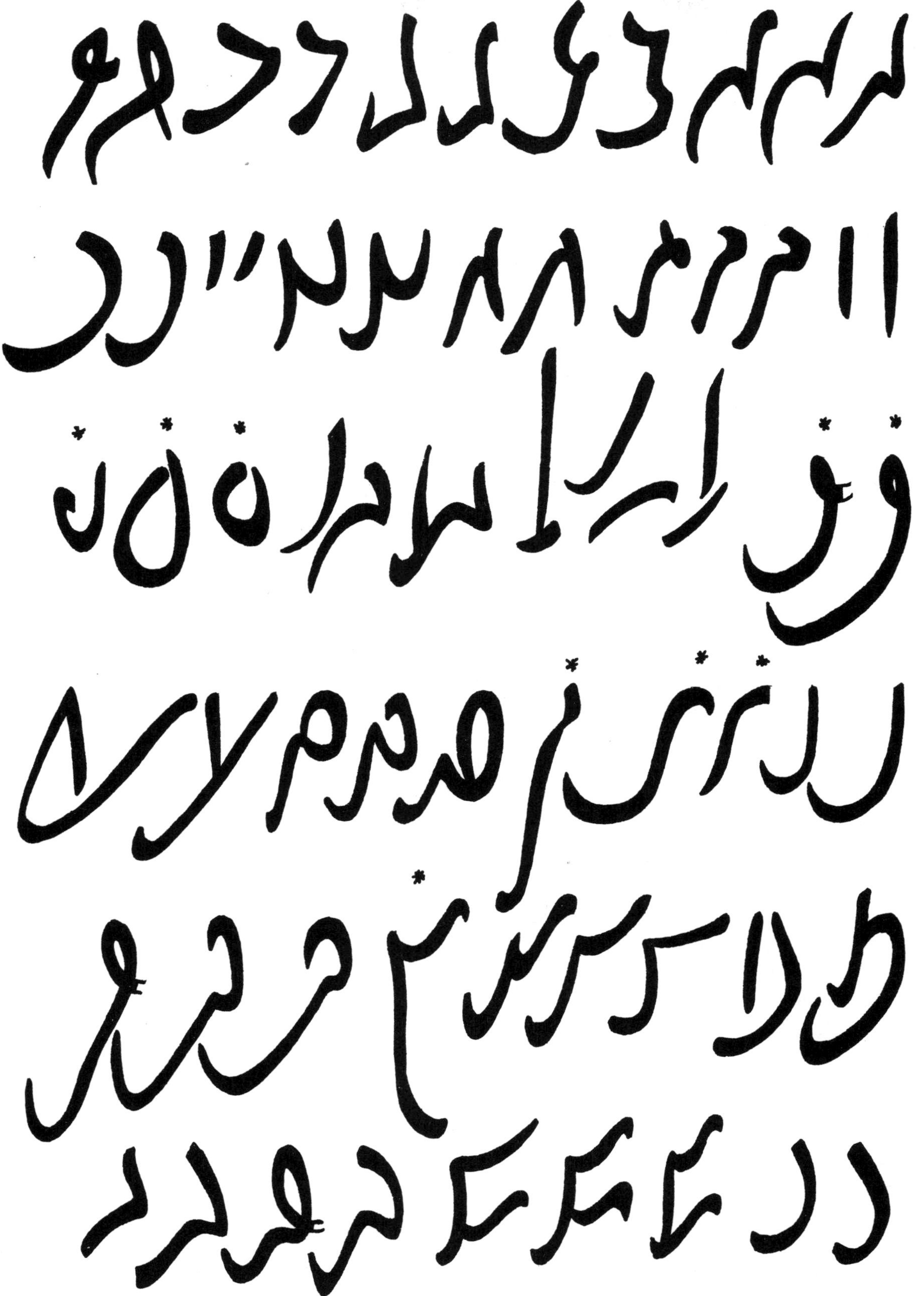

Chart 37. A 12th century cursive Sephardi script: a letter of Yehudah HaLevi

In ᵓAlef, the diagonal has merged with the left downstroke: . In Bet, all three basic strokes are recognizable. The serif is occasionally emphasized. In Gimel and Dalet the basic strokes are retained. In He, the three basic strokes merge together into a wavy downstroke: . The loop that was created when He was ligated with the letter immediately preceding it also occasionally appears when the letter stands alone: . Zayin retains the additional stroke at the top which was ligated with the downstroke. Ḥet loses its 'roof' which merges with the right downstroke: . In Ṭet the right downstroke and the 'base' together form a deep curve: . In medial Kaf all three basic strokes merge into one curve. Final Kaf has lost its 'roof' and become a long curved downstroke with a loop at its top: . Lamed has lost its 'roof', which has merged with the oblique downstroke: the 'mast' often extends towards the lower part of the letter immediately following, but without touching it: . In medial Mem, the left downstroke starts at the lower end of the right downstroke: while the former 'horn' becomes an additional long and high vertical stroke descending towards the lower left part of the letter, or towards the letter immediately following: . Final Mem becomes a circle drawn clockwise: . Final Nun occasionally has a large concave base. In Samekh, the 'roof', the right downstroke and the 'base' together form a circle drawn clockwise, and its left downstroke starts at its former base: . ᶜAyin retains its two strokes which are occasionally drawn without lifting the hand: . Pe becomes a curved downstroke with a vertical left stroke: . The right 'arm' of Ṣadi joins the top of the former diagonal: . The 'roof' and right downstroke of Qof become a small curve or loop, and its 'leg' starts at the lower end of the curve: . The two basic strokes of Resh become a single curved downstroke. In Shin the middle stroke joins the left downstroke and the right stroke forms an oblique, wavy base: . In Taw the 'roof' merges with the right downstroke, which curves leftwards and joins the top of the left downstroke: .
The extreme cursive forms of He, Qof and Taw occasionally resemble one another.

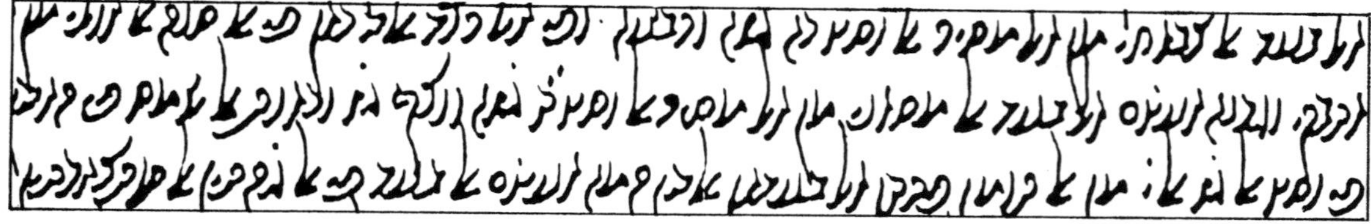

Fig. 227. Detail of a manuscript in an extreme cursive Sephardi script dating from 1475 (enlarged; see fig. 106)

The extreme cursive letter-forms in the manuscript of 1475 are the result of a more or less similar process, but the script is stylized and the letter-forms have a regular and rhythmical appearance. The influence of the elegant Arabic calligraphy is clearly recognizable; in fact, at first sight it looks like Arabic. As the language of the manuscript is Arabic, diacritic points appear above certain letters in order to indicate phonemes which do not exist in Hebrew, or to designate letters which stand for numerals.

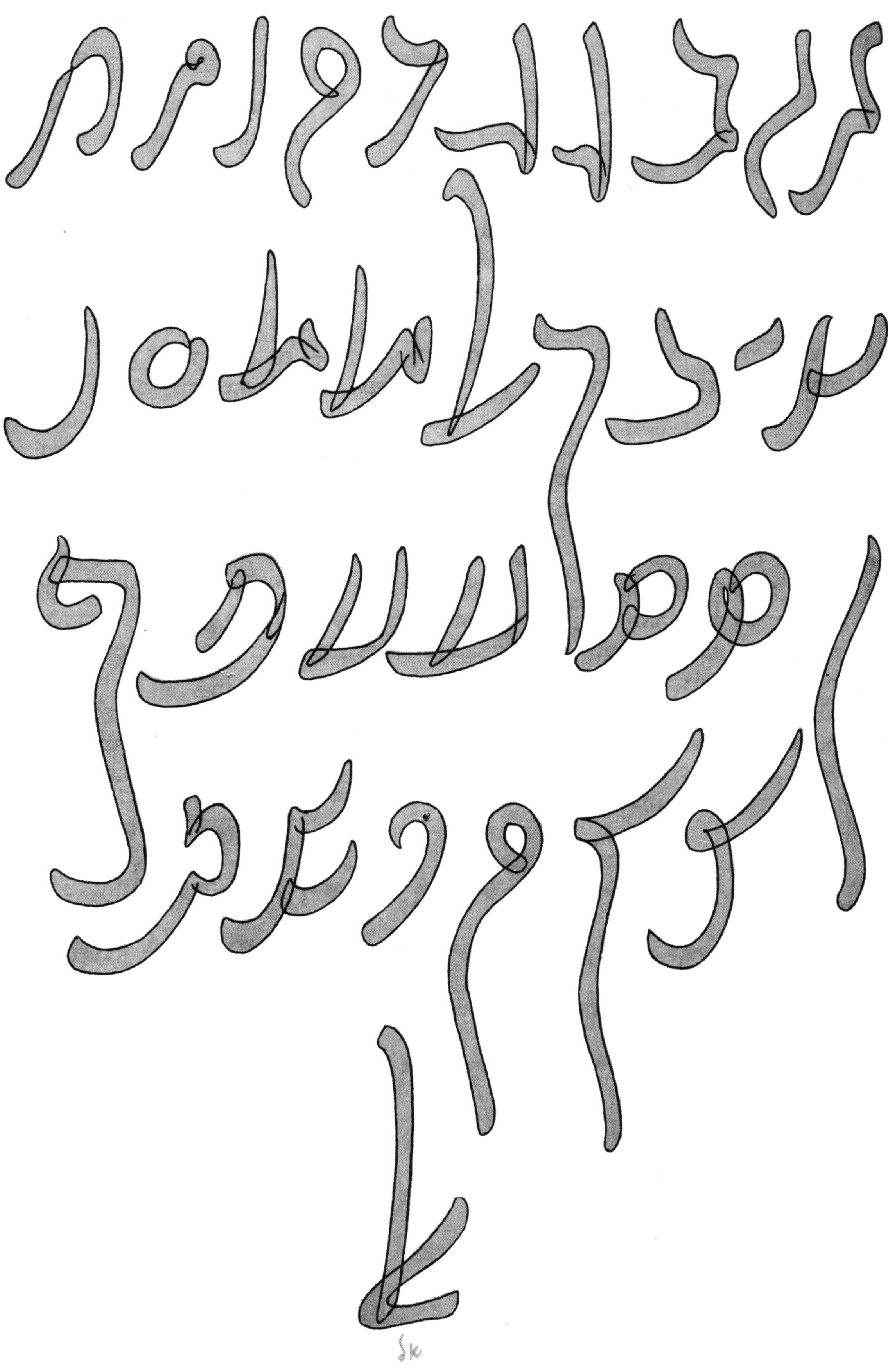

Chart 38. A 15th century cursive Sephardi script: a manuscript from Qalaʿat Aiyub dating from 1475

29. THE YEMENITE BOOK-HAND OF THE 13TH-15TH CENTURIES (CHARTS 39-41)

The 'Yemenite' script includes a variety of script-styles which differ from the group of scripts generally called the 'Eastern' script. The earliest dated manuscripts so far known in the 'Yemenite' script are from the 13th century. However, earlier undated manuscripts from Yemen apparently date from the early 12th century. As the 'Yemenite' script did not become definitely stylized, there is a large variety of handwritings, of which three main types, dating to the 13th-15th centuries, are represented here.

One of the prominent characteristics of most 'Yemenite' handwritings is the use of a flat calamus, the end of which was cut in a right angle and held perpendicularly to the guideline. As a result, the horizontal strokes are bold, in contrast to the thin downstrokes. The average height of the letters is equivalent to about two-and-a-half to three-and-a-half times the width of the calamus (in the 'Eastern' book-hand, the proportion is about three-and-a-half to four times).

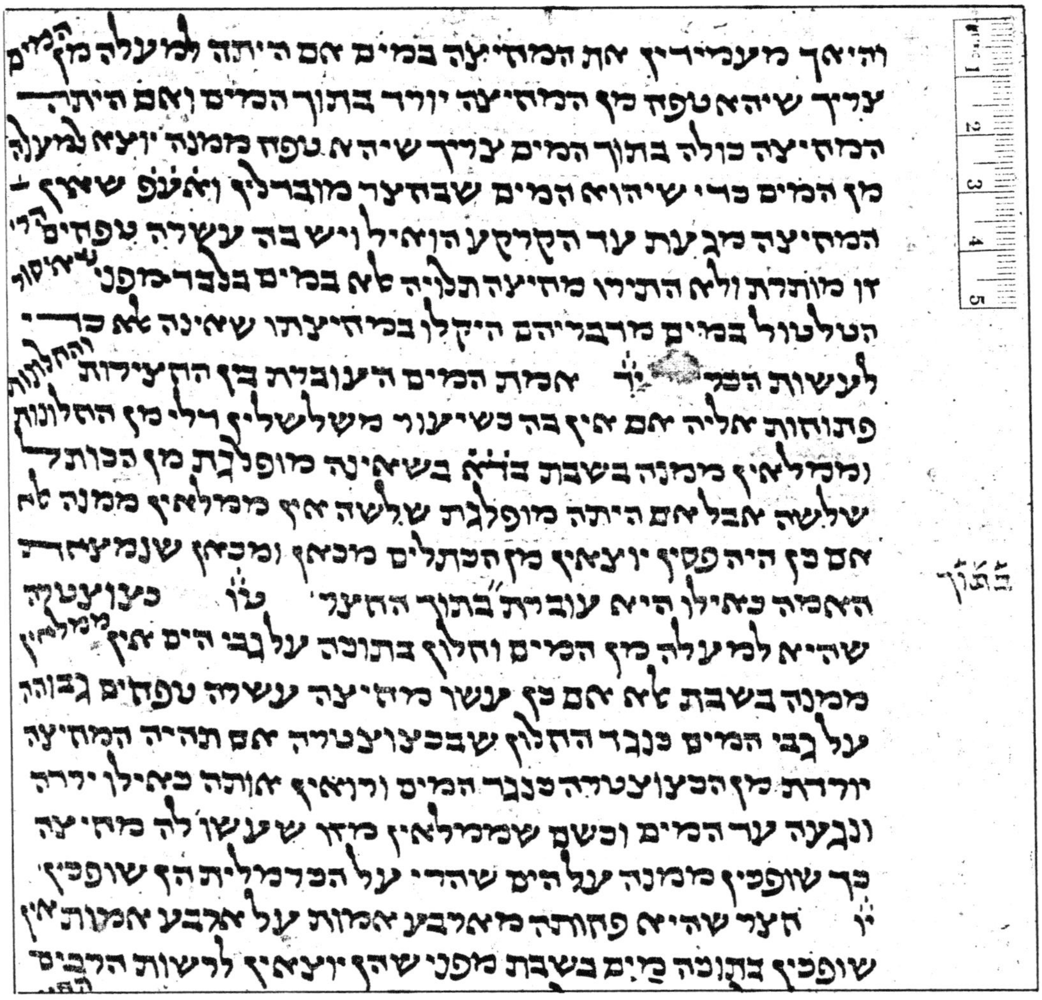

Fig, 228. Detail of a page of a Yemenite manuscript written 1386 in Al-Sud (New Haven, Yale Un. Beinecke L. Hebrew 1, fol. 32b (reduced)

פי סאדס נזירות ולא עליהא איצֿא רֿגב מתל אוכל חלב ונחוה פיתקרב לכפרה פלהדֿא אסכנ
ממשכנין אותו עליה· ותם עולה איצֿא אין ממשכנין עליהא והי עולת מצורע לאנה
לא תכמל לה טהרה חתי יקרב גמיע קראבינה פהו יתפז נפסה פי הבאתה··

פרק ששי

שום היתומים שלשים יום ושום ההקדש שש
יום ומכריזין בבקר ובערב· המקדיש נכסים והיתה עליו כתובת אשה ר׳ אליעזר אומר
כשיגרשנה ידיר הנייה ר׳ יהושע אומר אינו צריך כיוצא בו אמר רבן שמעון בן גמליא
הערב לאשה בכתובה והיה בעלה מגרשה ידיר הנייה שמא יעשו קנוניא על נכסיו של זה
ויחזיר את אשתו·· קד עלמת אן שום אלתקדיר פקט אן אלא כאנת ארץ ענד
אליתומים ולזם בית דין ביעהא עלי מא נבין או הקדיש אחד שדה מקנה אלתי תפדי כמא
אלתי תסוי כמא תקדם פלא תבאע הדה אלארצין חתי ינאדי עליהא אלעדה אלמדכורה כל
אליום בבקר ובערב אלדין המא וקתי אגתמאע אהל אלצנאיע פי אלמואקף והדה אלאיא
תכון מתואליה יום בעד יום ואדא נודי עלי נכסי יתומים ששים יום שני וחמישי פלא
חסן והו אלאולי והו קולהם א״ע״ג דכי חשיב ליומי דהכרזה לא הוי אלא תמני סר יומא כיון
דמשכא מילתא טובא שמעי אינאשי ויחתאג אן יכון פי אלנדא אלמוצע בחדודה
וכם סוי ומן אגל אי שי יבאע אעני את היקול ולדי ישתריה יעוול אן ידפע תמנה
פי דין פלאן או פי כתובת פלאנה לאן מן אגל דלך תבאע אמלאך אליתאם· ואעלם אן
אלאצל אלמעמול עליה אין נזקקין לנכסי יתומים ועלא אנהם יתמי דאכלי דרבית
דידהו ליזלו בתר שבקהו לכן קטוע אלהלכה אין נזקקין לנכסי יתומים ולא תבאע
בוגה אלא ואחד תלאתה אשיא לא גיר אמא פי כתובת אשה להספידה נפע כביר
לאנה [illegible] מא לא תאכל אלכתובה יש לה מזונות מנכסי יתומים כמא תבין פי חאד
עשר כתובות או לדין גוי יכון עליהם ברבית ותכון רבית אוכלת בנכסיהם פביעאצ̇הם
ונתודייה· דלך אלדין ילאחא בהם· או אדא תחקקנא אן דין הדא אלטאלב באקי עלא אביהם
אמא באקראר אביהם ענד מותה אן לפלאן ענדי או בכון בית דין קד שמתוה אלי אן
ידפע דינה ומת בנדויו· או אדא כאן אלדין מאגל ולם יחל אגלה לאן אלאצל ענדנא
חזקה לא עביד אינש דפרע בגו זמניה פאדא אראד בית דין אן יביעו פי אחד הדה

A. THE MANUSCRIPT OF 1414 (CHART 39)

We shall deal first with the latest of the three manuscripts, which was written in Gabla in 1414 (fig. 229). The letters are narrow and their height is equal to about three-and-a-half times the width of the flat end of the calamus. Most of the downstrokes slope downwards to the right and the letters lean forward. The 'roofs' are horizontal whereas many of the bases are oblique thick strokes, drawn upwards from left to right and sharpening at their tops. Most of the horizontal 'roofs' start with a small upright serif at their left end. The right 'arm' of ᵓAlef and Ṣadi and the middle stroke of Shin have a similar shape. The downstrokes of Gimel, Ṭet, Nun, and ᶜAyin, the right downstroke of Ṣadi and the right and left downstrokes of Shin, start with a thick, convex top. Waw and Yod are very narrow.

Fig. 229. Detail of a manuscript from Gabla dating from 1414, written in a Yemenite book-hand (London, British Library, Or. 2223)

These are the main features of some individual letter-signs: the relatively narrow ᵓAlef has a short, thin left downstroke descending vertically from the diagonal. Bet has no 'tail'. A thick, concave or straight base-stroke joins the downstroke, which curves somewhat to the right. Gimel has a convex, short base-stroke and a very short 'heel'. Dalet has a vertical downstroke starting a little above the 'roof'. He has a separated, thin left downstroke. Zayin has a short horizontal 'roof' with a small serif. Ṭet has a concave base. The downstroke of medial Kaf is short and its 'base' curves upwards to the right. Lamed has a narrow, convex 'roof' and its right downstroke descends vertically; an additional short, thick stroke slants downwards from the top of its 'mast' in a leftwards direction. The left downstroke of medial Mem curves down vertically and ends at the base-line. Final Mem has a rectangular form. Medial Nun is curved. Final Nun has a thick stroke at its top, sloping downwards to the right; its leg curves downwards towards the right. Samekh is composed of three strokes, the 'base' and the right downstroke together forming a single oblique stroke. ᶜAyin is relatively short. Medial Pe has a convex or pointed top with a small serif; its left stroke curves to the left in a convex manner and is thick at both ends. The 'roof' of final Pe is a straight stroke, slanting downwards slightly to the right. Its leg is a thin, straight stroke sloping downwards to the right. Its left stroke is relatively long and has an additional small stroke at its bottom. Medial Ṣadi has a short, concave base. The 'leg' of Qof generally starts at the 'roof'. The downstroke of Resh either descends vertically or curves downwards to the left. Shin has an oblique base-stroke. Its left downstroke slants downwards to the right. The lower part of the left downstroke of Taw slopes to the left.

Chart 39. A 15th century Yemenite book-hand: a manuscript from Gabla dating from 1414

B. THE MANUSCRIPT OF 1320 (CHART 40)

The manuscript from Ṣanʿaʾ, dating from 1320 (fig. 230), represents a different stylistic type. The height of the average letters measures about three times the width of the calamus, which was held perpendicularly to the guideline. The horizontal strokes are therefore very thick in comparison to the thin downstrokes. The letters are short and wide. The script apparently evolved from one of the semi-cursive 'Eastern' styles used in the 11th and 12th centuries. In the 'Yemenite' version, some of the characteristic letter-forms of that semi-cursive script developed into peculiar new forms. Thus, for example, the typical large serifs of the 'Eastern' semi-cursive left their impression on the form of some of the 'roofs', which are made with two consecutive concave strokes. The long 'legs' of final Kaf, Nun and Pe occasionally curve to the left at the bottom, whereas those of final Ṣadi and Qof slope downwards to the right. Gimel, Waw, Yod and Nun have thick horizontal 'roofs' pointing to the left from the top of their downstrokes, while Zayin has a thick horizontal 'roof' on its top, or occasionally to the right of its downstroke. ʿAyin, and sometimes Pe have a very short concave base, while the long right downstroke slants downwards to the left. ʿAyin, Pe and Ṣadi are relatively long. The top-strokes of ʿAyin and of Ṣadi point in opposite directions. Lamed also has a thick, concave base. The 'mast' of Lamed leans forward and its 'flag' is a thick horizontal stroke. Medial Mem has a broad horizontal 'roof', a short horizontal 'base' and two vertical downstrokes. The forms of Shin and ʾAlef are most peculiar. The middle stroke of Shin joins its left top-stroke. The former diagonal of ʾAlef has turned into two separate strokes – a 'roof' and a vertical downstroke, while the former right 'arm' has become a short, thick stroke, slanting downwards to the right in the upper right-hand corner. Here is an illustration of the main stages in the evolution of that form:

Fig. 230. Detail of a manuscript from Ṣanʿaʾ dating from 1320, written in a Yemenite book-hand (Jerusalem, HaRav Kook Institute 314)

Chart 40. A 14th century Yemenite script: a manuscript from Ṣanʿaʾ dating from 1320

C. THE MANUSCRIPT OF 1222 (CHART 41)

A manuscript written in ʿAden in 1222 (fig. 231) represents yet another type of 'Yemenite' script. Some of the letter-forms may be traced back to those in a 12th century semi-cursive type of the 'Eastern' script, appearing in manuscripts from Fuṣṭāṭ (chart 25). The most prominent characteristic of this 'Yemenite' script is its curved strokes. The letters are short and wide, their height measuring about two-and-a-half to three times the width of the flat end of the calamus, which was held perpendicularly to the guideline. The thickness of the strokes varies in accordance with their direction and the horizontal strokes are thicker than vertical strokes. Another major characteristic is the long curved serif at the left end of the 'roof' in the letters Bet, Dalet, He, Ḥet, Kaf, final Mem, Samekh, Qof, Resh and Taw, which has its origin in the semi-cursive 'Eastern' script. Most of the bases are concave strokes. The long 'legs' of the final forms of Kaf, Nun, Pe, Ṣadi and Qof occasionally curve at their bottom to the left, forming a thick concave base. ʾAlef has a most peculiar form, in which the former diagonal becomes a horizontal stroke, adorned with a large curved serif at its left end. The letter leans forward, standing on its curved left leg, which curves backwards at the bottom. Its small upper right stroke curves backwards at the top. Gimel has a thick, convex base-stroke that joins the bottom of the downstroke. Waw is long, extending below the base-line. Zayin, and occasionally final Nun, have a short, thick 'roof' with a thin serif slanting downwards towards its left end. Ṭet has a small serif slanting downwards to the left towards the left end of the convex right stroke. Yod is very short. Lamed has a large 'hook' at the top of its 'mast', and a thick concave 'base'. Medial Mem has a pointed top. Final Mem is very short and has a concave base. Samekh resembles a narrow final Mem with an extra left downstroke. Pe has a thin left downstroke curving slightly inwards. Ṣadi has a thick, almost horizontal right 'arm' which joins the top of the downstroke. The 'leg' of Qof generally starts at the 'roof', but occasionally starts at the left end of the 'base', curving leftwards at the bottom. Resh has a curved shoulder. The almost horizontal middle stroke of Shin joins the left downstroke near its top. The left downstroke of Taw curves downwards to the left.

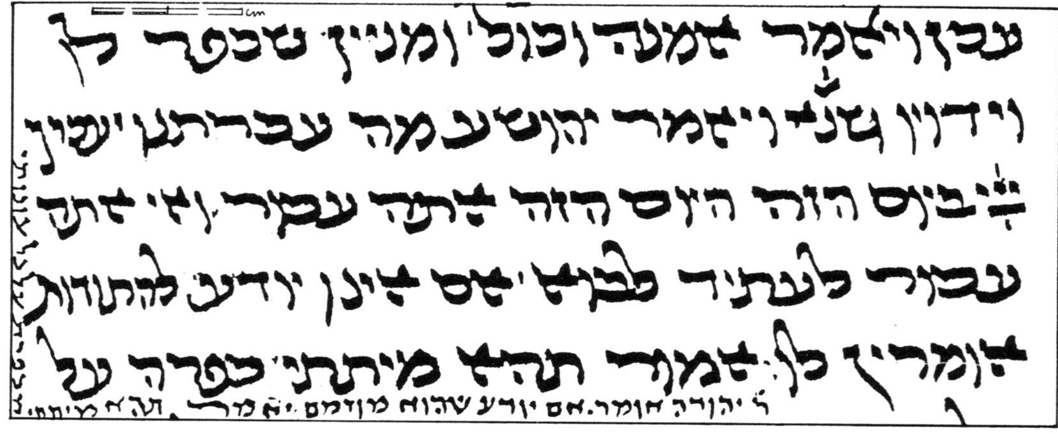

Fig. 231. Detail of a manuscript from ʿAden dating from 1222, written in a semi-cursive Yemenite hand (enlarged; see fig. 118)

Chart 41. A 13th century semi-cursive Yemenite script: a manuscript from ʿAden dating from 1222

30. THE CURSIVE 'BYZANTINE' SCRIPT OF THE 14TH CENTURY (CHART 42)

The 'Byzantine' script displays certain distinctive local features which distinguish it from contemporary handwritings in other regions. It was not stylized, however. A manuscript from Salonica, dating from 1329 (fig. 232), is representative here of the cursive 'Byzantine' script. Its salient feature is its combination of Ashkenazi and 'Eastern' elements. The small letters were drawn with a thin, flat writing implement, held parallel to the guideline, thus creating thick downstrokes and thin horizontal strokes, as in the Ashkenazi cursive script. Another characteristic that links that script to the Ashkenazi tradition is the backwards turn of the lower part of Dalet and Zayin. The large, convex serifs, however, are characteristic of the semi-cursive 'Eastern' script. The form of ʾAlef with the low, almost horizontal middle stroke is reminiscent of the 'Persian' cursive ʾAlef. The curving to the left of the downstrokes of the 'long-legged' letters occurs in cursive 'Eastern' handwritings. Except for the large serifs, which became integral parts of the letter-signs, no ornaments have been added. The curved 'roofs' and the right downstrokes in most of the letters are drawn as one continuous curved stroke. However, Bet and Samekh have an angular right 'shoulder'. The thin base-strokes appear to have been drawn from right to left. The upper part of Dalet, He, medial Kaf, final Mem, Samekh, Pe, Qof, Resh and Taw is shaped identically.

These are some major features of individual letters: the right 'arm' of ʾAlef curves downwards to the right and joins the right end of the almost horizontal middle stroke, which is drawn from right to left, meeting the wavy left downstroke in its lower half. The downstroke of Bet curves downwards to the right, creating a thick 'tail' at its meeting-point with the thin base. Gimel is long, its 'heel' extending below the base-line and its left stroke forming a thin horizontal 'base' drawn in a leftwards direction. Ṭet has an unusual high left downstroke. Final Kaf has a large concave base. Lamed is very narrow. Its 'mast' leans forward and its top is a large convex curve. Medial Mem has no base. Samekh differs from final Mem in that it has no serif and its form is almost triangular. Final Pe has a large concave base. Medial Ṣadi has no base and resembles the final form except for its short 'leg'. The left downstroke of Taw curves downwards to the left, extending below the base-line.

Fig. 232. Detail of a manuscript from Salonica dating from 1329, written in a semi-cursive script of Byzantine style (enlarged; see fig. 120)

Chart 42. A 14th century cursive 'Byzantine' script: a manuscript from Salonica dating from 1329

31. THE SEMI-CURSIVE 'ITALIAN' SCRIPT OF THE 15TH CENTURY (CHART 43)

The semi-cursive 'Italian' script of the 15th century is represented here by a manuscript written by Abraham Fariṣol (fig. 233). Early manuscripts written by him are in the Sephardi script-style. After he immigrated to Italy from Spain, he started to write in the 'Italian' script-style. His handwriting is very beautiful in both styles. The semi-cursive 'Italian' script appears to have evolved from the semi-cursive Gothic Ashkenazi, whose angular and rhomboid strokes became smooth and rounded, and whose narrow letters became spacious and clearly legible. Rhomboid strokes have been retained in the 'heel' of Gimel, the lower part of Zayin and the 'mast' of Lamed, the lower part of the downstroke in Bet and Dalet and the left stroke of He. The writing implement was cut obliquely and held perpendicularly to the guideline. The horizontal strokes are consequently thicker than the thin vertical strokes. The thickness of the curved strokes changes according to their direction. Most of the 'roofs' are convex and most of the bases are concave. The script is homogeneous, with almost no variations in the forms of the letters and most of the letters are of equal height.

These are some major features of individual letter-signs: the former diagonal of ʾAlef becomes a curved stroke, starting at the centre of the left downstroke, while what remains of the right 'arm' is a short stroke slanting downwards to the left. The left downstroke resembles the letter Waw. Gimel has a long 'heel' which curves downwards and continues below the base-line. The downstroke of Dalet curves at its bottom to the right. The left stroke of He is a small rhombus. Zayin and final Nun have a rhomboid 'head' with a narrow 'neck'. Ṭet is closed, with the pointed left end of the convex 'roof' touching the left downstroke below its top. Yod is very short. Lamed has a complex 'mast' made of two strokes – a convex curve on top of a rhombus, the pointed bottom of which meets the left end of the 'roof'. It has a short, thick base. Final Mem differs from Samekh in that its 'roof' extends a little beyond its meeting-point with the downstroke. The top-strokes of ʿAyin touch each other as do the top strokes of Shin. The top-strokes of Ṣadi are drawn in opposite directions. The 'leg' of Qof starts at the 'roof', and slants downwards to the right. The right downstrokes of He, Ḥet, Qof, Resh and Taw curve leftwards.

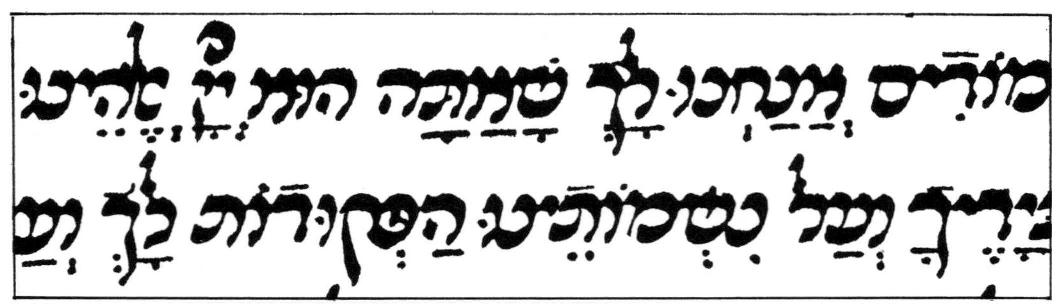

Fig. 233. Detail of a manuscript dating from 1488, written by the scribe Abraham Fariṣol in a semi-cursive script of Italian style (enlarged; see fig. 116)

Chart 43. A 15th century semi-cursive Italian script: a manuscript dating from 1488 written by Abraham Farișol

32. THE MODERN 'STAM' SCRIPT (CHARTS 44-45)

The modern Ashkenazi and Sephardi 'Stam' script is represented here by letter-forms designed on the basis of the literary sources (*Likkut Sifrei Stam* by Zvi Kahana, Jerusalem 1984). The Ashkenazi and Sephardi scripts used for sacred writings today are relatively late script-styles based on the Ashkenazi and Sephardi script-styles as well as on the descriptions of the letter-forms in early Jewish literary sources. After the weakening of the Jewish scribal tradition in the second millennium, the scribes attempted to revive the old tradition. However, because of the lack of authentic early scripts revealing the forms of the early letter-signs used for sacred purposes, the scribes had to rely on the literary sources and to interpret them according to their understanding. The earliest known work dealing with the ornamental additions to the letter-signs is *Sefer Tagei* ('The Book of Crowns'), ascribed to Rabbi Naḥum the copyist, who lived at the end of the Second Temple period. This book, which is mentioned in literary sources, survived in manuscripts and was printed in Paris in 1866. The relatively late tractate *Sofrim* ('Scribes') appears to have been written in the period of the Geʾonim. In the course of time, the verbal descriptions of the letter-forms and their components ceased to be clearly understood, and artificial forms were created which differ completely from the letter-forms of the early Jewish book-hand found in biblical scrolls of the late Second Temple period and in papyrus fragments of the post-Herodian period discovered in the Judean Desert (see above, charts 6, 7 and 10). The letter-forms in these sources also differ from the script of the early biblical scroll fragments discovered in the Cairo Genizah, the earliest of which appears to date from the 8th century (see above, chart 22). However, the latter demonstrate the existence of a continuous scribal tradition which underwent certain changes in the course of time.

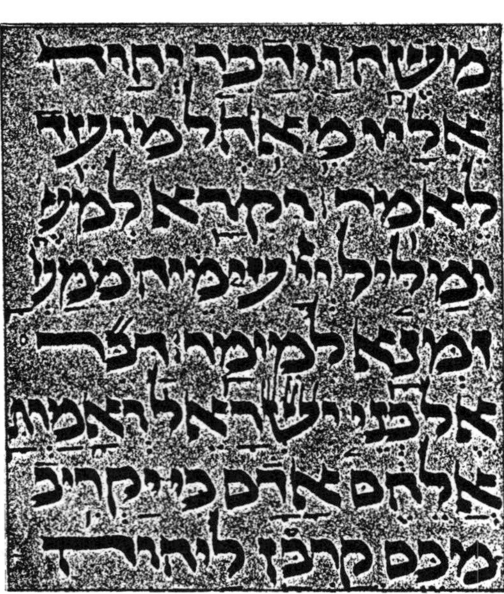

Fig. 234. Adorned letters in a manuscript from England dating from 1189 (Valmadonna MS. I; see fig. 213) and in a manuscript of unknown provenance dating from 1430

אאבבגג

דהוזזחחט

טייכךכלל

מםםנןןסע

עףפצצץץק

קרששתת

Chart 44. A modern Ashkenazi 'Stam' script

ובין ברד ותלד הגר לאברם בן ויקרא אברם
שם בנו אשר ילדה הגר ישמעאל ואברם בן
שמנים שנה ושש שנים בלדת הגר את ישמעאל
לאברם ויהי אברם בן תשעים
שנה ותשע שנים וירא יהוה אל אברם ויאמר
אליו אני אל שדי התהלך לפני והיה תמים ואתנה
בריתי ביני ובינך וארבה אותך במאד מאד ויפל
אברם על פניו וידבר אתו אלהים לאמר אני הנה
בריתי אתך והיית לאב המון גוים ולא יקרא עוד
את שמך אברם והיה שמך אברהם כי אב המון
גוים נתתיך והפרתי אתך במאד מאד ונתתיך לגוים
ומלכים ממך יצאו והקמתי את בריתי ביני ובינך
ובין זרעך אחריך לדרתם לברית עולם להיות לך
לאלהים ולזרעך אחריך ונתתי לך ולזרעך אחריך
את ארץ מגריך את כל ארץ כנען לאחזת עולם
והייתי להם לאלהים ויאמר אלהים אל אברהם
ואתה את בריתי תשמר אתה וזרעך אחריך
לדרתם זאת בריתי אשר תשמרו ביני וביניכם
ובין זרעך אחריך המול לכם כל זכר ונמלתם
את בשר ערלתכם והיה לאות ברית ביני וביניכם
ובן שמנת ימים ימול לכם כל זכר לדרתיכם יליד
בית ומקנת כסף מכל בן נכר אשר לא מזרעך
הוא המול ימול יליד ביתך ומקנת כספך והיתה
בריתי בבשרכם לברית עולם וערל זכר אשר
לא ימול את בשר ערלתו ונכרתה הנפש ההוא
מעמיה את בריתי הפר ויאמר
אלהים אל אברהם שרי אשתך לא תקרא את
שמה שרי כי שרה שמה וברכתי אתה וגם נתתי
ממנה לך בן וברכתיה והיתה לגוים מלכי עמים
ממנה יהיו ויפל אברהם על פניו ויצחק ויאמר
בלבו הלבן מאה שנה יולד ואם שרה הבת
תשעים שנה תלד ויאמר אברהם אל האלהים
לו ישמעאל יחיה לפניך ויאמר אלהים אבל
שרה אשתך ילדת לך בן וקראת את שמו יצחק
והקמתי את בריתי אתו לברית עולם לזרעו אחריו
ולישמעאל שמעתיך הנה ברכתי אתו והפריתי
אתו והרביתי אתו במאד מאד שנים עשר נשיאם
יוליד ונתתיו לגוי גדול ואת בריתי אקים את יצחק
אשר תלד לך שרה למועד הזה בשנה האחרת
ויכל לדבר אתו ויעל אלהים מעל אברהם ויקח
אברהם את ישמעאל בנו ואת כל ילידי ביתו
ואת כל מקנת כספו כל זכר באנשי בית אברהם

Fig. 235. Modern 'Stam' letters in an exemplar text for Torah scribes ('Tikun Sofrim')

Chart 45. A modern Sephardi 'Stam' script

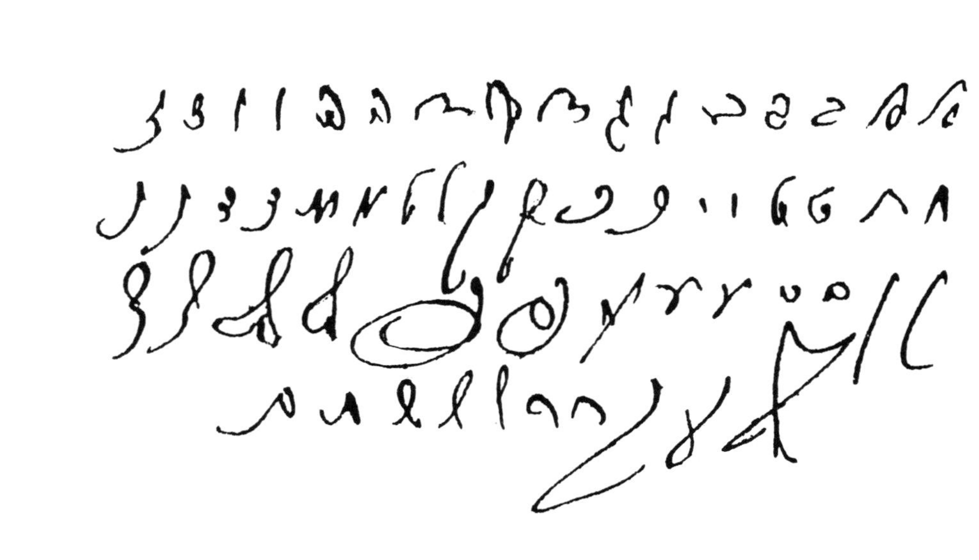

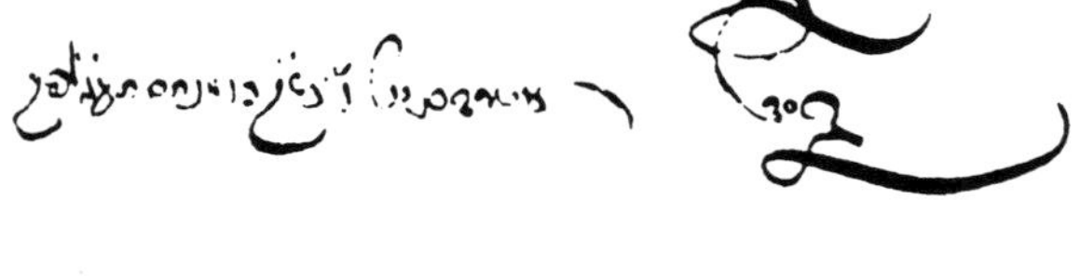

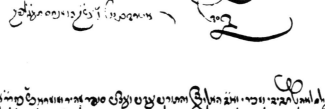

Fig. 236. A cursive Ashkenazi script in a document from Amsterdam dating from 1713

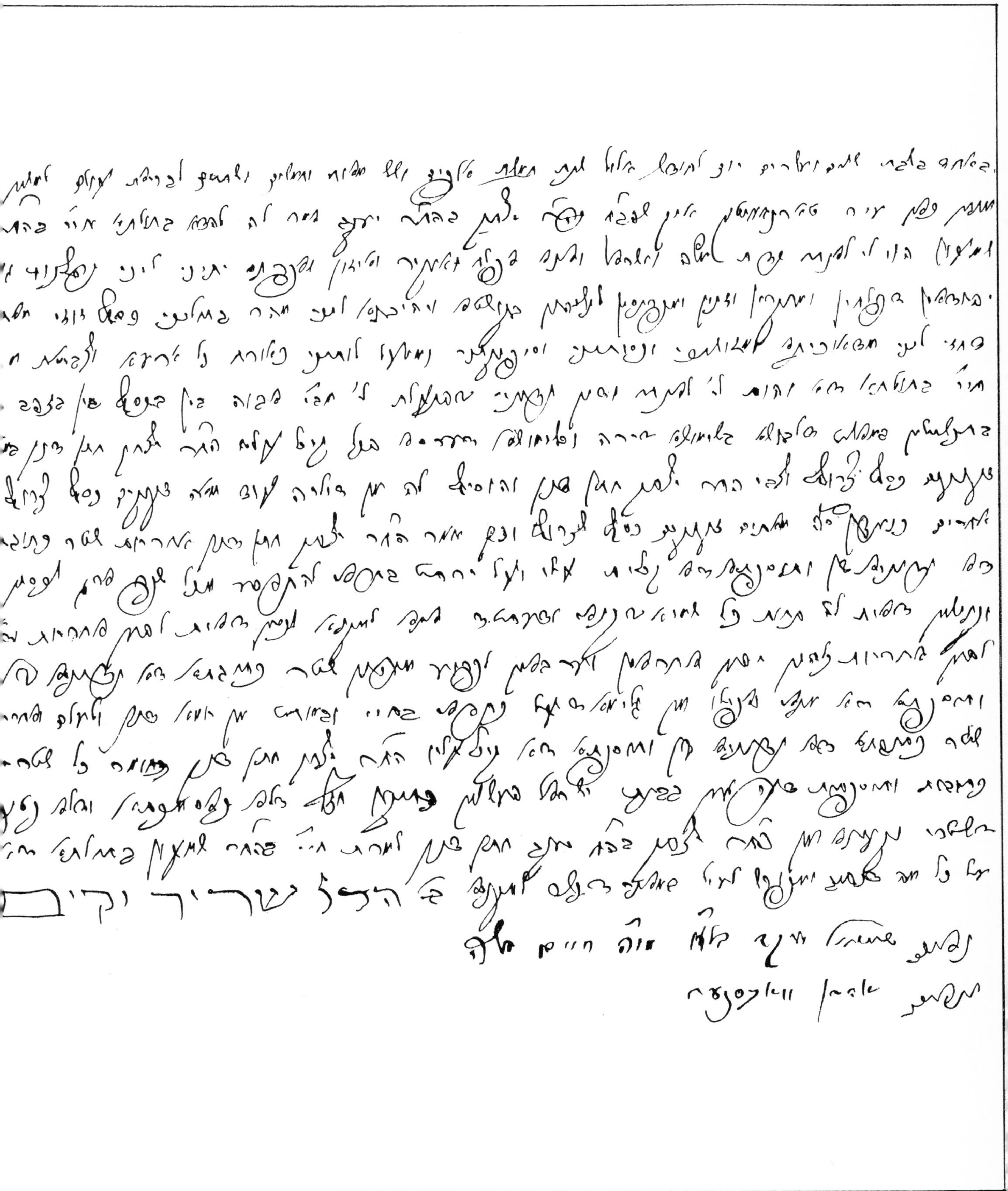

Fig. 237. A cursive Ashkenazi script in a *Ketubbah* from Germany dating from 1893

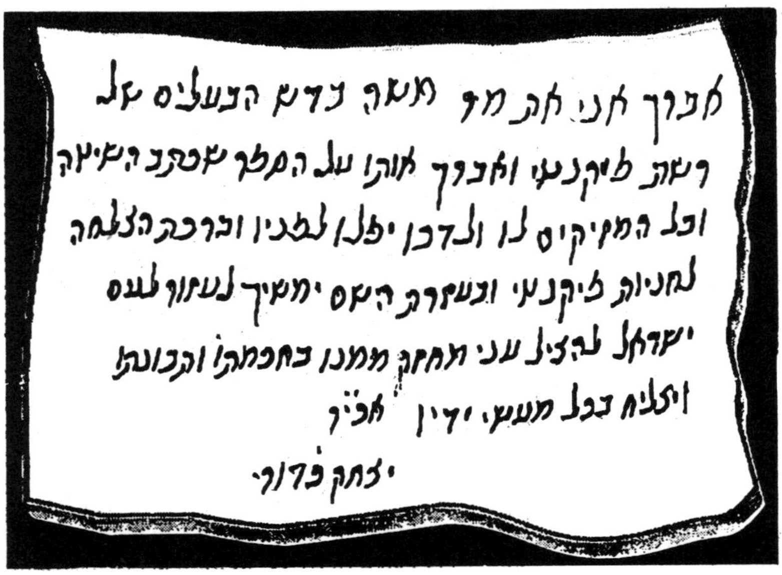

Fig. 238. A modern semi-cursive Sephardi script (ca. 1995)

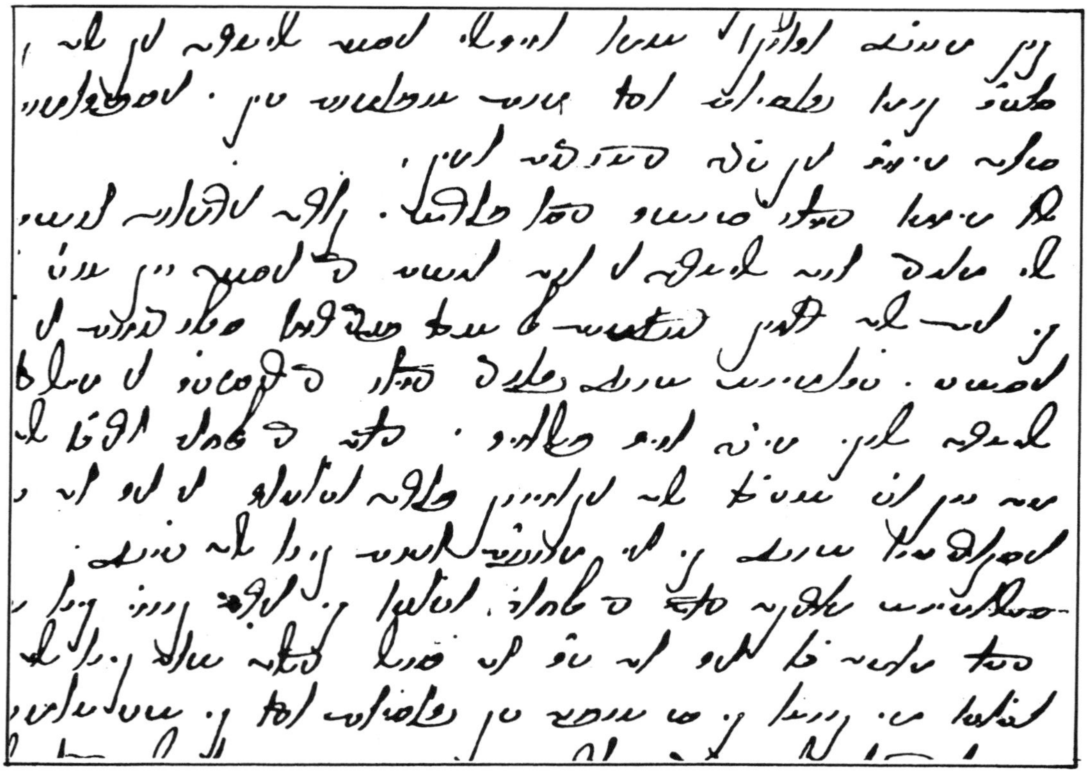

Fig. 239. An extreme cursive Sephardi script in a document dating from 1939

אבגדהו

זחטיכך

למםנןס

עפףצץק

רשת

Chart 46. Stylized modern Hebrew cursive letter-forms based on the Ashkenazi cursive script

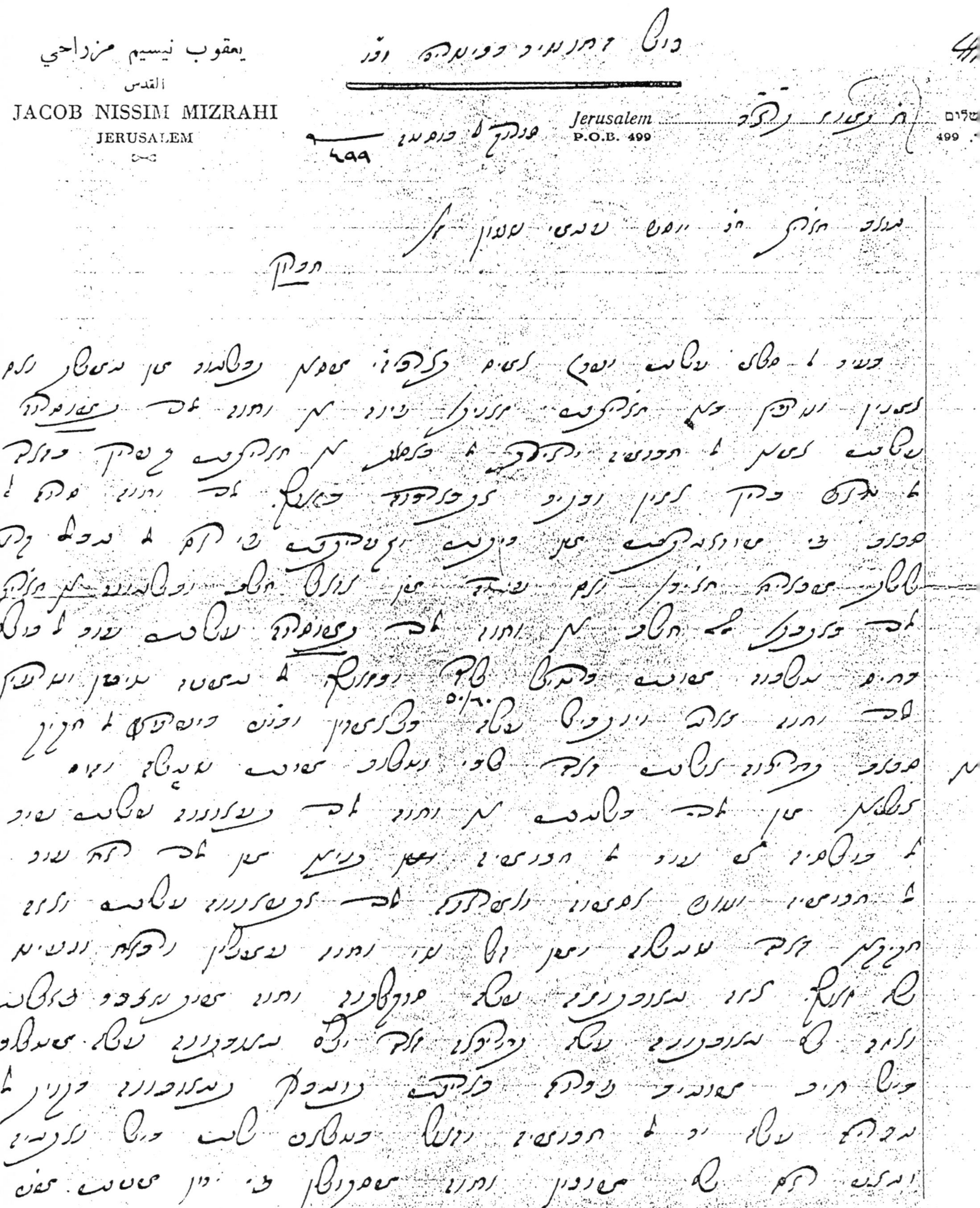

يعقوب نيسيم مزراحي

القدس

JACOB NISSIM MIZRAHI

JERUSALEM

Jerusalem ....

P.O.B. 499

...שלום

499

Fig. 240. A modern cursive Sephardi script in a document dating from 1934

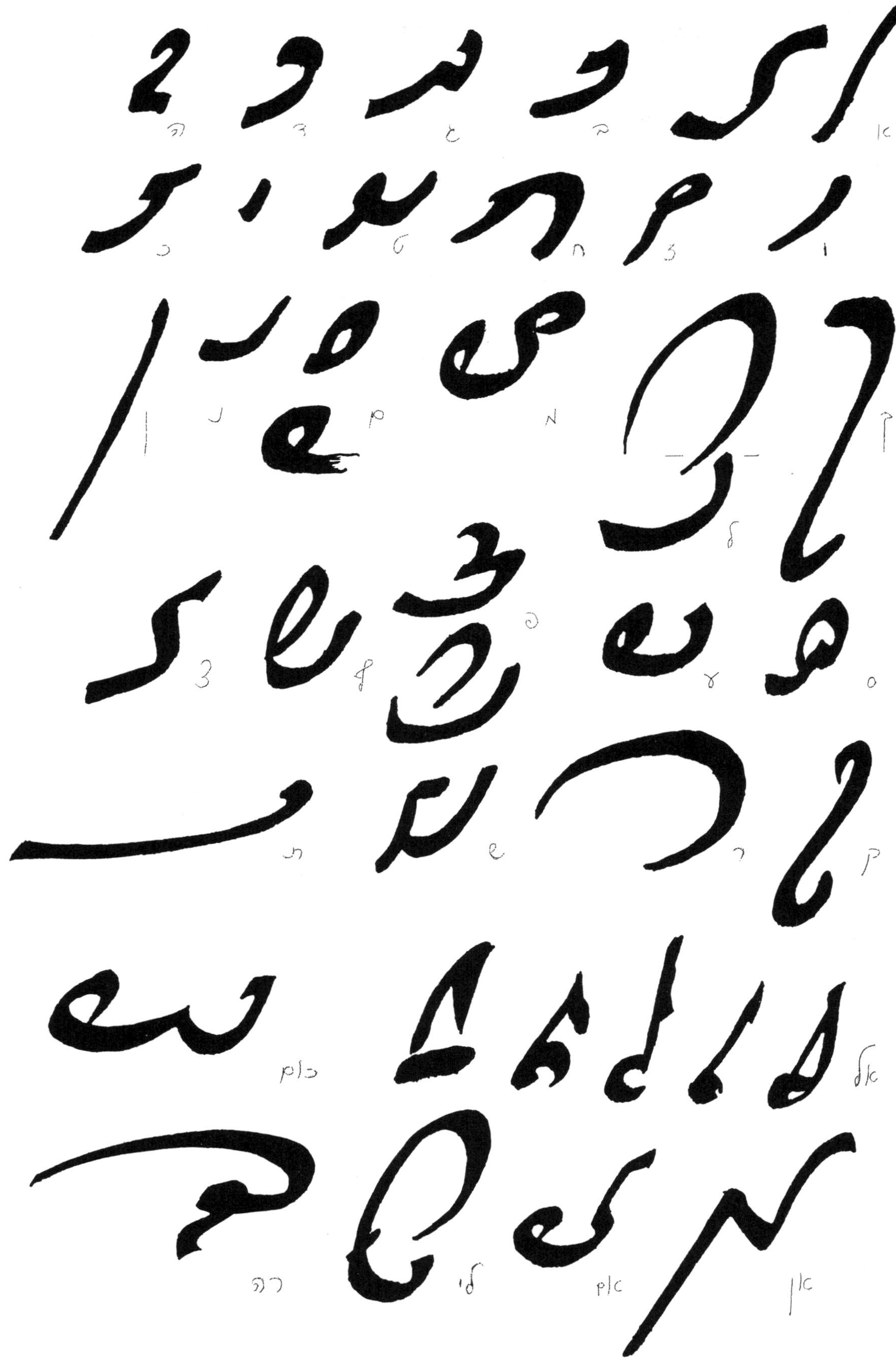

Chart 47. A modern Hebrew Sephardi cursive script: a document from Hebron dating from 1934

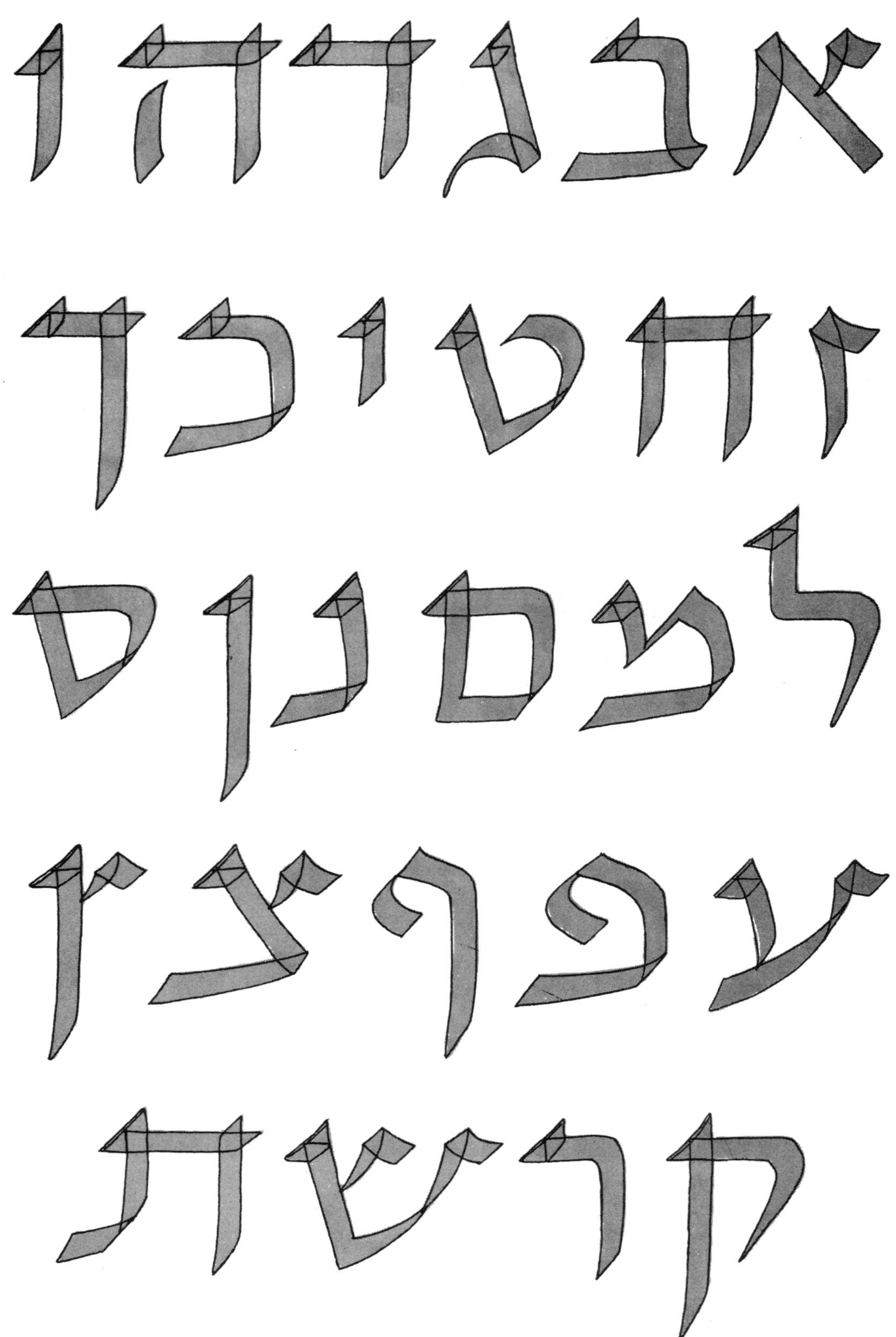

Chart 48. 'Yerushalmi' calligraphic script, designed in the first half of the 20th century

Chart 49. 'Rolit' calligraphic script, designed in the first half of the 20th century

בָּרֵךְ עָלֵינוּ יְיָ אֱלֹהֵינוּ
אֶת הַשָּׁנָה הַזֹּאת
וְאֶת כָּל מִינֵי תְבוּאָתָהּ
לְטוֹבָה

וְתֵן טַל וּמָטָר לִבְרָכָה עַל כָּל פְּנֵי הָאֲדָמָה
וְרַוֵּה פְּנֵי תֵבֵל וְשַׂבַּע אֶת הָעוֹלָם כֻּלּוֹ מִטּוּבֶךְ
וּמַלֵּא יָדֵינוּ מִבִּרְכוֹתֶיךָ וּמֵעֹשֶׁר מַתְּנוֹת יָדֶיךָ

שָׁמְרָה וְהַצִּילָה שָׁנָה זוּ

מִכָּל דָּבָר רָע וּמִכָּל מִינֵי מַשְׁחִית וּמִכָּל מִינֵי פּוּרְעָנוּת
וַעֲשֵׂה לָהּ תִּקְוָה טוֹבָה וְאַחֲרִית שָׁלוֹם
חוּס וְרַחֵם עָלֶיהָ וְעַל כָּל תְּבוּאָתָהּ וּפֵירוֹתֶיהָ
וּבָרְכָהּ בְּגִשְׁמֵי רָצוֹן בְּרָכָה וּנְדָבָה
וּתְהִי אַחֲרִיתָהּ חַיִּים וְשָׂבָע וְשָׁלוֹם
כַּשָּׁנִים הַטּוֹבוֹת לִבְרָכָה
כִּי אֵל טוֹב וּמֵטִיב אַתָּה וּמְבָרֵךְ הַשָּׁנִים

בָּרוּךְ אַתָּה יְיָ
מְבָרֵךְ הַשָּׁנִים

Chart 50. 'Ḥagit' calligraphic script (designed by Ada Yardeni)

הַלְלוּיָהּ

הַלְלוּ עַבְדֵי יְיָ
הַלְלוּ אֶת־שֵׁם יְיָ
יְהִי שֵׁם יְיָ מְבֹרָךְ
מֵעַתָּה וְעַד־עוֹלָם
מִמִּזְרַח־שֶׁמֶשׁ עַד־מְבוֹאוֹ
מְהֻלָּל שֵׁם יְיָ
רָם עַל־כָּל־גּוֹיִם יְיָ
עַל־הַשָּׁמַיִם כְּבוֹדוֹ
מִי כַּיְיָ אֱלֹהֵינוּ
הַמַּגְבִּיהִי לָשָׁבֶת
הַמַּשְׁפִּילִי לִרְאוֹת
בַּשָּׁמַיִם וּבָאָרֶץ
מְקִימִי מֵעָפָר דָּל
מֵאַשְׁפֹּת יָרִים אֶבְיוֹן
לְהוֹשִׁיבִי עִם־נְדִיבִים
עִם נְדִיבֵי עַמּוֹ
מוֹשִׁיבִי עֲקֶרֶת הַבַּיִת
אֵם־הַבָּנִים שְׂמֵחָה

הַלְלוּיָהּ

שָׂא נָא עֵינֶיךָ וּרְאֵה
מִן־הַמָּקוֹם אֲשֶׁר־אַתָּה שָׁם
צָפוֹנָה וָנֶגְבָּה וָקֵדְמָה וָיָמָּה
כִּי אֶת־כָּל־הָאָרֶץ אֲשֶׁר־אַתָּה רוֹאֶה
לְךָ אֶתְּנֶנָּה וּלְזַרְעֲךָ עַד־עוֹלָם

בראשית יג, יד־טו

תזמורת סימפונית חיפה

הילטון תל־אביב

10 המכונה מחשבת וקובעת לי
מתקרב לקצה השורה, נשמי

11 המכונה מחשבת וקובעת
הסדר מתקרב לקצה השו

12 המכונה מחשבת וקובע
כאשר הסדר מתקרב ל

14 המכונה מחשבת וקו
רושים. כאשר הסדר

לְפִיכָךְ

אֲנַחְנוּ חַיָּבִים לְהוֹדוֹת
לְהַלֵּל לְשַׁבֵּחַ
לְפָאֵר לְרוֹמֵם
לְהַדֵּר לְבָרֵךְ
לְעַלֵּה וּלְקַלֵּס
לְמִי שֶׁעָשָׂה לַאֲבוֹתֵינוּ וְלָנוּ
אֶת כָּל הַנִּסִּים הָאֵלֶּה
הוֹצִיאָנוּ מֵעַבְדוּת לְחֵרוּת
מִיָּגוֹן לְשִׂמְחָה
מֵאֵבֶל לְיוֹם טוֹב
וּמֵאֲפֵלָה לְאוֹר גָּדוֹל
וּמִשִּׁעְבּוּד לִגְאֻלָּה
וְנֹאמַר לְפָנָיו
שִׁירָה חֲדָשָׁה
הַלְלוּיָהּ

אבגדהו

זחטיכך

למםנןס

עפףצץ

קרשת

Chart 51. 'Ada' typeface (designed by Ada Yardeni)

האוניברסיטה העברית בירושלים
הפקולטה למדעי הרוח — החוג להיסטוריה של עם ישראל

אוסף
תעודות ארמיות
ממצרים
העתיקה

עריכה, ציור
ותרגום מחדש לעברית ולאנגלית
בצלאל פורטן · עדה ירדני

א

אגרות
נספח: אגרות ארמיות מן המקרא

אבגדהו
זחטיכך
למםנןס
עפףצץ
קרשת

יוסף נוה
ראשית תולדותיו של האלפבית

ז׳ורז׳ יפרח
סְפָרוֹת וּמִסְפָּרִים
הסטוריה של המצאה גאונית

Chart 52. 'Dafna' typeface (designed by Ada Yardeni)

הודו ליי
כי טוב
כי
לעולם
חסדו

Chart 53. 'Rephael' typeface (designed by Ada Yardeni)

Fig. 241. A codex and a stylus in a Pompeian wall-painting

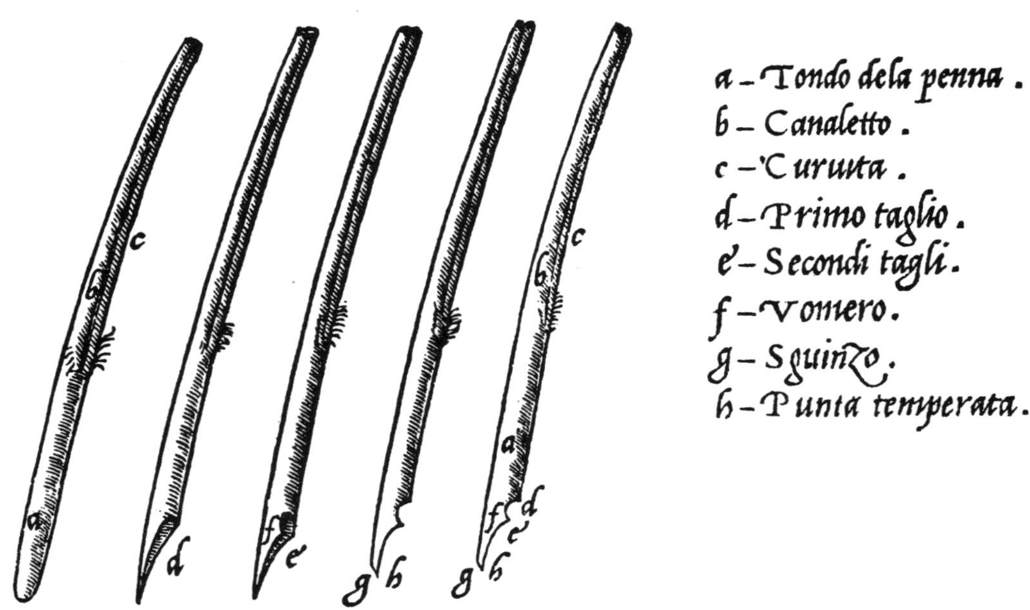

Fig. 242. Instructions for the cutting of a quill-feather in
Ludovico Arrighi's *La Operina da Imparare di scriuere littera Cancellarescha* printed in Rome in 1522

Part 4

CALLIGRAPHY, SCRIPT-COMPOSITION AND THE DESIGNING OF TYPEFACES

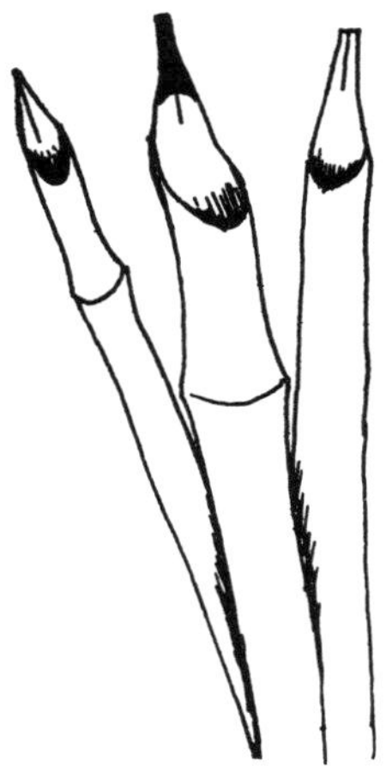

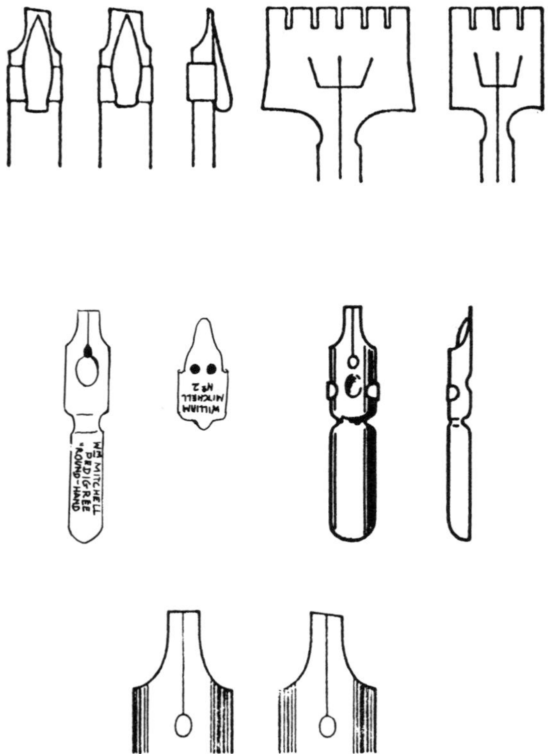

Fig. 243. Metal nibs for calligraphy

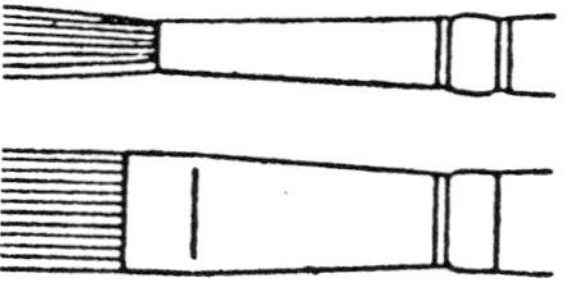

Fig. 244. Flat brushes for the writing of large letters

CHAPTER ONE: CALLIGRAPHY

Calligraphy is the art of fine writing. The calligrapher pays special attention to the stylistic features of the letter-forms and to their components and structure. The drawing of beautiful letter-forms with a pen or a brush and with ink or paint, differs from the designing of letter-forms for inscriptions or typefaces. Calligraphy requires special practice in the writing of certain script-styles, mainly through imitation of existing forms and by reducing the individual characteristics of the writer. Despite the vigorous activity in Hebrew manuscript illustration during the Middle Ages, it seems that the artistic factor never really became a prominent factor in the designing of the Hebrew letter-forms. The emphasis was placed on the preservation of the scribal tradition, which became sanctified at a certain stage of the natural evolution of the letter-forms. Due to historical circumstances, that tradition was for part of the time transmitted in a literary way rather than practically, and the exact details of the early forms were forgotten. The scribes in later times, relying on the early literary sources dealing with the scribal instructions for writing sacred texts, interpreted them according to their understanding. With the invention of printing, Hebrew calligraphy remained in the hands of orthodox, professional scribes, and was used mainly for the writing of the Torah, phylacteries and mezuzot. Only in the 20th century did artists begin to revive Hebrew calligraphy following the design of new Hebrew typefaces. However, the traditional 'Stam' script is still used, mainly by orthodox scribes, while other artistic letter-forms occasionally appear in various handwritten texts, although none of them has so far become a widely accepted style. Apart from the basic study of writing in schools and a few calligraphy courses, the art of Hebrew writing is neglected. Handwritten official texts which appear from time to time on various documents and certificates, are usually executed in modern individual handwritings which are often imitations of types appearing in print. Most of these handwritings reflect an ignorance of the history of the Hebrew letter-forms. In fact, no modern Hebrew calligraphic script-style has been crystallized so far. Although it may be claimed that there is no need for such a style, many will agree that a hand-written text should be legible and possess a beautiful appearance. This could be achieved by observing some basic rules, listed below:

1. Each letter of the alphabet should appear in one and the same form wherever it occurs in the text. For this purpose, much practice is needed in the writing of the letter-signs.
2. In order to achieve a homogeneous appearance, the writing should be rhythmical.
3. A balanced spacing of the letter-signs and their components – i.e., a balance between the strokes and their background – is essential for the harmony of the written text. This balance, as well as the feeling for it, may be achieved through constant practice.
4. In keeping with the tradition, the script-style may have groups of letter-forms with similar graphic components.

A. THE WRITING IMPLEMENTS

Special writing implements are needed for calligraphy. A reed-pen or a quill-pen may be purchased from professional 'Stam' scribes who prepare them for writing. It is also possible to prepare a calamus or a quill-pen by cutting their ends in a proper way. For beginners, however, we recommend the use of modern metallic nibs for calligraphy which may be purchased in special shops for art and writing materials. It is advisable to buy holders separately as well as several sizes of nibs. The nibs that are most recommended are those of William Mitchell with the trademark 'Round Hand Pedigree' (fig. 243). These are produced in various sizes. One should begin practicing with relatively broad nibs (e.g., 1, 1.5, 2 mm.). The nibs need an additional ink holder, which may be acquired separately. These metallic nibs have an advantage over other calligraphic pens in that they permit the drawing of very fine strokes. The ink to be used with these pens is china ink (e.g., Pelikan's 'Encre de Chine' A No. 17), which is available in large or small bottles. 'Stam' scribes use a special ink with extra brilliance. The writing surface may be parchment or special paper that does not absorb the ink. Parchment is too expensive for practicing. For writing large letters one may use flat, smooth brushes. These are available in various sizes (e.g. 16, 18, etc.). Gouache or plastic paints on a water basis may be used for writing with a brush on cardboard. Paper with marked guidelines or millimeter-paper is necessary for practicing. The table should be comfortable and both elbows have to lean on the table while one is writing. Some scribes prefer a slanting table but this is not essential. It is possible to use a light table, and to put millimeter-paper underneath the writing surface in order to avoid the marking of guidelines.

We may mention here that from early days scribes used various methods to mark guidelines as well as vertical margin-lines. Already in ancient scrolls from the Judean Desert, small holes were pierced in the hide scroll on both margins and guidelines were drawn or scratched between them. In the Middle East during the Middle Ages, they used ruling-boards upon which threads were stretched, and paper was then pressed against the threads which would leave their marks on it (this board was called 'masṭara' in Arabic). (On ruling devices and on other technical practices employed in medieval Hebrew manuscripts, see M. Beit-Arié, *Hebrew Codicology*, Jerusalem 1981.)

B. PRACTICING WRITING

How shall we begin? It is recommended to start practicing by drawing single strokes rather than letters. Straight and curved strokes should be drawn in different directions – horizontally to the right, vertically downwards, and obliquely. Later the strokes may be combined with each other in different ways. When drawing the strokes in lines from right to left, one should take care not to smear the ink with the hand. Left-handed people may have difficulty in drawing the strokes horizontally from left to

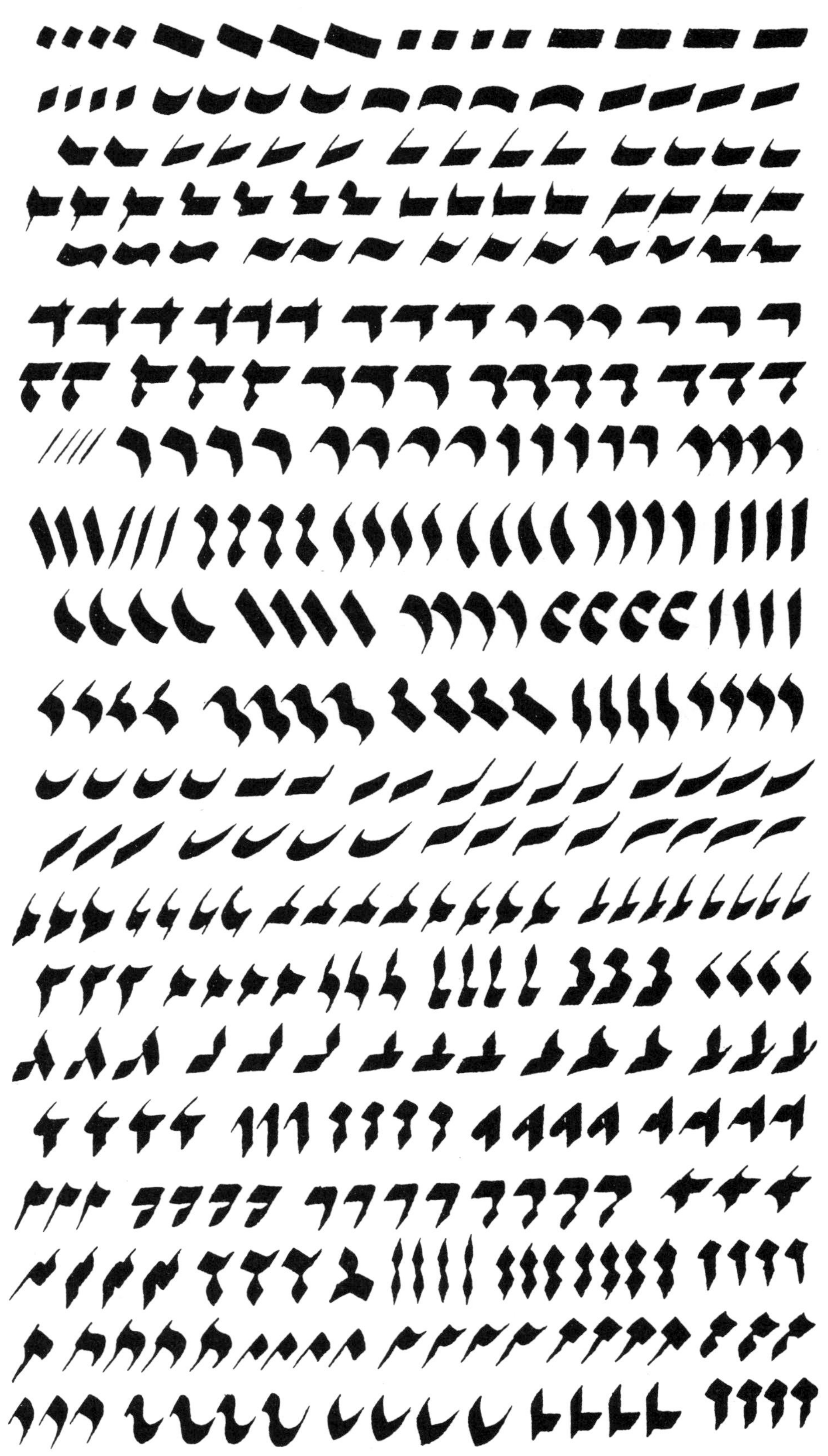

Fig. 245 First exercise in Hebrew calligraphy: the drawing of strokes in different directions

right because of the angle at which the implement is held in relation to the guideline. Drawing the strokes in the opposite direction will result in a different appearance of the letter-forms. Thus, left-handed people will have to turn the writing surface clockwise in order to draw the horizontal strokes from left to right. The angle between the writing implement and the guideline depends on personal preference. One should try different angles in order to achieve the best results.

As the holding of the implement has a major influence on its proper handling, it is recommended to grasp it near its lower end, but at a safe distance from the ink. If possible, it should be grasped with the tops of three fingers – the thumb, the index finger and the middle finger – while leaning the side of the palm and the small finger on the writing surface. However, each person has to choose the most comfortable position according to the size and form of the hand.

The writing implement should be held in a stable position, so that the difference in the thickness of the strokes will be the direct result of a change in their direction. The angle between the flat end of the writing implement and the guideline will be determined by the script-style (see, for example, the Ashkenazi and Sephardi Alefs in fig. 246).

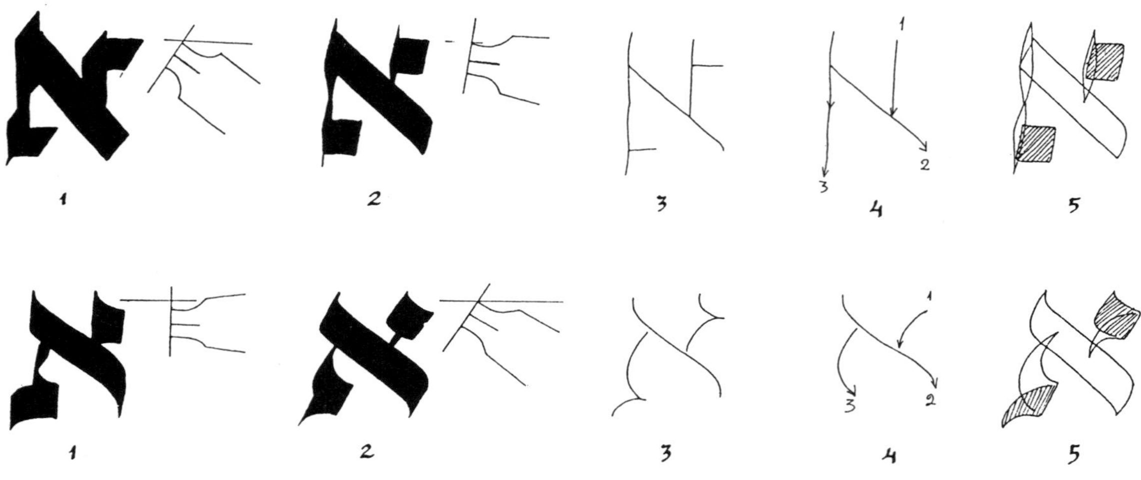

Fig. 246. A change in the angle in which the writing implement is held results in a change in the thickness of the stroke

1. Wrong 2. Right 3. The 'skeleton' with additions 4. The basic strokes without ornamental additions 5. The letter with the ornamental additions

C. WRITING IN A GIVEN SCRIPT-STYLE

After having practiced the drawing of individual strokes, one may choose a certain script-style and try to copy the letter-forms, starting with the different components of each letter – the 'roofs' and the 'bases', the

Fig. 247. Second exercise in Hebrew calligraphy: practicing the drawing of parts of letters in the 'Eastern' book-hand of the 10th century CE

downstrokes, the diagonals and the additional ornaments. Calligraphy requires slow writing; a certain fluency will be achieved through practice. Rapid writing can result in the irregular formation of the individual strokes. In the course of time, the writer will become more sensitive to proper spacing. The eyes will learn to perceive the elements which disturb the general harmony, and the hand will acquire skill in drawing homogeneous strokes.

After having practiced the drawing of the components of the letter-forms, one may begin practicing the drawing of individual letter-signs. Before trying to draw a series of different letters, each letter-form should be practiced separately. Various letters should then be drawn in sequence while correcting the spacing and the balance between them. One may discover that in a sequence of letter-forms the balance is disturbed, even though the components of the individual characters are perfectly balanced. A letter may have to be enlarged or reduced in size in order to prevent spots or excessively large spaces within the word as a whole. One may also discover that the spacing between the letters is ill-balanced and that the spaces between certain letter-forms have to be enlarged or reduced in order to make them appear harmonious. The ability to discern the details which influence the result of the work will gradually increase and the writer will soon be able to create an attractive-looking text.

D. SPACING

The spaces between letters as well as between the individual strokes of each letter should be properly balanced. This may be achieved through constant practice. The space inside the letters is determined, inter alia, by the relation between the thickness of the strokes and the height and width of the individual letter-forms. The width of the average letter should not be more than four times that of the flat end of the writing implement, while the height should not be less than three times that of the flat end of the implement (see fig. 248).

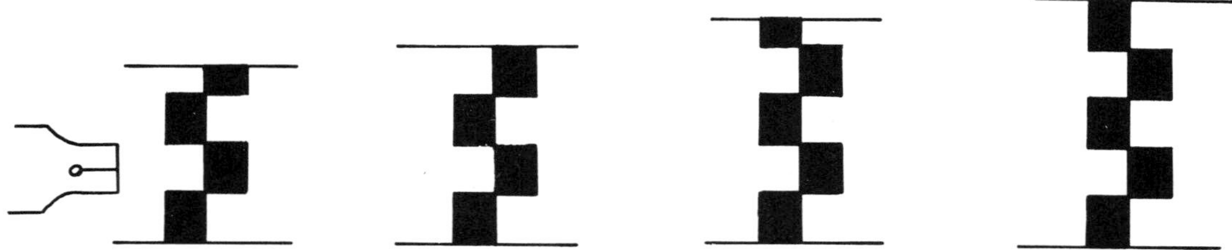

Fig. 248. The height of the letter in relation to the width of the implement's flat end

Although the spacing may possibly be calculated, perhaps with the help of a computer, the eyes act more quickly than any mechanical means, especially as one has to take into account the optical illusions which play a major role in visual impressions. For example, even a minute difference in the thickness of strokes of equal length, facing the same direction, may upset the balance between them (see the section on optical illusions below).

Fig. 249. Optically right and wrong relationships between the height and width of different letters

Fig. 250. Optically right and wrong relationships between strokes and spaces

Fig. 251. Correcting the spacing between letters in order to achieve a balanced appearance

The longer the text, the larger should be the space between the lines. The space should be somewhat (20% – 50%) larger than the average height of the letters. Enough space would thus be left for the long downstrokes.

Different script-styles require different spacing. Too large or too small a space may disturb legibility. In a short text with large characters, the lines may be placed close together to form an attractively-spaced composition. In decorative lettering, additional thin strokes may be drawn to connect certain characters (see below). (See fig. 252, examples of hand-written texts differing in their spacing.)

Fig. 252. Examples of hand-written text differing in their spacing

בָּרוּךְ אַתָּה
יי אֱלֹהֵינוּ מֶלֶךְ הָעוֹלָם
אֲשֶׁר קִדְּשָׁנוּ בְּמִצְוֹתָיו
וְצִוָּנוּ לְהַדְלִיק נֵר
שֶׁל שַׁבָּת

Fig. 253. The spacing of lines of a short text may be smaller than that in a long text

CHAPTER TWO: OPTICAL ILLUSIONS AND FACTORS INFLUENCING THE HARMONY OF THE SCRIPT

Each form that we see is influenced by its background or the space surrounding it. Identical forms may look different in different postures or against different backgrounds. This natural phenomenon is known as an 'optical illusion' and is the result of the physical structure of the eye and the brain. An awareness of certain optical illusions may help us to exploit their advantages and avoid difficulties when dealing with various forms, and, in this case, when dealing with letter-forms in two dimensions. There is a difference between what is 'right' according to mathematical calculations and what appears right from the visual point of view. In this case, the appearance of the letter-form is what we aim at.

Here are some examples of common optical illusions (most of them were taken from the book *Schriftschreiben, Schriftzeichnen*; see the bibliography):

1. Different forms of identical height may appear different in their height when placed side by side. For example, if we draw a circle, a triangle and a rectangle, all of identical height, between two parallel lines, the rectangle will touch the lines with two of its four sides, the triangle will touch the lower line with one side and the upper line at one point, while the circle will touch both lines at two points only. In order to make all the forms appear to our eyes as being of one and the same height we have to enlarge the triangle and the circle so that the triangle extends above the upper line and the circle extends both above the upper line and below the lower line.

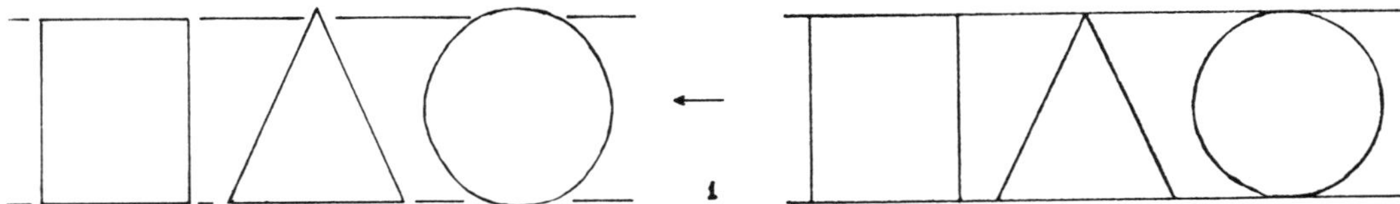

2. Identical forms of an asymmetrical shape, when placed side by side in a certain position, may look different in size. In the following example, the three trapezoidal forms are identical but the right one looks larger than the middle one and that one looks larger than the left one.

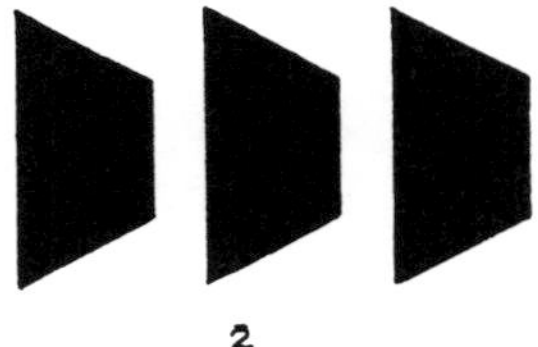

3. A short stroke will look thicker than a long one of a similar thickness.

4-5. Identical strokes may look different in their length as well as their thickness when drawn in different directions.

6-7. A mathematical square (with four identical sides) looks wider than it is in reality. In order that we should perceive it as a real square, it has to be made somewhat narrower (the horizontal strokes should be shorter than the vertical ones).

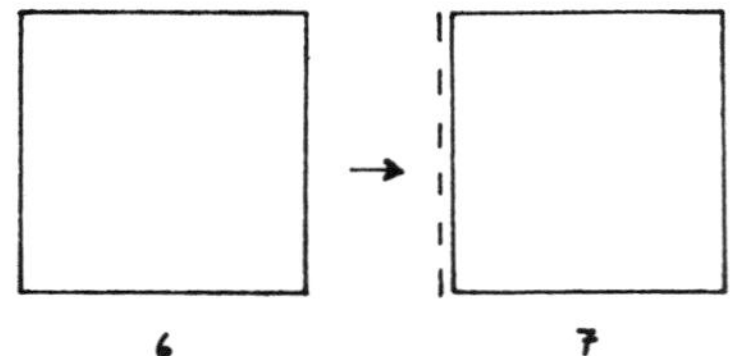

8. The optical centre differs from the mathematical centre, being somewhat higher.

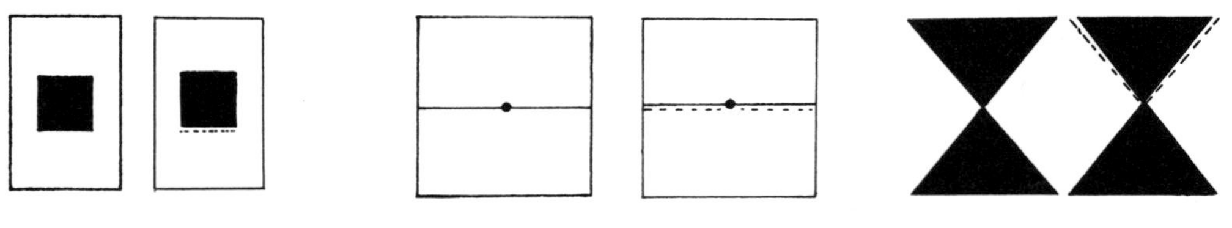

Thus, for example, a horizontal row of letters on a square sheet of paper will appear to be in the centre when it is somewhat higher than the real centre.

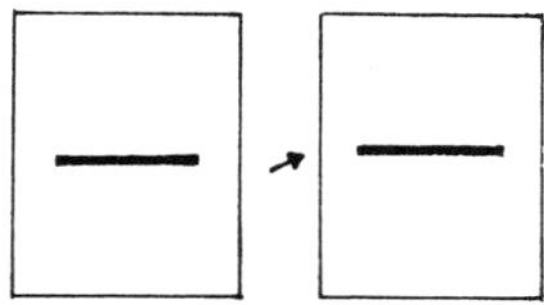

9. A line divided into segments looks longer than a continuous line of the same length.

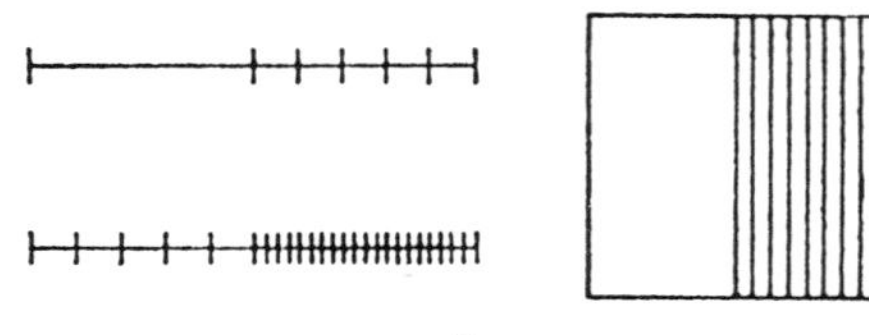

Similarly, a line of narrow and crowded letters looks longer than a line of the same length in which the letters are wide and spacious (but see below no. 19).

10-11. Two identical forms, striped in different directions, look different in their size. Similarly, a square divided vertically looks narrower than the identical square divided horizontally.

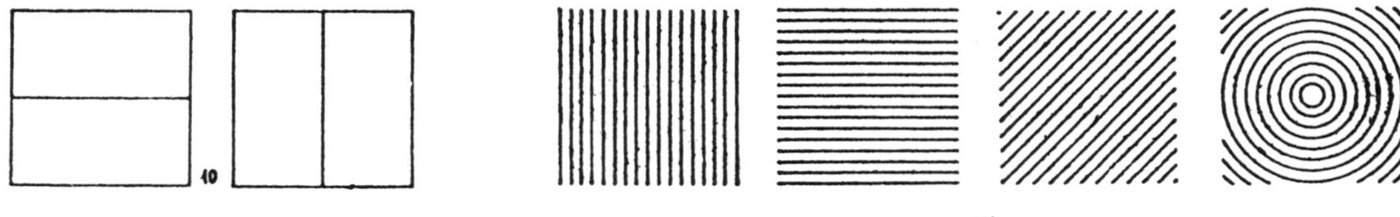

This phenomenon is famous for its use in the design of clothing – e.g., a shirt patterned with horizontal stripes looks wider than the same shirt patterned with vertical stripes. And generally, identical forms with different patterns look different in their sizes.

12. The appearance of a form may be influenced by the neighbouring forms. For example, two identical line-segments adjacent to corners pointing in opposite directions will look different in length.

Thus, ornaments added to a letter-sign will influence our impression of its size. This phenomenon may be used for balancing the strokes and spaces in a written text or in a composition of letter-forms.

כמה
מעלות
טובות
למקום
עלינו

13-15. A meeting of lines drawn in different directions may influence their form as perceived with our eyes. Thus, for example, segments of a diagonal cut by two parallel lines will look as if they belong to two different diagonals; parallel lines crossed by lines drawn in different directions will not look parallel; strokes of letters crossed by lines drawn in different directions may look unequal in their thickness. Thus, any addition to the letter-strokes influences our impression of their thickness, their size and their direction.

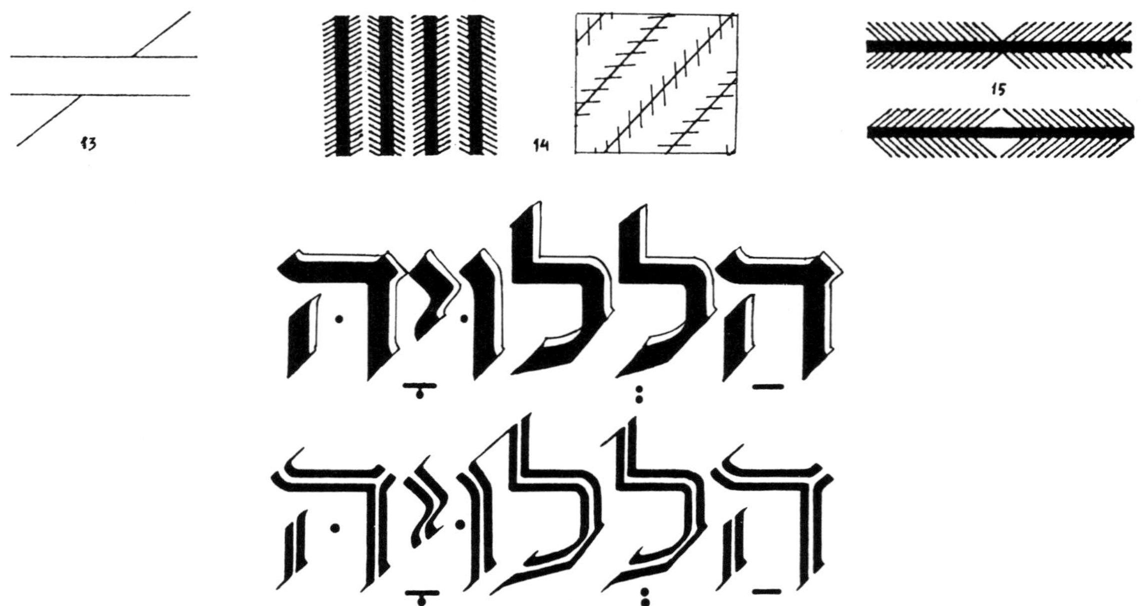

16. Because of our natural sense of perspective, a meeting between forms and radiating lines may deceive our eyes: forms of identical height appear higher the more they approach the point of focus. Thus, a square will look like a trapezoid with the long side closer to the point of focus; a circle may look pressed between corners. Parallel lines look curved when drawn over radiating lines.

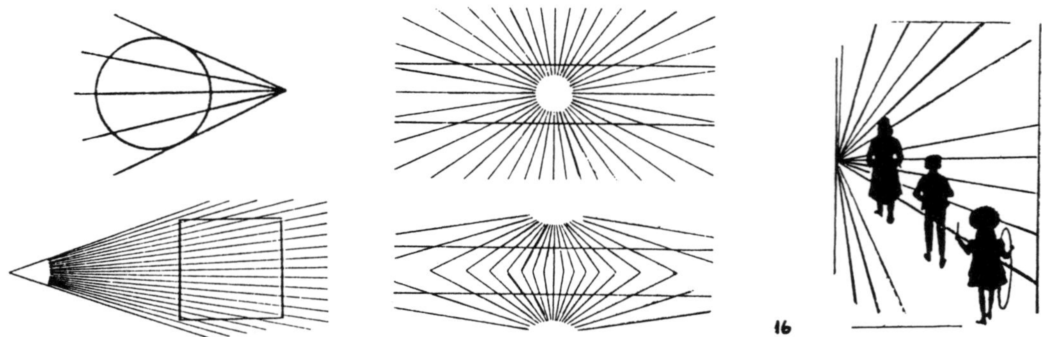

17. Straight lines appear curved when drawn over curved lines or circles.

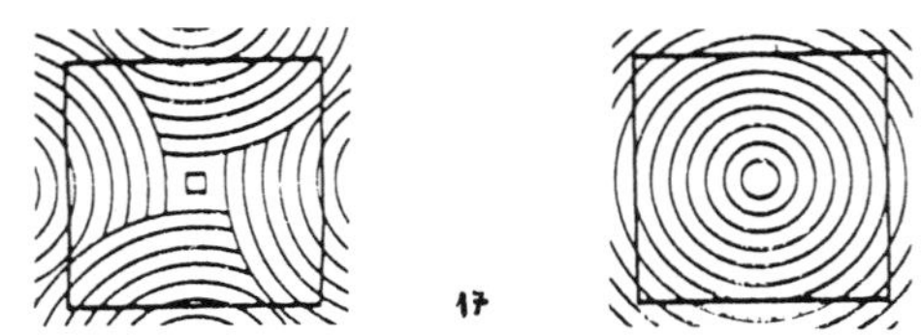

18. A phenomenon known to every draftsman is the 'breaking-point' at the joint of a straight and a curved line or of curved lines drawn in different directions. A gradual curving toward the meeting-point will avoid that 'breaking'.

19-20. Identical forms in different colours appear different in their size. Thus, a bright form on a dark background appears larger than the identical form when dark on a bright background.

This phenomenon should also be taken into account when dealing with letter-forms. It influences the balance between the strokes and their background (i.e., the spaces within and around the letter-signs), as well as our impression of their sizes.

In compositions of negative and positive forms our eyes perceive the dark and the bright forms alternately.

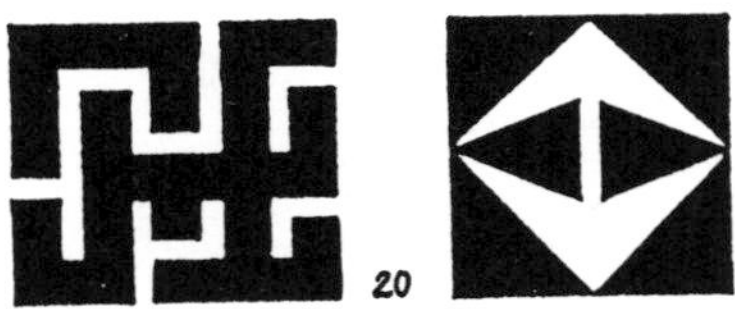

21. The eye reconstructs missing parts of forms. A form may occasionally be recognized by parts of its contours only.

This phenomenon is often exploited in the field of graphic arts.

שלום · שלום · שלום · שלום · שלום · שלום · שלום · שלום · שלום

יברכך ה׳
וישמרך
יאר ה׳
פניו אליך
ויחנך
ישא ה׳
פניו אליך
וישם לך

Ada Yardeni

Ada Yardeni

CHAPTER THREE: THE DESIGNING OF INSCRIPTIONS AND TYPEFACES

Two factors, in addition to the technical factor, should be considered when dealing with the design of letter-forms – the historical factor, i.e., the evolution of the various script-styles, and the graphic or visual factor, i.e., legibility, balanced spacing, formal harmony, the nature of the script (gentle, aggressive, etc.), colour, rhythm – in short, all the elements influencing the appearance of the script. Having already discussed in detail the history of the Hebrew script and its different styles, we shall now discuss the graphic factors to be considered when designing letter-forms.
The question may be asked: what is the purpose of designing a new script-style, when various Hebrew types and fonts are already available for printing and the graphic arts? We may answer that, in fact, the number of these fonts is relatively small, and most of them have been designed on the basis of the Sephardi or the Ashkenazi types, together with a certain influence from the Latin scripts. We hope that a graphic artist, after having studied the various script-styles which have evolved from the Jewish script in the course of its long history, would gain inspiration from the large variety of Hebrew letter-forms when designing a modern script or typeface. Although the personality and individual taste of the artist are undoubtedly the major factors in the design of a script, it is nevertheless true that the study of the evolution of the Hebrew script-styles and of the visual factors influencing the appearance of the script will deepen our acquaintance with the components of the Hebrew letters and develop our feeling for the beauty and harmony of a letter-form as well as our aesthetic sense in general.

A. SCRIPT AS A PRACTICAL INSTRUMENT

A script is used for practical purposes and, as such, should be functional and convenient. Every product made by human hands and used in everyday life, whether a chair or a house, a cup or a fork, a road or a signpost, a computer or a television set, a car or a washing machine, etc., influences our aesthetic sense, generally on an unconscious level. We react to the sights in our environment in a similar way as we react to sounds. There are sounds of which we are aware, and which may be more or less pleasant to our ears, whereas other sounds reach our ears without our being aware of hearing them, usually because we have become used to them. Sometimes we become aware of their existence only after they have stopped. Something similar happens with sights. There are forms or colours which we perceive consciously and which are more or less pleasant to our eyes, and others which our eyes perceive unconsciously. In the domain of writing we may distinguish between pure artistic writing and practical writing. Letter-signs may be used for transmitting an artistic message. The most beautiful letter-forms may be created by an artist without his ever having studied their formal evolution or the visual factors influencing their appearance. A pleasant and intelligent personality and an artistic talent may reveal themselves in a beautiful personal handwriting. However, the study of the evolution of a script and of the techniques for designing letter-forms aims at creating a practical tool that is beautiful at the same time. Artistic and practical values sometimes go together. Thus, a product intended for practical use may have artistic qualities, while a work of art occasionally serves practical purposes.

A few practical suggestions, based on my experience, are presented here in the hope that they will be of assistance to the reader who is interested in the field of letter-design.

Designing a script means the designing of the individual letter-forms belonging to a certain alphabetic system, in an original or an accepted script-style, for current use in print or some other technique, or for some project such as a book-cover, a sign, a trademark, a poster, a heading, a stone inscription, a label on a bottle or a box, an inscription on a vehicle, etc. The rules in these different assignments are quite similar, although more artistic freedom or creative imagination is allowable in designing a short inscription than in fonts for current use. In any case, we are dealing here with a practical use rather than with pure art. The artistic qualities depend on the talents and personality of the designer.

Fig. 254. A rough draft of the letter-forms in a size large enough for our eyes to perceive all its details

B. DESIGNING AN INSCRIPTION

An inscription is designed in stages, the first of which is the planning of the entire composition. Then a draft is made of the general structure of the letters. The letter-forms should be designed in a size that enables one to work on their details. A height of about three centimetres will permit both the form and the details of the letters to be properly handled. For the first

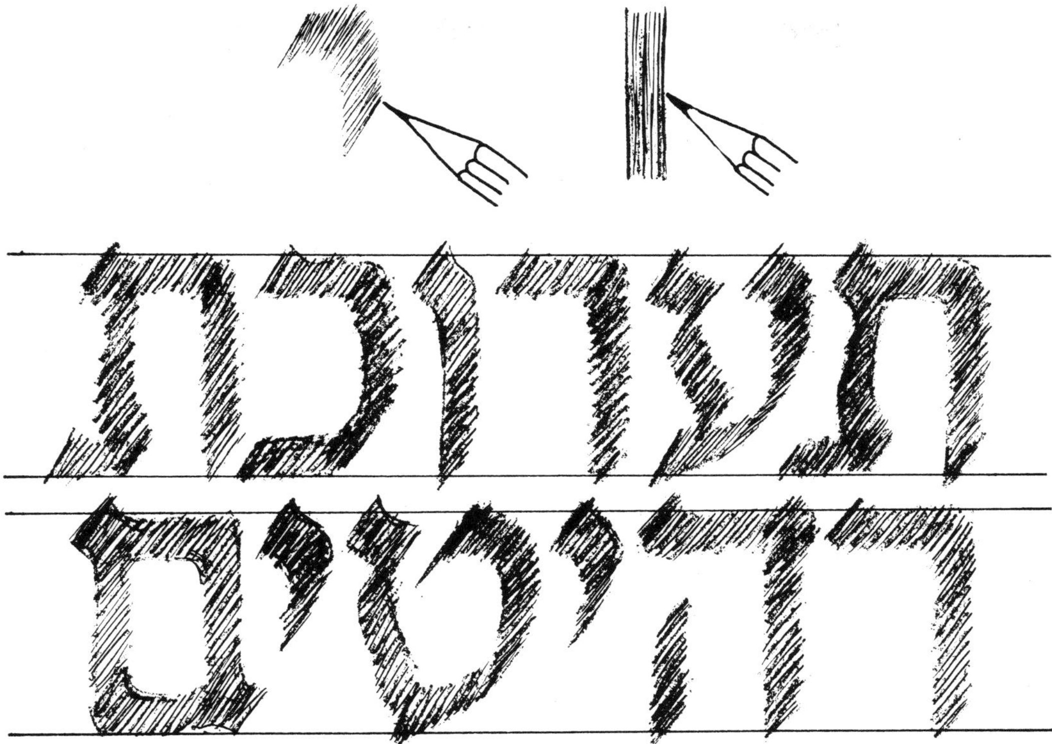

draft, the letters may be drawn with a flat writing-implement such as a flat brush, a flat nib or a chalk. Another method is to use a pencil or a thin brush and draw the strokes with thin parallel lines until the desired thickness is achieved. It is not recommended to start with the contours and then fill in the spaces, because in that way one does not gain an impression of the thickness of strokes that is suitable.

Here are a few basic rules for designing inscriptions:

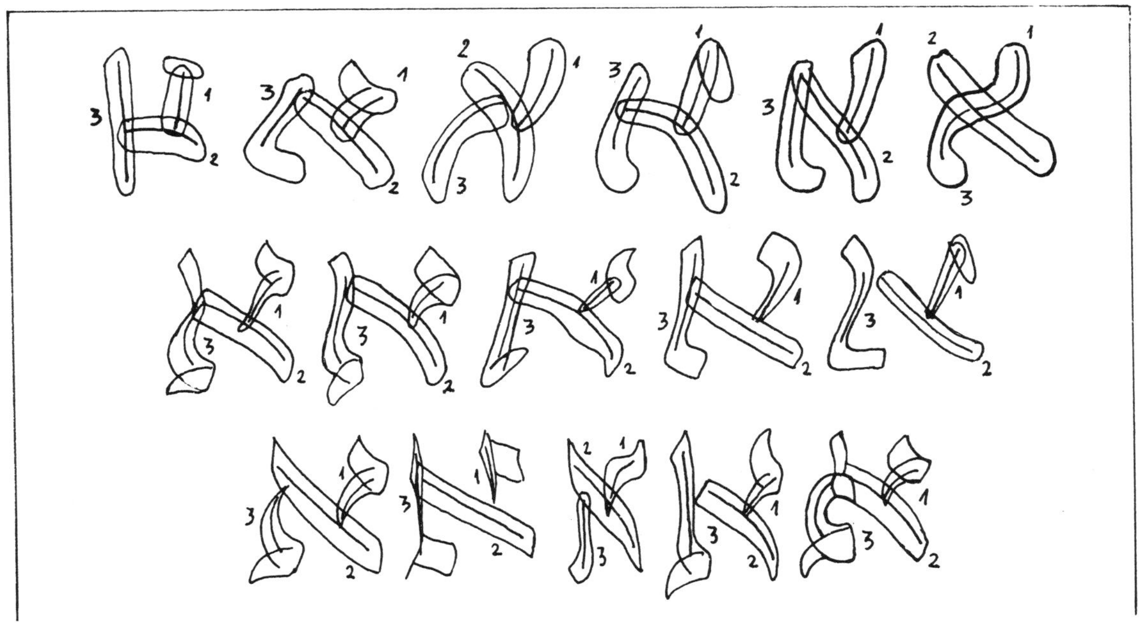

Fig. 255. Various examples of Alef: stroke 3 usually does not start beneath the meeting-point of strokes 1 and 2

1. Legibility

The script should be legible. Distortion of the basic forms of the letters will cause difficulties in reading. One has therefore to study the basic structure of the letter-forms (see above, part 2). Here is an example: if we examine the different styles of the square Alef in the course of its evolution we will see that stroke No. 3 does not usually start below the meeting-point between strokes No. 1 and No. 2. In cursive styles, in which that rule was not kept, it is difficult to identify the letter. Freedom in creating original letter-forms should be kept within certain limits.

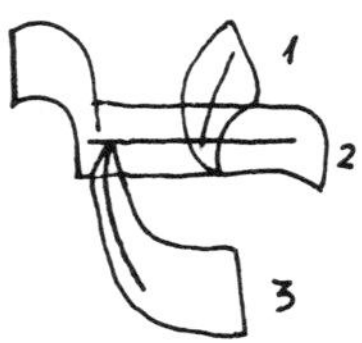

2. Spacing

The letter-form does not exist by itself; the form we see is determined by the background. Thus, the background and the letter-strokes are of equal importance in the composition and the same attention should be given to both. In order to create a harmonious composition we must balance the

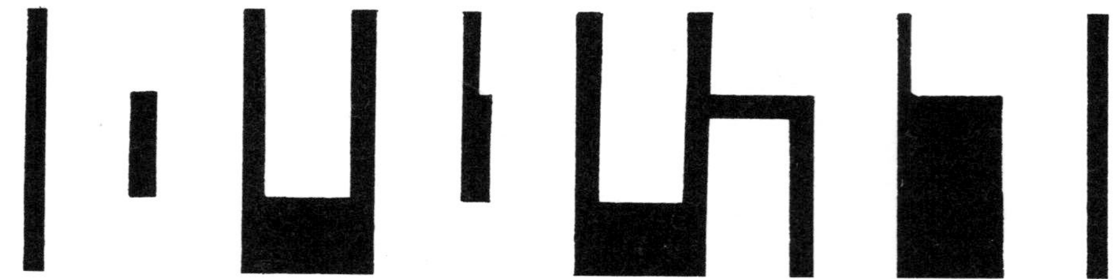

strokes and the spaces. Although this balance can be attained through a complex calculation, it is advisable to train one's eyes to sense the proper spacing between the strokes and between the letter-signs. There are a few basic rules which may help us in achieving this goal (see also the discussion of optical illusions above):

a. The distance between two straight, parallel strokes appears to be smaller than the same distance between two curved strokes or between a curved and a straight stroke, or between a straight stroke and a diagonal. One has therefore to balance the spacing between the letters (this could be done in the draft by separating the individual letter-forms from each other and moving them until the desired spacing is achieved).

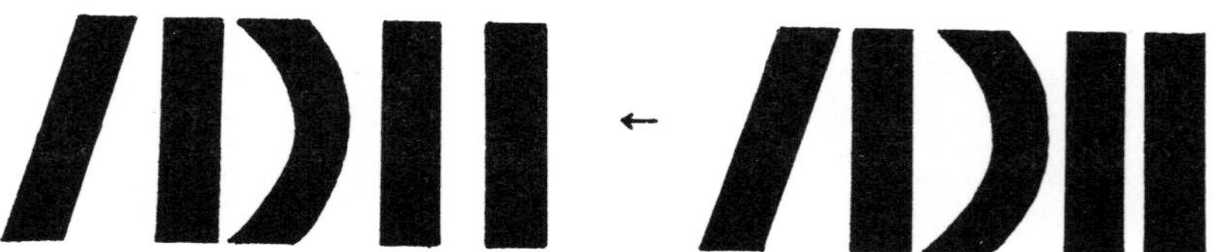

Fig. 256. The distance between two straight, parallel strokes appears smaller than a similar distance between two curved strokes or between a straight stroke and an oblique one, the space being in fact smaller in the first case

b. A stroke sharpening or curving at its end appears to be shorter than a stroke of the same length terminating with a flat end. The stroke with the sharp or curved end should therefore be longer and may extend a little beyond the guideline.

Fig. 257. A stroke with a pointed or curved end appears shorter than a stroke of similar height with a flat end. A fitting elongation of the first ones will correct the impression

c. Attention should be paid to the spaces in and around the letter-forms within the word, in the line and between the lines. The spacing between the letters in a line will be balanced and determined in accordance with the largest space created by two adjacent letter-forms (e.g., Resh followed by Yod, or Lamed below Qof, etc.).

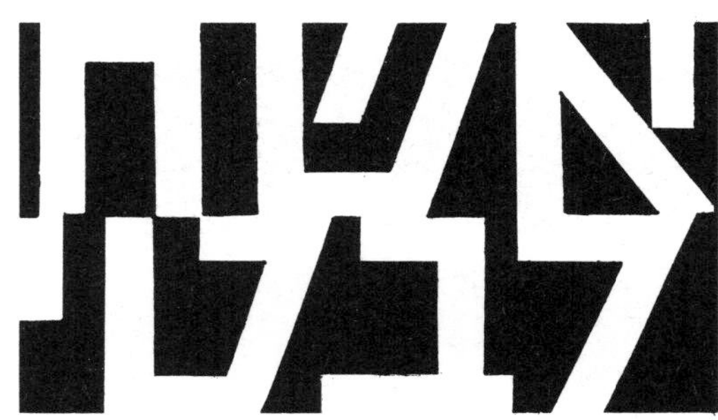

Fig. 258. An example of a balanced spacing between letters and background

In order to appear stable, a letter-form should rest on its centre of gravity. For this purpose, we may imagine the letter-form to be bordered by a rectangle. We can thus build it up like the composition of a black-and-white picture. The spaces will be balanced with the strokes until a harmonious composition is achieved.

Fig. 259. The letter as a composition of a picture in black-and-white

3. The 'Character' of the Script

In writing, as in the designing of a script, the personal character of the artist is naturally and unintentionally revealed. However, when designing an inscription the artist should be aware of the message which is to be conveyed. In order that the script should transmit the desired message, the artist should pay attention to its character. A script can be gentle or aggressive, dramatic or lyrical, dynamic or calm, luxurious or modest, 'noisy' or 'quiet', pretentious or modest, elegant or crude, beautiful or ugly, monumental or simple, heavy or light, modern or traditional, 'humorous' or 'serious', 'rough' or 'smooth', 'masculine' or 'feminine', etc. Thus, for example, the script on the cover of an art book should be more decorative than the script on the cover of a book about physics; a technical script will be suitable for the package of a computer; a fine and elegant script may be appropriate for an expensive piece of women's jewellery; a monumental script suits a burial inscription; an angular and heavy script is fitting for the sign on a menswear shop, etc.

When designing a script, we should imagine a human face and body with its different moods. In our sub-consciousness we draw an analogy between the forms we see and the expression of the human face and body. Thus, for example, a concave line ◡ reminds us of a smiling mouth and a convex line ◠ of a sad mouth; sharp angles convey stiffness and impatience while broad, horizontal forms express stability; a thin vertical line | is associated with elegance and a thin, wavy line ∼ with lightness, etc. The sensitive designer can develop the ability to make such analogies and use them in order to adapt the script to its purpose.

Fig. 260. Examples of scripts of various characters

4. The Combination of Different Types of Scripts

When a combination of different scripts is called for, the contrast between them should be appropriate in extent, i.e., a reasonable contrast in size, colour and inclination. Too small or too large a contrast will miss the right effect. Thus, for example, two different cursive scripts in a single inscription will create a sense of uneasiness. It is preferable to combine a cursive script with a solid and angular script. A combination of scripts whose sizes are too similar will be felt as an error of design, while too great a contrast in their sizes will spoil the harmony of the inscription. Light and bold letter-forms of the same type of script may be combined provided that the contrast is not too small or too great. In fig. 261 there are a few examples of more and of less successful combinations.

בכינוס "צבאות השם"

ביום שלישי ב׳ דר״ח טבת (18.12.90)   בשעה 9.00 בערב
ברחבת הכותל המערבי

Three different fonts in sizes too similar to one another to form an agreeable contrast

אתה נוהג להצליח?

יש לך עסק, ואתה רוצה להצליח.

Two fonts differing in character and in size, forming together an agreeable contrast

שָׂא נָא עֵינֶיךָ

Modern calligraphic square script
and modern cursive script,
differing enough in their character
but not enough in their size

אבגרהו
נחטיכק

Ashkenazi book-hand and modern cursive script
of Ashkenazi origin, too different in their character
and in the tilting of the letters and too similar in their size
to form an agreeable contrast

אבגרהו
דרבגהו|ן אח

Ashkenazi book-hand and Ashkenazi cursive script
fitting in character and size

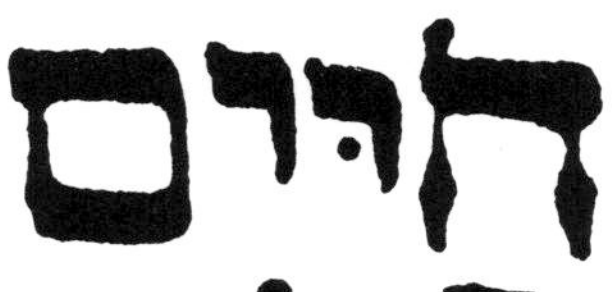

חיים

שָׁקַן הָתִי־דָרֵ״ש רַב נִתְחֹסֵי בְּנֵו עַבְדוֹהִי: כֹא וְאָתִיב יַת־רַב
שָׁקַן עַל־שׁקֻיָתֵיה וְיַהַב יַת־כַּסָא עַל־יִדָא דְּפַרְעֹה: כֹּה וְיָת
רַב נְתָחוֹסֵי צְלַב כְּמָא דְּר־פֵשׁר לְהֹן יֹסֵף: כֹּו וְלָא־דְּכִיר

Too great a difference in the size of the scripts

כתב היד האבוד

בעליית גג בהוליווד
נמצאה המחצית
הראשונה של
"האקלברי פין"

בפיסוק של טוויין. "הברקתי מיד
להוציא את האיש להורג בירייה
מבלי לתת לו שהות להתפלל".
המדפיס הוא גם האשם באובדן
כתב היד המקורי. ג׳יימס פרייזר
גלוק, תורם למוסד שהפך במשך
השנים לספרייה המחוזית של

One font in various sizes forming an agreeable contrast

אבגדהוזחטי

י וְהִגֵּה מִן־הַיְאֹר עֹלֹת שֶׁבַע פָּרֹות יְפֹות
מַרְאֶה וּבְרִיאֹת בָּשָׂר וַתִּרְעֶינָה בָּאָחוּ:
י וְהִגֵּה שֶׁבַע פָּרֹות אֲחֵרֹות עֹלֹות
אַחֲרֵיהֶן מִן־הַיְאֹר רָעֹות מַרְאֶה וְדַקֹּות
בָּשָׂר וַתַּעֲמֹדְנָה אֵצֶל הַפָּרֹות עַל־שְׂפַת

Two fonts differing enough in their sizes
but too similar in their appearance

Fig. 261. Examples of optically right and wrong compositions of scripts of various sizes

5. The Adjustment of the Inscription to Its Background

We have already mentioned the importance of the background in balancing the strokes and spaces. We should now speak of the adjustment of the inscription to its background: i.e., the relationship between the size of the inscription and that of the background, as well as the arrangement of the inscription on its background. In order that the inscription should catch the eye and its message be perceived, the inscription should be positioned in a way that takes the factor of optical illusion into account, and the background should always be considered an equally important factor in the composition. Thus, for example, when designing a sign to be placed in front of a shop, the general appearance of the shop-front should be considered; the inscription on a building should be made to fit its architectural style as well as its size; a heading in a newspaper should be designed in accordance with the size of the columns of the text and the type of script used for it, etc. In fig. 262 there are a few examples of the adaptation of an inscription to its background.

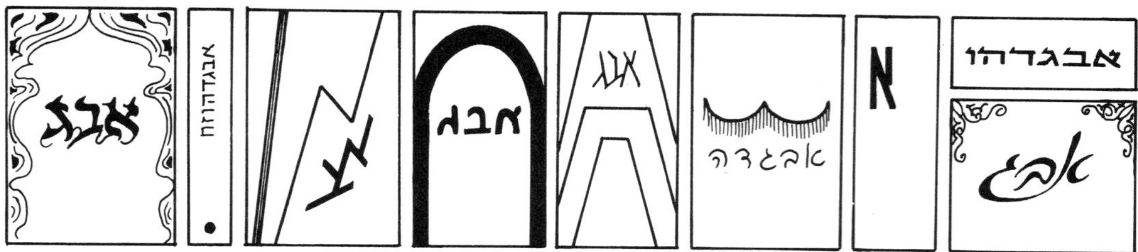

Fig. 262. Examples of an adjustment of an inscription and its background

An inscription may be designed as an elaborate composition: i.e., the words as well as the lines of the inscription combine to form a single composite unit. This may sometimes involve a certain distortion of the letter-forms, because the composition is constructed like a picture in which all the spaces and strokes are balanced. Such compositions, in which the form rather than the content is emphasized, may sometimes become a real work of art, and the designer can freely use his imagination and artistic creativity.

6. Designing Stone-Inscriptions

The two main types of stone inscriptions are those in deep and high relief: i.e., inscriptions in which the letters are incised and inscriptions in which the background is carved away and the letters raised above the background. In preparing the draft of the inscription, transparent paper may be used. There are two main methods of engraving the letters in the stone. One is to remove a layer to the width of the individual strokes,

Fig. 263. A letter-composition sometimes requires a certain distortion of the letter-forms

Fig. 264. An example of a design of letters to be incised in stone

which will then be bordered by straight, erect 'walls'. The other is to gradually deepen the individual strokes towards their central line, creating slanting 'walls'. At the ends of the strokes, the central line branches into two lines running towards the corners (figs. 73, 264).

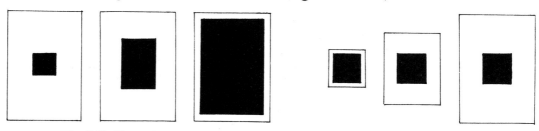

Fig. 265. Size relationships of the area covered with script and its background

The proportional relationship of the inscription to the background should also be considered (see “the layout of the text” below, and fig. 265).

C. DESIGNING A TYPEFACE

When designing a typeface, the final appearance of the printed text should be considered. In addition to the factors discussed above, the arrangement of the text on the page, the colour of the text and the size of the letters, and the regularity and rhythm of the strokes have to be taken into account. Difficulties in reading may be caused by various factors resulting from faults in the design of the letter-forms as well as their arrangement on the page. A font that is not properly designed tires the eyes. The designer should avoid obstacles to uninterrupted reading.

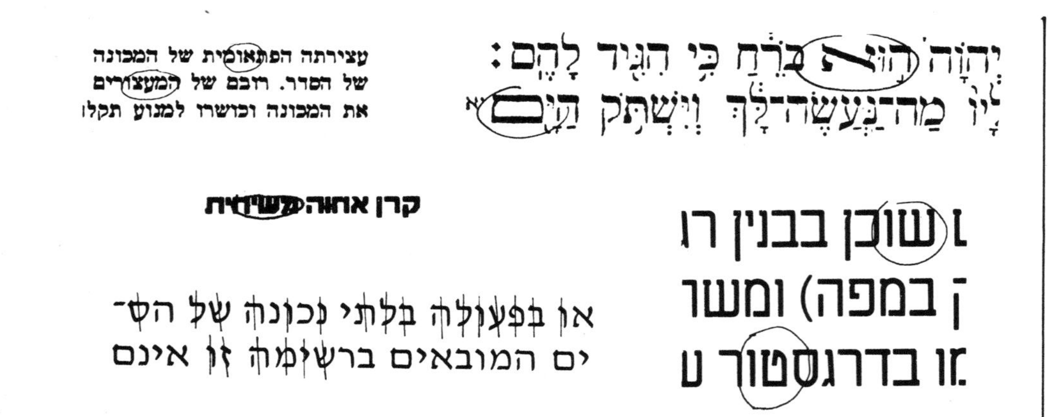

Fig. 266. Examples of difficulties in reading due to errors in the design of the letter-forms

Listed below are the faults in letter-design most likely to cause difficulties in reading:

1. Irregular forms.
2. Differences in the inclination of the letter-forms.
3. A lack of stylistic unity.
4. An extreme similarity in the forms of different letters of the alphabet.
5. Spots and excessively large spaces resulting from ill-balanced spacing.
6. A text too dark or light in colour as a result of excessively bold or light letter-forms.

We will now give a detailed description of each of the faults listed above:

1. Irregular forms. – In designing a typeface, an excess of ornament as well as a distortion of the basic strokes of the letter-forms should be avoided. Irregular letter-forms distract one's attention and interrupt the reading. One should remember that a practiced reader generally reads entire words rather than single letters.

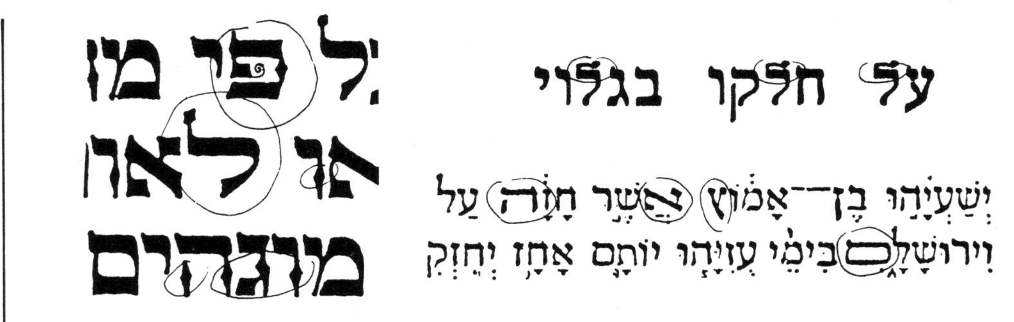

Fig. 267. Outstanding letter-forms

2. Differences in the inclination of the letter-forms. – These disturb the orderly 'rhythm' of the script. Strokes or part of strokes of different letter-forms which run in the same direction should be parallel. The letter-forms should be designed in such a way that their axial lines are parallel.

Fig. 268. Uneven inclination of letter-forms in a font

3. A lack of stylistic unity. – The stylistic unity of a script results from a similar formation of the letter-strokes and ornaments and their joints with each other, and, in general, from a similar character of the letter-forms. Certain script-styles are characterized by groups of letters with similar graphic components. Despite the natural difference in the structure of the individual letters, they should be uniform in their stylistic character in order to prevent difficulty in reading.

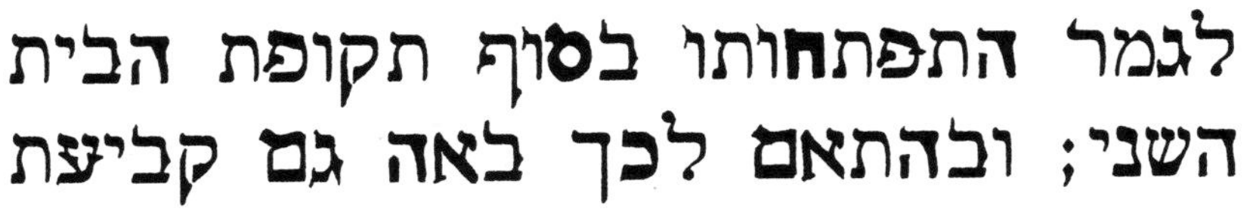

לגמר התפתחותו בסוף תקופת הבית
השני; ובהתאם לכך באה גם קביעת

Fig. 269. Lack of stylistic uniformity in the appearance of the letter strokes and of their graphical elements

4. An extreme similarity between the letter-forms. – Stylistic uniformity can result in an extreme similarity of the letter-signs which can be detrimental to their legibility. It is therefore necessary to preserve the special structural characteristics of the individual letters (e.g., in the Hebrew square script special attention should be given to Bet and Kaf, Dalet and Resh, Gimel and Nun, Waw and Zayin, Ḥet and Taw, as well as Ṭet, Samekh and final Mem).

יפגש עם חותחים

Fig. 270. Excessive resemblance in the form of certain letters

5. Spots and excessively large spaces. – Strokes which are drawn too close together, as well as the meeting-points between two or more strokes may appear as spots (particularly in small characters), and uneven spacing may disturb the balance of the script. Spots and excessively large spaces may be avoided through a careful design of letter-forms.

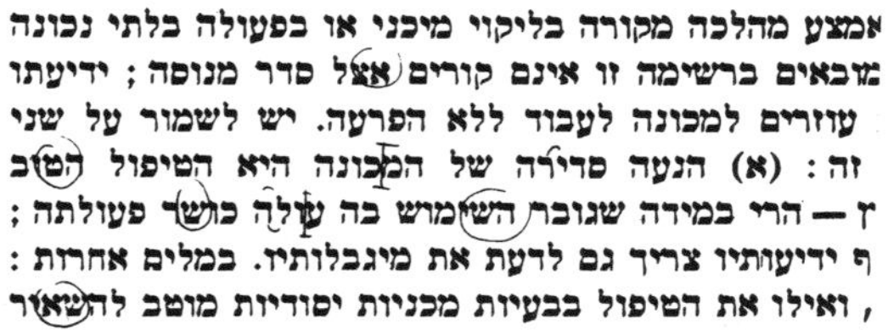

אמצע מהלכה מקורה בליקוי מיכני או בפעולה בלתי נכונה
מובאים ברשימה זו אינם קורים אצל סדר מנוסה ; ידיעתו
עוזרים למכונה לעבוד ללא הפרעה. יש לשמור על שני
זה : (א) הנעה סדירה של המכונה היא הטיפול הטוב
ץ — הרי במידה שגובר השימוש בה עולה כושר פעולתה ;
ף ידיעותיו צריך גם לדעת את מיגבלותיו. במלים אחרות :
ואילו את הטיפול בבעיות מכניות יסודיות מוטב להשאיר ,

Fig. 271. Spots or excessive large spaces resulting from ill-balanced spacing of the strokes and their background, and from the uneven sizes of different letter-forms

Listed below are a few devices which may be useful for that purpose:

a. The treatment of the meeting-point between two straight strokes:
When two straight strokes of the same thickness meet at a sharp angle, a 'spot' is created at their meeting-point. In order to avoid this, the strokes should gradually narrow towards their meeting-point.

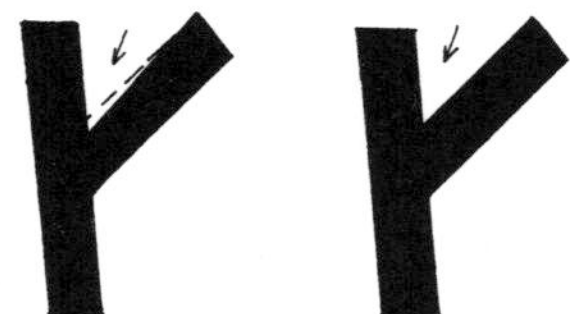

Fig. 272. The prevention of a spot at the meeting-point of two diagonals

The meeting-point of two straight strokes of different thickness should be at the intersection of their central lines.

Fig. 273. The correct meeting-point of a straight stroke and the corner of an angle is at the intersection of their central lines

The meeting-point between a straight stroke and the corner of an angle should be where the intersection of the central lines of the strokes making up the angle touches the nearest edge of the straight stroke.

Fig. 274. The correct meeting-point is where the central lines of the corner touch the edge of the straight stroke

b. The treating of the junction of a curved stroke with a straight stroke: in order to avoid a 'spot' at the meeting-point of a curved stroke and a straight stroke, the curved stroke should gradually narrow towards the meeting-point.

Fig. 275. The prevention of a spot at the meeting-point of two curved strokes or a curved and a straight stroke

c. Balancing the spaces: when designing a typeface, the spaces in and around the letters should be calculated in such a way that they fit each other when arranged in any sequence.

As most letter-forms differ from each other in their width, they may be classified in groups according to their width. The system will then have a harmonious appearance. As already mentioned, the formal differences between the letter-signs determine the spacing between them. In a printed text, unlike a handwritten text, the spacing is usually not completely balanced, because the letter-forms are geometrically designed within rectangles which do not allow the strokes of one letter to penetrate into the borders of another letter. The minimal spacing needed around each letter depends on its optical central axis. In order to achieve the best spacing, the individual letters should be placed inside rectangles in such a way that the optical central axis of each letter fits the vertical centre of its rectangle. The letter-form should be composed like a black-and-white picture. Its strokes will divide the rectangle into optically equivalent areas.

In order to emphasize certain letters or words in a text, a secondary font, with cursive, inclined letter-forms, may be designed together with the standard typeface. The inclination of the parallelograms should not exceed an angle of 20-30 degrees.

Fig. 276. The letter-form as a composition in black-and-white

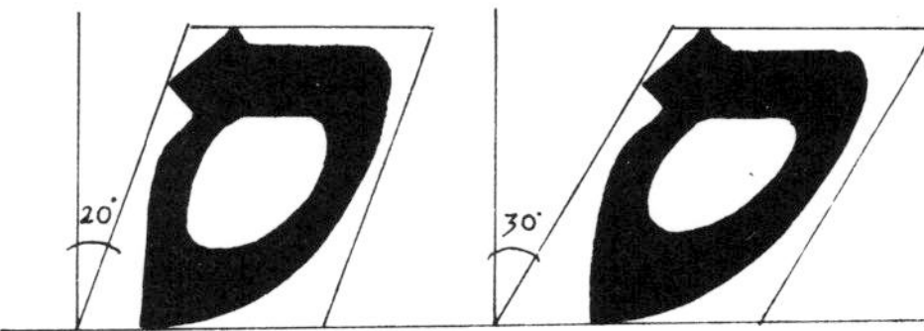

Fig. 277. The design of an inclined letter

The stability of the letter-form can only be achieved by taking optical illusions into account (see above). The vertical sides of the rectangles will serve as the borders between the individual letter-signs when arranged at a

Fig. 278. Stability resulting from the widening of the letter-form towards the bottom

minimal distance from each other. A vertical stroke will need a larger spacing than a curved or an oblique stroke. A letter opening to the left should be placed near the left side of the rectangle. A proper division of the rectangles will provide the desired spacing between the letters (see examples in fig. 279).

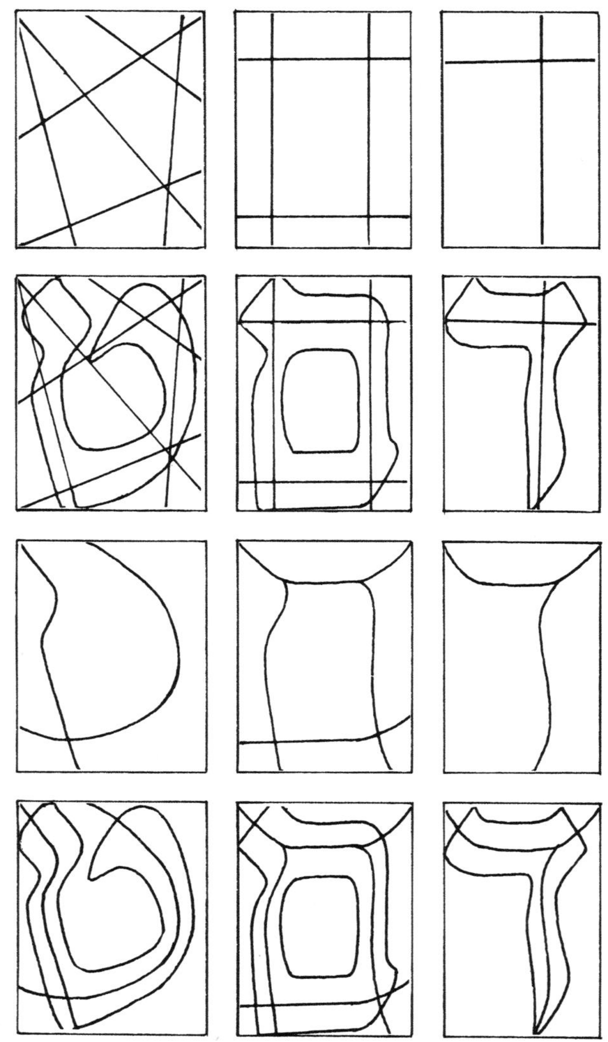

Fig. 279. The placement of the letter within a rectangle in accordance with an optically correct division of the background

6. The 'tone' of a printed text depends on the thickness and density of the letter-strokes. Fonts are usually made in two or three 'weights' – light, bold and medium or normal. Excessively bold letters may not only have a dark and heavy appearance but may also disturb the balance between the text and the background. On the other hand, if the letters are too light, the text may look 'pale' and be dominated by the background (see fig. 280).

These facts should be kept in mind when designing the fonts.

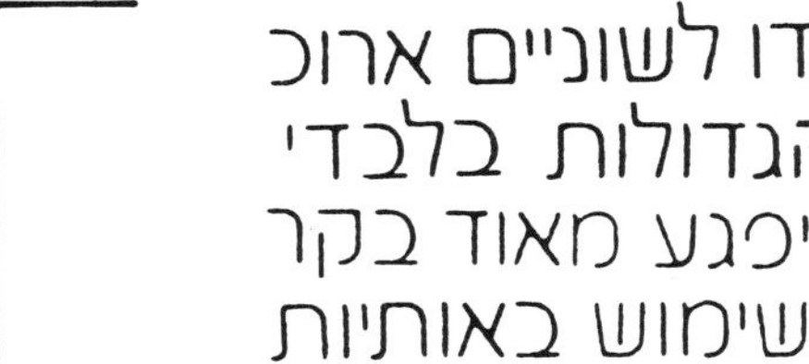

מהלכה מקורה בליקוי נ
יל המעצורים המובאים ב
נתו את המכונה וכושרו ל
• יש לשמור על שני כללים
רה של המכונה היא הט
— הרי במידה שגובר השי
ה, המכיר את היקף ידיע

Fig. 280. Excessively dark and light texts resulting from excessively thick or thin strokes of the letters

D. CORRECTING OR CHANGING THE DESIGN OF GIVEN LETTER-FORMS

One may occasionally want to change or correct certain features of a given script. Here are some common changes:

1. Alterations in the height or width of the letter-signs.
2. Alterations in the thickness of the strokes.
3. Alterations in the finish, such as smoothing-out corners at the meeting-points of the strokes, etc.
4. Ornamental additions, etc.

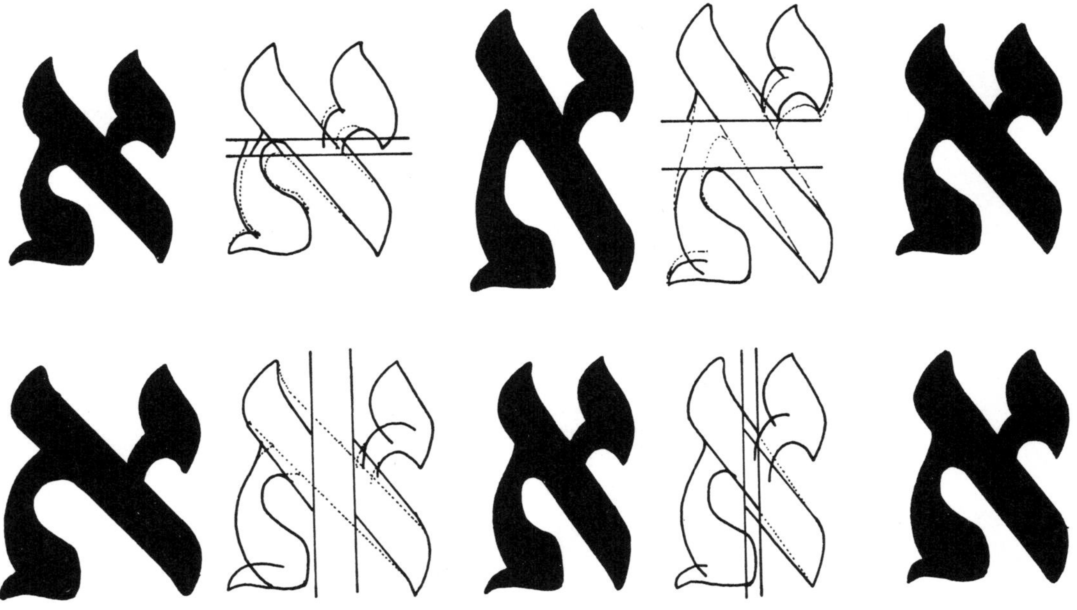

Fig. 281. An example of the enlarging and reducing of an ᾿Alef

1. In order to change the height or width of a letter-form, some of the strokes will have to be remade. Straight, horizontal or vertical strokes will simply be elongated or shortened. However, in the case of an oblique or a curved stroke, its angle has to be changed, as well as its meeting-points with other strokes. For this purpose we may divide the form into halves and move them together or apart in the desired direction, and then join the parts of the strokes while changing their angle (fig. 281). The more complex the form of the letter is, the more complex the change in its proportions will be.

In order to change its inclination, the letter-form will have to be redesigned in a parallelogram. We do not recommend taking a given script and automatically changing the inclination of the strokes, because that may disturb the balance between the strokes and the spaces.

2. Thin letter-forms may be thickened; bold ones may be made thinner. This change should not be an automatic one either. One must remember that a bold letter-form on a bright background looks smaller than a thin one of identical height. This is because the bright space inside the letter appears larger. The spaces therefore have to be balanced. A closed letter form, such as final Mem, when thickened, has to become wider than an open letter such as Dalet (fig. 282). An oblique stroke must be thickened on both its sides and change its angle. Thick strokes can be made thin by a reverse process. All strokes of a letter-form must be thickened or made thin proportionally. In certain letter-forms, strokes will have to be moved in order to keep their balance. For example, in a certain form of Dalet the 'leg' has to be moved to the left in order to preserve the proportional relationship between the projection of the right shoulder and the other parts of the letter-form.

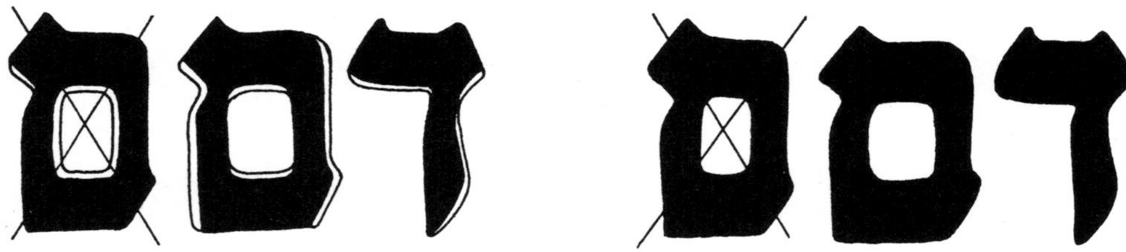

Fig. 282. Changing the thickness of the strokes

Of course, each script-style has its own problems, most of which may be solved by balancing the letter-forms within rectangles or parallelograms.

Fig. 283. The smoothing-out of corners at the meeting points of strokes is part of the 'finish'

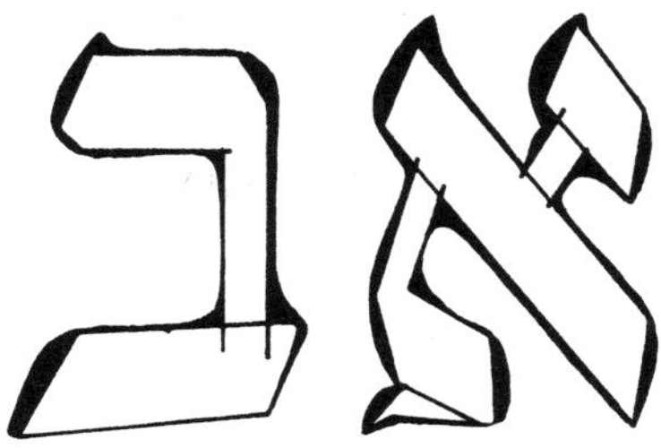

Fig. 284. Adding elegance with a free hand to mechanically-drawn strokes

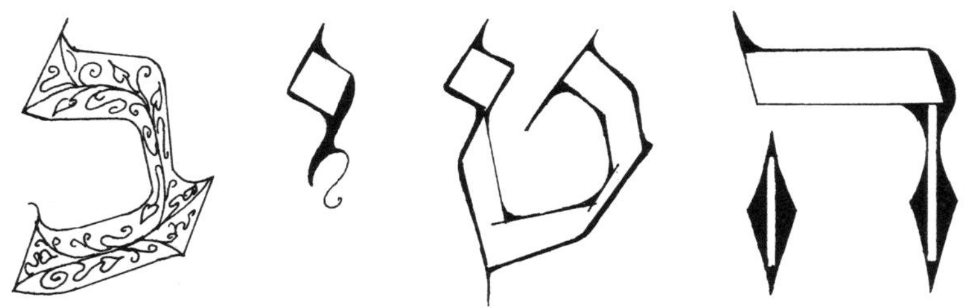

Fig. 285. Adding ornaments to plain strokes

3-4. The 'finish': e.g., the smoothing-out or emphasizing of corners and angles, or the addition of ornaments etc. In designing types for print, the straight and curved contours of the letter-forms may be made mechanically with the help of a computer, or of tools such as a ruler and a template or former, etc. However, the 'finish', which may add elegance to the plain strokes, and the addition of extra ornaments, should be done with a free hand (figs. 283-285) and may later be worked over with the computer.

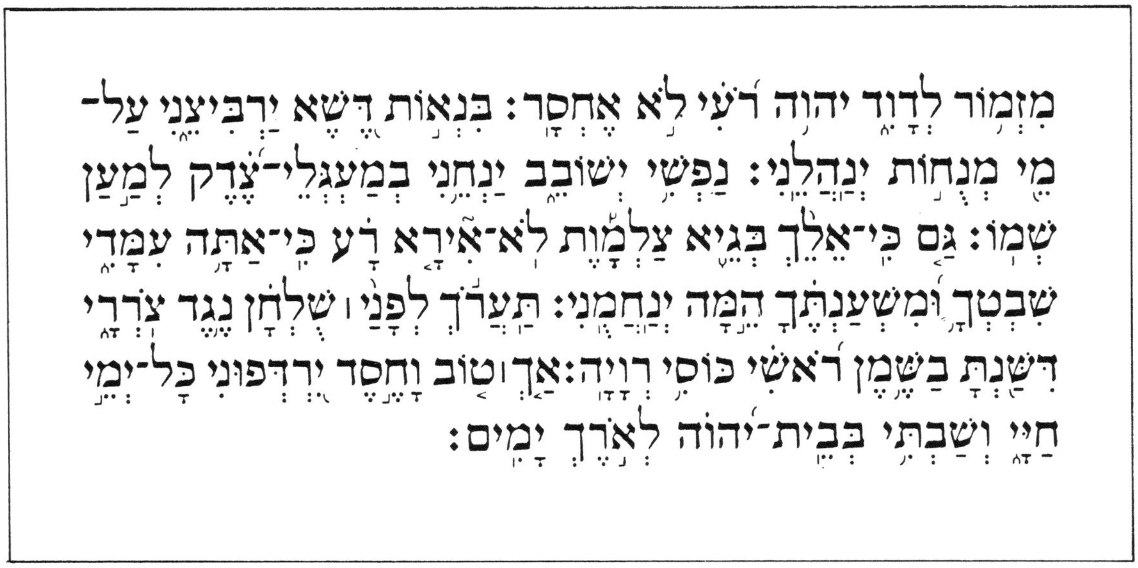

מִזְמוֹר לְדָוִד יְהוָה רֹעִי לֹא אֶחְסָר: בִּנְאוֹת דֶּשֶׁא יַרְבִּיצֵנִי עַל־
מֵי מְנֻחוֹת יְנַהֲלֵנִי: נַפְשִׁי יְשׁוֹבֵב יַנְחֵנִי בְמַעְגְּלֵי־צֶדֶק לְמַעַן
שְׁמוֹ: גַּם כִּי־אֵלֵךְ בְּגֵיא צַלְמָוֶת לֹא־אִירָא רָע כִּי־אַתָּה עִמָּדִי
שִׁבְטְךָ וּמִשְׁעַנְתֶּךָ הֵמָּה יְנַחֲמֻנִי: תַּעֲרֹךְ לְפָנַי ו שֻׁלְחָן נֶגֶד צֹרְרָי
דִּשַּׁנְתָּ בַשֶּׁמֶן רֹאשִׁי כּוֹסִי רְוָיָה: אַךְ ו טוֹב וָחֶסֶד יִרְדְּפוּנִי כָּל־יְמֵי
חַיָּי וְשַׁבְתִּי בְּבֵית־יְהוָה לְאֹרֶךְ יָמִים:

Fig. 286. An example of a text with vowelization marks

323

E. PUNCTUATION AND VOWELIZATION MARKS

When designing fonts for printing, one should also design punctuation marks and a system of vowelization marks fitting the style of the fonts.

The Hebrew vowelization system consists of short horizontal lines and dots placed below the letters, as well as dots placed above and inside the letters. The vowelization marks are as follows: Pataḥ – a short horizontal line; Kamatz – a short horizontal line with a dot placed in the centre below it; Ḥirik – a single dot; Tsere – two dots placed horizontally; Shewa – two dots placed vertically; Kubutz – three dots placed obliquely, descending to the right; Segol – three dots placed in the form of a reversed triangle; Ḥataf-Pataḥ, Ḥataf-Kamatz and Ḥataf-Segol – the respective vowel-sign with a Shewa on its right-hand side. Ḥolam – a dot above a Waw or to the left of the upper corner of any letter; Shuruk – Waw with a dot to the left of its centre. In addition to these vowelization marks, there is the Dagesh-mark, which is a dot placed inside a letter to indicate that it is doubled or pronounced in a different way. A consonantal He at the end of a word is also marked with a dot, called Mappik. Shin and Sin are marked with diacritical points.

The dots inside the letters should be placed at the optical centre of the letter-form. All the marks should fit the style and size of the letters; marks which are too large upset the balance between the strokes and the spaces, while ones which are too small are not sufficiently clear.

Generally, the marks beneath the letters should be placed below their optical centre. The marks beneath Dalet, Waw, Zayin, Yod and Resh should be situated directly below the 'leg'.

The dots of Shewa and of the Ḥatafs, as well as of the Ḥolam, the Shuruk, the Dagesh, the Mappik and the diacritical points of Shin and Sin may be somewhat smaller than the other dots. The Ḥolam on the Waw should be placed above the centre of its 'head', while the Ḥolam on other letters should be placed to the left of their upper corners. The Pataḥ and Kamatz should be narrower than the narrow letters. The punctuation marks should also fit the script-style and be in proportion to the size of the letters. Their spacing should be calculated according to the spacing of the letter-signs.

F. THE LAYOUT OF THE TEXT

The legibility of a text also depends on its layout against its background. The spacing of the letters and the lines has already been discussed above. In addition, one should consider the length of the lines and the layout of the text on the page, the headings, and, in the case of a book, the appearance of the text on a double page. The layout of the text will take into account its proportions in relation to the background and the factor of optical illusion as well as that of spacing and balancing.

These are the three most common forms of relationship between the text and the background (see above, fig. 265):

1. The text covers a large part of the background.
2. The text and the background appear similar in size.
3. The text covers a small part of the background.

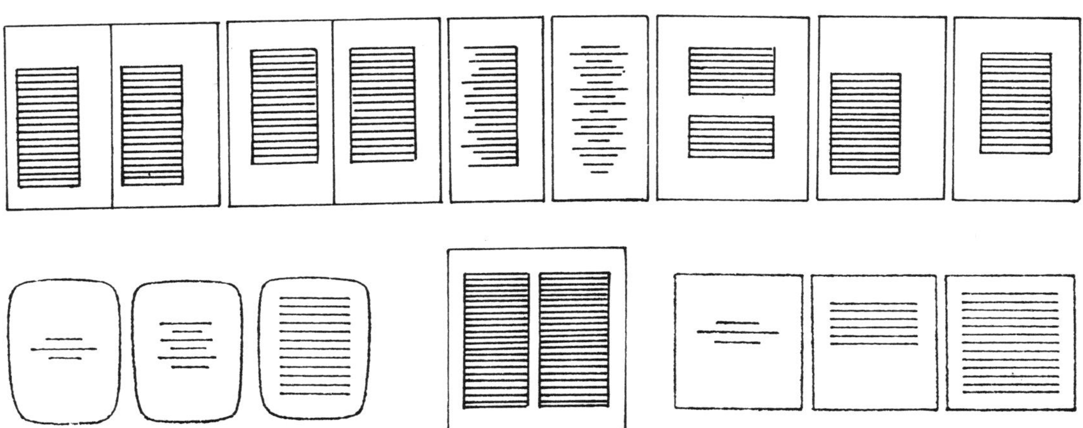

Fig. 287. Examples of the arrangement of the text on the page

The text may be laid out symmetrically or asymmetrically. In both cases there should be an optical balance between the text and the background. In fig. 288 there are a few examples of the division of a rectangular surface, including the combination of a continuous text with headings or with emphasized words or sentences.

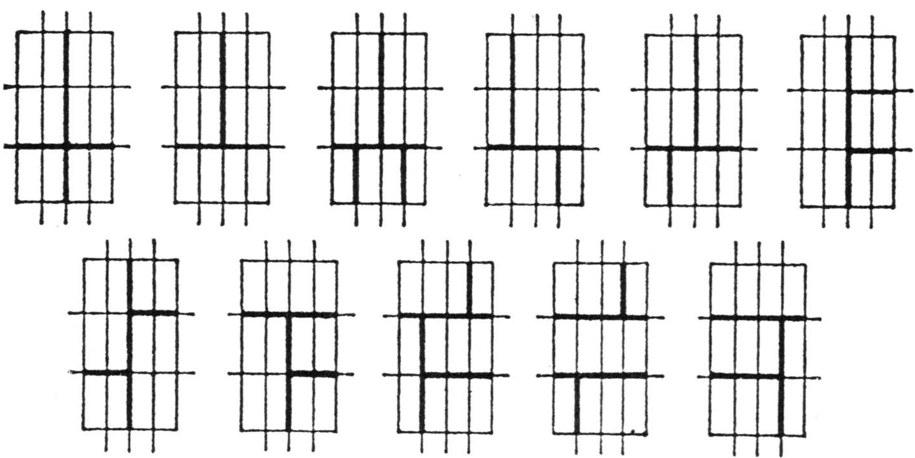

Fig. 288. Examples of a proportional division of a page

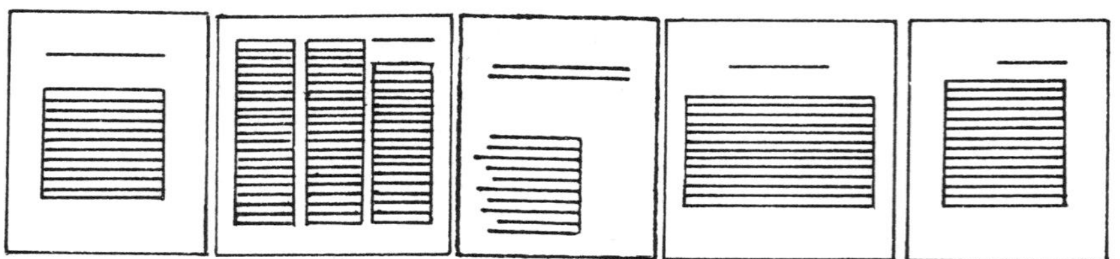

Fig. 289. Examples of the composition of a text with its heading

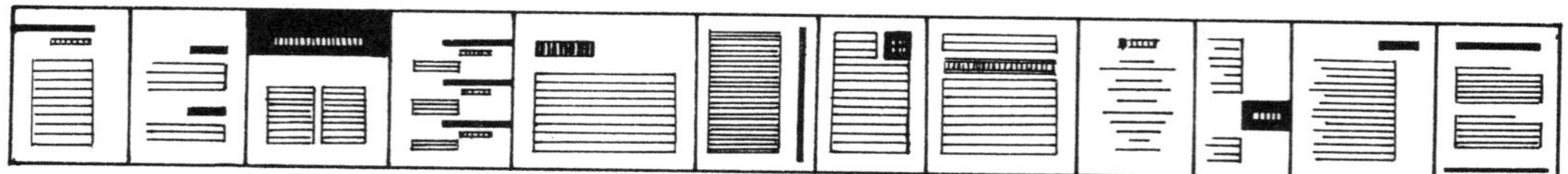

Fig. 290. Examples of an emphasized text by means of contrast

One should remember that an excessive number of emphasized words or sentences cancels out the effect of the emphasis. Too large a heading may dominate the text and disturb the balance, while too small a heading will lose its effect unless separated from the text by a large space. The effect depends on the contrast. A real contrast creates a certain tension as a result of the juxtaposition of different forms or colours, sizes and directions and the positioning of a form against its background or in space. The same rules of surface-division, balance, optical illusion and contrast apply to the layout of a text with illustrations.

SUMMING-UP

When dealing with forms, including letter-forms, we should remember that the visual perception of a form depends on at least four major factors which influence the harmonious appearance of the composition. These should be taken into account by the calligrapher or the designer of letter-forms. They derive from the physical structure of the human eye and are therefore common to all seeing people.

The factors are as follows:

BALANCE
SYMMETRY
CONTRAST
OPTICAL ILLUSIONS

The aesthetic sense is linked to a feeling for harmony, although individual taste depends on character and temperament, which differ from one person to another. Human imagination and creativity permit almost endless innovations in the area of design, including the design of scripts. But one has to keep in mind the fact that script serves for communication between people and is connected to a certain culture.

Despite fashions and technical innovations, the basic structure of the Hebrew letter-forms reflects an ancient tradition and the changes they underwent were the product of an evolution and the influences of the scripts and styles of other cultures.

The study of the evolution of the Hebrew letters may help us to understand their formal changes and will provide a firm and solid basis for modern Hebrew calligraphy and the design of modern Hebrew script-styles.

List of Alphabetic Charts

List of Illustrations

Selected Bibliography

Albright, W.F., 'A Biblical Fragment from the Maccabaean Age – The Nash Papyrus', *Journal of Biblical Literature* 56 (1937), 145-176

Beit-Arié, M., *HEBREW CODICOLOGY*[2] (Jerusalem 1981)

Beit-Arié, M., 'Palaeographical Identification of Hebrew Manuscripts: Methodology and Practice', *Jewish Art* 12-13 (Jerusalem 1986-1987), 15-44

Beit-Arié, M., *THE ONLY DATED MEDIEVAL MANUSCRIPT WRITTEN IN ENGLAND* (London 1985)

Birnbaum, S.A., *THE HEBREW SCRIPTS* I-II (London-Leiden 1954-1971)

Corpus Inscriptionum Semiticarum (Paris 1881-1951)

Cross Jr., F.M., 'The Development of the Jewish Scripts', in: G.E. Wright (ed.), *The Bible and the Ancient Near East*, Essays in honor of W.F. Albright (Garden City 1961), 133-202

Cross Jr., F.M., 'The Oldest Manuscripts from Qumran', *Journal of Biblical Literature* 74 (1955), 147-172

Dinstein, I. and Shapira, Y., 'Ancient Hebraic Handwriting Identification with Run-Length Histograms', *IEEE Transactions on System, Man and Cybernetics*, Vol. SMC-12, No. 3, May-June 1982 (Ben-Gurion University of the Negev, Beersheva, Israel, Electrical Engineering Dept.)

Diringer, D., *THE ALPHABET*[2] (Watford, Herts. 1949)

Diringer, D., *THE BOOK BEFORE PRINTING*[2] (New York 1982)

Discoveries in the Judaean Desert (Oxford)

Eshel, E., Eshel, H. and Yardeni, A., ʿA Qumran Composition Containing Part of Ps. 154 and a Prayer for the Welfare of King Jonathan and his Kingdomʾ, *Israel Exploration Journal* 42 (1992), 199-229

Frey, J.B., *Corpus Inscriptionum Iudaicarum* II, (Roma 1952)

Gilissen, L., *'L'expertise des écritures medievales', Réchèrch d'une methode avec application à un du XIe siecle: Le lectionnaire de Lobbes, codex Bruxellensis 18018* (Gand 1973)

Glatzer, M., 'Early Hebrew Printing', in: L.S. Gold (ed.), *A Sign and a Witness* (New York and Oxford 1983)

Israel Bibliophiles (eds. R. Weiser, L. Avrin et al.), nos. 2-4 (Jerusalem 1982-1984)

LA PALEOGRAPHIE HÉBRAÏQUE MEDIEVALE, colloques internationaux du Centre National de la Réchèrche Scientifique, no. 547 (Paris 1972)

LES TECHNIQUES DE LABORATIORE DANS L'ETUDE DE MANUSCRITS, colloques internationaux du Centre National de la Réchèrche Scientifique, no. 548 (Paris 1972)

Mallon, J., *DE L'ECRITURE* (Paris 1982)

Mounin, G., Quelques observations sur la notion d'articulation', *Introduction a la sémiologie* (Paris 1970), 135-148

Naveh, J., *EARLY HISTORY OF THE ALPHABET* (Jerusalem 1982)

Naveh, J. and Shaked, S., *AMULETS AND MAGIC BOWLS* (Jerusalem 1985)

Naveh, J. and Shaked, S., *MAGIC SPELLS AND FORMULAE* (Jerusalem 1993)

Nerdinger, E. and Beck, L., *SCHRIFT SCHREIBEN, SCHRIFT ZEICHNEN* (Munich 1964)

Plantin of Antwerp, cat. no. 211, The Israel Museum Jerusalem (1981)

Porten, B. and Yardeni, A., *TEXTBOOK OF ARAMAIC DOCUMENTS FROM ANCIENT EGYPT* vols. 1-3 (Jerusalem 1986-1993); vol. 4 (forthcoming)

Posner, R. and Ta-Shema, I., *THE HEBREW BOOK* (Jerusalem 1975)

Puech, E., 'Inscriptions funeraires palestiniennes - Tombeau de Jason et ossuaires', *Revue Biblique* 90 (1983), 481-533

Rahmani, L.Y., *A CATALOGUE OF JEWISH OSSUARIES IN THE COLLECTIONS OF THE STATE OF ISRAEL* (Jerusalem 1994)

Renov, I., *Changes in Hebrew Script, 6th cent. B.C.E. - 2nd cent. C.E.* Yeshiva University Ph.D., 1967 (Ann Arbor Michigan USA, University Microfilms International, 67-9680, London)

Sirat, C., Beit-Arié, M. and Glatzer, M., *MANUSCRITS MÉDIÉVAUX EN CARACTÈRES HÉBRAÏQUE portant des indications de date jusqu'à 1540*, vol. I-III (Jerusalem and Paris 1972-1986)

Sirat, C. (avec la colaboration de M. Dukan), *ECRITURE ET CIVILISATIONS* (Paris 1976)

Sirat, C., *L'EXAMEN DES ECRITURES: L'OEIL ET LA MACHINE* , Essai de methodologie, (PARIS 1981)

Sirat, C. and Hinzelin, R., 'Medecine et paleographie', *Le Courrier du CNRS* 39 (Pari 1981), 29-32

Sirat, C., *LES PAPYRUS EN CARACTÈRES HÉBRAÏQUE TROUVÉS EN ÉGYPTE* (Paris 1985)

Sirat, C., Cauderlier, P., Dukan, M. and Friedman, M.A., 'La Ketouba de Cologne', *Abhandlungen der Rheinisch-westfälischen Akademie der Wissenschaften*, Sonderreihe Papyrologica Coloniensia, vol. XII (Opladen 1986)

Yadin, Y. and Naveh, J., *MASADAH* I (Jerusalem 1989)

Yardeni, A., 'New Jewish Aramaic Ostraca', *Israel Exploration Journal* 40 (1990), 130-152

Yardeni, A., 'Les mouvements de la main et la diréction des traits dans l'écriture Hebraïque', *Bibliologia* 10 (1990), 377-401

Yardeni, A., *The Aramaic and Hebrew Documents in Cursive Script from Wadi Murabba*ʿ*at and Naḥal Ḥever and Related material - A Palaeographic and Epigraphic Examination*, Hebrew University Ph.D. (Jerusalem 1991)

Yardeni, A., 'The Palaeography of 4QJer.a: a Comparative Study', *Textus* 15 (1991), 233-268

Yardeni, A., 'Remarks on the Priestly Blessing on Two Amulets from Jerusalem', *Vetus Testamentum* 41 (1991), 176-185

Yardeni, A., 'The Paleo-Hebrew and Jewish Scripts', in:Catalogue of the Exhibition *Scrolls from the Dead Sea* (Jerusalem, 1993)

Yardeni, A., 'The Script of 4Q397 and 4Q398', in: E. Qimron and J. Strugnell, Qumran Cave 4, V: Miqṣat Maʿase Ha'Torah, *DJD* X (1994), 21-25; 29-34

Yardeni, A., 'Palaeographic Analysis' in: J.C. Greenfield and M. Sokoloff, 'An Astrological Text from Qumran (4Q318) and Reflections on Some Zodiacal Names', *Revue de Qumran* 64/16 (December 1995), 520-522, 524

Yardeni, A., 'The Aramaic and Hebrew Documents', in: Cotton, H. and Yardeni, A., *ARAMAIC, HEBREW AND GREEK DOCUMENTARY TEXTS FROM NAḤAL ḤEVER AND OTHER SITES* (The Seiyāl Collection II), *DJD* XXVII

Yardeni, A. and Levine, B., *THE DOCUMENTS FROM THE BAR KOKHBA PERIOD IN THE CAVE OF LETTERS II* (forthcoming)

Yardeni, A., *TEXTBOOK OF ARAMAIC AND HEBREW DOCUMENTARY TEXTS FROM THE JUDAEAN DESERT AND RELATED MATERIAL* (forthcoming)

אביגד, נ׳, ׳הפליאוגרפיה של מגילות ים המלח ותעודות קרובות׳, *מחקרים במגילות הגנוזות* (1961), 107–139

אביגד, נ׳, *בית–שערים*, כרך ג: מערכות הקברים מס׳ 12–24 (ירושלים תשל״ב)

אות היא לעולם, קובץ מאמרים מוקדש לעיצוב האות העברית (ירושלים תשמ״א)

אות עברית חדשה, אוניברסיטת תל אביב, הגלריה האוניברסיטאית (תל–אביב תשמ״ה)

אחיטוב, ש׳, *אסופת כתובות עבריות* (ירושלים תשנ״ג)

אפפלדורפר, ח׳ ולנגה, א׳, *זיהוי כתבי יד לפי צורת האותיות*, המעבדה הישראלית לפיסיקה, משרד התעשייה, המסחר והתיירות (1979)

בית–אריה, מ׳, ׳הספר העברי בימי הבינים׳, *זמנים* 8 (1982), 25–36

בית–אריה, מ׳ (בהשתתפות ע׳ אנגל וע׳ ירדני), *אסופות כתבים עבריים מימי הבינים* כרך א: כתב מזרחי וכתב תימני (ירושלים תשמ״ח)

בית–אריה, מ׳, *מקורות לקודיקולוגיה ופליאוגרפיה עברית* (ירושלים תשנ״ד)

גלצר, מ׳, מלאכת הספר של כתר ארם צובה והשלכותיה׳, *ספונות* יט (תשמ״ט), 167–276

דירינגר, ד׳, ׳כתב׳, האנציקלופדיה העברית, כרך כ (ירושלים תשל״א), 1094–1107

הברמן, א״מ, *המדפיסים בני שונצינו* (וינה תרצ״ג)

הברמן, א״מ, *הספר העברי בהתפתחותו* (ירושלים 1968)

זילברג, ג׳ (בהשתתפות מ׳ שפיצר, מ׳ בן–יהודה, ש׳ פרץ, א׳ לוטן), *תורת הדפוס*, הוצאת ארגון מפעלי הדפוס בישראל (תשכ״ח)

טובי, ל״פ, *כתב אמנותי עברי* (תל אביב 1951)

ידין, י׳, *החיפושים אחר בר כוכבא* (ירושלים תשל״א)

ירדני, ע׳, *הרפתקאות* (ירושלים 1983, 1993)

ירדני, ע׳, ׳שעטנ״ז ג״ץ ופרשות פתוחות וסתומות בקטע חדש של ספר בראשית מן הגניזה׳, דברי הקונגרס העולמי העשירי למדעי היהדות, חטיבה ד, כרך ראשון (ירושלים תש״ן), 173–180

ירדני, ע׳, ׳הכתב בשני קטעי השטרות ממערת אביאור׳, ארץ–ישראל כג (ירושלים תשנ״ב), 327–330

ירדני, ע׳, *תעודות ׳נחל צאלים׳* (באר–שבע וירושלים תשנ״ה)

כשר, מ״מ, *תורה שלמה*, כרך י״ט: כתב התורה ואותיותיה (ירושלים תשל״ח)

כתובות מספרות, מוזיאון ישראל ירושלים, קט. מס׳ 100 (ירושלים תשל״ג)

משקפיים, רבעון של אגף הנוער, מוזיאון ישראל, ירושלים, בשיתוף עם ׳כותרת ראשית׳, כרך 2: כתב (ירושלים תשמ״ח)

נגיד, א׳, ׳*משמעותם הטיפוגרפית של עיוותי ראייה*׳, *דפוסגרף* 38, חוברת מס׳ 7, 38–39

נוה, י׳, ׳התפתחות הכתב הארמי׳, *דברי האקדמיה הלאומית הישראלית למדעים*, כרך חמישי חוברת 4 (ירושלים תשל״ד)

נוה, י׳, *על פסיפס ואבן*, הכתובות הארמיות והעבריות מבתי–הכנסת העתיקים (ירושלים תשל״ח)

נוה, י׳, *אותיות ותולדותיהן* (ירושלים תשמ״ט)

נוה, י׳, *על חרס וגומא*, כתובות ארמיות ועבריות מימי בית שני, המשנה והתלמוד (ירושלים תשנ״ב)

נוה, י׳, ׳מצבות צוער׳, תרביץ סד (תשנ״ה), 477–497

סוקניק, א״ל, *אוצר המגילות הגנוזות שבידי האוניברסיטה העברית* (ירושלים תשט״ו)

סיראט, ק׳, *מן הכתב אל הספר*, הצצה אל עולם כתבי–היד העבריים של ימי–הביניים (ירושלים תשנ״ב)

פרידמן, ד״א, ׳אלף בית׳, *לשוננו* א (תרפ״ח), 275–290

קורן (קורנגולד), א׳, *הרעיון וההגשמה*, הדפסת ספר התנ״ך – המהדורה היהודית הראשונה (ירושלים תשנ״א)

שטיבנר, ארהרדט ד׳, *ספר הדפוס* (ירושלים 1992)

שפיצר, מ׳, ׳על האותיות שלנו׳, *עלי עי״ן*, מנחת דברים לשלמה זלמן שוקן אחרי מלאות לו שבעים שנה (ירושלים תש״ח–תשי״ב), 481–501

שפירא, י׳, *זיהוי סגנונות כתבי יד*, עבודה לשם קבלת תואר מוסמך בהדרכת יצחק דינשטיין, אוניברסיטת בן גוריון בנגב, הפקולטה למדעי הטכנולוגיה, המחלקה להנדסת חשמל

ששון, ס״ד, *מחקר מקיף על כתב ידו של הרמב״ם* (ירושלים תש״ן)

Index

D